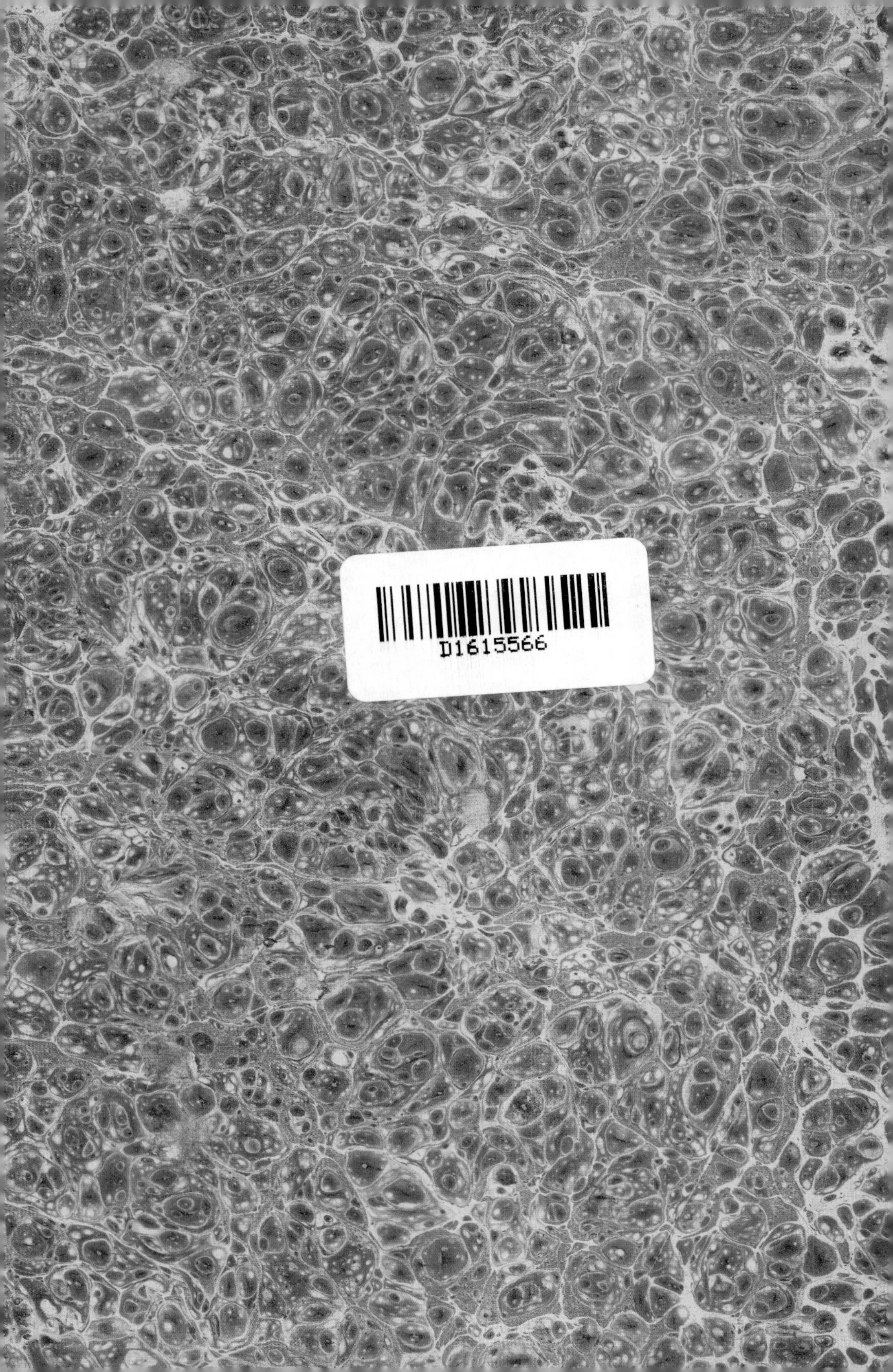
D1615566

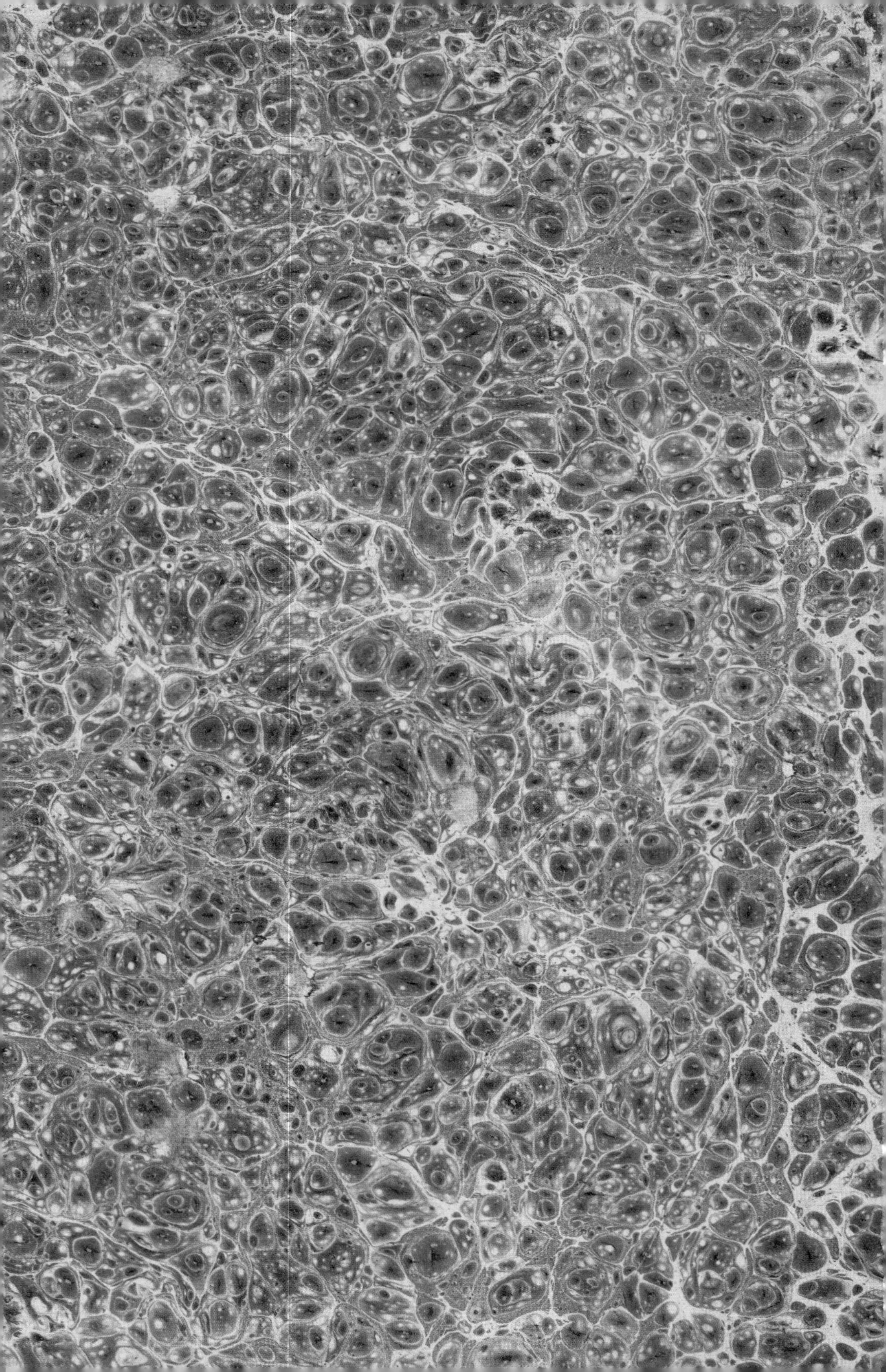

IMAGINING ENGLAND'S PAST

SUSAN OWENS

IMAGINING ENGLAND'S PAST

INSPIRATION, ENCHANTMENT, OBSESSION

P. 2: Julia Margaret Cameron, *King Arthur*, 1874.

P. 14: Title page (detail) from Thomas Percy's *Reliques of Ancient English Poetry*, 1765.

P. 266: 'Tumbling' (detail) from Joseph Strutt, *Sports and Pastimes of the People of England*, 1801.

First published in the United Kingdom in 2023
by Thames & Hudson Ltd,
181A High Holborn, London WC1V 7QX

First published in the United States of America in 2023
by Thames & Hudson Inc.,
500 Fifth Avenue, New York, New York 10110

Designed by Peter Burgess

British Library Cataloguing-in-Publication Data

A catalogue record for this book is available from the British Library

Library of Congress Control Number 2022945685

ISBN 978-0-500-02433-1

Printed in China by Shanghai Offset Printing Products Limited

CONTENTS

Alan Ronald, *Bolsover Castle in Derbyshire*, c. 1940.

PROLOGUE

'The past is never dead. It's not even past.'

William Faulkner, *Requiem for a Nun* (1951)

When is a medieval castle not a medieval castle?

I have come to Bolsover in Derbyshire, where the imposing silhouette of the castle dominates the skyline. There are battlements and arrow-slits and high stone walls. There is an outer court with state apartments that stand in ruins, and, within, a satisfyingly four-square keep. Even in the holiday warmth of a July day, there is no mistaking the insistent pressure of the past in this place. Step over the threshold and stand still for a moment: you can feel it gathering in the shadows, sense its cool breath on your cheek; it prickles through the soles of your shoes on the worn stone steps. Put your hand on the masonry there, just by the door, and think of all the other hands – gauntleted, red-raw with work, heavy with rings mounted with precious stones – that have rested there over the centuries.

But wait. In spite of appearances, Bolsover Castle is not ancient at all, but was in fact constructed in the early years of the seventeenth century. It might have been modelled on the twelfth-century castle that once stood on that spot, which gradually fell into ruins under the custodianship of successive farmers, although no one really knows. The men who built it, Charles Cavendish and his son, William, did so to celebrate the glamour and romance of medieval chivalry.[1] Go inside the Little Castle – the building modelled on a medieval keep – and you will find a suite of beguiling seventeenth-century rooms, spaces designed and decorated for the pursuit of pleasure, within which even today a playful, theatrical atmosphere lingers. Bolsover wears its fancy dress with aplomb. It is an outrageously extravagant love letter to the days of old.

I should, really, have expected it. In England, romantic versions of the past are always edging their way into our lives. The church I attended as a child had been built in the middle of the nineteenth century in what I came to learn was called the Gothic Revival style. My school occupied a rambling Edwardian building in Derbyshire that tried its hardest to resemble seventeenth-century collegiate premises. And I vividly remember being taken on a school trip to Riber Castle near Matlock, which to my eyes was the very essence of a romantic medieval ruin. Again, no. It was actually built in 1862 by John Smedley, wealthy manufacturer of fine knitwear, and was once described by the distinguished architectural historian John Summerson as 'an object of indecipherable bastardy'.[2] What chance, then, did I have? Things were made more confusing still by the blackened stone of all these edifices, which added greatly to their air of ancient decay – even though the soot was actually a by-product of the area's mills: the Derwent Valley was the engine room of the industrial revolution, the place the modern world came into being. To a child these surroundings were distinctly disquieting. Why were all these buildings pretending to be older than they were?

After the church, the largest building in the Suffolk village in which I now live is the meeting hall of a friendly society, the Ancient Order of Foresters. The Foresters sold it in the 1960s, but the most elderly village residents tell me they remember going to dances there. It was built in 1905 by an architect who based it on the architectural style known as Palladianism – both because he thought the large windows and high ceilings characteristic of this classically inspired style were suitable for an assembly room, and because he believed it conferred an air of grandeur. Palladianism was derived from the designs of a sixteenth-century Venetian architect, Andrea Palladio, who in turn was inspired by ancient Roman and Greek buildings. Foresters' Hall shouldered its way in between small-windowed, timber-framed medieval houses to sit like a fat cuckoo in the village nest; and thus today an echo of the ancient Mediterranean world can be heard in rural Suffolk. It was not just the hall that dressed up in borrowed clothes: the Foresters themselves were so ambitious for their history that, with some audacity, given that they were not very ancient at all but only founded in the late eighteenth century, they traced their ancestry all the way back to the biblical Adam – the 'first forester', as the author of an early members' manual confidently puts it.[3]

The past has been – and remains – one of English culture's most invigorating sources of inspiration, a self-renewing treasure trove to be dipped into again and again. This is not to argue that, as a nation, England is unusually preoccupied; the concept of a long-lost golden age is common to many cultures, and movements such as the Gothic Revival and Romanticism, which offered poets, artists and architects ways of delving into and reworking history, were at least Europe-wide. I have chosen to focus on England because the particularities of its profound and passionate relationship with the past have always fascinated me. Although many other books have been written about specific instances of historicism in English culture, I sensed that a longer trawl through the centuries would allow me to gather the widest variety of examples in my net and use them to tell a fresh story. Much of my thinking for this book was done during the years I spent as a curator at the Victoria and Albert Museum, when I could hardly open a Solander box or pull out a rack in the paintings store without finding a watercolour of a ruined abbey or a picture reimagining some aspect of the 'olden time'. The galleries were full of ceramics, textiles and jewelry that revived styles of the past, whether remote or more recent. I knew I had to investigate this phenomenon, and when I began to read, look and ask questions for this book, a surprising, absorbing and profoundly human story began to unfold.

Imagining England's Past is about those who have, over the centuries, been inspired, enchanted and, yes, obsessed by the past and have attempted to bring its spirit into their work and their lives. I have woven my narrative around their encounters with history, asking what they reveal about each individual and the times in which they lived. I have tried to look over their shoulders to see the beguiling visions they saw, asking what these reveal about their preoccupations and aspirations, their dreams and anxieties.

What drives this perpetual turn to the past? One answer, of course, is nostalgia. English culture has been shaped by a recurrent harking back to a golden age, a time of perceived comfort, stability, safety or community spirit. The emotional pull of the past can be felt in histories, stories, poems and pictures. From the earliest of written records, it is evident that people have looked back on the days of old in a mood of intense longing, whether the lost lamented time was distant or heartbreakingly close. The migrants from northern Germany and southern Scandinavia who from the fifth century onwards crossed the North Sea to the land that would become England felt it. A story such as *Beowulf*, that celebrated a glorious warrior culture of the past, was a talisman, reinforcing identity through its retelling: each hearer would receive a precious portion of their shared, imagined past like a holy relic. The British, many of whom had been pushed to the western edges of the land and overseas to Brittany, needed to bring a hero of their own out of the misty obscurity of time. Their champion emerged in the form of the warlord Arthur – later reinvented as King Arthur – about whom tales were told not only of immense bravery, but of his mystical relationship with the land itself. It was hinted that he might, one day, return. Identity, legitimacy, belonging and hope are at the heart of these stories.

Every subsequent age has been nostalgic for an earlier period – it is a condition apparently hard-wired into the human psyche. Today it is common to hear people speak fondly of the 'Blitz spirit', while some living through the Second World War itself looked wistfully back to the Victorian era, little thinking that the Victorians themselves had assiduously cultivated a romantic obsession with medieval England.[4] Nostalgia has many faces. Compare, for example, the young artist Samuel Palmer with the political radical William Cobbett, both of whom walked or rode through the rural Kent of the 1820s – though from the way they represented it one would be hard-pressed to recognize it as the same place. Looking at Palmer's Edenic, visionary pictures, one would not imagine that the countryside was in reality an edgy, troubled place in which appalling working conditions and agricultural mechanization would shortly lead to the Swing Riots; he allowed dreams, legends and archetypes to block out the rural unrest that was breaking out all around. Cobbett, on the other hand, who was firmly on the side of the labourers, crossly pointed out some 'shabby-genteel houses, surrounded with dead fences and things called gardens...rubbishly flimsy things' that had been stuck up on former common land, and sighed for a rural England, remembered from his childhood in the 1760s and 1770s, where, he thought, none of the problems could have happened in the first place.[5]

At times, the emotional pinch of nostalgia could become agonizingly acute. Tennyson wrote *In Memoriam*, one of the greatest elegies of the Victorian age, for his close friend Arthur Hallam, who had died young. As he wrote in 'Break, Break, Break', 'the tender grace of a day that is dead / Will never come back to me'.[6] It could also be a tool of passionate protest against a changing world: Edward Burne-Jones spent his last years covering up as much of the industrial nineteenth century as he could with vast, dreamy Arthurian canvases, tapestries and stained glass, coming to wish that he had been born in the Middle Ages – 'People would then have known how to use me,' he lamented; 'now they don't know what on earth to do with me.'[7] Ironically, today's steampunks are nostalgic for the trappings of the same industry that appalled Burne-Jones, in their own protest against an increasingly bland and digitized world.

Nostalgia is part of my story here, but so too are curiosity, wonder and imaginative speculation. Over the centuries, people have had a passionate desire to know who was here before. The antiquarians of the sixteenth and seventeenth centuries were entranced by the material remains of the distant past they could plainly see in the English landscape – the stone circles and the long barrows – but had few tools beyond observation and conjecture that would help them to understand what they were. So these scholars projected their minds back in time until the imaginary inhabitants of England's ancient hills, valleys, woods and plains swam into view in their mental divining mirrors.

Others have been fascinated by the human stories of the past and have attempted to get inside the minds of individual men and women. Sir Walter Scott changed the cultural landscape by writing historical figures from the inside out; for the first time, his readers experienced them as feeling, thinking human beings. In the early 2000s Hilary Mantel inhabited the head, the heart and indeed the stomach of Thomas Cromwell, and magnificently reimagined a slice of Tudor history from his perspective. It is perhaps a little sobering, in fact, to reflect on how much of a sense of national history has been shaped by fiction and subsequent television adaptations, from Scott and Dickens to Bernard Cornwell, Alison Weir and Mantel herself.

My story is also about the sense of place that is so central to English art and literature, often amplified into the visionary mysticism that seems happily to coexist with pragmatism in the national psyche. For many, the sound of ancient history can still be heard in the echo-chambers of the country's hills and valleys. 'And did those feet in ancient time / Walk upon England's mountains green?' asked William Blake in the poem of 1804 that has become known as 'Jerusalem', drawing on an apocryphal legend. Almost certainly not. And yet the story that Jesus had visited Glastonbury with his uncle Joseph of Arimathea, a tin merchant, has flourished along with the Glastonbury thorn, because it invests the landscape with a profoundly spiritual dimension. The twentieth century saw a new and intense focus on prehistory, as artists and writers such as Ithell Colquhoun and Paul Nash sought to connect with the ancient forces of the land that they sensed reverberating through standing stones, hill figures and long barrows, and to channel the mysterious and magical power they found there into their own work. It was felt at this time that something of great importance was in danger of being lost, tidied up and concreted over; in response, they willed numinous historical forces, long-buried, to bubble up through the surface. Today, stories of ghosts – especially those connected with historic sites and great houses – are as popular as ever, reflecting a desire for the past to be not *entirely* past.

This book, then, is about the urge to make sense of and forge deep emotional connections with place, to feel part of a meaningful historical continuum, to recover and preserve the past and to establish relationships with the dead as well as the living.

Our relationship with the past has reached a critical point. As I write, the ways in which English history is interpreted are being examined and rethought with unprecedented rigour, passion and originality.[8] New stories are being researched and told. Those engaged in writing history are seeking to uncover complex and uncomfortable truths that allow marginalized or silenced voices to be heard. The flattering mirror that has so long framed traditional ideas of England's past has been taken out into the daylight, and discomfiting images have appeared in it; and while some resent the disruption to long-established stories that has followed, others have been horrified and stirred into action by the racial and colonial biases they see reflected.[9] For many today, the past has for too long been pictured in ways that conceal its uglier dimensions, and needs urgently to be retold. A new generation of writers and artists is taking hold of stale ideas, shaking colonial assumptions out of them and offering instead an alternative, more nuanced picture. All of this matters because our concept of the past is the fabric from which our present and our future are made.[10]

Custodians of the past's material culture have found themselves at the crux of the debate. Museums are taking a fresh look at their historical collections and finding much that is compromised, whether made in exploitative conditions, acquired in questionable circumstances or, as in the notorious case of the Benin bronzes, looted. As one reviewer remarked of the British Galleries at the Metropolitan Museum of Art, New York, 'Viewed through this particular historical lens, the objects in the Met can look like the hood ornaments of a capitalist death machine.'[11] Heritage organizations such as the National Trust are researching and publishing connections between the properties they manage and fortunes made from the slave trade.[12] Statues of public figures with connections to slavery are being toppled by those who can no longer tolerate the culture of respect these monuments imply. And while the manner in which the statue of the slave trader Edward Colston was pulled down and pushed into Bristol's docks has divided opinion, it seems reasonable to ask why, in 2020, a tribute to a man who made a fortune from a company with a monopoly on the West African slave trade was still there at all. Statuary in public places is not inert, but interactive, put in place to convey a message to successive generations; that message will not fall silent of its own accord.

These necessary and urgent dialogues with the past are taking place as Britain takes its first steps into a future outside the European Union; the English are newly thrown back on historical imaginings to define their collective identity. So it seems like a good moment to shine a light on the individuals who, at different times and in different places, have composed, painted, built and dreamed up the visions that have got us this far.

DURAT OPUS VATUM

I

ONCE UPON A TIME

I am looking at sheets of vellum so ragged, scuffed and blotted that parts are difficult to read. Over its thousand-year existence, the manuscript of *Beowulf* – the earliest surviving epic poem in English – has had a rough time. It was among the treasures kept at Ashburnham House when a fire broke out there one dreadful October night in 1731; rescued, it suffered more over subsequent years through the touch of eager fingers, both those of the scholarly and the merely curious. Letters at the edge of pages began to part company from words and drop unnoticed to the ground like tiny dead leaves, to be swept up with the dust and mouse-droppings. And yet this ancient document records a poem composed perhaps centuries before its scribe sat down with his quill to inscribe the stirring opening word, 'Hwæt' – listen! Some scholars suggest a date at the outset of the eighth century, some later – no one knows for sure. But standing in front of the manuscript, what makes me catch my breath is a single word on its second line. *Beowulf* begins with the poet inviting us to contemplate the *geardagum* – the days of old. In an image that flares in my mind, I am a hill-walker approaching a summit only to see further peaks, some unimaginably distant, fading into a haze at the far-off horizon. These scraps of vellum now in the care of the British Library, so ancient and fragile that one is half-afraid even to look at them, are only the foreground; behind them can be sensed two more distant pasts. One is a real history, in which audiences in halls and homes listened raptly to a poet's rousing tales of kings and comrades, weapons and treasure; the other, which reaches still further back into the past, is a history crafted in the imagination. Thirteen centuries ago, in the place that was becoming England, a poet wondered about the distant past of his people on the other side of the North Sea, and in his imagination he conjured up a world of myth and legend, a time and place in which glorious heroes fought monsters and dragons. His story was set close enough to grip the attention of an audience by what it promised to reveal about their ancestry, and yet far enough away for the events and characters he described to be magnified and distorted by the enchanted lens of the olden days.

Fascination with the romance of the long-ago is no invention of the modern age. English literature as we know it begins by looking back.

Perhaps there is nothing strange in that. For many of the early English, it would have been hard to avoid thinking about the might and glory of former civilizations. The days of old were not a nebulous concept for those living near the physical remains of the Roman occupation, but right there, in stone, in the landscape. For a people who built primarily with wood, this masonry was to be marvelled at – or cursed, when it got in the way of the plough. It was certainly regarded as a curiosity to be shown off and discussed: an early biography of Saint Cuthbert describes a visit he made along with his priests and deacons to Carlisle, where one morning Waga, the local official, showed them 'the city wall and the well formerly built in a wonderful manner by the Romans'.[1]

For those with the leisure to stand and contemplate the scene, Roman ruins could open a window onto the past through which a distant glamour could still be discerned. 'Cities are visible from afar', observed one poet, awed by the scale of the buildings, 'the cunning work of giants, the wondrous fortifications in stone which are on this earth.'[2] 'Wrætlic is þes wealstan,' mused another, perhaps contemplating the Roman city of Bath, 'wyrde gebræcon; / burgstede burston, brosnað enta geweorc' – wondrous is this masonry, shattered by fate; the battlements are broken, the work of giants corrupted. The sight inspires this poet to send his imagination soaring back into the past. He mentally rebuilds the walls, imagining the exhilarating sights and sounds that once animated them:

Beorht wæron burgræced, burnsele monige,
heah horngestreon, heresweg micel,
meodoheall monig dreama full,
oþþæt þæt onwende wyrd seo swiþe.[3]

Bright were the city dwellings, many the bath-houses,
All the high pinnacles resounded with trumpets,
Many the banqueting halls full of pleasures,
Until that was overturned by mighty fate.

The ruined city is a tangible elegy; the poet's initial wonder and delight are soon shadowed by reflections on the transitory nature of earthly glory. No matter how splendid the city – and the poet goes on to describe the proud warriors in shining armour, the silver, pearls and precious gems, the stone courts and the hot streams that have momentarily dazzled his mind's eye – treasures such as these always pass away. For him, the ruins were a *memento mori* in stone, a reminder that, given time, all earthly things decay and crumble. One must fix one's thoughts on the heavenly kingdom, they taught: the only reliable place in which to put one's trust.

The early English were predisposed to seek moral lessons in the relics of former civilizations. Widely circulated literary works such as Saint Augustine's *The City of God*, which exhorted its readers to contemplate heaven rather than earthly cities, and the cleric Gildas's doomy

Hadrian's Wall, a relic of the Roman past in the landscape.

diatribe *On the Ruin and Conquest of Britain*, probably written around the year 540, were part of their mental furniture. In addition to this, books of the Old Testament – Jeremiah, Lamentations, Isaiah and Ezekiel, among others – were littered with the broken walls of sinful cities, felled by the righteous wrecking-ball of an angry and disappointed God.[4]

But another aspect of this frame of mind, just as deeply rooted in the culture, was a more secular preoccupation with the contrast between former times and the present. The idea of decline from a splendid past has affected most cultures, and was certainly there in classical literature. From Hesiod onwards, the present has often been regarded as an impoverished shadow of a glorious past. The tenth-century manuscript of the poem quoted above, now known as *The Ruin* – badly damaged and only partly legible, which seems strangely appropriate – shares pages with several of the most emotionally charged of Old English elegies. A seafarer describes his bleak and lonely exile; a woman separated from her husband laments her dreary solitude. Things were not always like this, they each say: once there was fellowship and belonging; once there was love. In the grip of desperate longing, they send their minds back to former times despite the pain memories bring, as though compulsively probing a bruise. But among all the melancholy voices that sigh through the leaves of this manuscript book, one rings out like a hammer on gold. 'Hwær cwom mearg, hwær cwom mago?,' it demands. Where has the horse gone? Where the young rider?

> Hwær cwom maþþumgyfa?
> Hwær cwom symbla gesetu? hwær sindon seledreamas?

> Where the giver of treasure?
> Where are the seats at the feasts? Where are the revels in the hall?

This despairing cry bursts from a poem now known as *The Wanderer*, which hymns a sort of cosmic belatedness. The narrator ponders his own sad experience of losing his lord and becoming separated from his people. There is no way out of this narrow, binding path of exile. 'Wyn eal gedreas!' he exclaims: all joy has died. Before long, his desolation seems to him to reflect the world at large. Lifting his head for a moment from contemplating the *geardagum*, he can see how everything is falling into decay. Momentarily his vantage point changes – rather than looking back, he looks towards the future – but it turns out only to provide a better view of the end of things. 'Hu gaestlic bið, / þonne ealre þisse worulde wela / weste stondeð', he observes: how terrible it will be, when all the wealth of this world stands waste.

> Eala beorht bune, eala byrnwiga,
> Eala þeodnes þrymm! hu seo þrag gewat,
> genap under nihthelm, swa heo no wære!

> Alas, the bright cup, alas, the mailed warrior,
> Alas, the glory of the prince! How the time has passed away,
> darkened under the cover of night, as if it had never been![5]

Eala! These glorious things are – can only be – in the days gone by. And perhaps, in truth, that great and much-lamented time never really was.

The English may have found a melancholy pleasure in peering nostalgically back into the dim past and contemplating the brevity of this earthly life, *eala, eala*. But what did the existing inhabitants of the land, some of whom had been pushed westwards into Wales and Cornwall while others were living alongside the Saxon settlers, see when they looked back? Were the British also obsessed with a sense of belatedness? Did they, too, look for moral lessons – or were they searching for something else? Many Britons surveying the last few centuries would only have seen the gloomy picture of dispossession. If they were to find a more positive story they would need to delve deeply into history, to reach back before boats carrying Germanic settlers began to arrive in the east. Ideally what they would find there would be a past that put Britain on a global map; one that supplied some glorious ancestors for their indigenous princes.

There was an ancient legend that did exactly that. The earliest surviving record of it is a laconic mention in a history of Britain written in Wales – probably the kingdom of Gwynedd – in the early ninth century and traditionally attributed to an author called Nennius.[6] But the legend reached stratospheric popularity in the twelfth century, when it was included in a bestselling work written by an Anglo-Norman cleric living in Oxford called Geoffrey of Monmouth. Now known as the *Historia regum Britanniae*, the History of the Kings of Britain, his book was completed by

1139; today, over two hundred manuscript copies survive, roughly a third of which were created before the end of the twelfth century.[7] Geoffrey gave the tale he tells in the *Historia* authority by claiming an extraordinary source – 'a very old book in the British tongue' given to him by a certain Walter, Archdeacon of Oxford – that he was translating into Latin. Be that as it may – and it was certainly not as simple as that – the story he unfolds supplies a glamorous past.[8]

Britain, writes Geoffrey, was founded by Brutus, a great-grandson of the Trojan hero Aeneas, who became the first British king and the ancestor of the royal line. It happened like this: exiled from Italy for accidentally shooting his father, the young Brutus lived in Greece, where, learning of his ancestry, he sought out and lived among the surviving, enslaved Trojans. 'He began to manifest so much soldierly prowess and virtue', Geoffrey tells us, 'that their kings and chiefs loved him above all the youths in that country; to wise men he displayed his wisdom, to warriors his aggression and, whenever he acquired gold, silver and ornaments, he used to present everything to his men.' He became the leader of the Trojans, and after decisively defeating the Greeks in battle, married the king's daughter, Innogin, and set sail from the shores of Greece. After two days he and his crew stopped at an uninhabited island called Leogetia, where they discovered a temple to Diana containing a statue of the goddess, which had the power to answer questions put to it. Brutus made offerings to Diana, and asked her to 'say in which lands you wish us to dwell'. During the night, Geoffrey writes, he seemed to see Diana standing before him and to hear her say:

> Brutus, to the west, beyond the kingdoms of Gaul,
> lies an island of the ocean, surrounded by the sea;
> an island of the ocean, where giants once lived,
> but now it is deserted and waiting for your people.
> Sail to it; it will be your home for ever.
> It will furnish your children with a new Troy,
> From your descendants will arise kings, who
> will be masters of the whole world.

So the Trojan refugees joyfully set sail in search of their new home in the west that was prophesied for them. After an eventful voyage – the body-count resulting from Brutus's aggressive skirmishes with the locals wherever he weighed anchor would impress a teenaged video-gamer – the Trojans reached the south coast of Albion, as it was then called, at Totnes (Plate 1). Brutus named the island Britain after himself, and so it was that the Trojans became Britons and their language was renamed British. Searching for a suitable place to build a city, he came upon a spot on the River Thames and called it Troynovant – the New Troy, a name that later morphed into Trinovantum.[9] It was a glorious beginning.

Britain being uninhabited (apart from a few remaining giants), subsequently all Britons could point to illustrious Trojan forebears. 'For noble Britons sprang from Trojans bold, / And Troynovant was built of old Troy's ashes cold', as Edmund Spenser was to put it in *The Faerie Queene*. It was a coveted ancestry, and one that seemed entirely plausible: at the time Geoffrey was writing, the Trojan War was regarded as a historical event calculated to have occurred between 1334 and 1135 BC.[10] Nor were Britons alone in claiming it: the Trojan diaspora offered numerous dazzling opportunities. Both Virgil in the *Aeneid* and Livy in his history of the city had sought to entrench a Trojan back story for Rome, in which the hero Aeneas began a dynasty that led eventually to the birth of its legendary founders, Romulus and Remus; and the great history of the world known as the *Nuremberg Chronicle* (1493) cites Franco, a son of Hector, as the founder of France, and Turcus, a son of Troilus, as the founder of Turkey.

But the glorious tale of Britain's foundation was only the beginning of Geoffrey's story. He goes on to tell the tales of Brutus's successors who formed the British royal line, some of whose names would resonate down the centuries: King Leir and his three daughters Gonorilla, Regau and Cordeilla; King Lud, who 'repaired the walls of Trinovantum and surrounded it with numerous towers', and after whom the city was renamed as Kaerlud, a name corrupted to Kaerlundein and later to Lundene; and finally the glorious British kings Uther Pendragon and his son Arthur, who fought so valiantly against the invading English. The *Historia* is a gripping read. Even now, nine centuries later, Geoffrey's skills as a raconteur keep us turning the pages.

Take, for instance, his account of Stonehenge, and compare it with that of his contemporary, the historian Henry of Huntingdon, whose *Historia Anglorum* begins at the point of the Roman invasion. Listing

Stonehenge – 'Staneges' – among four 'wonders which may be seen in England', Henry marvels over its construction, and can only declare that 'no one can work out how the stones were so skilfully lifted up to such a height or why they were erected there'.[11] Geoffrey, on the other hand, provides a fulsome, almost novelistic account of the monument's original purpose and its construction, using it to build his epic national myth.

He begins the story at Caerleon, later Salisbury: Ambrosius Aurelianus, a British military leader of the fifth century – and also king, according to Geoffrey – is looking sadly at a burial place of many of Britain's noblemen, massacred by the Saxons. Ambrosius summons stonemasons and carpenters from all around, seeking someone to build a monument that will stand forever as their memorial. But it is no good; no one has the confidence to begin a project of such magnitude. The only person who can help, suggests the archbishop of Caerleon, is the prophet Merlin, who answers the King thus:

> If you wish to mark their graves with a lasting monument, send for the Giants' Ring, which is on Mount Killaraus in Ireland. There is there a ring of stones, which no man of this era could erect save by skill and art combined. The stones are huge, beyond the strength of any man. If you set them up in the same pattern around the burial-place, they will stand forever.

Merlin describes how the stones have magical healing properties and were 'brought long ago from the farthest shores of Africa by giants, who erected them in Ireland while they lived there'. At his words, fifteen thousand armed men under the King's brother, Uther Pendragon, are sent to Ireland to fetch the stones. Merlin is sent with them, 'to supply them with brains and advice'. After a battle with the Irish, they arrive at the ring of stones and stand in wonder. At this point Merlin decides to have some fun at the expense of these muscly simpletons: 'Employ your might, men,' he commands, 'to take down the stones and we shall see whether brains yield to brawn or vice versa.' The men try ropes, pulleys and ladders, but nothing will shift them – an illustration of this episode in a later version of Geoffrey's story, Wace's *Roman de Brut*, shows a diminutive Merlin addressing two powerful men who ineffectually attempt to get a grip of the stones (Plate II). Finally, Merlin, whether through engineering prowess or supernatural strength, 'took down the stones with incredible ease and had them carried to the ships and loaded'. They all return to England and make their way to Caerleon, where Merlin erects the stones around the cemetery exactly as they had stood on Mount Killaraus – 'so proving', adds Geoffrey with a satisfied air, 'the superiority of brains over brawn'.[12]

How could Geoffrey know all this? As Henry of Huntingdon sadly recounted to a friend, 'although I searched again and again, I was unable to find any report of those times, either oral or written. Such is the destructive oblivion that in the course of the ages obscures and extinguishes the glory of mortals.' When he describes his 'amazement' at discovering Geoffrey's 'written account of those very matters', one can only sympathize.[13] Is Geoffrey's claim merely to have translated stories from a much older book remotely credible? No one can know, although it is generally thought likely to be a fiction designed to lend authority to his story. How much had he assembled from folklore and traditional tales and songs, of which Henry had either been unaware or had thought unworthy of notice? One is left helplessly asking questions, entranced by the depth and detail of his stories but suspecting that the joke is on us.

Although Geoffrey's book was hugely popular, it was severely criticized by other historians of the era. William of Newburgh vehemently attacked the *Historia* as a 'laughable web of fiction'.[14] The most elaborate put-down, however, occurs in Gerald of Wales's 1188 *Journey Through Wales*, in which he tells the story of a man called Meilyr who had an unusual gift. 'Whenever anyone told a lie in his presence, Meilyr was immediately aware of it, for he saw a demon dancing and exulting on the liar's tongue.' These unclean spirits could be made to fly away by placing Saint John's Gospel in the subject's lap. This suggested the following experiment, recounted by Gerald with barely suppressed glee: on one such occasion the Gospel was taken away and immediately replaced with Geoffrey's *History of the Kings of Britain*. The result was conclusive: the demons flew back, alighting 'all over his body, and on the book, too, staying there longer than usual and being even more demanding'.[15]

When poor, scrupulous Henry of Huntingdon tried to look into the distant past, he saw only featureless darkness; when Geoffrey turned his mind back, he had a vision of a colourful, noisy arena filled with people speaking, laughing, arguing, fighting, building, doing. His stories gave shape and meaning to those otherwise blank years. And this proto-novelist was such an accomplished storyteller that the distant past he dramatized has its own past; in his description of the Giants' Ring, for instance, he gestures back to the hazy 'long ago' when the giants took their stones to Ireland from Africa – which in itself implies an even longer ago, when they lived with them there. The history he lays out for us is given greater credibility by this background, like the shadow an artist draws beneath an object to make it appear three-dimensional.

He is as insubstantial as mist, and slides like a shadow through woods and over water. His spirit is in cairns and boulders, caves and streams. His voice is in the rising of the wind and the growl of thunder. He lives in the fierce rocks and the salt spray of the sea. He wanders with the stars. He was wounded and borne over water. He is sleeping, but one day will wake.

Many have believed that Arthur – King Arthur, if you will – is not subject to the laws of nature. Across England, wrote Thomas Malory at the end of his *Morte d'Arthur*, there are those who say he 'ys nat dede'; and there are also those who say his tomb bears the prophetic legend 'REX QUONDAM REXQUE FUTURUS' – the once and future king. Arthur seems to exist both in the days of old and in some mysterious, equivalent period in the future. So what do we see when we look at the historical record? Is it possible to make out a real figure slipping among the mist-soaked hills of the distant past?

There is nothing insubstantial about the Arthur who first bursts aggressively into written history early in the ninth century as a hero and protector of the British. 'Then Arthur fought against them [the Saxons] in those days', writes Nennius, 'together with the kings of the British; but he was their leader in battle.' Describing Arthur as a *dux bellorum*, or war-leader, Nennius goes on to list twelve battles that he commanded, in each of which he was victorious. At the eighth, we are told, Arthur carried the image of the Virgin Mary on his shoulders (probably a misunderstanding for her image on his shield) and with the powerful backing of Christ and the holy Virgin slaughtered a great many pagans; at the twelfth, on the mountain of Badon, he alone killed 960 men. But his account is overlaid with melancholy; these triumphs, splendid though they were, were ultimately hollow. The Saxons began to seek powerful reinforcements from their homelands, who came to the British Isles in unremitting waves. Through sheer force of numbers, he says, they established their dominance.[16]

Already some essential Arthurian characteristics are present. At first he seems all too rooted in a warrior culture, an able man of flesh and blood whose thoughts run on strategy, weapons and slaughter. And yet another dimension flickers into view; he seems to slip from the grip of cold, muddy reality and into the distorting mirror-world of fable. For one thing, there is the roll-call of battles that takes us on a topographical tour of the land, to the rivers of Glein and Dubglas and Bassas, the Scottish wood Cat Coit Celidon, a castle, a city, another river, and finally to the hills of Agned and Badon. This is more than a list; as it goes on, Arthur is ever more firmly associated with the land itself through its rivers, woods and hills. For another, there is a spiritual dimension, with Arthur fighting under the protection of the Virgin Mary's image. And then there is that extraordinary feat at the end: slaughter of the enemy by a single man on a scale unimaginable before the early twentieth century brought mechanization to the battlefield. It has been observed that 960 can be expressed poetically as three three-hundreds and three score, which suggests that the origin of this story may lie in verse or song.[17] The final note of defeat is also significant. Even at this first mention, Arthur is ultimately a tragic hero – no matter how many battles he wins, he will lose the war.

To write this account, Nennius was delving far back into history, describing events that supposedly occurred some three hundred years before, in the late fifth or early sixth centuries. So how did he know what happened? What written sources, now lost, was he using – and could any have been based in fact? What poems were recited, what songs were sung, handed down from one generation to the next, transforming Arthur into a folk hero and mythologizing his deeds until any historical traces were thoroughly kicked over? The Welsh poem *Y Gododdin*, thought to have been written between 600 and 1100 (though more probably around 1000) hints tantalizingly at a world of lost fable with a single line that follows a description of the great achievements in battle of the warrior Gwawrddur: 'though he was no Arthur', the poet remarks.[18] Arthur was evidently still a major figure in twelfth-century popular culture, judging by the exasperation of William of Malmesbury in his *History of the English Kings* (*c*.1125), as he underlines the importance of separating fact from fantasy:

> This Arthur is the hero of many wild tales among the Britons even in our own day, but assuredly deserves to be the subject of reliable history rather than of false and dreaming fable....[19]

It is, perhaps, unwise to expect Nennius's ideas of 'history' to bear much relation to today's; given the milieu in which he was writing, it would be more accurate to think of it as a concoction of oral history and folklore, heavily laced with rhetoric spun for the benefit of his princely patrons.

Amid all these questions and speculations, however, is a small but inconvenient fact: Gildas, the one historian contemporary with Arthur, makes no apparent mention of him, even though he describes the siege of Badon Hill itself, which centuries later was hymned as Arthur's great victory. When one comes to weigh up the available evidence, the distinct possibility has to be faced that the historical warrior Arthur might never have existed at all.[20] There may be a lot of smoke drifting about among the mirrors, but today most scholars agree that there is no fire.

Never mind. Arthur may never have lived, but he certainly shows no sign of dying. From being a fabled figure in the early Middle Ages, he passed through the hands of historians (of varying degrees of reliability) until he grew into one of the greatest legends of the olden times. Nennius's description of a military leader and his list of conquests, with its hints at Arthur's superhuman ability, was the grit in the oyster that later generations of writers embellished into a magnificent pearl.

For the Welsh of the ninth century, to whom the Saxons still posed a threat, anyone who was fabled to have killed 960 of them in one charge was an obvious folk hero. Three hundred years later, Arthur was naturally of interest to another group, the Anglo-Norman elite: the grandsons of the Norman barons who had so swiftly dismantled what had so often been hymned as God-given Saxon power. But Arthur the ferocious *dux bellorum*, slashing his way through Saxon flesh in Britain's woods and hills, was not quite sophisticated enough for the High Middle Ages. This elusive man's life was ripe for embellishment.

Geoffrey of Monmouth audaciously transformed Arthur from Dark Age warrior to glorious king, providing him with a royal pedigree that stretched back all the way to Brutus himself. It was in this guise that Arthur shot to international fame. Geoffrey's manuscript was copied, passed from hand to hand and read avidly both in Britain and on the Continent. Here is Arthur's introduction into the narrative when he came to the throne on the death of his father, Uther Pendragon:

> He was a youth of fifteen, of great promise and generosity, whose innate goodness ensured that he was loved by almost everybody. As newly crowned king, he displayed his customary open-handedness. Such a crowd of knights flocked to him that he ran out of gifts.

Arthur himself – or at least a line drawing of him – makes an appearance in the margin of one manuscript copy of Geoffrey's story, made soon after he composed it. A dignified figure with a long beard – an older Arthur come to comment on his youthful self – he makes an elegant gesture towards this particular passage as if to give Geoffrey's story his imprimatur: yes, he seems to say, these words are true.

The Arthur Geoffrey creates is a suitably war-like king: at Kaerluidcoit, he 'inflicted unparalleled losses on them [the Saxons]'; near Bath, armed with his sword Caliburnus, he alone 'laid low four hundred and seventy men' (Plate IV).[21] And yet he is also wise. Geoffrey pointedly mentions the occasions on which he seeks, and takes, advice from his retainers, the clergy and the nobles as he devises strategies against the Saxons.[22] Another dimension is an unexpectedly tender humanity; after a savage battle against the Scots and Picts, their priests 'knelt and implored him to take pity on their shattered people', at which Arthur was 'moved to tears of pity, agreed to the holy men's request and granted them pardon'.[23] But what gives Arthur a wholly new dimension is the sophistication and poise of his court, here assembled at his coronation:

> So noble was Britain then that it surpassed other kingdoms in its stores of wealth, the ostentation of its dress and the sophistication of its inhabitants. All its doughty knights wore clothes and armour of a single colour. Its elegant ladies, similarly dressed, spurned the love of any man who had not proved himself three times in battle. So the ladies were chaste and better women, whilst the knights conducted themselves more virtuously for the sake of their love.[24]

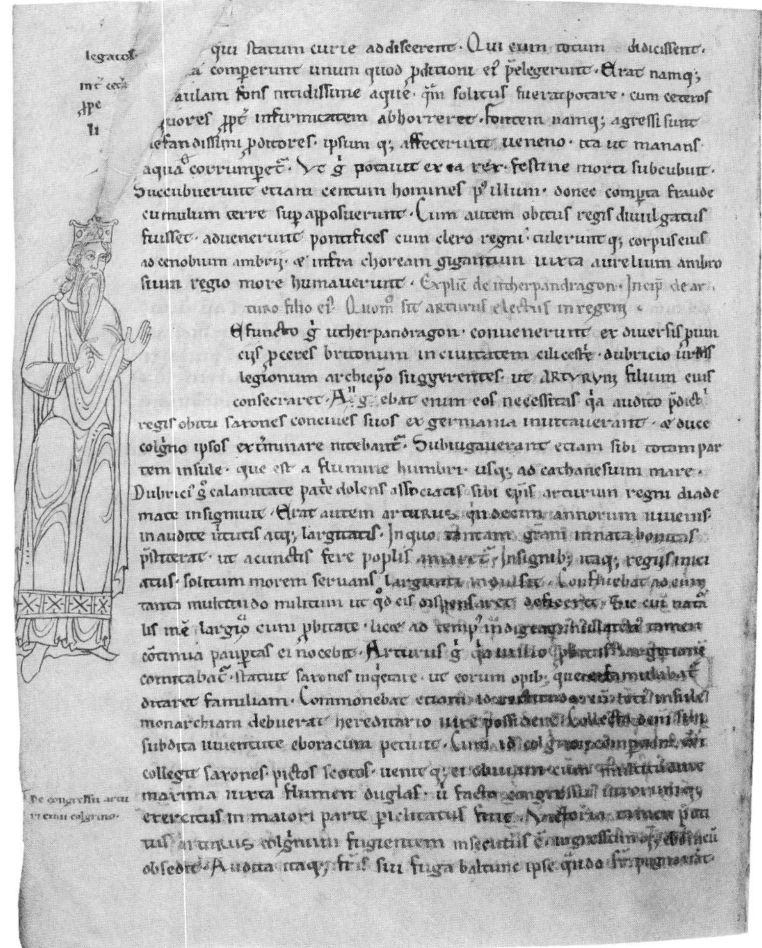

King Arthur in the margin of a late twelfth-century copy of Geoffrey of Monmouth's *History of the Kings of England*.

In plucking Arthur out of the mud of the battlefield and moving his military campaigns overseas, giving him imperial ambitions and putting him on a royal throne, Geoffrey created a character that chimed with the aspirations of the times. His Arthur was a fitting figurehead for an age in which the tougher, sometimes brutal militaristic aspects of the feudal system were being transformed by new aristocratic ideals of chivalry, courtly elegance and civility. As the taste for more refined living and sophisticated entertainment grew, Geoffrey borrowed from the tradition of Provençal poets and writers of romances to turn the old provincial warlord into a kingly leader, his behaviour guided by high ideals. The supernatural dimension that formerly shimmered around him like reflections on a stream is only vestigially present in Geoffrey's telling. A hint of it flashes from his sword Caliburnus (the precursor of Excalibur), a blade 'forged on the isle of Avallon'.[25] And it briefly shadows the text again at the end, when Arthur is mortally injured at the last battle against his nephew and 'taken away to the island of Avallon to have his wounds tended'.[26] But Geoffrey's interest is principally in the valour of Arthur's conduct in battle and the splendour of his court.

Geoffrey's tale was a live culture bubbling with potential, and it was not long before writers on both sides of the Channel took a little of it and went on to bake their own Arthurian stories, each adding distinctive new flavourings. In these new versions, mostly French at first, individual knights of Arthur's court become more prominent and are endowed with psychological depth and character, while Arthur's militarism reacquires a mystical dimension with the addition of the stories of the Lady of the Lake and the sword in the stone. In the twelfth century there was the Norman poet Wace, who finished the popular and widely read *Roman de Brut* in 1155 – the year Geoffrey died – 'translating' his *Historia* into French, adding the Round Table and making Arthur's knights a veritable European Union, bringing together 'Britons, Frenchmen, Normans, Angevins [from Anjou], Flemings, Burgundians and Loherins [from Lotharingia, a territory that included present-day Lorraine and Luxembourg]'. Following Wace were Chrétien de Troyes, who mined the psychological dimension suggested to him by King Arthur's flawed knights, composing exciting stories concerning Lancelot, Perceval and Yvain; and his contemporary Marie de France, in whose *Lais* the Arthurian court is the backdrop to the romantic trials of Lanval (Lancelot) and Tristan. In the thirteenth century, the English poet Layamon translated Wace's *Brut* back into English, doubling its length and embellishing the story yet further, describing the birth of Merlin and Arthur's departure to Avalon. These and a host of other romances grafted legends onto Arthur's story: the quest for the Holy Grail became a key feature of the Arthurian legend, as did the adulterous passion between Lancelot and Guinevere. One of the greatest of all Middle English poems, the late fourteenth-century *Sir Gawain and the Green Knight*, begins in Camelot on New Year's Day with King Arthur calling for a strange and marvellous tale – or for an unknown challenger to appear. Like puppets in a toy theatre, Arthur and his knights could be assembled in different combinations and sent out on new adventures. The 'false fables' that William of Malmesbury had worried were being spun around the figure of Arthur had apparently won a decisive victory.[27]

But then, in 1191, reality asserted itself when the remains of King Arthur and his queen Guinevere were purportedly discovered at Glastonbury Abbey. Five metres underground was found the great trunk of an oak tree, hollowed out and containing two skeletons. On top of the stone that covered it was a lead cross that, according to an account by Gerald of Wales, was inscribed with the words 'Hic jacet sepultus inclitus rex Arthurus in insula Avalonia' – here lies buried the renowned King Arthur on the Isle of Avalon. How did the monks know where to look? Gerald, a writer and former courtier to Henry II, who had visited Glastonbury within three or four years of the discovery and spoken to those involved, added a note of mystery by recording that an aged Welsh bard had conveyed the information to the King, which had prompted the search.[28] A more prosaic account simply noted that it had been discovered in the digging of another grave – although five metres seems an unwarranted depth. The truth is now generally thought to have been of a more secular nature: a publicity stunt dreamed up by the Abbot, designed to attract pilgrims and their money to the abbey in the wake of a devastating fire that had led to a costly rebuilding project.

But just suppose, for a moment, that it is not quite as cut and dried as that. How, in the twelfth century, did people frame the past? Imagine a Norman abbot and his colleagues picturing a tomb for King Arthur. Would they have thought of a coffin made from a hollowed-out oak? Would it not have been more likely for them to have imagined a grand stone vault and an effigy? The twelfth-century Arthur was Geoffrey of Monmouth's King Arthur, presiding over a superb, elegant and wealthy court. A hollowed-out oak seems better suited to Nennius's *dux bellorum*, with his semi-mystical connection to the land. Similarly, the inscription, eventually illustrated in William Camden's *Britannia*, is in archaic sub-Roman lettering of a kind that the abbot and his monks are unlikely to

Roger Fenton, *Glastonbury Abbey*, 1858. The abbey was the site of the 'discovery' of King Arthur's grave in 1191.

have thought to emulate. Monasteries in this period appear to have spent a considerable amount of time faking charters and other documents in order to attest and protect land-holdings or to burnish their prestige, but they rarely attempted anything more elaborate than smearing deeds with dirt or carrying them around for a few weeks in a coat pocket to give them the superficial appearance of age.[29] It is not impossible that the monks of Glastonbury, anxious to prove the abbey's antiquity, were unusually sophisticated in this respect. But as with other aspects of Arthur's life and death, a lingering suggestion of uncanniness cannot quite be dispelled.

As time went on, although the armour still shone, the atmosphere of the Arthurian legends began to darken. The fourteenth century saw the composition of the Alliterative *Morte Arthure* and the Stanzaic *Morte Arthur*, both of which focus on the final years of Arthur's reign and his fall on the field of battle. The catastrophes of the age – plague, famine and a seemingly endless war with France – had created a climate of intense nostalgia that led writers both to evoke past golden ages and to overshadow them with transience. In the late fifteenth century, a time of political upheaval and civil war, with the rival houses of Lancaster and York fighting for the throne, the days of King Arthur and an imagined chivalric past for England exerted a renewed fascination. The most comprehensive and influential of the era's retellings was composed by Sir Thomas Malory during a period of imprisonment between 1468 and 1470, possibly in the Tower of London, for his part in a plot against Edward IV. Wherever it was, it appears to have had an excellent library: Malory drew upon a wide range of English and French sources as he orchestrated his comprehensive retelling of the Arthurian legends, *Le Morte d'Arthur*. His book received its valedictory title by accident; Malory had given it the more fitting title *The Whole Book of King Arthur and his Noble Knights of the Round Table*, but when it was printed in 1485, William Caxton took the name of the last section for that of the whole, and it stuck. In his preface, Caxton promises a tale of 'noble chivalry, courtesy, humanity, friendliness, hardiness, love, friendship, cowardice, murder, hate, virtue and sin' – human experiences and emotions that, he emphasizes, were every bit as relevant to the late fifteenth century as they were in those far-off times.[30] Malory's text, printed rather than circulated in manuscript copies, reached a significantly wider audience; tales of the olden days were given wings by this new technology.

The question of Arthur's status as a historical figure arose again at this time. Back in 1191, when his grave was 'discovered' at Glastonbury, Gerald of Wales reported it with an air of triumph because he saw it as proof that Arthur was dead; it put paid once and for all, he thought, to the ridiculous tales circulating among the British that he was still alive. By the time of *Le Morte d'Arthur* the situation had been turned inside out. In his preface, Caxton feels the need to assert the reality of Arthur, which many had come to doubt: 'divers men', he writes, 'hold opinion that there was no such Arthur, and that all such books as been made of him, be but feigned and fables, because that some chronicles make of him no mention, nor remember him nothing, nor of his knights'. Countering this, he goes on to cite 'many evidences of the contrary' – one only need look, Caxton says, at his tomb at Glastonbury, to read history books such as Geoffrey's, to remember his seal at Saint Edward's shrine in Westminster and his round table at Winchester and to recall all those books celebrating his noble acts written not only in English but in Dutch, Italian, Spanish, Greek and French. It was important, Caxton thought, for *Le Morte d'Arthur* to be rooted in fact; it gave meaning and heft to the stories, especially important because most works to have been printed at this date were religious.

Arthur stood on the threshold, at the hinge between man and myth. He shimmered between the two, like a ghost: neither real nor fabulous, neither living nor dead. But whether ordinary people thought of Arthur as a great chieftain, a semi-supernatural figure who had never died, or a mythical figure who had never lived in the first place, there was no doubt that he was kept in their minds by stories and legends that were passed on through the generations. A vital part of his enduring power was his shaping of the landscape. According to place names, Arthur left his mark on hills and boulders up and down the land. In his ninth-century history of Britain, Nennius describes one such 'wonder' in the region of Builth in Brecknockshire:

> There is a heap of stones there, and one of the stones placed on top of the pile has the footprint of a dog on it. When he hunted Twrch Trwyth [a legendary wild boar], Cabal, the warrior Arthur's hound, impressed his footprint on the stone, and Arthur later brought together the pile of stones, under the stone in which was his dog's footprint, and it is called Carn Cabal. And men come and take the stone in their hands for the space of a day and a night, and on the morrow it is found upon the stone pile.[31]

In the general way of place names, many such examples have endured. Great boulders acquired the names Arthur's Oven, Arthur's Seat or Arthur's Stone, while a circle of tall stones on Bodmin Moor, sunk into the turf like the backs of gigantic chairs, became known as King Arthur's Hall. Even Arthur's reputed coffin, imagined as the hollowed-out trunk of an oak, connects him to the land and associates him with oaky qualities: ruggedness, solidity, endurance. At the heart of these names is the suggestion that Arthur had been transformed into an elemental being, become a part of the landscape, which still vibrated with his personality – we are reminded of Nennius, and his description of Arthur fighting battles by rivers, woods and hills. He was – surely – too great a figure to have gone entirely. If, indeed, he had gone at all. The wealthy and the educated had their Arthurian romances; for those without the means to read them, here instead were tales about particular, familiar places. The landscape itself was the book in which they learned of King Arthur. The great stones in wild places, symbols of his watchful presence, can be seen as placeholders in case of his return.

Arthur was a shape-shifting hero for many generations; he could be dressed up or down to meet the particular needs of any given era. And this ever-expanding fabric of Arthurian story, legend and folklore that had come to occupy a central place in English history had political resonances, too. Henry VII, who came to the throne the year that Malory's *Morte d'Arthur* was published, named his eldest son Arthur in a move to cement links with this legendary British king, who after all was prophesied to return – and to lay claim to a dynasty that led all the way back to Brutus himself.

It is exacting work, such delicate drawing. Pen in hand, his long parchment scroll draped over his desk and tumbling onto the floor, John Rous is pursing his lips and furrowing his eyebrows in concentration. It is sometime between 1477 and 1485, and he has been asked by the Beauchamp family to draw up the genealogy of the earls of Warwick: he has represented each figure with a portrait drawn in pen, a coat of arms above and a brief written description below. When Rous has finished, he turns the parchment over and, as a grace note, adds a portrait of himself: a pleasant-looking, rather stout man dressed in ecclesiastical robes sitting at his desk in a sturdy armchair, he presents a comfortable contrast to the armoured figures of the other side, beginning with the legendary founders of Warwick, going by way of various kings and concluding with the powerful earls of Rous's day, Richard III and Edward, Prince of Wales.

Roll chronicles were fishing lines designed to descend through the still waters of time, dropping from generation to generation until they dipped into the fertile, if somewhat murky, sediment of myth. By Rous's time, rolls had been used to represent genealogies for centuries, and they continued to be popular: one spectacular illustrated chronicle, begun in the middle of the fifteenth century for Henry VI, was added to as late as 1665 to include Charles II. Intended to demonstrate Henry's claim to the throne – contested by his Yorkist opponents – it begins with Adam and Eve in the Garden of Eden and makes its way to the present via Noah. Comparable rolls made for James I demonstrate his descent from Brutus.[32]

But Rous's was different. In its quiet way, it introduced a new way of understanding the past. It had not occurred to most other writers and illuminators that fashions changed – and that, as a result, one could make

Self-portrait by John Rous on the back of a roll chronicle, *c.* 1477–85.

a reasonably accurate guess at the date of a monument by looking at what the people represented on it were wearing. In medieval illustrations of the story of Troy, for instance, the figures generally wear contemporary costume: wooden horses are pushed through the gates of medieval towns, while Greek soldiers clad in medieval armour sail into medieval Trojan harbours.[33] But rather than drawing the Saxon contingent, the Norman Newburghs and the more recent Beauchamps all wearing armour of the mid-fifteenth century, Rous imagines them in garb they might actually have worn.[34]

A priest in the chantry of Guy's Cliffe outside Warwick, Rous was able to devote much of his time to antiquarian research. He saw the past not only in manuscripts, but in physical objects. He went into churches and looked hard at memorial brasses and effigies, where the information he sought was engraved in metal and sculpted in stone. The first of the warrior-earls he depicts, such as the mythical Arthgallus – perhaps another name for Arthur himself – are in long chainmail surcoats of the kind he saw represented in the earliest surviving effigies.[35] It was a reasonable guess. He was able to plot the date at which mail coats began to be superseded by plate armour, when the visored bassinet was developed (although he was a few decades adrift in that respect) and when cuisses and greaves started to be worn.[36] He may have been invited to Warwick Castle to see actual suits of armour worn by individual earls – the current incumbents were, after all, employing him. Rous evidently enjoyed making connections between legends and the objects that had somehow drifted through time and washed up in the present. He mentions a cup that played an important part in the story of Sir Enyas, then kept in the Beauchamps' 'tresori', confiding: 'I have dronk of the same I dar the better wryghten.'[37]

The patience with which Rous established facts about the past by looking around for evidence co-existed apparently comfortably with his belief in old legends and fables. Even in his daily life, fact and fancy were woven together: Guy's Cliffe was where the legendary Guy of Warwick, a folkloric English hero who was 'adopted' by the Beauchamps and written into their family history, supposedly ended his days as a hermit. Rous himself wrote a history of England in which the old legend of Brutus and his successors was stirred in with contemporary politics and urgent protests against park enclosures. Another of his books – now lost – was about giants, perhaps inspired by Guy, who, according to fable, fought and killed the Danish giant Colbrand. There was nothing unusual about Rous's belief in these great creatures. There was biblical authority for their existence: they were mentioned in various books of the Old Testament, including Genesis, where it is clearly stated that 'There were giants in the earth in those days' (6:4). They also played a key part in 'the British History', as the Brutus myth and related stories had come to be known, having allegedly inhabited the island before the conqueror's arrival. But what might have appealed particularly to Rous was the tangible evidence that these enormous beings had once lumbered around Britain. For one thing, there was the ancient outline of Gogmagog, the giant fought by Brutus's follower Corineus and subsequently thrown over the cliff into the sea, that was carved into the turf at Plymouth Hoe as a memorial of this event and kept scoured in Rous's day. And there were the immense bones that were sometimes found; the thirteenth-century chronicler Ralph of Coggeshall discovered what he took to be the rib of a giant on the Essex seashore, and naturally thought it worth recording. For a historian such as Rous, physical records such as these told their own story.

Although a number of scholars had begun to be sceptical, in Rous's day, the British History was still part of people's mental furniture.[38] Thanks to William Caxton the stories even went into print in 1480, in his popular *Chronicles of England*, which became the standard history for its era. But change was coming. New and rigorous ways of looking at the world had begun to transform understanding of science, nature and history. First-hand accounts came to be valued above old fables. These ideas originated in Italy and spread throughout Europe; appropriately enough, the man who first publicly took a keen-edged scythe to the overgrown garden of legend, folklore and downright nonsense that passed for British history was an Italian scholar, Polydore Vergil.

Vergil was fascinated by how things began. In an earlier book, written with the aid of the well-stocked library shelves in Urbino belonging to his patron Duke Guidobaldo, he had posed the kinds of difficult questions that would not have crossed most people's minds: where did the ancient gods come from? What are the origins of the institution of marriage? He scrutinized music, poetry and philosophy. He wondered who divided the day into hours and who had come up with the letters of the alphabet. More ordinary things, in his view, were no less worthy of research; with the help of Greek and Latin texts as well as the Bible and the works of early historians, Vergil explored the origins of everything under the sun from books and buildings to buttons, bellows and warm baths. He assembled his discoveries in an ambitious book titled *De inventoribus rerum* (On the inventors of all things), essentially a cultural history of humanity that covered ideas, crafts, traditions and religious practices. It was a bestseller, going through more than thirty editions in his lifetime. As far as Vergil was concerned, no aspect of human life, history or tradition was beyond keen and critical questioning, not even the church. He did not support practices such as the sale of indulgences, for example, and as a result *De inventoribus rerum* was eventually placed on the papal index of forbidden books.

This was the man – sceptical, mercurial, intellectually audacious – who was sent to England in 1502 by the Borgia pope Alexander VI as a sub-collector of 'Peter's pence', or donations made to the Catholic Church.[39] Vergil's illustrious continental connections, including the great humanist scholar Erasmus, enabled him to make friends in England in a learned circle that included Thomas More and the scholar and physician Thomas Linacre. He was received by Henry VII – the same Henry who had sought Arthurian legitimacy for his firstborn son – and claimed 'ever after' to have been 'entertained by him kindly'. The King encouraged Vergil to write a new history of England, which he began to research in earnest in 1506 to 1507; it was first published in Basel in 1534, with revised editions appearing over the following two decades.

In researching the subject, Vergil applied the same rigorous method that he had brought to the origins of human culture. Rather than contenting himself with retelling the usual legends, he scoured classical authorities such as Caesar's *Gallic Wars*, Tacitus's *Agricola* and Pliny's *Natural History* to discover what they had to say about early Britain; for the sub-Roman period he used Gildas and Bede; and for the medieval period he mined the writings of respected historians such as William of Malmesbury, William of Newburgh and Matthew Paris. From the outset, his determination to cut through colourful fantasies about the early history of the British was clear. 'What kinde of people were the first inhabitants of Brittaine, whether thei that were bredde in the contrie or otherwise straungers, it was never yet sufficientlie knowne or determined', writes Vergil in his *Anglica historia*, and states his intention to return to the earliest sources and to 'repete there sentences in order, and to laye them beefore the ieys of the reader...bie cause an Historie is a full rehersall and declaration of things don, not a gesse or divination.'[40] Or, indeed, a complete fiction. He read a great deal about Brutus's triumphant arrival in Albion in early British histories. But when he turned to the bookshelves to consult works by the great classical historians in search of this illustrious founder, Vergil found him to be strangely elusive: 'nether Livie, nether Dionisius Halicarnaseus, who writt diligentlie of the Romane antiquities, nor divers other writers, did ever once make rehersall of this Brutus'. Armed with acute new methods of scholarship, with one well-aimed prod Vergil had punctured the gaudy bubble of the

British History. Brutus had, apparently, never existed and Geoffrey of Monmouth was guilty of 'moste impudent lyeing'.[41]

Vergil would not, however, have lasted long in the pope's employment without a good measure of charm and diplomacy, and he goes on to suggest that Britain was by no means alone in seeking a great figure for a foundation myth, and it was easy to see how one thing led to another until everyone believed it:

> But in olde time [the British] did presume on this fraunchise and libertie that manie nations weare so bowlde as to derive the beginninge of theire stocke from the Goddes (as especiallie the Romaines did), to thentent the originall of there people and citties mighte bee the more princlie and prosperus, which things, albeit thei sownded more like fabels then the sincere witnesses of noble acts, yet weare thei receaved for trewthe; for the which cause even those things which last of all were committed to writinge of the antiquities of Britaines, were with soe easye credit receaved of the common sorte that thei have ascribid the fownteine of theire genialogie to Brutus....[42]

Vergil had, also, to admit that his intellectual triumph left him with a problem. As soon as one pushed Brutus out of the way and took a long, hard look at the space where he used to be, it became grimly apparent that 'all things are full of darcknes. Trulie ther is nothinge more obscure, more uncertaine, or unknowne then the affaires of the Brittons from the beginninge.'[43] There were no extant records from this early period, he acknowledges sadly – Gildas, one of the earliest British historians, had testified to that. According to him they had all been destroyed. All he could suggest – reasonably enough, one might think – was that tribes had come across the Channel from northern Gaul. No matter how rigorous Vergil's intellectual method, and with what devastating effect he applied it to the British History, he was in the unenviable position of knocking down a bold, dazzling, status-enhancing founder and replacing him with a rabble of Gaulish invaders.

When he embarks on his list of British kings, for the sake of tradition – and so as not to upset his readers too much – Vergil decides to fill this void with brief mentions of Brutus and his sons, although he does so, he admits, 'not altogether without indignation'. We can well imagine. He takes a slightly different tack when it comes to Arthur; as with Brutus, he would probably rather have left him out entirely, but instead decides on summarizing Geoffrey's version of the story with heavy sarcasm. The 'common people', he remarks,

> extol Arthure unto the heavens, alleginge that hee daunted three capitans of the Saxons in plaine feelde; that hee subdewed Scotlande with the Iles adjoyninge; that in the teritorie of the Parisiens hee manfullie overthrew the Romaines, with there capitan Lucius; that hee didd depopulat Fraunce; that finallie hee slewe giauntes, and appalled the hartes of sterne and warlike menne.[44]

It was ironic that it should have been Henry VII who set this in motion by his encouragement of Vergil. While over the years people had gradually come to be less inclined to accept the British History as fact rather than fable – as we have seen, in his 1485 preface to Malory's *Morte d'Arthur* Caxton felt it necessary to assert Arthur's status as a historical figure – Henry's accession changed the cultural climate and gave impetus to its revival. Here was a monarch with Welsh ancestry, who claimed descent from Cadwaladr ap Cadwallon, the seventh-century king described in Welsh tradition as the last king of the Britons. It fulfilled a prophecy made to Cadwaladr that the British line would one day return to the throne, delivering the Welsh from their Saxon oppressors.[45] In calling his first son Arthur, Henry VII created the impression of mystic destiny, proclaiming the Prince as a legitimate successor to the most glorious of British heroes. Merlin's prophecy that Arthur would one day return was, in a sense, fulfilled. Events in Prince Arthur's short life were celebrated in poems and pageants that revelled in Arthurian symbolism. One of the pageants celebrating his marriage in 1501 was presided over by the figure of King Arthur on a gold throne. Someone declaimed a poem that described Britain as 'The lond of Arthure', and the palace was decorated for the marriage with 'the picturs of the noble Kings of this realme', which included Brutus and Arthur.[46] When this promising young man tragically died in 1502, his arms were displayed alongside those of his illustrious ancestors Brutus and Cadwaladr.

It was not an auspicious time for Vergil to point out that it was all nonsense. Indeed, he is careful to promote the idea of Henry VII's British lineage, referring to the prophecy made to Cadwaladr from an 'apparition' lent authority by its 'heavenly appearance': 'Thus Henry acquired the kingdom,' he wrote, 'an event of which foreknowledge had been possible both many centuries earlier and also soon after his birth.' For the Tudors themselves, King Arthur's potent symbolism was far too precious to jettison.

It is 6 June 1522, early evening in the City of London. But rather than the usual slackening of tension, the emptying, dusty space that comes in summer with the working day's end, the streets have erupted into colour and noise. Crowds gather and disperse just as quickly, hurrying to better vantage points. Necks are stretched and tiptoes stood upon as each person strains to see. The smell of bonfires is in the air, and there are stalls selling cakes and ale. Members of the clergy and city livery companies line the roadside, attempting to maintain a dignified composure. And suddenly, with a fanfare of trumpets and a collective intake of breath, here they come: two young leaders, side by side, mounted on matching horses. In a touch of theatre so unexpected it could almost make you laugh, they are dressed identically. King Henry VIII is escorting his visitor, the Holy Roman Emperor Charles V – one of the most powerful men in the world – in a procession through his city, and as they make their way through the streets they are welcomed by a series of magnificent pageants.[48] At the drawbridge on the approach to London Bridge they meet the giants Hercules and Samson who, in a welcoming mood, hold between them a great board inscribed in splendid gold letters with the names of the lands and dominions belonging to Charles. On the bridge the King and Emperor pass Jason and Medea, who are celebrating the chivalric Order of the Golden Fleece; on Gracechurch Street they are greeted by Charles's illustrious ancestor Charlemagne, who graciously presents swords and crowns to each; and at Leadenhall they encounter a genealogical tree that demonstrates their mutual lineage from John of Gaunt. Figures from myth and history keep bursting into spectacular, three-dimensional life to greet, delight and flatter these two men. Keep on, though: edge your way back through the crowds, the torch-bearers and the men dancing the morris to Cornhill, because that is where you will see one of the most spectacular sights of all. On each side of the street great towers have been built, over which banners stream and into which trumpeters and sackbut-players have crowded. Between these, a palace has been constructed for King Arthur himself to hold court at the Round Table, surrounded by 'all the noble pryncces that were under his obeisaunce', as a contemporary witness said.[49] Arthur has taken his place at the heart of this festival of living history.

This was not the only time Henry brought his guest face to face with Arthur. Later that month, after a state visit to Windsor, they travelled on to Winchester, where Henry proudly took the Emperor to see one of the most spectacular relics of England's medieval past, hanging high on the wall of Winchester Castle's Great Hall: King Arthur's round table itself (Plate III). Seventeen feet wide, the great board famously proclaimed each knight's equal status: 'Tuit esteient assis meain', as the poet Wace, who introduced it into the Arthurian story, had put it – all were seated alike. Had the table been real, it would have almost vibrated under the strain of the emotions it had absorbed; in fact, it was probably made in 1290 for Edward I, a notable Arthurian enthusiast who held 'round table' feasts and tournaments for which his knights played the parts of Sir Gawain, Sir Lancelot, Sir Perceval and so on.[50] No matter. What was important was what people believed it to be – a precious relic that represented Britain's enchanted Arthurian past. But Henry had gone a step further. As he and his guest stood admiring the table, Charles would have studied the large portrait of King Arthur himself, enthroned and seated under a canopy, painted on the table. Was he struck by the distinct facial resemblance between the venerable king and his host? If not, he should have been. Henry had recently had the table repainted, and that was precisely the effect that the portrait, which depicted a remarkably young-looking, vigorous Arthur, was intended to achieve.[51] King Arthur of the Cornhill pageant was one thing; but here, apparently, was clear evidence that the king of England had precious Arthurian blood charging through his veins.

Dearly held ideas about the past – particularly when they touched on King Arthur – mattered because they related so keenly to the present in the form of Henry VIII and the Tudor dynasty. Lineage was all. In claiming a bloodline, the sovereign claimed for him or herself the essential essence of former monarchs all the way back to Brutus; after the Reformation, when precedents justifying the new dispensation were keenly sought, the stakes were even higher.[52] The intemperance with which some scholars greeted Polydore Vergil's scepticism was, then, entirely predictable.[53]

Among the first to respond was John Leland, a scholar and antiquarian connected to Henry VIII's court, who wrote first an angry pamphlet and then a book that made a spirited case for Arthur's historical existence. Pointedly disparaging 'the fond fables or base stuffe of forraine writers', he imagines himself as the wind, whose breath will 'drive darke shadowes away' so that everyone will be dazzled anew by the 'bright shining sun' that was Arthur. Apart from a downright intimidating array of scholarly sources, prominently displayed in list form near the beginning, an important part of Leland's intellectual artillery was his first-hand knowledge of British places. It gave him a distinct advantage when it came to delving into 'the Misteries of sacred Antiquitie', as he put it. The physical remains of history mattered to Leland, and unusually, he was not reliant on mere hearsay concerning Arthurian relics. When he visited Westminster, where King Arthur's seal was kept, it was, as he said, 'to the end that what so as an eare witnesse I had heard, I might at length also as an eye witnesse behold the same'.[54] And not only look, but touch; when he visited Glastonbury he was shown the inscribed lead plate that had been found on Arthur's tomb when it was discovered some three hundred and fifty years before. Gingerly he took it in his hands, 'with feareful joyntes in each part,' he admitted, 'being moved both with the Antiquitie and worthinesse of the thing'.[55]

Leland did not know it, but he was standing on a fault-line, as the medieval and the Renaissance clashed and ground together and old and new ways of thinking were compounded. Although alive to the value of first-hand observation rather than reliance on time-honoured stories as a way of understanding the past, he was also capable of bringing all his intellectual acuity to the defence of a fable.

It was one thing to defend the British History; it was quite another to add to it. But Leland's close friend, the Protestant convert and passionate religious reformer John Bale – so splenetic in his speech he came to be known as 'Bilious Bale' – did just that. Accusing Vergil of 'polutynge oure Englyshe chronycles most shamefullye with his Romishe lyes and other Italyshe beggerye', he bolstered the 'chronycles' in two ingenious ways.[56] In a catalogue of British authors published in 1548, he delved into the early history of Britain and explained one of the more puzzling aspects of the well-known tale: why Albion had been inhabited by giants when the Trojans arrived. At the same time, he supplied a biblical connection, neatly filling in the gap between the Flood, survived only by Noah, his family and a representative group of animals, and the arrival of Brutus. After the Flood, Bale argued, the world was repopulated by the sons of Noah: Shem, Ham and Japhet. Japhet had a son, Samothes, who became the first king of the continental Celts and of Britannia. He provided laws and taught the Britons and the Gauls about the stars and politics. His son Magus gave the people knowledge of building. His son Sarron brought philosophy. His son Druys founded the Druids. His son Bardus introduced music and poetry. Are you still with me? Agriculture was taught by Osiris, a descendant of Ham, who visited Britain. His descendant Albion, an evil giant, taught the science of navigation and, becoming king of Britain, it was he, of course, who gave his name to the island. During the five centuries between Albion's death in 1708 BC and the arrival of Brutus around 1140 BC, giants populated the land and things went badly downhill. In fact, even as far back as the days of Sarron, the Golden Age had become the Age of Silver; with Albion the Age of Iron began.[57]

Bale did not invent this back story for Britain. He was taken in by a literary hoax in the form of a book of the late fifteenth century about the post-Flood peopling of the world that purported to be written by two great sages: the Chaldæan historian and astrologer Berosus, and the Egyptian historian Manetho.[58] By both filling an otherwise mysterious gap and situating Britain within the biblical chronology, this book had an irresistible allure. Now that Brutus and his descendants, including Arthur, had been linked with such apparent certainty to biblical authority, it seemed as though they were here to stay.

When in 1575 Elizabeth I arrived at Kenilworth Castle in Warwickshire as a guest of the Earl of Leicester, the days that lay ahead offered a magnificent prospect of plays, dances, masques, hunting and firework displays, each intricately stage-managed event bristling with allusions to literature and legend, and every corner of the gardens sprouting emblems and allegories. Ovid's *Metamorphoses* was evoked, as was the elaborate Venetian story of 1499, *Hypnerotomachia Poliphili*, which described the pursuit of love through a dreamlike landscape.[59] But that summer's evening, when in the twilight her horse's hooves first struck Kenilworth's grounds, the atmosphere in which the Queen was immersed was an unmistakeably Arthurian one. Crossing the bridge that stretched over an ornamental pool towards the castle, she was greeted by the Lady of the Lake, who, the eyewitness Robert Langham reported, was 'famous in king Arthurz book'. The Lady was standing on a 'moovabl Iland, bright blazing with torches', which appeared to float to the shore at the Queen's approach, upon which she addressed the sovereign with some 'well penned' verses that introduced the ancient history of the castle and then herself. 'I am the Lady of this pleasant lake', she sang,

> Who, since the time of great King Arthur's reign
> That here with royal court abode did make,
> Have led a lowering life in restless pain.

Elizabeth's presence has, she says, renewed her joy, and she concludes with the lines:

> And as my love to Arthur did appear,
> So shall't to you, in earnest and in sport,
> Pass on, Madame, you need no longer stand –
> The Lake, the Lodge, the Lord, are yours for to command.[60]

Her words are a masterpiece of diplomacy. Although the setting is richly Arthurian, there is no Arthur here who could rival the Queen. As his successor, Queen Elizabeth steps into the richly fabled but sad, 'lowering' world and redeems it, becoming, herself, a new Arthur.

The Elizabethan court loved to reimagine medieval chivalry. The annual Accession Day Tilts, in which the Queen's knights jousted before her, were opportunities for theatrical display expertly stage-managed by Sir Henry Lee, the Queen's ceremonial Champion and Master of the Armouries. Those taking part commissioned spectacular armour, fashioned elaborate disguises and had their shields painted with allegorical emblems. These pageants slipped into literature such as Sir Philip Sidney's *Arcadia* (1590), which describes annual tournaments in which the knights appear in ingenious costumes: one, along with his horse, is encased inside an image of a phoenix that is set on fire, so that when he emerges he appears to rise

The Redcrosse Knight, woodcut illustrating Edmund Spenser's *Faerie Queene* (1590).

out of the ashes, while his opponent is a Frozen Knight with icicles on his armour.[61] Edmund Spenser claimed in a letter to Sir Walter Raleigh that the structure of his epic poem the *Faerie Queene* derived from the Tilts, the number of chapters, knights and adventures corresponding to the number of days 'the Faery Queene kept her Annuall feast'.[62] In this world of fire and ice, threaded with allegory and emblazoned with emblems, the dividing line between fiction and reality kept slipping out of sight. If a spectacle could be imagined, it could be realized.

Like the Accession Day Tilts, Spenser's *Faerie Queene* links Queen Elizabeth to a chivalric past, delving deeply into Arthurian legend and recounting a version of the British History. Even the language he chooses to use in the poem is deliberately archaic, drawing on expressions used by earlier poets like Chaucer, Lydgate and Skelton, and adapting familiar words in ways that would, to a contemporary ear, have sounded quaint and antiquated.[63] Spenser's collaborator E. K. explained his use of archaisms as a natural, even unconscious consequence of his familiarity with poets of earlier generations: 'how could it be', he wrote, 'but that walking in the sonne although for other cause he walked, yet needes he mought be sunburnt; and having the sound of those auncient Poetes still ringing in his eares, he mought needes in singing hit out some of theyr tunes'. And anyway, he concluded, these 'olde and obsolete wordes bring great grace and, as one would say, auctoritie to the verse'.[64] In the Elizabethan court, the past was a giant golden mirror, held up to reflect a glorious radiance over the present.

The Elizabethan habit of allegory ran deep. When Spenser wrote 'Thus *Brute* this Realme unto his rule subdewd, / And raigned long in great felicitie' he was describing not an actual past, but a poetic one of myth and symbol. The British History had evolved into a shared national legend, valuable not because it was literal truth but because these heroic tales encapsulated values that bolstered a cherished collective identity.[65] Raphael Holinshed included a detailed run-through of the whole saga, including Bale's pre-Brutus material, in his popular and influential *Chronicles of England, Scotland and Ireland* (1577, revised 1587), the great compendium of stories and legends that William Shakespeare mined not only for his history plays but also for the tragedies *King Lear* and *Macbeth*. Holinshed does, however, include a disclaimer in his introduction:

> sith the originall in maner of all nations is doubtful, and even the same for the more parte fabulous (that always excepted which we fynde in the holy scriptures) I wishe not any man to leane to that whiche shall be heere set downe, as to an infallible truth, sith I do but only shewe other mennes conjectures, grounded neverthelesse uppon likely reasons (concernyng that matter whereof there is now left but little other certaynti [...]), or rather none at all.[66]

This uncertainty weighed on the conscience of Ben Jonson in 1603, when he and Thomas Dekker wrote the script for the 'Magnificent Entertainment', a pageant for the triumphal entrance of James I into London (delayed because of the plague until 1604), in which the Genius Loci mentions Brutus in his speech of 'Gratulation'. This evocation of Brutus was all very well in words declaimed to accompany a dazzling spectacle – but in the published script Jonson felt bound to explain himself: 'Rather than the City should want a founder,' he notes fastidiously, 'we choose to follow the received story of Brute, whether fabulous, or true, and not altogether unwarranted in poetry: since it is a favour of antiquity to few cities to let them know their first authors.'[67]

So did Brutus and the Trojans begin to fade from the scene? Not for some time. Between 1597 and 1607, Richard White, a distinguished Professor of Law at Douai University and one of Europe's most respected historians, published a *Historium Britanniae* – in Latin and therefore aimed at a Continental readership – that presented all the legends surrounding Brutus and the glorious lineage of kings. This magisterial swansong of the British History far outshone its contemporary, the diligently researched *Britannia* by the comparatively little-known antiquarian William Camden.[68] Even John Milton gave the old legends a degree of credence in his *History of Britain, that Part Especially now call'd England* (1670, though composed in the 1640s). Although he is dismissive of many early fables – an 'Outlandish figment' he calls one, 'too absurd' another – when it comes to 'Brutus and his Line, with the whole Progeny of Kings, to the entrance of Julius Caesar', he admits that 'we cannot so easily be discharg'd'.[69]

As Polydore Vergil had reluctantly conceded in his history, although Brutus and his entourage were rooted in evidence so shallow that they could be toppled with the first gust of fresh Renaissance air, a blank was never going to be accepted as a substitute. Nothing was going to replace the Trojans and their illustrious descendants until an arresting new figure could step out of the shadows of the past.

II
THE TREASURES OF TIME

For many years, those who were sceptical about the British History had been straining their inner eyes in vain as they sought to discern the shades of early Britons in the darkness that concealed the past. The 'ancient inhabitours of the Iland', lamented the Elizabethan antiquary William Camden, 'lie so hidden in the utmost nooke and secretest closet of Antiquitie, as it were in a most thicke wood, where no pathwaies are to be seene'.[1] Sometimes, however, breakthroughs come from unexpected places. And when this one came, it was not so much from the past as from a distant shore.

But before we go there, we should make Camden's acquaintance.

When Camden was a student at Oxford in the 1560s he had great difficulty staying indoors. One minute he would be at his desk in the library, apparently absorbed in a book. But before he knew what was happening he would find himself on his feet, reaching for his hat and heading for the door. There was one sort of history within the pages of books, yes, but Camden was alive to a kind that was written into Britain's landscapes and buildings. Outdoors were the remains of ancient military encampments, were barrows and stone circles, were the ruins of ancient castles, all waiting to be explored.[2] In Camden's mind, geography leaked into history – history coloured geography – and any excursion was a journey into the past. Others might regard landscapes and townscapes merely as the familiar backdrop to their lives, or look at unusual features like long barrows or stone circles through a prism of folklore and fables; but he wanted to use his pen as a needle and thread to stitch places to the historical events that had occurred in them.

The works of classical authors such as Caesar and Tacitus were becoming available in England, bringing much-needed fresh information and giving Camden a distinct advantage over his predecessors. It was now more possible than before to restore 'antiquity to Britaine, and Britaine to his antiquity', as he neatly described his ambition in the introduction to his book *Britannia, or a Chorographicall Description of the most Flourishing Kingdomes, England, Scotland, and Ireland* (first published in 1586). In this great undertaking he promised to 'renew ancientrie, enlighten obscuritie, cleare doubts, and recall home veritie by way of recovery, which the negligence of writers and credulitie of the common sort had in a manner proscribed and utterly banished from amongst us'. Given the colourful kaleidoscope of fable and local legend through which most people viewed the British past, this project was a lot to take on, and he was well aware of it. 'A painfull matter, I assure you', he admits, and promises us that he has carried out thorough research, having 'travailed over all England... conferred with most skillful observers in each county...studiously read over our owne countrie writers, old and new, all Greeke and Latine authors which have once made mention of Britaine...had conference with learned men in other parts of Christendome...looked into most Libraries, Registers, and memorials of Churches, Cities, and Corporations [and] poored upon many an old Rowle'.[3]

Camden – the most vigorous new broom in the history of British history – was determined to sweep away the dingy old layers of myth and fable that had accrued over the centuries. One reason for this resolve was his coming-of-age in the aftermath of the dissolution of the monasteries, the first major phase of Protestant iconoclasm which under Edward VI extended the depredations of monastic property to parish churches. In this new era, the catastrophic destruction of countless manuscripts, records, paintings, sculpture, stained glass and precious objects of all kinds was shockingly recent, and the material remnants of the past were newly precious. What Camden was looking for on his excursions was material evidence that would allow him to piece together the shattered fragments. The landscapes through which he rode as he researched *Britannia* county by county were, to him, surfaces upon which he could read history – quite literally, in the case of the coins he found and the Roman stone inscriptions he transcribed. Camden was not a polemicist after the fashion of Polydore Vergil, stacking up evidence like so much ammunition; rather, he was an antiquarian, laying out the facts as he understood them like exhibits in a cabinet of curiosities, for us to examine and wonder about. To an extent he was obliged to make it up as he went along; as his first biographer put it, it was 'a sort of Learning, that was then but just appearing in the world'.[4]

Despite Camden's businesslike tone as he trots briskly from place to place, a melancholy undertow often interrupts the flow of *Britannia*. The extent to which ancient books and 'old Rowles' had been neglected and inscriptions allowed to crumble into illegibility caused him genuine distress; time and again he had cause to lament that centuries-old voices, still capable of communicating vital bits of information, had fallen silent almost within living memory. Sometimes he came tantalizingly close to these ancient historians whose accounts he so longed to hear. In his section on Wiltshire, he recalls finding in a church a hollowed-out block of wood with its interior lined in lead and 'a booke therein of very thicke parchment, all written in Capitall Romane letters. but', records Camden sadly,

> it had lien so long that when the leaves were touched they fouldered [crumbled] to dust. Sir Thomas Eliot, who saw it, judged it to be an Historie. No doubt hee that so carefully laied it up hoped it should be found and discover some things memorable to posteritie.[5]

In Cumbria he describes his exploration of a Roman encampment: 'But now Corne growes where the towne stood, nevertheless many expresse footings thereof are evidently to be seene. The ancient vaults stand open, and many altars, stones with inscriptions, and Statues are heere gotten out of the ground.' He made a survey of it with his friend Robert Cotton – 'a singular lover of antiquity' – and yet his account is tinged with sadness about the wealth of things he is unable to save and the many precious objects that, through ignorance, have been 'defaced, broken, and converted to other uses'.[6] Virtually everywhere he went Camden must have been confronted with the sad reality of how few people shared his own reverence for history.

There were some parts of the landscape, however, that remained stubbornly taciturn even under Camden's inquisitive questioning. Despite his fascination with the ancient past, time and time again when he looked at barrows and hillforts, the Romans got in the way. At Yarnbury Camp near Wylye in Wiltshire, which we now know to be an Iron Age hillfort, he declares confidently that 'by the forme and maner of making, a man

Ancient Roman inscriptions found in Northumberland, engraving in William Camden's *Britannia* (1806 edition).

may easily know it was a Romane Campe'. Contemplating Julliberrie's Grave, a Neolithic long barrow near Chilham in Kent, he dismisses local legends that it was the tomb of a witch or a giant and, reasonably enough, speculates that it was the grave of the Roman military officer Laberius Durus, killed nearby during Caesar's second expedition to Britain. There were, frustratingly, just too few pieces of the jigsaw, and too many gaps that could only be filled with speculation. But as Camden himself put it, 'who is so skilfull that, strugling with Time in the foggie dark sea of Antiquity, may not run upon rockes?'[7] At Stonehenge, however – in the face of what he describes as 'a huge and monstrous peece of work' that offered no clear interpretation – he declines to 'argue and dispute', and instead laments 'with much griefe that the Authors of so notable a monument are thus buried in oblivion'. Yet again, he felt, this was the fault of those who had failed to preserve precious clues: in the time of Henry VIII, he relates, a metal tablet 'inscribed with many letters' had been found at the site, but the characters were 'in so strange a Character' that no one had been able to read them, and as a result the plate had been neglected. 'Had it been preserved', remarks Camden gloomily, 'somewhat happily might have been discovered as concerning Stoneheng, which now lieth obscured.'[8]

If Camden had a blind spot for landscapes shaped by ancient Britons, it could hardly have been otherwise. At the time there was barely any concept of what we now call 'prehistory' – what his assumptions reveal is a lack of intellectual framework to support it. And his focus on Roman Britain had a point. As far as he was concerned, it was the Romans, not the Trojans, who had brought glamour, culture and civilization to British shores. Britain – though admittedly a distant outpost – had indeed once been part of a great empire. And if you wanted charismatic figures, why keep conjuring up a mythical character when some of the greatest Roman emperors – Claudius, Vespasian, Hadrian, Severus, Constantine – had actually been to Britain?[9]

Another advantage of the Romans was their predisposition to compose accounts and leave records. Forget Geoffrey of Monmouth; if you were seeking descriptions from those who were alive at the time and did not mind the colonizer's tendency to simplify and exaggerate, look at what the classical historians had to say. In *Britannia*, Camden did just that. Julius Caesar had personally encountered the Britons during his invasions of

55 and 54 BC and wrote about them, noting that they did not sow crops but lived on milk and flesh, dressed in skins and painted their bodies with woad 'and thereby they are the more terrible to their enemies in fight'.[10] They had long hair, he records, and shaved their bodies – apart from the men their upper lips. Herodian, a Roman civil servant who, much later, wrote a history of the empire, adds further details to their appearance:

> They knowe no use at all of garments, but about their belly onely and necke they weare yron; supposing that to be a goodly ornament, and a proofe of their wealth, like as all other Barbarians esteeme of gold. Or why? Their very bare bodies they marke with sundry pictures, representing all maner of living creatures; and therefore it is verily that they will not be clad, for hiding (forsooth) that painting of their bodies.

They were also, he continues, 'a most warlike nation', who armed themselves for battle with swords, shields and spears.[11] Well, if he was relying on Julius Caesar's account, that aspect of their character would have been abundantly evident. The naturalist and philosopher Pliny, clearly captivated by the idea of the Britons' body-painting, embellishes further, declaring not only that women and girls 'anoint and die their bodies all over' with the juice of woad, but also that, as children, the 'Barbarians' have their skin incised with the images of beasts – a form of tattooing – so that as they become adult, 'these pictured characters likewise waxe'.[12] For Camden, when he first gathered these accounts together for his book, it must have seemed as though the ancient Britons – painted, tattooed and warlike – had broken down the doors of the 'secretest closet of Antiquitie' and come tumbling out.[13]

Even so, they might have remained largely words on the page, known only to other antiquarians, had it not been for expeditions to the 'New World'. In 1585, John White set sail for Roanoke Island, Virginia in an expedition promoted by Walter Raleigh. Almost nothing was known about the people, plants, birds, beasts and fish native to America, and as an artist, it was White's mission to get it all down on paper, in order to establish a framework of vital information that might benefit other prospective colonizers. His watercolours suggest that he became absorbed by the people he depicted: he not only drew villages, fishing methods and weapons, but also the ceremonies and festivals of the Carolina Algonquians; on paper he recorded women carrying children, men armed with bows and arrows and family groups sitting down to eat. But what seems to have caught his eye above all were the tattoos and paints transforming the bodies of those he portrayed. Painstakingly, and with the finest of brushes, White transcribed every detail of the individual patterns and symbols he saw.[14]

White brought his precious portfolio of watercolours safely back to England, where they were engraved by Theodore de Bry and, in 1590, published in a book by the mathematician and natural philosopher Thomas Harriot. At a time when people were fascinated by costume and customs from around the world, the insight that de Bry's engravings of White's images in *A Brief and True Report of the New Found Land of Virginia* gave into the life and culture of Native Americans caused a sensation. But it was the book's appendix that provided the biggest jolt of all. Here, as de Bry put it, were 'Som picture, of the Pictes which in the Olde Tyme dyd Habite one part of the Great Bretainne'. In publishing these images it was, of course, de Bry's intention to draw a parallel, and 'to showe', in his words, 'how that the Inhabitants of the great Britannie have bin in times past as savvage as those of Virginia'. In the text accompanying the image of a warrior, a 'truue picture of one Picte', he explains: 'In tymes past the Pictes, habitans of one part of great Bretainne, which is now nammed England, wear savvages, and did paint all their bodye after the maner followinge....And when they hath overcomme some of their ennemis, they did never felle to carye a we their heads with them.'[15]

For all their apparent barbarity, the 'Pictes' in White's watercolours, posing dramatically to reveal their elaborate and fearsome decoration, seem to have stepped out of an Elizabethan masque.[16] A painted warrior shouts in triumph as he grasps the severed head of his victim (the cut of his beard making him look suspiciously like an Elizabethan); a powerfully built, spear-carrying woman, with intricate images of moons and stars adorning her body, strides determinedly on her way.[17] According to de Bry, White had assured him that he had discovered these figures in an 'oolld English chronicle'. Whether he meant images or descriptions is unclear, although one does not need to be a hardened cynic to suspect White's 'chronicle' of being of the same nature as Geoffrey's 'very old book', invoked to create a smokescreen of authority. The images, however, tell their own story. When White tried to think himself into the mindset of

Jodocus Hondius, engraved title page to John Speed's *The Theatre of the Empire of Great Britaine* (1627).

these ancient representatives of the past and imagine the paintings and tattoos they might have created, the images he found had a strong flavour not only of the Native Americans of Virginia and Carolina but also of the Elizabethan age. At the time, elite armour was decorated with colourful, elaborate patterns and women's jackets were often richly embroidered with emblems and flowers.[18] Looking at a watercolour of a female 'Picte' attributed to the French artist Jacques le Moyne des Morgues, also a model for one of the figures illustrated in Harriot's appendix, it is hard not to interpret her body-painting as the kind of close-fitting jacket embroidered with meticulously observed flowers – irises, peonies, lilies – that was fashionable in England at the time (Plate v).[19] The illusion is so great that each time I see it I am taken aback afresh to realize that she is 'clothed' only with pictures. The problem for the historic credibility of this 'yonge dowgter of the Pictes', however, is that none of the flowers was a native species, and a number had recently been imported to Europe. Distant times and distant places were becoming ever more entangled in these visions of the past.

When de Bry compares 'the Inhabitants of the great Britannie' of 'times past' with the Algonquians of his day, he, too, manipulates time. If the Native Americans depicted in Harriot's book could be seen as the inhabitants not just of a different region of the globe but also an earlier time frame, then the Elizabethans could cast themselves as conquering Romans to their uncivilized Britons – or, perhaps, Saxons, from whom many in the later sixteenth century had begun to assume that they were descended – and thus justify their incursions.[20] Whichever guise the English adopted in these history-bending acts of colonial role-play, they took care to cast themselves as the bringers of civilization to 'savvages' in the form of administration, infrastructure and the rule of law.

In 1611, just over twenty years after his first appearance, White's tattooed and extravagantly moustachioed ancient Briton became a familiar figure when the cartographer John Speed included a version on the title page of his atlas *Theatre of the Empire of Great Britaine,* the first of its kind and so popular it went through numerous editions in the seventeenth century. Here, he presides as a dominant, even heroic figure over the land, surrounded by four smaller representatives of the others who had shaped British history: a 'Romane', a Saxon, a Dane and a Norman.

Standing where Brutus would have stood only a few years before, he seemed finally to have toppled one of the most pervasive myths of the era. Brutus had been relegated to odd appearances in poetry and drama like a once-celebrated actor reduced to provincial repertory.

The light that in the 1620s shone through the windowpanes of Sir Robert Cotton's house in Westminster, falling on the floor in patches like slow-drifting sheets of paper, did so on the greatest library in England. On the shelves, manuscripts of histories composed by Gildas, Bede, Nennius and Geoffrey of Monmouth rubbed up against Saxon legal charters and descriptions of the lives of saints and kings. There were chronicles relating to medieval history and others associated with the Norman Conquest, treatises on heraldry and, somewhere, rules setting out the correct form for jousting. The more material Cotton acquired for his library, the more compelling its centripetal force seemed to become: many manuscripts that had been removed from monastic libraries at the Dissolution found their way there, as did the libraries of deceased friends and acquaintances. Added to this were the papers of the Tudor antiquaries John Leland and John Bale, along with literary manuscripts of Chaucer, Hoccleve, Gower and Lydgate. Among Cotton's greatest treasures were a copy of the Magna Carta, an early transcript of the books of Moses and the magnificent Lindisfarne Gospels. Sadly, some precious volumes went astray; Cotton lent the ninth-century Utrecht Psalter to the Earl of Arundel, himself a collector on a heroic scale, who – understandably, perhaps, if not commendably – failed to return it. Some curious ancient oddities ended up in Cotton's library too, such as the sole remaining manuscript of *Beowulf*, its covers containing the last precious echo of a remote world of heroes, dragons and monsters; not only that, but also the unique and precious volume through which trotted the spellbinding fable of Sir Gawain's encounter with the Green Knight. Above each individual bookcase Cotton placed the bust of a Roman emperor – Julius, Augustus, Tiberius, Caligula, Nero, Vespasian and so on – which allowed him to devise a simple finding-guide for the books. *Beowulf*, for example, was (and, indeed, remains in the catalogue of the British Library) 'Vitellius A.xv', meaning that it was on the top shelf under the bust of Vitellius and the fifteenth volume along; if you were looking for Ælfwine's prayer book, you would need to head for Titus and then count four shelves down and twenty-six books along.

The Roman emperors presided over a place of sociable browsing. Cotton was among the original members of the first Society of Antiquaries, founded in 1586 – probably in response to the publication of Camden's *Britannia* that same year – which gathered every Friday to discuss subjects ranging from land tenure and lineages to colleges and collections. Around 1602, Cotton petitioned the Queen for an academy 'for the study of antiquity and history' and suggested that his own library be merged with the royal library.[21] This scheme failed to find favour, but nonetheless he seems to have thought of his library as a national resource and opened the doors to a community of scholars, lawyers, politicians and antiquaries.[22] A visitor might find Cotton's friend Ben Jonson there, consulting volumes of classical texts in order that he might get the details of Roman politics and customs just right in a masque he was writing for the new king. Or clerks and politicians from the Palace of Westminster next door, in search of information about protocol and ceremonies. Camden, Cotton's lifelong friend and mentor, would call in for a bookish conversation by the fire in the adjoining room. It was a place in which the pursuit of knowledge and the reconstruction of the past outweighed the political and religious disputes so rife in the era: the Benedictine mystic Fr. Augustine Baker, for instance, researching the history of the Benedictine order in England, was made as welcome as the fiercely Calvinist Archbishop of Armagh, James Ussher.[23]

Many scholars came to Cotton's library in order to encounter the past; but there were few with ambitions to match Ussher's. His project, among the most admired of the age, was nothing less than a detailed chronology of the world, beginning with the moment of its creation and ending a few years after Christ's Crucifixion with the reign of the Emperor Vespasian, AD 69 to 79. Drawing on his extensive knowledge of ancient languages and calendars, Ussher pegged enough episodes from the ancient past to known biblical dates and events to construct a slender ladder leading into the remotest history. From one rung to the next, century to century, he moved carefully back through countless begettings, saw the flood waters rise and fall, stepped into the garden of Eden and watched as the earth was dismantled and there was nothing. The moment of creation, he reckoned, had occurred in 4004 BC, on 'the night preceding the twenty third day of Octob.', which was, as it happened, a Saturday.[24] On its first publication in Latin in 1650 (an English translation came in 1658), Ussher's book was acknowledged as a staggering feat of scholarship, and his ingenious calculations adopted so wholeheartedly that his dates began to be printed in the margins of the Authorized Version of the Bible. Ussher's pursuit of precision may have enabled him to join the dots on a doggedly heroic scale, and yet it caused him to discount the poetic use of language in which a 'day' might stand for a hundred or a thousand years; ever the literalist, he decided that Adam and Eve were probably escorted out of Paradise within twenty-four hours of their arrival. If Genesis said it was a day, then, in his view, it was a day; no more and no less.[25] Looking back into the past, now rendered fully compatible with biblical time, was like gazing up at a domed ceiling painted with a thousand figures enacting scenes familiar from the scriptures, and a thousand more enacting scenes from history, your eye rising up the interior, higher and higher, earlier and earlier, until it arrives at God's act of creation, pulsing away at the apex. Ussher's vision was dazzlingly beautiful and absorbing in its wealth of incident, and its span was finite. There could be nothing outside the room, no prehistory; everything that had ever happened was accommodated within the God-given time frame.

Ussher's achievement, however, was the swansong of this airless, labyrinthine research. The cultural climate was changing fast, and as time went on, more and more scholars were throwing open the doors and seeking news of the past elsewhere.

In November 1660, the Royal Society was founded with the motto '*Nullius in verba*': take no one's word for it. Authority was challenged and experiment held to be the key to knowledge. For the philosopher Francis Bacon, 'the searching out, inventing and discovering of all whatsoever is hid in secret in the World' was vitally important. But how was one to achieve this? A library, said Bacon, was essential, that one may consult 'whatsoever the Wit of Man hath heretofore committed to Books of worth'. But literature, he thought, was only part of a larger mechanism for discovery;

one must try to bring representative examples of the world to oneself in order to study it in microcosm. For this, physical examples of nature were needed, both living and inert. Firstly, a 'spacious, wonderful Garden...so you may have, in a small Compass, a Model of Universal Nature made private', and secondly,

> A goodly huge Cabinet, wherein whatsoever the Hand of Man, by exquisite Art or Engine, hath made rare in Stuff, Form, or Motion, whatsoever Singularity, Chance and the Shuffle of things hath produced, whatsoever Nature hath wrought in things that want Life, and may be kept, shall be sorted and included.[26]

As the seventeenth century progressed, scholars spent less time in the library and more time poking about on field margins, talking to farmers about the curious objects they had ploughed up and prowling around in quarries and along beaches in search of strangely shaped stones. Flints and fossils were picked up, brushed down, taken home and scrutinized like never before. Could these things reveal secrets about the past? The physician and writer Sir Thomas Browne thought so. He summed up this new attitude when, in 1643, he described nature as 'that universall and publike Manuscript, that lies expans'd unto the eyes of all'.[27] But how could one read this manuscript if one were not fluent in the language in which it was written?

Collections grew as attempts were made to learn it. In his library, Cotton displayed a spectacular example of a fossilized fish, discovered when the fens near the Cambridgeshire village of Conington were drained.[28] His contemporary, the gardener John Tradescant the Elder, established a vast collection of strange and wonderful examples of natural history and ethnography at his house in Lambeth, which came to be known as 'the Ark'; it was opened to the public, the first museum in England. Attached to the house was a botanical garden in which Tradescant grew plants and trees from seeds sent from the American colonies. His son, John Tradescant the Younger, added to his father's collection of costumes, weapons, coins, medals, taxidermy, fossils, shells, seeds and more dubious curiosities such as a mermaid's hand and a dragon's egg; in 1677 the *Musaeum Tradescantianum* was given by Elias Ashmole to Oxford University, where it formed the nucleus of the Ashmolean Museum.[29]

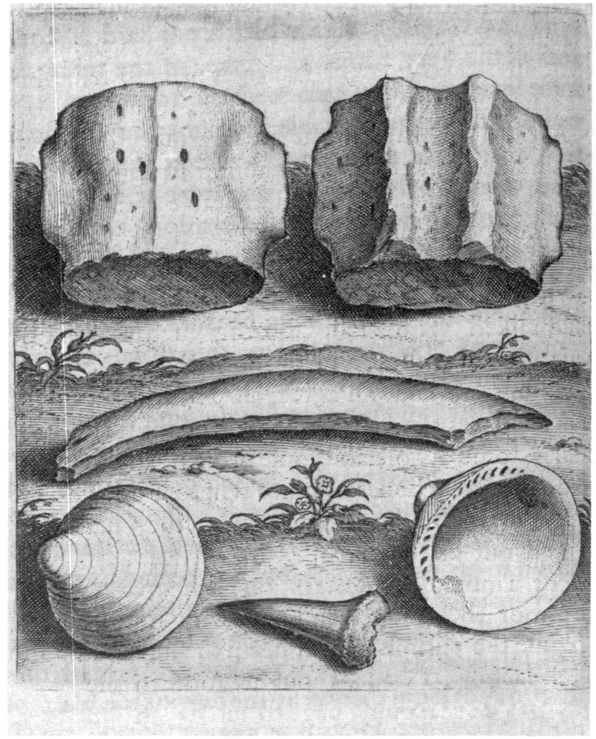

Richard Verstegan, 'Great bones of fishes found in the earth', illustration to *The Restitution of Decayed Intelligence in Antiquities* (1605).

Fossils, generally known as 'formed stones', came under intense scrutiny at this time. These puzzling and enigmatic objects revealed the seventeenth-century mind in all its imaginative ingenuity and speculative play. The first to find fossils intriguing enough to illustrate them in a book was Richard Verstegan, a correspondent of Cotton's and one of the earliest scholars of early English history and language. In his book *The Restitution of Decayed Intelligence in Antiquities* (1605), he describes them as 'great bones of fishes found in the earth' and cites them as evidence that parts of the Low Countries, where they were found, were once under the sea.[30] Camden, who had found examples near Whitby during his perambulations, had come up with various interpretations. He first describes them as 'faschioned like serpents folded and wrapped round as in a wreathe', and suggests that they might be the result of Nature getting tired of serious business and, as a pastime, 'disporting her selfe' by making these curious things. With his second idea he comes oddly close to the truth: 'A man would thinke verily they had beene sometime serpents, which a coate or crust of stone had now covered all over' – although what an aeon of time was actually covered in that 'sometime' would have staggered Camden.[31]

From the mid-1660s, the Oxford chemist Robert Plot, who was to become the Ashmolean's first curator, made a concerted effort to collect fossils, rocks and minerals and to organize them in an attempt to make sense of these strange and beautiful things. He was fascinated by natural history and antiquities, and his initial ambition had been to write a study that encompassed the entire country; but in the end he decided to focus on his own county, examining its rivers, testing its echoes, puzzling over the phenomenon of salt springs and delving around in quarries to examine types of local stone. When his *Natural History of Oxfordshire* was published in 1677 he devoted a chapter to 'Formed Stones', posing a question that was being hotly debated at the time: whether the stones that looked like shellfish were naturally produced by strange powers at work within the earth, or were the result of shells being distributed over the earth by a great flood, 'and there being filled with mud, clay, and petrifying juices' which 'have in tract of time been turned into stones, as we now find them, still retaining the same shape in the whole, with the same lineations, futures, eminencies, cavities, orifices, points, that they had whil'st they were shells'?[32] On balance, he decided that their resemblance to living creatures was coincidental. The biblical Flood, he reasoned, was probably not universal but seemed only to have affected Asia. And anyway, it lasted for a mere forty days – 'too small a time for so many shell-fish, so dispersed, as they must be presumed to be by so violent a motion, to get together and sequester themselves from all other company, and set themselves down, each sort, in a convenient station'.[33] As a chemist, he thought it most likely that formed stones were the result of mineral salts crystallizing and forming extraordinary patterns – in the same way, he argues, that 'Nitre always shoots into Pyramids, salt Marine into Cubes, Alum into octo, and Sal Armoniac into Hexaedrums.'[34] But his imagination was captured by these stones, and in particular by those that bore remarkable resemblances to plants and animals: he found one

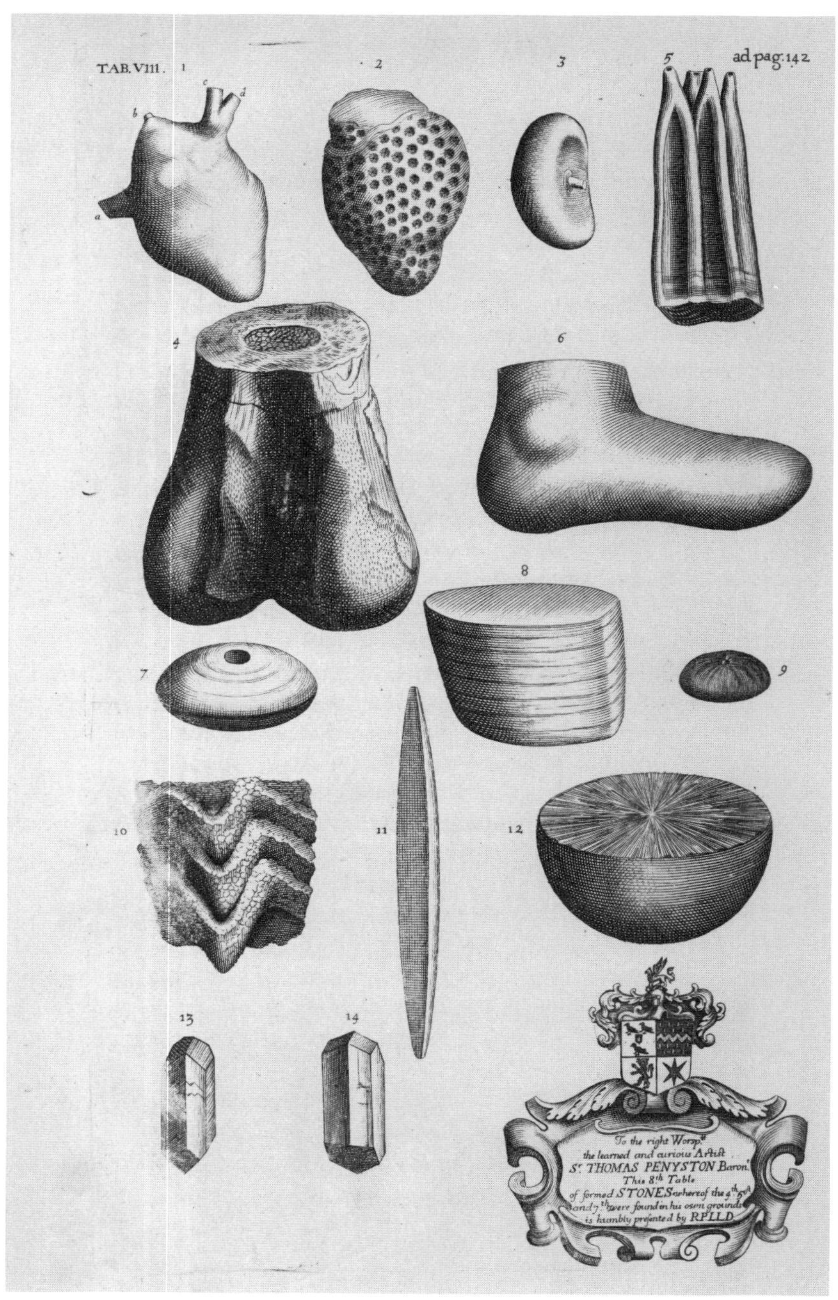

Above and opposite: Robert Plot, 'formed stones' illustrated in *The Natural History of Oxfordshire* (1677).

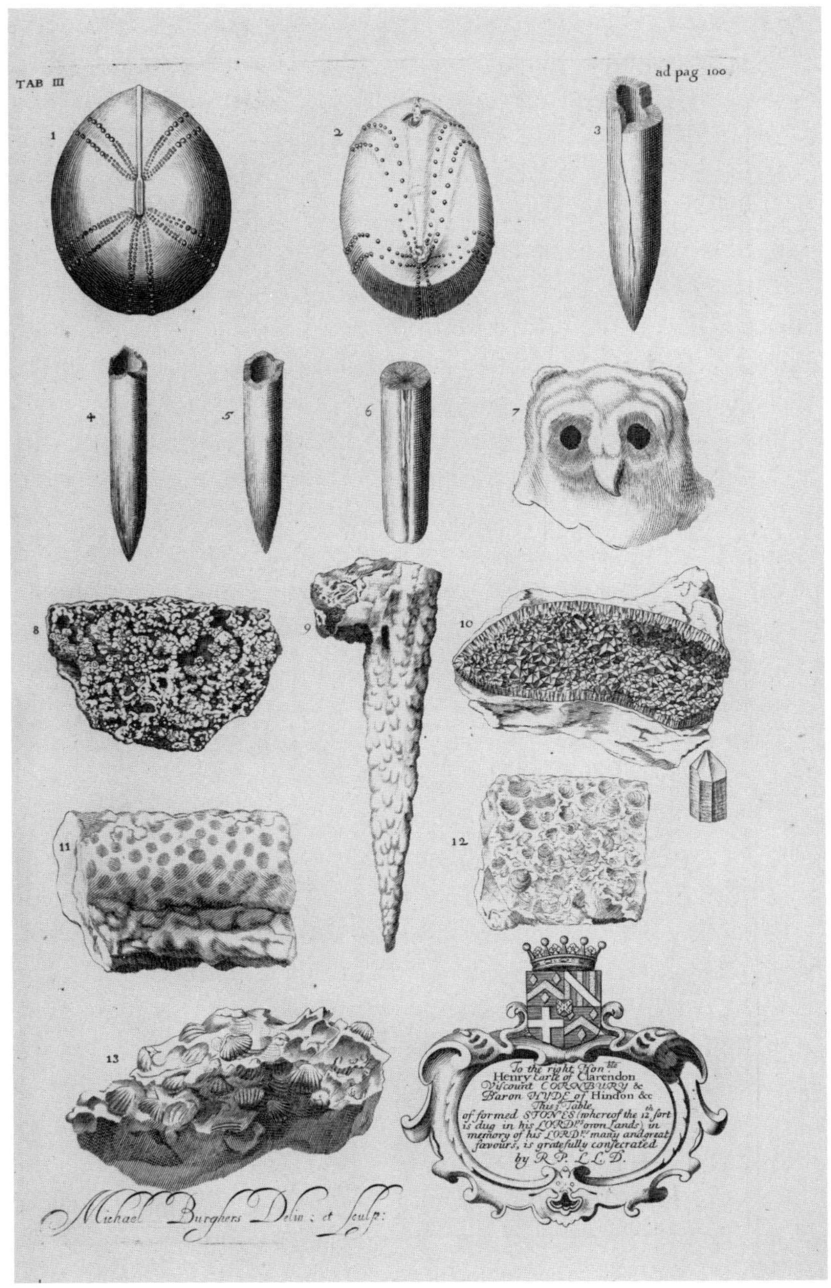
TAB III
ad pag 100
1
2
3
4
5
6
7
8
9
10
11
12
13
To the right Honble
Henry Earle of Clarendon
Viscount CORNBURY &
Baron HYDE of Hindon &c
This Table
of formed STONES (whereof the 12th sort
is dug in his LORD^ps own Lands) in
memory of his LORD^ps many and great
favours, is gratefully consecrated
by R.P. LL.D.
Michael Burghers Delin: et sculp:

near Stokenchurch in the Chilterns that looked like a tuber, and another in the quarry pits near Shotover Hill in the shape of a bryony root. Others were like fruits – his acquaintance the 'Learned and Ingenious' Sir George Croke found a pebble in the shape of a pear near his home, and close to Hardwick House Plot himself discovered a stone 'in the form of an Apricock'. There were stones that looked like eyes; those that mimicked the heads of horses and owls; others that mysteriously adopted the form of human hearts, breasts or feet. Neoplatonic ideas current at the time proposed the existence of a web of affinities stretching across the natural world – so perhaps these kinds of likenesses were only to be expected. The most telling of these were engraved in his *Natural History*.

It was not easy to separate fact from folklore. Plot was working in a climate in which the prehistoric flint arrowheads that regularly turned up in fields could still be explained as elf-bolts aimed at cattle, and he himself thought that circular crop-markings in north Oxford might well be caused by witches dancing at their Sabbaths.[35] Of the stones that most puzzled Plot was one he ferreted out of a quarry near the village of Cornwell that had, he wrote, 'exactly the figure of the lowermost part of the thigh-bone of a Man'. What made it exceed 'the ordinary course of nature' was its gigantic size: 'In compass near the *capita femoris* just two foot, and at the top above the *sinus* (where the thigh-bone is as small as any where) about 15 inches.'[36] Was its shape down to some 'sportive plastic power of the Earth'? Or was it the remains of an enormous beast? He considers the possibility that it might have been 'the bone of some Elephant brought hither during the Government of the Romans in Britain', but dismisses the idea, not least because as he was debating the matter a real elephant happened to be brought to Oxford; he examined it, and found the bones of the living animal to be much bigger. There was, however, another explanation: giants. Reasoning that huge remains of this kind 'must have been the bones of Men or Women', Plot backs up his hypothesis by citing instances of giants in the Bible, in classical literature and in other more recent histories and anecdotal accounts.[37] They were considerably smaller nowadays than in earlier times, it was true, but surely that was only to be expected 'in these parts of the World, where Luxury has crept in, together with Civility'.[38] Modern mores, it seemed, were taking their toll even on colossi.

Plot's guess, however, was astute enough in the context of the imaginative constraints imposed by a biblical time frame: he was right that it was the remains of a femoral bone, and he was also right in his surmise that it belonged to a giant of sorts. What he could not have known was that the giant in question was a Megalosaurus that had been bounding ferociously around Oxfordshire in the Middle Jurassic period – millions of years before 4004 BC. But as we watch Plot rummaging through his trays of 'formed stones' found in Oxfordshire quarries, choosing favourites to illustrate and speculating about their origins, the range – and limits – of his imagination tell us more about the tenor of the times than any amount of literal correctness.

In the open space of Hay Hill in the centre of Norwich sits the gigantic marble brain of Sir Thomas Browne, vulnerable outside its skull but somehow, with its enormous coils and folds, still intimidating. Words and phrases generated by the brain, often cryptic, are scattered about. A polished marble bean says 'BRAMPTON URNS', a blocky seat 'ETERNITIE'. A bench made for two – perhaps best avoided – bears the dismaying words 'VULGAR ERRORS'. The components are arranged in the form of a quincunx, five points set out in a cross like a five on a playing card, a geometric pattern that Browne encountered again and again in his experiments and came to believe was a key to unlocking the secrets of the natural world. *A Homage to Sir Thomas Browne*, a work by the French artists Anne and Patrick Poirier commissioned in 2005, is close to the site of Browne's house in Norwich. It was there that he ran a successful medical practice; there that he conducted experiments surrounded by books and pictures; and there that he wrote his books, making profound and original reflections on life, death and the past. 'His whole house and garden', marvelled John Evelyn in 1671, 'is a paradise and Cabinet of rarities and that of the best collection, amongst Medails, books, Plants, natural things.'

If 'BRAMPTON URNS' are gnomic words to find inscribed on a giant marble bean in central Norwich, the original objects were no less mysterious. It all began with a discovery, as Browne gets around to telling us in the second chapter of his strange and wonderful book on the subject, *Hydriotaphia, Urne-Buriall*, of 1658.

> In a field of old Walsingham, not many moneths past, were digged up between fourty and fifty Urnes, desposited in a dry and sandy soile, not a yard deep, nor farre from one another; Not all strictly of one figure, but most answering these described; Some containing two pounds of bones, distinguishable in skulls, ribs, jawes, thigh-bones, and teeth, with fresh impressions of their combustion.[39]

Found with the funerary urns, Browne writes, were objects that had belonged to the deceased, 'things wherein they excelled, delighted, or which were dear unto them': fragments of a hair comb, small boxes and, in one particular urn sent to Browne by a friend, a jewel: 'some kind of *Opale*' – though whether 'burnt upon the finger of the dead, or cast into the fire by some affectionate friend', he cannot say.[40] The urns are Roman, he decides, since it is known that the Romans practised cremation, and he has no other artefacts or illustrations with which to compare them. 'Remembring the early civility they brought upon these Countreys,' he remarks, 'and forgetting long passed mischiefs; We mercifully preserve their bones, and pisse not upon their ashes.'[41] Today they are known to have been Saxon, but that is beside the point. Like Proust's madeleine, these sad relics of the long dead were a catalyst. The bones wreathed about with dogs' grass, the burnt fragments of possessions, the echoes of distant customs and the thought of ancient tears shed sent Browne's imagination spiralling up and out and into the past, his idiosyncratic mind ranging over a staggering array of obscure burial customs and the 'wilde enormities' of funerary ceremonies practised in antiquity. Browne is a metaphysical tour guide, whisking us on an exhilarating ride through the ancient world, where we examine pyres and pyramids, before we finally find ourselves deposited, blinking in bewilderment, back in his study. His book is a lesson in the use and value of conjecture: 'What Song the *Syrens* sang, or what name *Achilles* assumed when he hid himself among women, though puzzling Questions are not beyond all conjecture,' he writes.[42] Through the digressive and humane prose of *Urn-Buriall* we are invited to contemplate the universal hope of immortality and the desire to evade oblivion – which, Browne remarks, is so often overturned by the ironies of fate. 'Time hath spared the Epitaph of *Adrians* horse,' he observes in a wry aside, 'confounded that of himself.'[43] Whether he is looking at an ancient epitaph or an urn, Browne senses the human presence behind it, recognizing the emotion underlying the antiquity.[44]

In a magnificently melancholy final chapter Browne thinks about how these obscure urns survived, somehow, 'in a yard under ground, and thin walls of clay'. He imagines 'the drums and tramplings of three conquests' above ground, and as he does so his mind turns to the mysterious relationship between past, present and eternity.[45] The past is liable to be blotted out with such rapidity, he muses, that 'Grave stones tell truth scarce fourty years; Generations pass while some trees stand, and old Families last not three Oaks.'[46] And as we contemplate the past and turn its relics over in our hands, we may do well to acknowledge that time is catching up with us. 'The number of the dead long exceedeth all that shall live,' Browne concludes. 'The night of time far surpasseth the day, and who knows when was the Equinox?'[47]

'Time', writes Browne as he considers the fragile urns, 'which antiquitates Antiquities, and hath an art to make dust of all things, hath yet spared these *minor* Monuments.'[48] Around two hundred miles southwest of Norwich, Time had also spared a *major* monument; and the new intellectual climate of the seventeenth century would no longer permit it to be hurried past with a baffled shrug. As objects of all kinds were increasingly scrutinized, tapped and held up to the light in an effort to persuade them to divulge their stories, it was no longer enough to think of the great mysterious antiquity that stood on Salisbury Plain merely as a symbol of the unknowable past – a 'Huge dumb heape, that cannot tell us how, / Nor what, nor whence it is', as Samuel Daniel put it in his 1599 poem *Musophilus*.[49] Stonehenge now presented an irresistible challenge. It posed a puzzling Question, certainly, but not, as Browne would have said, one beyond all conjecture.

Welcome to my theatre! Come in, sit down. The production of *Stonehenge* is about to commence. There are six acts in this play: six theories concerning the origins and purpose of that monument, presented to you in the order in which they were broadcast to the world. Each is more intriguing than the last, and every single one deploys an extraordinary and glittering cast of characters.

Drawing of Stonehenge by the Flemish painter Lucas de Heere, from a sketch made on the spot around 1572 to illustrate a guidebook to the history and costumes of England.

But first, let us return for a moment to William Camden, who was uncharacteristically reticent on this subject; in fact it is possible that he never actually went to Stonehenge.[50] There is a slightly stale quality to his description of it, like a painting copied from a photograph. Even so, Camden accomplishes the feat of ushering Stonehenge out of the medieval age and into the margins of modern ways of thinking. He dutifully records the two principal bits of folklore – first, that it was built by Ambrosius Aurelianus or his brother Uther Pendragon (father of King Arthur) to commemorate Britons slain by the Saxons; second, that it commemorates Ambrosius himself, killed on that spot – but is not convinced by any of it. The truth, he laments, is hidden from view. At which point he shrugs and turns his attention to an interesting warren of hares near Amesbury.

So by the beginning of the seventeenth century, the traditional props and scenery had been cleared away, leaving just the stones and an empty stage.

Enter Edmund Bolton. A historian and scholar closely acquainted with Camden, the cartographer John Speed, and Sir Robert Cotton, he was, one can assume, a man frequently to be found browsing under the emperors' noses in the latter's library. Bolton was dismissive of the old chronicles that made little distinction between fact and folklore, and critical of the 'vast vulgar Tomes' produced by Holinshed and other Elizabethan historians.[51] He wanted to read and write a new kind of history, one pinned securely to archival records and bolstered by evidence provided by old coins and inscriptions – although imaginative conjecture still played a significant part. Bolton's particular fascination was with ancient Roman history, and it was when he embarked on a book about the reign of Nero, *Nero Caesar* (1624), that his interest grew in the 'most great, and noble ladie' Boudicca, the queen of the East Anglian Iceni tribe, who had fiercely resisted Roman rule. Her death, Bolton tells us, 'was vehemently lamented of her surviving friends, who honoured her funerall with stately rites, and buried her remaines ambitiously brave'. But where? Bolton believed he may have found the answer: 'without averring any thing precisely,' he begins with becoming modesty, 'no other toombe seemes to mee so likely to be hers, as the admirable monument of the stones upon SALISBURIE plaine'. For one thing, he argues, there is no visible inscription, as one would naturally expect from a *Roman* structure. There is a stylistic argument to be made, too: 'That Stonage was a worke of the BRITANNS, the rudenesse it selfe perswades'. His theory did not necessarily negate the old story that it was a tomb to Aurelius Ambrosius – there was no reason why it should not 'at first have beene erected in honour of that most heroicall championesse of BRITAIN, BOADICIA', and then later made the grave of Aurelius and his men. Bolton throws the weight of the Roman historian Cassius Dio behind his argument; Dio affirms, he says, that they buried her 'with much magnificence' (repeating himself more emphatically two pages later: 'with *much magnificence*') – and where else would fit the description but these 'orderly irregular, and formless uniforme heapes of massive marble'?

Bolton's final piece of conjecture recalls the metal plate inscribed with ancient, illegible lettering mentioned by Camden. Was it not very probable that it bore 'some old BRITISH inscription, dedicated to the immortall fame of some or other great Worthie' – who was most likely to have been Boudicca herself?[52]

Inigo Jones, architect, connoisseur of paintings, masque-designer, Surveyor of the King's Works and a man so steeped in the principles of classical building he could be called 'the Vitruvius of his age', had his own views on the matter.[53] In 1655, three years after Jones's death, his pupil John Webb published his theories in *The Most Notable Antiquity of Great Britain, Vulgarly Called Stone-Heng on Salisbury Plain, Restored by Inigo Jones Esquire*, a book written as though by Jones himself, but actually compiled by Webb from notes made on their conversations. According to the text, it made no sense to suggest that Stonehenge, in the south-west of England, was Boudicca's tomb, when she was 'no doubt, buried in her own territories, among the graves of her renowned Ancestors'. And in any case, the ancient Britons were, in Jones's opinion, wholly barbarous, with no knowledge of building in stone.[54] So much for Bolton's averring.

Jones had a yet more audacious theory of his own. He had spent a considerable amount of time in Italy, where he sought out ancient buildings: in Rome he made a particularly close study of the Pantheon and the temple of Fortuna Virilis, and in Naples he admired the temple of Castor and Pollux. With this experience, he had got into the habit of looking back at the past not in speculative wonder, but with the sharp eyes and acutely mathematical brain of an architect; and it was this professional focus that he applied to Stonehenge. As ventriloquized by Webb, he asks us to consider a few points in favour of the ancient Romans, whose 'powerfull means for effecting great works: together with their *Order* in building, and manner of workmanship' suggested them as obvious candidates. Stonehenge, he continues, 'in my judgement was a work, built by the *Romans*, and they the sole *Founders* thereof. For, if [we] look upon this *Antiquity*, as an admired and magnificent building, who more magnificent than the *Romans*?'[55] The stones may now be rough, but their current appearance is simply the result of their 'long contest with the violence of time, and injury of weather'.[56] Exposed as they have been not only 'to the fury of all devouring Age, but the rage of men likewise', is it any wonder they have been 'subject to ruine'? Stonehenge, then, is the battered and weather-beaten remains of a building that had once been the acme of polished, geometrical perfection. To demonstrate his point Webb includes a drawing of Stonehenge not as it looked in the early years of the seventeenth century, but as Jones surmised it appeared when it was first built. The outer circle of sarsens is complete, their lintels forming a continuous ring: they have been transformed into an elegant colonnade. Within, the inner group of trilithons no longer describes a horseshoe shape but an open inner circle; to achieve this, the five extant trilithons have been joined by a sixth. Within, smaller bluestones stand at regular intervals like neat bollards. The contours of all the stones are decisively straight. Jones's plan of the monument as seen from above is the clincher: it demonstrates that Stonehenge forms a perfect circle. And look: one can draw four equilateral triangles within the outer circle that determine the exact position of the inner trilithons. Consider this mathematical precision, the book asks, and compare it with certain ancient temples described in Vitruvius's great treatise on architecture, *De architectura* – could any doubt remain? Furthermore, Stonehenge was clearly designed to have no roof, which, to Jones, strongly suggested that it was built as a temple dedicated to Coelus, the primal Roman god of the sky.[57]

The next theory is delivered by a dapper figure with a neatly trimmed moustache and a shrewd expression; a courtier who had been made physician to Charles II when still in exile.[58] In 1663 Walter Charleton published a rebuttal of Jones's ideas in the form of *Chorea Gigantum, or, The most Famous Antiquity of Great Britain, vulgarly called Stone-Heng, Standing on Salisbury Plain, Restored to the Danes*. Though purportedly on the subject of Stonehenge, this was largely a bid (one of several) for royal approval. Another book, *Danicorum monumentorum* (1643), by a Danish physician and antiquary, Ole Worm, on the megalithic tomb monuments of Denmark, had given Charleton an idea about Stonehenge. '*Who were the Authors of this stupendious Building*,' he asks, 'that doth so amaze and amuse its beholders'? Well, 'of all Nations in the world, none was so much addicted to Monuments of huge and unhewn stones, as the *Danes* appear to have been'.[59]

Stonehenge was no longer a melancholy memorial, nor a temple to a pagan god. It was remade by Charleton as the chief ceremonial centre of the Danes, their coronation place, where the mighty institution of monarchy had for centuries been upheld and celebrated. 'It is not improbable', he suggests, pointing to the lintels, that these stones were used as elevated platforms by the nobility when voting to elect their king.[60]

The poet John Dryden was evidently convinced. His lines praising Charleton's achievement are included as a preface to the book – 'Stone-Heng, once thought a Temple, You have found / A Throne, where Kings, our Earthly Gods, were Crown'd'. Getting to the heart of Charleton's desire to connect Stonehenge with royalty, Dryden goes on to refer to an episode of 1651, after the battle of Worcester, when the King himself visited the stones:

> These Ruins sheltered oınce *His* Sacred Head,
> Then when from *Wor'ster*'s fatal Field *He* fled;
> Watch'd by the Genius of this Kingly Place,
> And mighty Visions of the Danish Race.
> His *Refuge* then was for a *Temple* shown:
> But, *He* Restor'd, 'tis now become a *Throne*.[61]

Charleton disarmingly admits that he may be wrong, while still retaining grounds for optimism – 'Sure I am of thus much, that this Opinion of mine, if it be erroneous, is yet highly plausible.'[62] And yet this wily courtier was right about the political value of bringing the past to bear on the concerns of the present, especially in the atmosphere of the post-Restoration court, which was naturally keen to reassert its legitimacy.

The next actor in this drama introduces a distinct change of approach. 'There have been several Books, writt by learned men concerning Stonehenge,' begins the antiquary John Aubrey equably, 'much differing from one another some affirming one thing, some another.'[63] He had read Jones and Webb's *Stonehenge Restored* 'with great delight', he declares, but found that Jones 'framed the monument to his own hypothesis, which is much differing from the thing itself. This gave me an edge to make more researches'.[64]

Determined not to fall into the same trap of putting theory before 'the thing itself', Aubrey got on his horse. 'I was', he wrote, 'for relying on my owne Eiesight.'[65] He began his research with fieldwork, comparing Stonehenge with other stone circles around Britain, including Avebury in Wiltshire, Nine Stones in Dorset, the Devil's Quoits at Stanton Harcourt in Oxfordshire, Boscawen-Un in Cornwall and Long Meg and her Daughters in Cumbria. 'These Antiquities are so exceeding old,' he explains, 'that no Books doe reach them: so that there is no way to retrive them but by comparative antiquitie, which I have writt upon the spott, from the monuments themselves.'[66] He got to know ancient Wiltshire so well that he was able to draw a map of it, and through the careful survey he conducted of Stonehenge he discovered the ring of chalk pits just inside the surrounding ditch, which are now called Aubrey holes after him.

Aubrey's comparative method revealed that there were stone circles in parts of the British Isles reached by neither the Romans, the Saxons nor the Danes, and so – partly by a process of elimination – he was able to conclude that they were constructed by the ancient Britons. But what were they for? His fieldwork provided him, he explained, with 'clear evidence that these monuments were Pagan Temples', and he goes on '(with humble subscription to better judgement)' to offer 'a probability that they were Temples of the Druids', on the grounds that druids were 'the most eminent Priests (or Order of Priests) among the Britaines'.[67]

Aubrey incorporated his observations on Stonehenge and Avebury, completed by 1665, into his study of stone circles, 'Templa Druidum', which eventually formed part of his ambitious archaeological survey *Monumenta Britannica*. But despite being commanded by Charles II in 1663 to publish his findings, and the encouragement of those such as Sir Thomas Browne, who wrote 'Sir your friends who persuade you to print your Templa Druidum &c do butt what is fitt & reasonable', *Monumenta Britannica* remained unpublished at his death in 1697 – although copies did circulate in manuscript.[68]

What set Aubrey apart in his speculations about Stonehenge was his insightful historical imagination. He was less wary than his contemporaries of entertaining the possibility of a distant past unconstrained by biblical time: 'the world is much older than is commonly supposed', he once noted.[69] And he had an unusual degree of empathy with the past, which, in another area of research, led him to collect stories of the supernatural generally derided as old wives' tales, regarding them as important and vanishing relics of folklore. All this allowed him to picture ancient Britons and to reconstruct their landscape. 'Let us imagine', he wrote in the notes he made for *Monumenta Britannica*,

> what kind of countrie this was in the time of the ancient Britons, by the nature of the soile, which is a soure, woodsere land, very natural for the production of oaks especially. One may conclude that this North-division was a shady dismall wood; and the inhabitants almost as salvage as the Beasts, whose Skins were their only rayment....[70]

Aubrey was beguiled by the imaginative act of evoking the past; 'the retrieving of these forgotten things from Oblivion in some sort resembles the Art of a Conjurer,' he wrote, 'who makes those walke & appeare that have layen in their graves many hundreds of yeares: and to represent as it were to the eie the places, Customes and Fashions, that were of old Time'.

Friendship and collaboration were vitally important to seventeenth-century antiquaries. Early in the century, Cotton's library was a hotspot; later, affairs migrated to the Royal Society. Inigo Jones was in the thick of court life; John Aubrey talked and smoked away numerous ideas for projects in the company of his many antiquarian friends – one particularly ambitious book idea 'vanish't in Fumo sc: Tabaci [tobacco smoke]', he ruefully admitted, '& was never thought on since'.[71] Aylett Sammes, on the other hand, preferred to nurture his ideas alone. Had he been meshed into the sociable world of ideas, discoveries and correspondence, his own theories – for which, it must be said, he produces not a shred of material evidence – may not have developed in so eccentric a manner.

In his book of 1676, *Britannia Antiqua Illustrata*, Sammes asks us to consider Stonehenge's traditional name, *Chorea gigantum*, the giants' dance. What if it referred to 'an Ancient Tradition, wrapt up in ignorant and idle Tales' – in other words, did the old name contain a crucial clue? If there really had been giants, who were they? As for the old fable, related by Geoffrey of Monmouth, that the stones had originated in Africa, what if it were not the stones themselves, but the art of erecting them, that had come from that part of the world – 'the known habitations of the *Phoenicians*?'[72]

He fleshes out the background to his ingenious theory: Britain's earliest settlers were Phoenicians, who sailed to Western Europe to trade with the Celtic tribes of Britain and France. 'Not only the name of Britain itself', he continues ('Barat-anac', since you ask, the land of tin),

> but of most places therein of ancient denomination are purely derived from the Phoenician Tongue, and...the Language itself for the most part, as well as the Customs, Religions, Idols, Offices, Dignities of the Ancient Britons are all clearly Phoenician, as likewise their instruments of war.[73]

Sammes did not invent the idea that the Phoenicians – whose ancient civilization originated in modern-day Lebanon – had travelled to the British Isles to trade for tin, and subsequently settled.[74] Deriving from the ancient Greek historian Herodotus, it had been mentioned by a number of writers. But, by relying heavily on wild speculation, dubious etymologies and highly selective readings of classical texts, Sammes inflated the idea until he had imagined an entire Phoenician culture that permeated every aspect of British life and included the construction of Stonehenge as a temple dedicated to Hercules.[75] Had the inscribed tablet mentioned by Camden survived – made of tin and lead, those favourite metals of the Phoenicians – it is possible, is it not, that those ancient letters, so difficult to decipher, would have been found to be in the Phoenician tongue.[76]

One might expect Sammes's outlandish and entirely unverifiable theories about the Phoenicians to have drifted away like Aubrey's tobacco smoke. And yet the scent of them lingered in the fabric of the mind. His ideas were even taken seriously – though, it must be said, not accepted – by Edmund Gibson when in 1695 he was editing a scholarly new edition of Camden's *Britannia*. While the majority of other theories drew upon a known past that post-dated the Roman conquest, Sammes offered the

An 'Antient Britain' from Aylett Sammes's
Britannia Antiqua Illustrata (1676).

tantalizing glimmer of a distant, glamorous world in which anything seemed possible. In some ways his book must have tapped into the old, thwarted desire for an illustrious European ancestry for Britain – the very thing that had kept the Brutus myth alive for so long.[77]

The illustrations advertised in the title of Sammes's book had a similar impact. One of them remains familiar, indelible even, as the inspiration for the 1973 folk horror film *The Wicker Man*, directed by Robin Hardy: a frightening image of a giant, hollow, standing figure, into which men and women are crowded before it is set alight to make a mass human sacrifice. In another illustration, a shaggy-haired ancient Briton presides over a mountainous landscape precociously equipped with a viaduct and towns with towers and steeples. Clad in an ankle-length black cloak, he is a figure one would not be particularly surprised to encounter today. Another image established the appearance of a druid – a long-bearded sage carrying a staff and wearing a hooded robe – and it is this figure who would dominate the mind of one William Stukeley.[78]

When the physician, antiquarian and, later, clergyman Dr William Stukeley finally published his book *Stonehenge: A Temple Restor'd to the British Druids* in 1740, he provided his engraver with an authorial self-portrait.[79] It was an unusual image. While other authors of the period might appear holding a pen as if caught in the act of composition, or elegantly resting an elbow on a pile of books, Stukeley elected to present himself as a druid, wearing a leafy wreath on his head. The name he adopted, Chyndonax, came from an old French book; he chose it when in 1722 he formed a 'Society of Roman Knights' for friends devoted to saving Roman remains, each of whom took a Roman or Celtic sobriquet. Stukeley was alone in taking a druidic one, and Chyndonax would become something of an alter ego for him.[80] The portrait was an outward sign of his inner identification with the druids, who were, to his mind, the undoubted 'true authors' of Stonehenge; what had been a 'probability' in Aubrey's mind became a certainty in Stukeley's.[81] A clergyman posing as a druid was admittedly eccentric. And yet it could be justified: leaving aside the druids' regrettable taste for human sacrifice, Stukeley believed that the druidic religion was essentially Abrahamic, and so not incompatible with Christianity. In druidic religion, he had discovered the origins of the Church of England.

William Stukeley, engraving in *Stonehenge: A Temple Restor'd to the British Druids* (1740).

Stukeley's interest had in fact been fired around 1717 when he was lent a manuscript of Aubrey's *Monumenta Britannica*, sections of which he had enthusiastically copied into his notebook. For the engravings in his book, Stukeley made sketches on the spot, spending his summers 'viewing, measuring, and considering the works of the ancient Druids in our Island'.[82] A keen draughtsman who always had a sketchbook to hand, he was the first Stonehenge scholar to make pictures central to his treatise. In *Stonehenge: A Temple Restor'd to the British Druids*, the monument was observed not only in close-up, but in relation to the wider landscape; and while some views are peopled with small groups of elegant contemporary visitors, others are inhabited by ancient Britons in tunics.[83] In this visual history, past and present perform a graceful dance; the monument is imaginatively reconstructed, then falls back into familiar semi-ruin. Stukeley's time-travelling imagination was not matched until 1815, when Charles Hamilton Smith imagined crowds of Britons attending a grand festival at Stonehenge for Samuel Rush Meyrick's book *Costume of the Original Inhabitants of the British Islands* (Plate VI). Stukeley's engravings alone give his book a lasting importance, not least for the record they offer of Stonehenge's appearance during an era in which depredation and vandalism were common.

Between 1719 and 1724 he made not only accurate measurements but numerous important discoveries. It was Stukeley who noticed two important earthworks, the avenue and the cursus (which he named); Stukeley who recognized the astronomical alignment of the stones; Stukeley who coined the word 'trilithon' from the Greek *tri* (three) and *lithos* (stone) to describe the stones arranged as two uprights joined by a horizontal lintel.

If the book's illustrations put us there, on the spot, amid the stones, so too does Stukeley's text, which sparkles with the excitement of spending days walking and looking, measuring and digging; and with stories such as how he and his patron Lord Winchelsea took their dinner one day on top of a lintel (their pipes, he speculates, were probably still there). This is how he describes his feelings as he arrived at the site:

> When you enter the building, whether on foot or horseback and cast your eyes around, upon the yawning ruins, you are struck into an exstatic reverie, which none can describe, and they only can be sensible of, that feel it. Other buildings fall by piece meal, but here a single stone is a ruin, and lies like the haughty carcase of Goliath...if you look upon the perfect part, you fancy intire quarries mounted up into the air: if upon the rude havock below, you see as it were the bowels of a mountain turn'd inside outwards.[84]

Combined, the visual and the emotional content of Stukeley's *Stonehenge* was irresistible. His interpretation of the monument balances awe and precision in a way that appealed to readers for generations. And for better or worse, it is thanks to Chyndonax that Stonehenge has been associated with druids in the public mind right up to the present day.

Before you go, Dr Stukeley, what about the metal tablet mentioned by Camden, that nobody had been able to decipher? 'No doubt but it was a memorial of the founders,' he informs us as he gathers his engravings together and prepares to leave the stage, 'wrote by the Druids: and had it been preserv'd till now, would have been an invaluable curiosity.'[85]

If not a single one of these imaginative theories turned out to be right (though some might be described as righter than others), we might reflect that, although many advances have been made since this flush of fervent antiquarianism in the seventeenth and early eighteenth centuries, Stonehenge remains, in Henry James's phrase, 'portentously unexplained'.[86] 'Each generation', the archaeologist Jacquetta Hawkes has observed, 'gets the Stonehenge it deserves – or desires.'[87]

III

LIVING IN THE PAST

You could contemplate ancient ruins in the English landscape. Or you could find a suitable spot in your grounds and build your own. The historical imagination that had led to some audaciously speculative leaps in the seventeenth century took on a whole new dimension in the eighteenth.

The Grand Tour, which served as a kind of ambulatory finishing school for the sons of the ruling class, sparked new ways of thinking about, and inhabiting, the past. Young 'milords' would travel through France and Italy on an itinerary that took in Paris, Florence, Naples, Venice and finally, for an extensive stay, Rome. During the seventeenth and eighteenth centuries the Tour established the conditions for supplying future leaders with a nuanced understanding of European politics, geography and history as well as a shared cultural frame of reference – although whether every young Grand Tourist took advantage of the more high-minded opportunities on offer is another matter. Above all, the experience – especially in Rome – of living surrounded by constant reminders of the Renaissance and the ancient world deeply impressed these visitors, who, once back at home, sought to recapture it. Perhaps the Tour's most obvious legacy was the built environment; in the early to mid-eighteenth century, up and down the country mansions were built to emulate sixteenth-century villas in the Veneto designed by the architect Andrea Palladio, who was himself emulating ancient Roman and Greek prototypes. The ancient world was taking root in British fields. And not only did men and women of wealth and status commission houses based on classical models, they also shipped a staggering number of works of art to Britain, amassing paintings by Claude Lorrain and his followers and adorning their rooms with antique marble sculpture until they were as redolent of classical antiquity as the buildings themselves.

Alfred's Hall in Cirencester Park.

Along with these grand visions of the long-ago and the far-away, a new and widespread interest in English history came in by the back door. Or perhaps that is the wrong figure of speech for an interest that was, at least at first, most readily expressed outdoors. England's grandest eighteenth-century houses may have been designed with classical culture in mind, but the grounds were demonstrably not Italian – a fact made only too clear with each passing shower or chilly gust of wind. As a result, they often became playful, even experimental places, with a certain licence to accommodate intriguing architectural features such as rustic grottoes, pretend hermitages and Gothic pavilions tucked away in the woods or placed where one might chance upon them on a winding walk. Among the most curious of these structures was the sham ruin, one of the earliest of which resulted from a collaboration between friends: Alexander Pope, who created his own extraordinary wild garden and grotto in Twickenham, and the Tory peer Lord Bathurst, who devised one of the first landscape gardens in the grounds of his house, Cirencester Park in Gloucestershire, and animated it with picturesque follies.

One October day in 1718, Pope sat down in one of these, a neoclassical pavilion that Bathurst had built especially for him, to write to his friends Martha and Teresa Blount. From this impressive vantage point, the poet described how every afternoon he and his host 'draw plans for houses and gardens, open avenues, cut glades, plant firs, contrive water-works'. These schemes may not always have come to fruition, but they were, he wrote, 'all very fine and beautiful in our own imagination'.[1] Among their more successful plans was a sham ruin. Three years later, this 'Venerable Structure of our Ancestours', as Pope ironically put it, went up in the heart of Oakley Wood. It was built in a Gothic style, with slender lancet windows, arched doorways and a parapet with battlements; Bathurst had its name, Alfred's Hall, carved in Gothic lettering over the door.[2] It looked as though it had stood in its wooded spot for centuries, gradually crumbling, each blackened stone murmuring of its great antiquity and royal associations. As Bathurst's friend, the poet Edward Stephens, wrote, 'This Pile the marks of rolling Cen'tries wears, / Sunk to Decay, – and built scarce twenty Years'.[3]

Over the years, Alfred's Hall grew, taking on fragments from the demolished Sapperton Manor, so that real ancient masonry joined modern dressed stone. As the bluestocking Mrs Pendarves, later Mrs Delany, told her friend Jonathan Swift: 'My lord Bathurst has greatly improved the wood-house, which you may remember but a cottage not a bit better than an Irish cabin. It is now a venerable castle, and has been taken by an antiquarian for one of king Arthur's "with thicket overgrown, grotesque and wild".'[4] For Bathurst, a friend to many of the leading wits and writers of the day, Alfred's Hall was a place for sociable gatherings over food and drink – even the walk there through the wood must have heightened the sense of occasion and theatre (although one pities the servants obliged to carry dishes there from the house's kitchens). Dining within the rustic stone walls, they could imaginatively inhabit the past as though putting on the costume of another era.

The Gothic style, regarded at the time as quintessentially English, was the clear choice for Bathurst, a Tory peer.[5] And in linking his rustic banqueting-house to King Alfred in particular, Bathurst was evoking the perceived English virtues of liberty and the rule of law – the Saxons were, at this time, generally believed to have been democratic and freedom-loving – as well as celebrating the Saxon king's connection with his local area. A print of the Hall from 1763 shows it overgrown with creepers and is inscribed: 'Tradition says that a treaty was sign'd here with Gormandus the Dane.' Legends were evidently planted around Alfred's Hall like ivy, in the hope that they would grow and spread.

With Alfred's Hall, Bathurst glorified the medieval origins of British liberties such as those brought by King John's signing of the Magna Carta; other eighteenth-century builders of sham ruins had different agendas. In the 1730s, at Stowe House, the Whig politician Lord Cobham had the architect and designer William Kent construct a ruined 'Temple of Modern Virtue' as a protest against political corruption, after he was dismissed from his ministerial position by the prime minister, Robert Walpole. To make quite sure no one misses the point, a decapitated statue of Walpole stands nearby. Cobham's nephew George Lyttelton, one of a group of rising Whig politicians known as 'Cobham's cubs' that also included William Pitt, built a number of sham ruins – among them one intended to make a point that may have been less *ad hominem*, but was just as vehement. In the 1740s, when Lyttelton came to landscape the grounds of Hagley Park in Worcestershire, among the hermitages, classical temples and Palladian bridges supplied by his architect Sanderson Miller was a ruined medieval castle built on high ground. For some, this might have been a thought-provoking symbol of the passage of time. For Lyttelton, however, it symbolized nothing less than the defeat of tyranny: a castle represented absolute monarchy, while the Whig revolution of 1688 had decisively asserted the primacy of Parliament over Crown. Robert Walpole's son Horace admired Lyttelton's ruin, remarking that 'it has the true rust of the Barons' Wars' – wars, that is, against Royalist forces.[6] In the years following the Jacobite uprising of 1745, sham ruins were built up and down the land to celebrate England's rejection of its feudal and Catholic past.[7]

Among these progressive ruins was one constructed by Miller at his own estate, Radway Grange in Warwickshire. It was built in stages: first came an impressive octagonal tower at the top of Edge Hill, joined a couple of years later by a ruined wall, a smaller square tower and a drawbridge – all giving the air of having grown over the course of centuries.[8] When the ruin was completed (if that is the word), Miller held a ball to celebrate, pointedly choosing 3 September 1750, the anniversary of the Battle of Worcester (1651), at which Oliver Cromwell defeated a Royalist force led by Charles II – Edge Hill itself being the site, in 1642, of a pitched battle of the First English Civil War.[9]

Real and make-believe history were becoming intimately intertwined, as Miller's neighbour, poet turned landscape gardener William Shenstone, recounted in a letter to the poet Richard Jago. Miller (arriving so early one morning to see Shenstone that he woke him up) announced that he had reluctantly left a surveyor engaged in measuring the field of battle. 'This', reports Shenstone with relish, 'he purposes to enrich with a number of anecdotes, gleaned from his neighbourhood; which must probably render it extremely entertaining: and surely Edge-hill fight was never more unfortunate to the nation, than it was lucky for Mr. Miller!' His energetic neighbour would, Shenstone predicted, 'turn every bank and hillock of his estate there, if not into *classical*, at least into *historical* ground'.[10] In 1767, Jago wrote 'Edge-Hill', a lengthy topographical poem about the area, in which he describes climbing the hill to Miller's sham ruin. It prompts Jago's thoughts to turn to actual medieval castles, and the unenlightened, brutal and – in the view of a respectable gentleman – altogether regrettable lives led within them by 'Britain's ancient Nobles', who:

Now o'er defenceless tribes, with wanton rage,
Tyrannic rul'd; and, in their castled halls
Secure, with wild excess their revels kept.[11]

Gazing out over the rural landscape from this vantage point, Jago sees not the leas of Warwickshire, but a scene of the present triumphing over the past. The peaceful 'open scenes, and cultur'd fields' in front of him remind him of 'Fair Liberty, and Freedom's gen'rous reign, / With guardian laws, and polish'd arts adorn'd'. A medieval castle, whether real or sham, speaks to him only of 'Distrust, barbarity, and Gothic rule'.[12]

When, in 1757, Shenstone built a sham ruin at his neighbouring Shropshire estate, the Leasowes, in one way he went further than Miller. Rather than a castle, he chose to construct 'the ruins of a Priory', even incorporating stones taken from the ruins of nearby Halesowen Abbey.[13] As with the ruined castles, his priory made a sharply anti-Catholic point. In his rather overheated poem 'The Ruined Abbey: or, the Effects of Superstition', Shenstone pictures the English Reformation as a great storm that lifts the roofs off corrupt abbeys and blows down their walls, leaving only ruins 'but of use to grace a rural scene, / To bound our vistas, and to glad the sons / Of George's reign, reserv'd for fairer times!'[14] Like the post-1745 ruined castles, Shenstone's 'priory' was a stage-set for a performance of triumphalist attitudes. The inclusion of masonry from Halesowen made the production all the more piquant: the old abbey was forced to play itself in a farce.

Wealthy landowners who could afford to build sham ruins were sent up by David Garrick and George Colman in their 1766 comedy *The Clandestine Marriage*. The play spears the absurdity of the craze in the character of Mr Sterling, who, conducting Lord Ogleby around his garden, boasts: 'Ay, ruins, my Lord! and they are reckoned very fine ones too. You would think them ready to tumble on your head. It has just cost me a hundred and fifty pounds to put my ruins in thorough repair.'[15] Some ruins were just badly constructed in the first place. As the self-appointed arbiter of taste, William Gilpin, declared, 'It is not every man, who can build a house, that can execute a ruin.'

To give the stone its mouldering appearance – to make the widening chink run naturally through all the joints – to mutilate the ornaments – to peel the facing from the internal structure – to shew

> how correspondent parts have once united; though now the chasm runs wide between them – and to scatter heaps of ruin around with negligence and ease; are great efforts of art; much too delicate for the hand of a common workman; and what we very rarely see performd.
>
> Besides, after all, that art can bestow, you must put your ruin at last into the hands of nature to adorn, and perfect it. If the mosses and lychens grown unkindly on your walls – if the streaming weather-stains have produced no variety of tints – if the ivy refuses to mantle over your buttress; or to creep among the ornaments of your Gothic window – if the ash cannot be brought to hang from the cleft; or long, spiry grass to wave over the shattered battlement – your ruin will be still incomplete – you may as well write over the gate, Built in the year 1772.[16]

In 1742, the sham ruin craze was (slightly) democratized. A middle-class reader flipping speculatively through the pages of the landscape gardener Batty Langley's *Ancient Architecture Restored and Improved by a Great Variety of Grand and Useful Designs, entirely New in the Gothick Mode for the Ornamenting of Buildings and Gardens* could choose an attractive garden pavilion and then pass the book directly over to their builder or craftsmen. Langley's book became extremely popular, and, along with a reissue of 1747 with the title *Gothic Architecture, Improved by Rules and Proportions*, it opened up a whole range of new possibilities, whether for those intending to introduce the air of history to their property or those who merely wished to be fashionable.[17] Langley's claim that his designs were based on lengthy researches into 'many of the most ancient Buildings, now standing in this Kingdom' was not always accepted by his more knowledgeable readers: Horace Walpole, for instance, complained that the book 'does not contain a single design of true or good Gothic', adding witheringly that 'the Goths never built summer-houses or temples in a garden'.[18] But nonetheless, Langley injected a powerful compound of Gothic arches, pinnacles and castellations into the nation's architectural bloodstream. Shenstone himself used *Ancient Architecture Restored*, telling Jago that 'by the assistance of some such treatise, I could sketch out some charming Gothic temples and Gothic benches for garden seats'.[19]

A seat inside one of Langley's Gothic pavilions would have been the perfect place to admire pictures of the actual ruins to be found in the

Batty Langley, plate from *New Principles of Gardening* (1728): 'An Avenue in Perspective terminated with the ruins of an ancient Building after the Roman manner'.

landscape, whether relics of pre-Reformation England or of old conflicts. Ruins of this kind had previously been of interest to few but obsessive antiquaries, a group once wryly regarded as the grubby-fingered metal-detectorists of their day; as John Earle, tutor to the future Charles II, noted with derision in 1628, an antiquary would 'go forty mile to see a Saint's Well, or ruin'd Abbey, and if there be but a cross, or stone footstool in the way, he will be poring on it so long till he forgett his journey'.[20] Now, these sites were attracting the attention of a wider public. The Yorkshire gentleman Samuel Buck was among the first to identify and nurture a nascent interest. In 1726, encouraged by the Society of Antiquaries, he published a group of etched views of the 'antiquities' of his native county, based on drawings that he had made on the spot; these were followed by further scenes of 'remarkable ruins' he found in Lincolnshire and Nottinghamshire. Their success gave him the idea for a more ambitious series of publications, in which he and his brother Nathaniel systematically recorded the remains of castles and abbeys in England and Wales. Every summer the Bucks bowled from one county to the next with their drawing boards, making sketches that they would etch in the autumn and publish in the winter. As Samuel put it in his

Batty Langley, design for a 'Gothic Umbrello' from *Ancient Architecture Restored* (1742).

Samuel Buck, *Tynemouth Abbey*, 1728.

prospectus, they wished to 'rescue the mangled remains' of 'these aged & venerable edifices from the inexorable jaws of time'.[21]

There was a keen market for each instalment; although the Bucks' draughtsmanship was frequently little better than rudimentary, their images still conveyed a new sense of the romance of ruins. Foliage waves decoratively along the uneven stones above the clerestory in Samuel's drawing of Tynemouth Abbey, where the Bucks stopped one late spring day in 1728, and long shadows suggest endings and the passage of time. And yet this is not the only story the Bucks tell in this image. Framed between the Gothic arches are ships – out in the bay, brisk commerce is taking place, contrasting with the calm of the ancient abbey. Two years earlier the Bucks had visited Louth in Lincolnshire, where Samuel had sat down to draw the abbey's crumbling walls. He put these sad remnants of ancient masonry in the foreground, where they stand like a line of broken teeth, but in the background he was careful to add a view of what he described in the print's inscription as the 'well Built, Rich, Populous, & Pleasant' town.

The Bucks knew their market, and frequently packaged their 'aged & venerable edifices' within a reassuring context of modernity and prosperity that heavily underlined the contrast between past and present.

The men and women who bought the Bucks' views were armchair (or, perhaps, Gothic bench) travellers, intrigued by these features of the landscape, but reassured by a mercantile context. Many of them would also have read the travel writings of one of the most prolific authors of the day. Daniel Defoe may well have crossed paths with the Bucks as he trundled from town to town making notes on 'the present state of the country' for his *Tour Through the Whole Island of Great Britain*, published between 1724 and 1727. Defoe's aim, however, was the exact reverse of the Bucks'. Modernity and progress were planted firmly in his foreground: 'improvement', as he puts it, 'in culture...in commerce, the encrease of people, and employment for them'. 'Encrease' was one of Defoe's favourite words. He was alert to signs of it in buildings, in towns and cities and in the houses of the nobility and the gentry. And yet he finds that he cannot entirely overlook the past. Time and again Defoe regrets his decision 'to decline the delightful view of antiquity'. The material remains left by the Romans, Saxons and Normans are, he writes, warming to his theme,

> like wounds hastily healed up, the calous spread over them being remov'd, they appear presently; and though the earth, which naturally eats into the strongest stones, metals, or whatever substance...has defaced the surface, the figures and inscriptions upon most of these things, yet they are beautiful, even in their decay, and the venerable face of antiquity has some thing so pleasing, so surprizing, so satisfactory in it, especially to those who have with any attention read the histories of pass'd ages, that I know nothing renders travelling more pleasant and more agreeable.[22]

To his own surprise, Defoe had fallen under the spell of the romance of the past; the slow diminishment of ancient buildings and artefacts is the gentle shade that tempers the glare of relentless 'encrease'. His course, however, is set and he regretfully turns away from this potentially absorbing subject. One wonders whether the Bucks read the first volumes of Defoe's *Tour* and spotted an opportunity to slip into the gaps he had left.

As the century progressed, Britain's ruins came more insistently into the foreground. Romanticism blustered over the North Sea from Europe, changing the cultural climate and bringing conditions that encouraged emotional responses to nature and history. The Bucks' adroit presentation of ancient structures within a framework of modern commercial life no longer suited the times. What now began to grip people's imaginations was the intensely romantic atmosphere to be found in ruined abbeys and priories, and the potential of these sites to offer precious insights into the medieval past. Hostility to the political and religious structures of pre-Reformation England dwindled in the face of the powerful appeal of ruins to the eye and the imagination. The past came to be regarded with a sense of wonder rather than in a spirit of judgment. Even William Shenstone was affected; a ruin, he wrote in his essay 'Unconnected Thoughts on Gardening', 'may be neither new to us, nor majestic, nor beautiful, yet afford that pleasing melancholy which proceeds from a reflection on decayed magnificence'.[23] In the later eighteenth century, a period in which fine aesthetic sensibilities were actively cultivated, many became gripped by a new condition – ruin-mania – of which 'pleasing melancholy' was the life-blood.

When the Gothic novelist Ann Radcliffe visited the ruins of Furness Abbey in Cumbria in 1794, she was profoundly impressed by the 'deep retirement of its situation' and 'the venerable grandeur of its gothic arches' shadowed by ancient trees, all of which created an atmosphere conducive to 'solemn yet delightful emotion'. In her travelogue she seems to take her reader by the arm and invite them to picture the abbey's 'beautiful gothic arch':

> A thick grove of plane-trees, with some oak and beech, overshadow it on the right, and lead the eye onward to the ruins of the Abbey, seen through this dark arch in remote perspective, over rough but verdant ground. The principal features are the great northern window and part of the eastern choir, with glimpses of shattered arches and stately walls beyond, caught between the gaping casements.

Steeped in the abbey's rich atmosphere of 'darkness and mystery', her imagination begins to work and 'the images and the manners of times, that were past' rise up in front of her:

> The midnight procession of monks, clothed in white and bearing lighted tapers, appeared to the 'mind's eye' issuing to the choir through the very door-case, by which such processions were wont to pass from the cloisters to perform the matin service, when, at the moment of their entering the church, the deep chanting of voices was heard, and the organ swelled a solemn peal.[24]

She could, she fancied, almost hear the sound echoing among the old stones and dying away in the breeze. The past was there, undisturbed (as long as one averted one's eyes from the 'small manor house of modern date' nearby). It was present in each shadowy doorway and overgrown arch. Every leaf whispered of it, and under the shade of the trees it pressed so close that one could virtually reach out and grasp it.

In the 1790s, Radcliffe and her companion were lucky to have the place to themselves. The French Revolution and subsequent military conflicts had made travel to the Continent exceptionally difficult, and instead British tourists set out to discover their own countries. Ruins were high

J. M. W. Turner, *Tintern Abbey, Monmouthshire*, watercolour, *c.* 1794.

on their itinerary, and places like the Lake District and the Wye Valley became popular destinations; guide books were published that provided historical details, entertaining anecdotes and information about how to get there.[25] This was a recent phenomenon; during a tour of South Wales as late as 1787, the diarist John Byng (later Viscount Torrington) had mused:

I Matthew Paris, Brutus arriving in Britain to the dismay of the resident giants.

II Merlin in Ireland, demonstrating to soldiers that Stonehenge cannot be moved by brute force alone. He is about to whisk the monument over the sea to Salisbury Plain.

III The Round Table in Winchester, made in the late thirteenth century and repainted in the reign of Henry VIII.

IV Portrait of King Arthur in Peter of Langtoft's *Chronicle of England*, *c.* 1307–27.
Each crown represents a conquest.

v *A Young Daughter of the Picts*, *c.* 1585,
watercolour attributed to Jacques le Moyne des Morgues.

VI Charles Hamilton Smith, 'Grand Conventional Festival of the Britons', illustration in Samuel Rush Meyrick's *Costume of the Original Inhabitants of the British Islands*, 1815.

VII Thomas Jones, *The Bard*, 1774.

VIII William Blake, title page design
to Thomas Gray's poem *The Bard*, 1797–8.

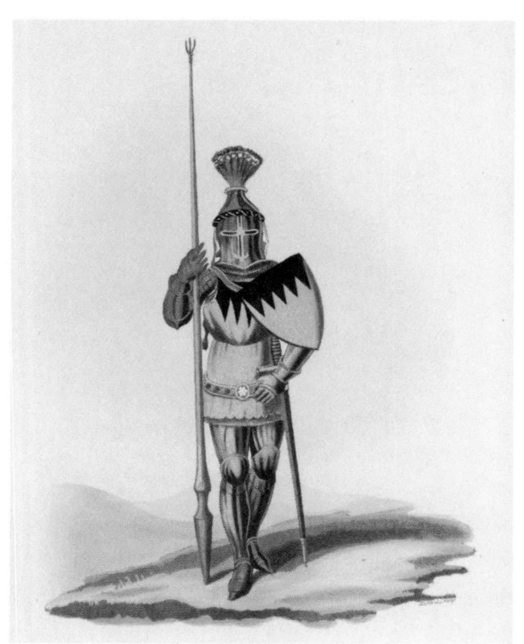

IX 'Sir John Arsich', plate from Samuel Rush Meyrick's *Critical Enquiry into Antient Armour*, 1842.

X Joseph Strutt, 'The Saxon King in his Martial Habit with his Armour Bearer', illustration to *A Complete View of the Dresses and Habits of the People of England*, 1796.

XI William Powell Frith, *An English Merry-Making a Hundred Years Ago*, 1847.

XII Edward Matthew Ward, *Interview between Charles II and Nell Gwyn as Witnessed by John Evelyn*, 1854.

XIII Henry Courbould, *Lord Eglinton dressed as Lord of the Tournament*, c. 1840.

> I have often thought that maps, merely for tourists might be made. And have wish'd that some intelligent traveller...wou'd mark on such touring maps, all the castles, Roman stations, views, canals, parks &c, &c...for till lately we had no inquisitive travellers and but few views of remarkable places.

The existing guides for tourists – often containing information gleaned from county histories assiduously compiled by local historians – were, according to Byng, 'too much in the stile of pompous history' with not enough local information.[26] When he came to compose the frontispiece for his first travel journal, Byng, who was passionately attached to historical sites, drew a landscape tellingly framed by crumbling arches.[27]

If not tourists, then it was artists busy with sketchbooks and drawing-boards, creating images of ruins for a public eager to buy watercolours or prints as souvenirs of an excursion. Three years after Radcliffe went there, the young J. M. W. Turner stopped at Furness Abbey on one of the summer drawing tours he took throughout Britain, and made a careful pencil study in his sketchbook. It was from sketches such as these that, back in his London painting room, Turner would create some of the most powerful and moving images of abbey ruins of the era. At Tate Britain is a watercolour he painted of Tintern Abbey in 1794. We, the viewers, are low down – perhaps perching on a chunk of broken masonry – and near to the soaring arches, too close to get any perspective on the structure as a whole. It surrounds us. We are no longer sitting back and getting the measure of it, as with the Bucks' views; instead we are given little choice but to breathe its air of melancholy magnificence. Our eyes are drawn vertically up the paper, until they rest on the Gothic arch framing the sky, a relic of an age of audacious faith.

It took the young Jane Austen to interrupt all this theatrical gaping with her burlesque 'History of England', written in 1791 at the age of fifteen: 'nothing can be said in [Henry VIII's] vindication,' she wrote with mock gravity, 'but that his abolishing Religious Houses & leaving them to the ruinous depredations of time has been of infinite use to the landscape of England in general, which probably was a principal motive for his doing it'.[28] There was also, she slyly suggested in *Northanger Abbey* (completed in 1803), a somewhat juvenile dimension to this desire to abandon oneself to the heady atmosphere of the medieval past. On being driven to Northanger

Paul Sandby, *Strawberry Hill from the East*, watercolour, *c.* 1769.

Abbey, where she is to stay with her friends the Tilneys, Austen's young heroine Catherine Morland looks forward to experiencing a sensation of 'solemn awe' when the 'massy walls of grey stone' become visible around the next bend, 'rising amidst a grove of ancient oaks, with the last beams of the sun playing in beautiful splendour on its high Gothic windows', and is disappointed when she arrives in the grounds 'without having discerned even an antique chimney'. Once inside, her expectations are again frustrated. Although the abbey's windows are suitably arched, they admit a distressing amount of cheerful light for someone who had 'hoped for the smallest divisions, and the heaviest stone-work, for painted glass, dirt and cobwebs'. Catherine's immersion in the sensational world of 'horrid' Gothic novels, with their ghosts, tyrants and curses, has left her emotionally ill-prepared for the more measured, nuanced prose of adult life. 'Charming as were all Mrs Radcliffe's works', she eventually concludes, 'it was not in them perhaps that human nature, at least in the midland counties of England, was to be looked for.'[29]

John Carter, *View of the hall and staircase at Strawberry Hill*, 1788.

May 1769: Horace Walpole is greeting a group of distinguished French, Spanish and Portuguese visitors at the gate of Strawberry Hill, his house on the banks of the Thames at Twickenham. It has been remarked that when this elegant connoisseur and man of letters enters a room it is with 'affected delicacy...knees bent, and feet upon tiptoe, as if afraid of a wet floor'.[30] To meet his guests today it can be imagined that his deportment is more extravagantly affected than ever, as he is wearing two extraordinary garments. The first, strictly speaking, is not a garment at all, but a piece of artistic virtuosity: a limewood carving of a cravat imitating Venetian needle-point lace, created around 1690 by the master wood-carver Grinling Gibbons. The second is a long pair of gloves trimmed with silk, metal and lace that once belonged to King James I. 'The French servants stared', he delightedly reported to a friend afterwards, 'and firmly believed that this was the dress of an English country gentleman.'[31]

Inside Strawberry Hill, Walpole conducted his guests through spaces and rooms designed to evoke a succession of subtly different historical moods.[32] Before entering the house itself, the scene would have been set as they walked through the Little Cloister, which, with its rib vaulting and pointed arches, breathed a monastic air; this continued in the entrance hall, a room hung with paper of a trompe-l'oeil Gothic design and lit by a lantern set with fragments of medieval stained glass. As Walpole's guests progressed, they would have noticed the atmosphere gradually changing into one more suited to a castle than a cloister; up the stairs was a rich display of arms and armour, most spectacularly a suit of gold parade armour purchased by Walpole as having belonged to Francis I, king of France. The Holbein Chamber was designed to have a Tudor character, to match the tracings of Holbein's images of Henry VIII's court that hung there (although chairs and tables Walpole believed to be Tudor were actually made in the seventeenth century in Goa or Sri Lanka, then Portuguese colonies). The long Gallery had oil paintings displayed in mirrored niches, and the vaulted Tribune – named after the room of Medici treasures in the Uffizi in Florence – was where Walpole displayed some of his most precious collections: his beloved portrait miniatures and enamels; objects with royal associations, such as – according to his own descriptions – Henry VIII's dagger and the 'precious prayer-book' which belonged to Francis I's queen; ancient bronzes, classical rings and a model of Thomas Becket's shrine.[33] It was also the usual home of his wooden cravat. One can only imagine the cumulative effect of the tour on his guests that day, guided as they were by a host who appeared to have stepped out of one of his own display cases.

So was Strawberry Hill constructed from the remains of an ancient abbey, its Gothic tracery carefully restored and its precious medieval spirit revived? Not even remotely. The house that in 1747 Walpole leased from Elizabeth Chenevix, a fashionable trinket-seller, was a small seventeenth-century building. 'It is', he wrote to a friend, 'a little play-thing-house that I got out of Mrs Chenevix's shop, and it is the prettiest bauble you ever saw.'[34] Over the following years he transformed the play-thing-house into 'a little Gothic castle', which developed lancet and quatrefoil windows, grew battlements and pinnacles and, in time, sprouted a pair of towers.[35] Strawberry Hill became, in Walpole's imagination, the ancient seat of the

Barons of Strawberry; he referred to it wryly as 'the castle (I am building) of my ancestors'.[36] And yet although it had no genuine medieval foundations, in many of its details it was closely based on actual ancient edifices and monuments. Walpole and the close friends who comprised his 'Committee of Taste' drew upon their knowledge of Gothic cathedrals in England and Europe, and used one of the greatest antiquarian publications of the seventeenth century, William Dugdale's *History of St Paul's Cathedral* (1658) with its large, impressively detailed illustrations by Wenceslaus Hollar, as a style manual. In Walpole's library, for instance, the bookcases were based on a print found in Dugdale's book representing a side door of the choir of Old St Paul's, while the chimney-piece combined details from medieval tombs in Westminster Abbey and Canterbury Cathedral. The Queen's Dressing Room at Windsor Castle provided the inspiration for the Tudor-style Holbein Chamber's decorative ceiling – the relief mouldings of which were made not of traditional plaster, but of papier-mâché.

Each individual room at Strawberry Hill exerted its own character through architecture, decoration and the light from arched or trefoil windows, often filtered through medieval stained glass to create the subtle effect, by turns pretty and theatrical, that Walpole called 'gloomth'. Some of the objects displayed exerted a fascinating aura not so much because of what they were, but because of their distinguished provenance: Cardinal Wolsey's broad-brimmed scarlet hat in the Holbein Room, or Anne Boleyn's clock, reputedly given to her by Henry VIII as a wedding gift. Other objects were part of a more elaborate game of make-believe. In Walpole's imagination, the armoury was composed of ancestral pieces that had been inherited, rather than purchased – as was the more prosaic case. Having discovered a distant relation through genealogical research, Walpole announced that the 'trophies of old coats of mail, Indian shields made of rhinoceros's hides, broadswords, quivers, long bows, arrows and spears' were 'all *supposed* to be taken by Sir Terry Robsart in the holy wars'.[37] Provided with a distinguished shared provenance, when displayed by candlelight, these formerly miscellaneous objects evoked a dramatic episode of medieval history.

Walpole composed his 'little Gothic castle' as one might a novel, arranging architecture, decoration, furniture, paintings and artefacts until they unfolded the tales he desired. It was really only a matter of time before

Strawberry Hill inspired a work of fiction. One morning in 1764, Walpole woke from a dream, 'of which all I could recover', he later related,

> was, that I had thought myself in an ancient castle (a very natural dream for a head filled like mine with Gothic story) and that on the uppermost bannister of a great staircase I saw a gigantic hand in armour. In the evening I sat down and began to write....[38]

The result, published later that year, was *The Castle of Otranto*, a supernatural story of obsession and pursuit set in the distant past. The plot relates how Conrad, son of the saturnine Prince of Otranto, is grotesquely crushed to death on the eve of his marriage to the beautiful Isabella when a gigantic helmet mysteriously crashes into the courtyard, at which point the Prince decides to marry the bride himself and grimly sets off in pursuit. At the heart of the book is the castle, which is haunted by supernatural figures including a cowled skeleton, an elusive giant and the subject of a portrait who, heaving a 'deep sigh', steps down out of his picture – an idea suggested to Walpole by a Jacobean oil painting of Henry Carey, Lord Falkland, that hung beneath the papier-mâché fan-vaulting in his Gallery.[39] The partly ruined Castle, which, like Strawberry Hill, is almost a character in its own right, is destroyed in the closing pages of the novel by the giant ghost of Alfonso, the ancient ruler of Otranto.

With *Otranto*, Walpole built – and then pulled down – a sham ruin in his imagination. A place in which to express fears about the past with its ghosts and superstitions, it was the dark flip-side of Strawberry Hill, the 'Gothic' atmosphere of which was designed to charm, not frighten. The past, Strawberry Hill suggested, far from being savage and barbarous, was a delightful place to be – in fact, it was the one dependable comfort in life. 'Visions, you know, have always been my pasture', wrote Walpole.

> And so far from growing old enough to quarrel with their emptiness, I almost think there is no wisdom comparable to that of exchanging what is called the realities of life for dreams. Old Castles, old pictures, old histories, and the babble of old people make one live back into centuries that cannot disappoint one. One holds fast and surely what is past.[40]

For Walpole, historical objects were not simply the keys that would unlock this enchanting past. They were the door itself and the floorboards under his feet; they covered every wall and occupied each cupboard of the room within. Portraits; furniture; clothes; ceramics; textiles; books; as long as these things had historic associations or interesting provenances, they were capable of providing a route to versions of the past that were more fascinating and magical than the present.

Walpole did not at first publish *The Castle of Otranto* under his own name. Instead, he contrived an elaborate device for bowling the 'original' text far back into the past – not once, but twice. Writing as the text's putative translator from Italian to English, 'William Marshal' (perhaps thinking of the Anglo-Norman soldier and 1st Earl of Pembroke of that name, whose tomb effigy is in the Temple Church in London), Walpole explains that the printed text of the story, a book that had been 'found in the library of an ancient Catholic family in the north of *England*', had been published in Naples in 1529. But then he points still further back, proposing that the original story – if 'written near the time when it is supposed to have happened' – was composed 'between 1095, the era of the first crusade, and 1243, the date of the last, or not long afterwards'. Having thought ourselves in the early sixteenth century, the floorboards beneath our feet give way, dramatically depositing us at an earlier date. To underline the point, for the second edition Walpole changed the subtitle 'A Story' to 'A Gothic Story'. He reserves a final flourish for the last few lines of his 'translator's preface': remarking on the author's specificity about the castle layout, he speculates not only that he 'had some certain building in his eye', but that some real-life 'catastrophe' had given rise to the story in the first place. It was precisely the kind of elaborate provenance that Walpole gave to so many of the items in his collection.

Otranto set the scene for subsequent generations of writers of Gothic fiction, from Ann Radcliffe and Matthew Lewis onwards. Gothic novelists played on the idea that it was not in the nature of the past to lie quietly buried, but rather to develop roots that would creep quietly beneath the topsoil of the present and send shoots bursting through, whether in the form of ghosts or ancient pagan practices. Old buildings in these books are always haunted, if only by the burden of the past; ghosts gather like dust in the dim turn of a turret stair or the damp recesses of the vaults. What you might think has been left in the distant past, whispers Gothic fiction, is never quite dead. In fact, it might even be undead; just over a

Merlin's Cave in the Royal Gardens at Richmond, created in 1735 by William Kent.

hundred years later, Bram Stoker's novel *Dracula* introduced a protagonist who exemplified the horrifyingly incongruous presence of the archaic amid the trains and typewriters of modern life.

Creating an imaginary version of the past was not just an esoteric pursuit at this time; it also became a fashionable one. Many wealthy English families built Gothic follies in secluded corners of their estates to be styled as 'hermitages'; some were furnished with props such as a rustic chair and table, a book and a pair of spectacles to imply a temporarily absent inhabitant, while others were occupied by full-size models of hermits, bent devoutly over religious texts. A few even boasted an actual hermit – or, at least, a household servant in an occasional rôle, forbidden to trim his hair and beard and obliged to dress in rough sackcloth. A trip to see the hermit would be part of the entertainment offered to guests; some ornamental hermits would be allowed to converse with visitors, answering questions and dispensing sage advice, while others were forbidden to speak. The hermit was a bit of flotsam from the medieval, pre-Reformation past that had apparently drifted into the present.

Occasionally the inhabitants of these kinds of spaces were imagined as particular individuals. In the 1730s, William Kent was commissioned by Queen Caroline, consort of George II, to build two hermitages in what was then Richmond Gardens. The first was a rustic stone building, 'very Grotesque,' according to one visitor, 'being a Heap of Stones thrown into a very artful Disorder, and curiously embellished with Moss and Shrubs, to represent rude Nature' while the second, Merlin's Cave, was a strange-looking house with conical thatched roofs.[41] Inside were rustic bookcases and vellum-bound books, while in the central hall were life-sized models representing the young Merlin and his secretary at his desk consulting instruments and books of magic, Elizabeth of York, Elizabeth I and Britomart from Spenser's *Faerie Queene*. Queen Caroline and the new Hanoverian dynasty were thus connected to England's past, both royal and mythical.[42]

Come with me: through the colonnade, past those antique capitals and into the north aisle of the museum. Narrow steps lead down to the basement storey, to the rooms once inhabited by the monk Padre Giovanni and preserved just as he left them. Look in here: this little room must have been his cell, with its carved wooden crucifix and small library; and that his oratory, with a niche for holy water. Step into his parlour, decorated, as John Soane, the house's owner, explains, with a painting of a martyred saint, 'Statues in terra cotta, and...numerous Models and Works of Art, taken chiefly from the ecclesiastical monuments'. It is almost like plunging into a different element, so golden is the light as it filters through yellow panes of glass and falls on the plaster casts of medieval fragments, curios and grotesque heads that cover the walls and ceiling; Soane himself called it '*lumière mystérieuse*'.[43] A door leads into a little courtyard with fragments of medieval masonry, the ruins of Padre Giovanni's monastery. 'The rich Canopy,' says Soane, 'and other Decorations of this venerable spot, are objects which cannot fail to produce the most powerful sensations in the minds of the admirers of the piety of our forefathers.' Here too is the old monk's tomb, which 'adds to the gloomy scenery of this hallowed place'. And look: at the head of his grave is that of his dog Fanny, his 'favourite companion, the delight, the solace of his leisure hours', to which is added a simple inscription: 'Alas, poor Fanny!'

So how long ago did Padre Giovanni die? And why are the splendid remains of his monastery to be found in the basement of a house in central London, in a small, dank area usually used for kitchen refuse? Well, Soane's monk was, in fact, imaginary (though Fanny had been Mrs Soane's lap-dog) and the ecclesiastical masonry posing as his monastery was made up of fragments he had acquired from the medieval Palace of Westminster. Soane himself was self-effacing about his fantasy, quoting the Roman poet Horace: 'Dulce est desipere in loco', he wrote – it is pleasant to be silly in such a place.[44] But there was more to it than that. Soane was the architect responsible for some of the greatest neoclassical buildings of the early nineteenth century, such as the Bank of England and Dulwich Picture Gallery, but when he created these spaces in his basement in Lincoln's Inn Fields he became nothing less than a Gothic novelist.[45] Elsewhere in his remarkable house – or rather, the three terraced houses Soane made into one – he assembled an astonishing collection of antiquities from Greece, Rome and Egypt, arranged with theatrical panache. The invention of Padre Giovanni allowed Soane to bring emotion into the mix, and to turn a museum of fragments and artefacts into an evocative stage-set. When visiting, it is hard not to turn one's head at the least sound, half-expecting the padre to appear in the doorway.

Spring 1757, and in a Cambridge room the Welsh harpist John Parry is playing to a group of dons. His repertoire is 'Antient British Music' – the name of his published collection of Welsh melodies – which, claimed Parry, was none other than the music of the ancient druids themselves. In the audience sits Thomas Gray, poet and fellow of Pembroke College. He is electrified by what he hears. That day, the early poetry he has been thinking about at his desk in his college rooms suddenly begins to breathe and live.

Two years earlier, inspired by his studies of early English and Welsh poetry and the history of rhyme, Gray had begun writing a poem, 'The Bard', set in late thirteenth-century Wales. The poem's brief preface tells us that it was based 'on a Tradition current in Wales, that EDWARD the First, when he compleated the conquest of that country, ordered all the Bards, that fell into his hands, to be put to death'. It relates a dramatic encounter between the King, marching his victorious army through Snowdonia near the river Conwy, and a Welsh bard (a figure thought to be descended from the Celtic druids) who curses him from a rocky outcrop – 'Ruin seize thee, ruthless King!' – and predicts the future Tudor dynasty and the flourishing of English poetry. The poem ends with the bard uttering a final curse – 'Be thine despair and sceptered care; / To triumph, and to die, are mine' – before throwing himself into the river. Initially Gray made such good progress that he seemed to be effortlessly ventriloquizing his central character, declaring: 'I felt myself the bard.' Difficulties with the third part had forced him to lay his poem aside; but that spring day, music resonant with history and ancient British mysticism filled his mind. Back in his rooms Gray retrieved his manuscript and finished his poem. 'Mr Parry has been here', he reported to his friend the poet William Mason shortly afterwards,

> & scratch'd out such ravishing blind Harmony, such tunes of a thousand year old, with names enough to choak you, as have set all this learned body a'dancing, & inspired them with due reverence for *Odikle* [i.e. 'The Bard', subtitled 'A Pindaric Ode'], whenever he shall appear. Mr Parry (you must know) it was, that has put Odikle in motion again, & with much exercise it has got a *tender Tail* grown...and here it is.[46]

Parry's strange music, unlike anything Gray had heard before, had given him a new imaginative sympathy with bards and their supposed predecessors, the druids. By the most fleeting and intangible means, the gap between the distant past and the present was bridged.

In the summer of 1757, Gray's friend Walpole printed 'The Bard' on his newly installed press at Strawberry Hill, in a slim, elegant volume simply called *Odes by Mr. Gray*. Critical reaction to the poem was not as wholeheartedly positive as Gray would have liked; some readers complained that his references and allusions were unfamiliar and even obscure. Nonetheless, the pathos and passion of Gray's bard introduced a distinctive new flavour into eighteenth-century poetry, and the poem's reputation grew. Gray had given the Britons a voice. It may have been a doomed voice, but it was exhilarating, even as it was uttering its last, defiant curses.

Artists responded enthusiastically to the poem's striking visual imagery. The landscape painter Paul Sandby was among the first to be inspired, exhibiting *The Bard* in 1761 at the Society of Artists. His painting is sadly now lost, but an echo of its extraordinary impact survives in Mason's breathless description of it in a letter to Lord Nuneham: 'Sandby has made such a picture! such a bard! such a headlong flood! such a Snowdon! such giant oaks! such desert caves!,' he exclaimed, and concluded that it might be 'the best picture that has been painted this century in any country' – such are the ones that get away.[47] A few years later, the Welsh artist Thomas Jones took up the theme with a painting of the same title (Plate VII). He frames the scene with two blasted oak trees, their branches broken and great roots breaking the ground. Under clouds the colour of trout skin, the bard, illuminated by a pale shaft of sunlight, steps towards the edge of a rocky precipice, while behind him rise higher mountain peaks. In the background, silhouetted against the rock face, are monoliths clearly based on Stonehenge. Gray's poem may have been set in the 1270s, but by including these ruins Jones associated the bards with the ancient druids, who, thanks to Stukeley, were generally thought at the time to have been responsible for stone circles. It was a gesture towards the more distant British past and a long tradition of individual heroism and resistance.

Occasionally a new voice is heard in poetry so startling and fresh it is like walking outside on a cold day and being struck smartly in the face by the icy air. Just three years after Cambridge dons were set a'dancing by ancient music, a publication had a similarly rousing effect on its readers; except it was not a new voice at all, but an exceptionally old one. In 1760 a young Highlander, James Macpherson, published *Fragments of Ancient Poetry*, a group of verses that he claimed were 'genuine remains of ancient Scottish poetry' composed by bards in an era of 'the most remote antiquity'. 'Every chief or great man had in his family a Bard or poet,' explains Macpherson in his preface, 'whose office it was to record in verse, the illustrious actions of that family. By the succession of these Bards, such poems were handed down from race to race; some in manuscript; but more by oral tradition.'[48]

Translated into spare English prose and biblical cadences, the poems in *Fragments* are strikingly elemental, full of lonely hills and scudding clouds, of sea and rushes and the blustering wind. Warriors meet and battles take place in a landscape of rock and water that is even more ancient than the passionate speakers who sit and wait on the hill, or wander the heath among the ghosts of those who lived there long ago. Or perhaps it is more accurate to say that the bleak landscape soaked in mists and fogs produces an atmosphere so heavy with foreboding and memory that it *is* the drama: the human events that take place within it are small in the context of this sublime stage-set.

> Autumn is dark on the mountains; grey mist rests on the hills. The whirlwind is heard on the heath. Dark rolls the river through the narrow plain. A tree stands alone on the hill, and marks the grave of Connal. The leaves whirl round with the wind, and strew the grave of the dead. At times are seen here the ghosts of the deceased, when the musing hunter alone stalks slowly over the heath.[49]

It seemed to its readers that Macpherson had discovered a vein of pure antiquity deep in the Highlands, one that had lain undisturbed for many centuries; what if this were only the beginning, and much more of this precious lode remained to be mined? Macpherson had hinted as much in his preface when he mentioned more that 'deserves to be recovered and translated', with a pointed mention of the 'encouragement' that would be needed for 'such an undertaking'.[50] Supporters duly mustered funds that enabled him to make trips to Perthshire, Argyll, Inverness-shire and the islands of Skye, North and South Uist, Benbecula and Mull to gather manuscripts, songs and ballads, and before long Macpherson published one epic, *Fingal* (1762), followed by another, *Temora* (1763). Both, he claimed, were his translations from the original Gaelic of a blind Scottish poet of the third century called Ossian.

Soon after the appearance of *Fingal*, the poet Anna Seward reflected on the attractive simplicity of these ancient verses:

John Sell Cotman, *A Subject from Ossian*, watercolour, 1803.
On the back are two lines from *Temora*: 'The moon looks abroad from her cloud. The grey-skirted mist is near, the dwelling of the ghosts'.

> Stranger, as was the author of these sombre dramas, to the sciences and arts, even to agriculture itself, and therefore excluded from the immense resources which they yield to the poet; yet, by the force of native genius, the grandly simple objects, which an uncultivated, and almost desert country could produce, are found sufficient for the sublimest purposes of illustration, description, and imagery.[51]

Seward was right about the striking images conjured up by Ossian's poems. Artists wishing to paint and draw landscape had for some time been caught between the demands of topography on the one hand – considered a lowly, plodding sort of art – and a fancifully Italianate treatment of the British landscape on the other. Ossian's many descriptions of the natural world offered a bracing alternative: a landscape that had the advantage of being real and historical, but could also be shaped entirely within the imagination.

The sombre mood of Macpherson's translations may have inspired artists, but *Fragments* had hardly been published before their authenticity began to be questioned. Were his discoveries simply too good to be true? Was 'Ossian' really their author – or was Macpherson rather more than the mere translator he claimed to be? In April 1760, Gray confessed to Walpole that he was 'charmed' by the 'specimens of Erse poetry', but, ever the scholar, mentioned that he would like to see 'a few lines of the original, that I may form some slight idea of the language, the measures, and the rhythm'. He did, however, add good-humouredly: 'if I were sure that any one now living in Scotland had written them to divert himself and laugh at the credulity of the world, I would undertake a journey into the Highlands only for the pleasure of seeing him'.[52] Gray made contact with Macpherson and received examples of the poems – and yet this did nothing to settle his mind. Were they authentic or not? 'What plagues me', he wrote to his friend Thomas Wharton a couple of months later,

> is, I can not come at any certainty on that head. I was so struck, so *extasié* with their infinite beauty, that I writ into Scotland to make a thousand enquiries. The letters I have in return are ill-wrote, ill-reason'd, unsatisfactory, calculated (one would imagine) to deceive one, & yet not cunning enough to do it cleverly. In short, the whole external evidence would make one believe these fragments (for so he calls them, tho' nothing can be more entire) counterfeit: but the internal is so strong on the other side, that I am resolved to believe them genuine, spite of the Devil & the Kirk.[53]

It was the Scottish antiquarian John Pinkerton who finally flapped away the Celtic mists that lingered around 'Ossian', briskly pointing out numerous anachronisms and citing an unaccountable lack of original texts. Even so, controversy has simmered away over the years – Macpherson certainly based his 'translations' on the actual Gaelic poetry he had collected and in which he had considerable expertise; inventing, yes, but within the parameters of tradition.[54] But what is perhaps most telling is how swiftly Macpherson's poetry had been able to seduce a society that had embraced Enlightenment values of progress and empiricism. The conditions had been perfect for an alternative to all this modernity, for an atmospheric mist to soften the searching glare of the Enlightenment. When Scotland was first offered its own Homer, it was as though it willingly suspended disbelief. 'Ossian' was a granite edifice to a marble

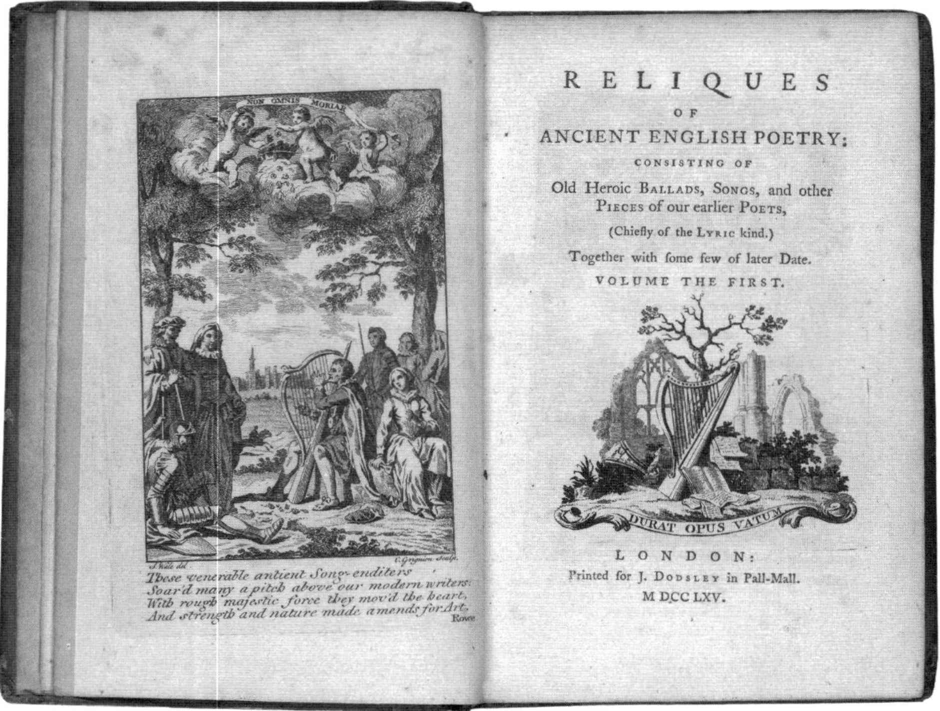

Frontispiece and title page to Thomas Percy's
Reliques of Ancient English Poetry (1765).

sculpture; heroic and stirring rather than refined and urbane. Ancient superstition, barbarism and a deep identification with nature had entered polite drawing-rooms within the leather-bound boards of a small book, and the passion with which they were received suggested an appetite that was otherwise going unfulfilled.[55]

Rip. Rip. Rrrrip. Scrunch; crackle.

For over half of every year sounds like these were heard two or three times a day, a harsh tuning-up before the fire could begin its comforting melody. For the most part they probably went unnoticed, automatically blocked out in much the same way as the presence of the servant lighting the fire would hardly have been remarked upon. We will never know what made the clergyman Thomas Percy, on a visit of around 1753 to his friend Humphrey Pitt, look up and take notice of a large book that was being used by the maids to light the fire. It was 'unbound and sadly torn', he later recalled, about two inches thick, 'lying dirty on the floor under a Bureau in ye Parlour'.[56] When he looked more closely he saw that the pages that were being torn from the book were covered in old songs, ballads and romances. They had been transcribed by hand, sometime in the previous century by the look of it. Whoever had done so had gathered the material together from many different sources, some evidently much older still.[57] Percy was astonished, and persuaded Pitt to allow him to rescue the volume; the maids would have to find something else to use. His timely action was eventually to change the course of English poetry.

Nothing happened very quickly, however. The volume, having been saved from the fire, probably remained in the Pitt household for some years. What reminded Percy of it seems to have been an old Scottish ballad, 'Gil Morrice', that his friend Shenstone recited to him in the summer of 1757. In November of that year, Percy wrote to Shenstone with the news that he had 'a very curious old MS. Collection of ancient Ballads' – Samuel Johnson had seen them, he reported, and advised him to publish and even offered to help him select and annotate the material, though in the end it was Shenstone himself who performed this task until his death in 1763. Far from sticking to the ballads found in the volume, Percy spread his net widely; his fireside find inspired him to search for more material, which he assembled from a variety of printed books, including Nicholas Ling's *England's Helicon* (1600 and 1614) and Thomas D'Urfey's *Wit and Mirth, or Pills to Purge Melancholy* (1698–1714), as well as archives including the ballads gathered by Samuel Pepys, a pioneering collector of popular 'broadsides' (printed ballad sheets), which occupied several volumes of the library he bequeathed to Magdalene College, Cambridge.[58]

Percy organized the material for *Reliques of Ancient English Poetry* (1765) in three volumes, loosely grouping together ballads with martial, supernatural, Arthurian or Shakespearean subjects, and interspersing them with Scottish ballads and love songs. In his preface he promises that 'such specimens of ancient poetry have been selected as either shew the gradation of our language, exhibit the progress of popular opinions, display the peculiar manners and customs of former ages, or throw light on our earliest classical poets'.[59] This tightly buttoned-up description hardly prepares the reader for the riot of sex and violence they are about to encounter. However Percy may have wished to dress it up, his ballads are, by their very nature, unruly and amoral. They take justice out of the hands of the authorities and give it to those directly involved. Open Percy's *Reliques* at random: meet Lord Barnard discovering his wife in bed with her lover Little Musgrave, and, after voyeuristically lifting up both the coverlet and the sheet to look at their bodies, cutting off her breasts so that she bleeds to death and running Musgrave through with his sword. Make the acquaintance of Robin Hood, who kills Guy of Gisborne, cuts off his head, sticks it on the end of his bow, then mutilates his face so badly 'That he was never on woman born, / Cold know whose head it was'. Let Percy introduce you to a stepmother who arranges for her husband's beautiful daughter to be knifed to death by her cook, minced, made into a pie and offered up to her unwitting father for dinner; the woman was burned at the stake, while her husband 'judg'd the master-cook / In boiling lead to stand'.[60] The pages of *Reliques* are clotted with gore. Cruelty is met with cruelty and summary justice dealt out with sickening frequency. Percy attempted to dignify the voice of the past in his introductory essay, in which he described the important role of the minstrel in English history, dwelling on his descent from the ancient bards and the 'great reverence' in which the post was held 'among the Saxon tribes, as well as among their Danish brethren'. King Alfred himself, he reminds us, disguised himself as a minstrel in order to infiltrate a Danish camp.[61] Even so, it is hard to avoid the conclusion that the voices that rise from the pages of the *Reliques* are ones that revel in bawdiness and unbridled violence.

'Trash' was the word Percy habitually used to describe the contents of *Reliques*, keenly aware that the publishing of popular ballads had to be squared with his status as a clergyman. 'I am content to perform the office of a scavenger for the public,' he announced rather defensively, 'and as Virgil found *Gold* among the *Dung* of *Ennius*, from all this learned Lumber I hope to extract something that shall please the most delicate and correct Taste.'[62] It was partly his anxiety on this front – coupled with additional nervousness about the reaction of the book's dedicatee, his patron Elizabeth Percy, Countess (later Duchess) of Northumberland, that led him to top and tail each ballad with a display of scholarly commentary. And it was perhaps this peculiar combination of serious structure and riotous content that made the *Reliques* such a spectacular success on its publication. A good proportion of Percy's material was not particularly obscure, but it had generally been dismissed as so much 'trash'; his innovation was to suggest that it was worthy of attention. He tied it into a native tradition and insisted that ancient English myth, folklore, story and superstition were interesting and significant. The account of ancient minstrels that Percy gives in his introduction may be fanciful, but his scholarly attention rehabilitated ballads, giving them a serious historical context that they had never before had. Poetry had long modelled itself on classical precedents, but here was a native alternative with its roots in an ancient bardic tradition, and one evidently in boisterously robust health. The old ballads that Percy had saved from the fire and rooted out of libraries burst into the refined tea-party of eighteenth-century verse, smashing the bone china and offering tankards of beer instead. English poetry was never quite the same again.

Reliques was only the beginning; the cantankerous antiquary Joseph Ritson, needled by what he saw as Percy's slipshod editorial methods and cavalier way with authentic texts, sought out and published many more examples of genuine verse in anthologies including *Pieces of Ancient Popular Poetry from Authentic Manuscripts and Old Printed Copies* (1791) and *Ancient Songs from the Time of King Henry the Third to the Revolution* (1792). Ritson's radical political opinions and sympathy for the principles of the French Revolution also led him to publish the exhaustive *Robin Hood: a Collection of all the Ancient Poems, Songs, and Ballads now Extant Related to that Celebrated English Outlaw* (1795).[63] But among the first to respond to Percy's *Reliques* was a boy in Bristol.

To say that Thomas Chatterton was bookish is like saying that Hamlet had a tendency to indecision. 'At eight years of age he was so eager for books that he read from the moment he waked, which was early, until he went to bed, if they would let him,' remembered his sister.[64] He borrowed books from the circulating libraries and read during breaks at his school, Colston's in Bristol, and at the end of the day in the churchyard of St Mary Redcliffe, next to his home.[65] On leaving school and being apprenticed as a scrivener to an attorney, John Lambert – a job that kept him in his master's house but left him with much time to fill – he read.

And a kind bookseller, who knew the boy had no money for books, allowed Chatterton to spend time in his shop, reading 'promiscuously works on religion, history, biography, poetry, heraldry – and, in short, the most abstruse treatises on every subject'.[66]

Chatterton may have read widely, but what absorbed him most of all was the Middle Ages. Lambert possessed a copy of Chaucer, and another favourite book of Chatterton's was the popular collection the *Muses Library, or, A Series of English Poetry, from the Saxons to the Reign of King Charles II* (1737), which included works by writers including William Langland, John Gower and Thomas Hoccleve.[67] He was also surrounded to an unusual degree by the material culture of the past. Not only did he live in the shadow of St Mary Redcliffe and attend a school for which his uniform was a Tudor-style bluecoat, his father, a writing master at a school attached to the church, who had died before Thomas was born, had taken from its muniments room a quantity of medieval manuscripts that he used to cover his pupils' books. At some point Chatterton discovered two boxes of the precious remaining documents and, announcing to his mother that he had 'found a treasure', afterwards 'was perpetually rummaging and ransacking every corner in the house for more parchments, and, from time to time, carried away those he had already found, by pockets-full'.[68]

Chatterton took up his apprenticeship in the summer of 1767, when he was fourteen. The previous few years – formative for this precocious boy – had seen the publication of Gray's *Bard* (1757), Macpherson's *Fragments of Ancient Poetry* (1760), Walpole's *Castle of Otranto* (1764) and Percy's *Reliques of Ancient English Poetry* (1765). Any young bookish person would have been excited by these new springs that had apparently begun to gush from Britain's ancient literary bedrock; Chatterton was inspired to act. He was a boy who existed in two worlds: on the one hand there was the dreary everyday reality of school, and later the drudgery of scrivening for an unsympathetic master; but on the other, and every bit as real to him, was the mental realm he inhabited, a great airy framework of history and poetry. At some point he had an idea that burst the membrane between the two: he would invent history and interleave it so cleverly into the world that it would be accepted as fact.

In the early autumn of 1768, Chatterton saw his chance. A new bridge had been constructed over the Avon in Bristol to replace a medieval one, and in September it was opened to foot passengers. Not long afterwards, a short letter appeared in the *Bristol Weekly Journal*, accompanied by an eyewitness account of the ceremony held at the time of the opening of the fourteenth-century bridge:

> Mr Printer,
>
> The following Description of the Mayor's first passing over the Old Bridge, taken from an old manuscript, may not at this time be unacceptable to the generality of your readers,
>
> Yours, &c.,
> Dunhelmus Bristoliensis
>
> On Fridaie was the Time fixed for passing the newe Brydge: Aboute the Time of the Tollynge the tenth Clock, Master Greggorie Dalbenye, monnted on a Fergreyne Horse, enformed Master Maior all Thynges were prepared: when two Beadils want fyrst streyng fresh stre, next came a Manne dressed up as follows: Hose of Goatskyn, erinepart outwards, Doublet and Waystcoat also, over which a white Robe without sleeves, much like an albe, but not so longe, reeching but to his Lends; a girdle of Azure over his left shoulder, rechde also to his Lends on the Ryght, and doubled back to his Left, bucklyng with a Gouldin Buckel, dangled to his knee; thereby representing a Saxon Eldermann. In his hande he bare a shield, the Maystrie of Gille a Brogton, who paincted the same, representyng Saincte Warburgh crossynge the Ford.

The account goes on to describe others in the procession: a strong man in armour, minstrels singing the song of Saint Werburgh and the mayor on a white horse, 'dight with sable Trappyng', city merchants, priests and friars. A Latin sermon was preached, after which 'with the sound of clarion theie agayne went to the Brydge, and there dined, spendying the rest of the Daie in Sportes and Plaies', and all was followed by the lighting of 'a greete Fire at Night on Kynwulph Hyll'.[69]

Having invented this picturesque description of the day, with ceremonies and costumes designed to knock the modern versions into a cocked hat, Chatterton realized he might be asked to provide some corroboration for this extraordinary, hitherto unknown account, so central to Bristol's history. So he faked material evidence, trimming the margins

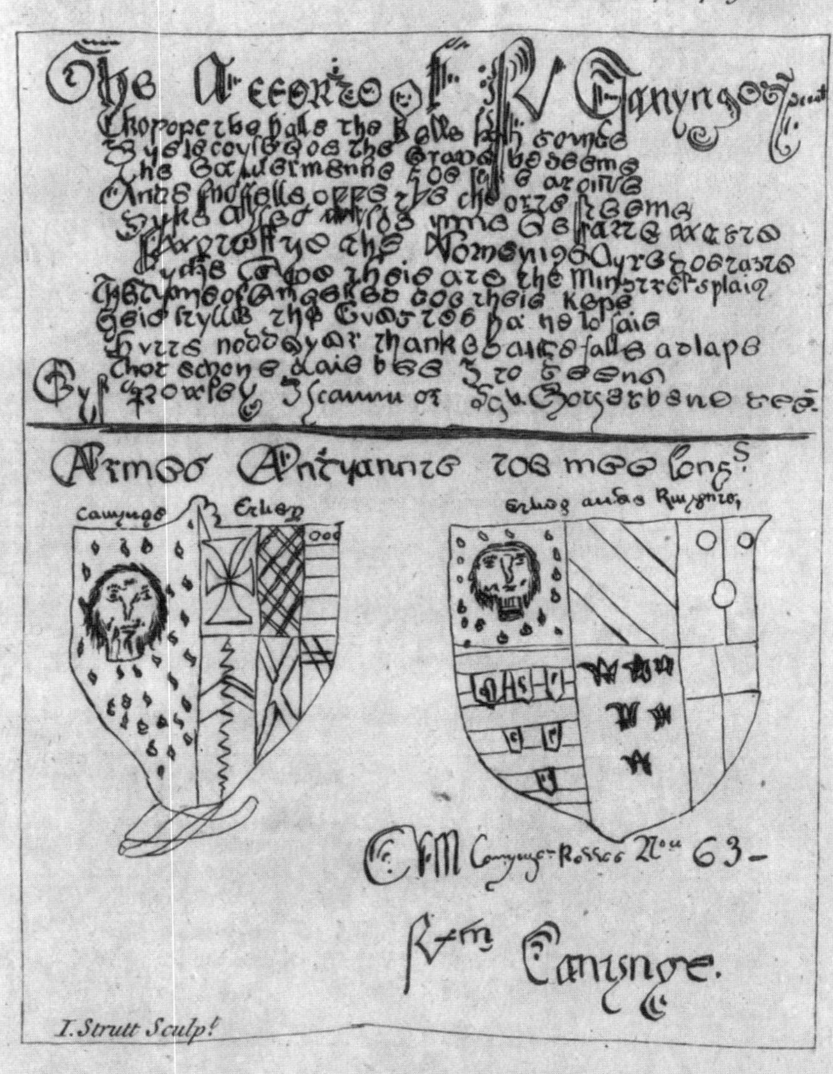

'The Accounte of W. Canynges Feast',
document forged by Thomas Chatterton.

from parchment documents in his master's office, inscribing them with a style of writing based on that of the medieval manuscripts he had salvaged from his late father's possessions and giving them the appearance of age by holding them above a candle-flame until they were distorted and blackened with soot.[70]

As a practical joke on the city, Chatterton's account of the medieval bridge-opening ceremony was audacious enough. But his greatest invention was far more wide-reaching. Having seen the name Thomas Rouley on a memorial brass at St John's Gate, Bristol, he invented a fifteenth-century writer, Thomas Rowley. And just as he made the medieval bridge-opening ceremony plausible by grafting it onto the modern event, Chatterton planted Rowley in relation to a famous local figure, making him the friend, biographer and correspondent of William Canynges, a successful merchant, MP, five-times mayor of Bristol and eventually, after his wife's death, a priest. There was a personal dimension for the young forger too; in the latter part of his life Canynges dwelt at St Mary Redcliffe, which served to bring Chatterton's fictional creation – one might even say his alter ego – to his very door.

One of the principal recipients of Chatterton's fabricated Rowley manuscripts was a local surgeon and antiquary, William Barrett, who had sought the source of the bridge-opening account after its publication because he was compiling material for a history of Bristol, although this was not to appear until 1789. Chatterton was only too happy to oblige. He was keen to root his poems in Bristol's landscape and history, and among the verses he fed Barrett was 'Song to Ælla, Lorde of the Castel of Brystowe ynne Daies of Yore', in which Rowley describes how the 'Brystowannes, menne of myght, / Ydar'd the bloudie fyghte, / And actedd deeds full quent.'[71] Another work, 'The Storie of William Canynge', begins with the common medieval conceit of the narrator lying down by the side of a stream – in this case, a tributary of the River Avon – and drifting into a vision-filled reverie: 'Anent a brooklette as I laie reclynd, / Listenynge to heare the water glyde alonge'. The Bristolian visions that appear to him are of the Saxon warrior Ælla and 'holie Wareburghus'.[72] But more than poetry, what Barrett was looking for were contemporary accounts of medieval Bristol for his book; and Rowley turned out to be a rich source of those, too. Chatterton provided Barrett with drawings, maps, inventories, deeds, accounts of churches, copies of inscriptions and correspondence between Rowley and Canynges.[73] He invented a cod-medieval language gleaned from his reading of medieval verse, frequently substituting 'ie' for 'y' and 'y' for 'i', doubling letters and adding redundant 'e's, and even assembled an extensive Rowley dictionary of useful old words gleaned from medieval glossaries. He was careful to make the physical objects as convincing as possible, and with his actual medieval manuscripts as a guide he wrote in varying colours of ink in crabbed characters. As well as darkening the parchment sheets with soot, he discoloured them with red or yellow pigment, rubbed them on the ground, crumpled them up in his hands and painted them with glue or varnish.[74] Even so, Barrett had his doubts; he decided against including some Rowleian manuscripts, such as a 'piece of parchment about 9 inches by 7, with several monumental stones and inscriptions upon it...given by Chatterton to Mr Barrett to illustrate his History of Bristol', perhaps because it bore a suspiciously close resemblance to certain illustrations in Camden's *Britannia*.[75] On the whole, though, these doubts were evidently suppressed by his desire to believe in this treasure-trove of manuscripts that was so helpful to his own project, and Rowley's name frequently crops up in his published book.

Not everyone, however, could be taken in. Having had such success with Barrett and other local antiquaries by tailoring material specifically to meet their dearest wishes, Chatterton set his sights higher. In 1762 the first two volumes had appeared of Walpole's pioneering work of art history, *Anecdotes of Painting in England*, a book that Chatterton probably encountered on the shelves of his local bookshop, and which begins with an account of wall paintings executed during the 1220s in the reign of Henry III. Chatterton decided to apply his tried and tested tactic to Walpole. He sat down to compose an account of 'The Ryse of Peyncteynge yn Englade', purportedly written in 1469 by 'T. Rowleie' for his patron Canynges, in which he ranged from ancient Britons painting their bodies with woad, to Johne Seconde Abbate of Seyncte Austyns Mynsterre being 'the fyrste Englyshe Paynctere yn Oyles'.[76] At first Walpole was astounded and delighted, offering Chatterton 'a thousand thanks for it', but before long he realized the account was forged and would have nothing further to do with it or its author.[77]

Chatterton himself left Rowley and, eventually, Bristol behind. He moved to London, wrote poetry of an astonishing variety and succeeded in getting it published in numerous journals. He was still only seventeen when in August 1770 he died suddenly, in the attic room he rented in a bawdy-house in Gray's Inn. Long thought to have taken his own life, he is now generally believed to have accidentally overdosed on laudanum, a tincture of opium, a drug he was consuming on top of the arsenic with which he was dosing a venereal disease.[78]

During the next decade controversy simmered about the authenticity or otherwise of Rowley, with numerous writers drawn into the debate; Chatterton would no doubt have thoroughly enjoyed the stir his creation had caused. His posthumous fame grew exponentially: he influenced Wordsworth, Coleridge, Keats and Shelley, and by the mid-nineteenth century had become a cult figure. In 1856 the artist Henry Wallis caused a sensation when he exhibited *The Death of Chatterton* at the Royal Academy, a painting for which the glamorous young novelist George Meredith posed, stretched out on a bed in the very garret in which Chatterton had died, torn papers and an empty poison phial littering the floor. The boy who had created the fictional Rowley now had his own brief life mythologized.

Chatterton had found a new way of reimagining history. While others had retrieved – or invented – samples of ancient literature and brought them to the light of day, he did something more complex, becoming a kind of playwright whose stage was fifteenth-century Bristol. Having invented a character, he inserted him into a complex historical world of known events, places and people, swiftly responding to changing requirements and even arranging for apparent physical remnants to drift into the present. In Chatterton's young hands, forgery became a theatrical act of creation.

A subdued light filtered through the high windows of Westminster Abbey, reflected off the ancient stone and fell dimly on the sketchbook of a young man as he sat drawing, eyes bulging slightly with the challenge of capturing the magnificence of a medieval tomb on a small oblong of paper. Visitors came and went with quiet voices; vergers passed by with swift officious footsteps; but when the displaced air with its drifting motes of dust settled it seemed to suspend him in a rich shared silence with the royal dead. The more intensely he looked and drew and looked again, the drag of his pencil pausing for a moment, the more tangible his communion with them became.

As a young apprentice, William Blake spent a lot of time alone at Westminster Abbey. He had been asked by his master, the engraver James Basire, to make careful drawings of the medieval monuments and wall paintings there for future engravings, and over the following three years, beginning in 1774, he worked his way from tomb to tomb; few people knew the interior of the abbey as well as he did. Basire, as engraver to the Society of Antiquaries, was asked to record the opening of Edward I's tomb in May of the same year, and among Blake's first known drawings are two haunting images of the King's body. In the right-hand sketch, drawn 'when some of the vestments were remov'd', according to an inscription, one can indistinctly discern his features shadowing the veil.[79] For the earnest young apprentice, a face-to-face meeting with Edward I was an auspicious beginning, and one that can only have reinforced his sense of the presence of the past.

Even before Blake was sent to Westminster Abbey, British history and legend occupied his thoughts; in his earliest known print, made in 1773, he shook the dust off an ancient myth to depict 'Joseph of Arimathea among the Rocks of Albion', and one of his first series of watercolours illustrated the history of England from the arrival of Brutus to the reign of Edward IV. Later, he planned a more extensive *History of England* in twenty-two engravings, to be published as a small book. Although no copies have ever been tracked down, Blake's subjects included the giants who lived in England before Brutus, Brutus's landing, Corineus throwing Gogmagog into the sea, King Lear, the Ancient Britons as described by Caesar and the druids.[80] Blake claimed to believe 'with Milton, the ancient British History' – although in truth he was approaching the myth from an entirely different direction.[81] While John Milton reasoned his way into including Brutus in his *History of Britain*, Blake gave the story reality through the force of his imagination. In 1797, when he was commissioned to create a series of watercolours illustrating Gray's works, his title-page design for *The Bard* gave this figure the same authoritative stature, flowing beard and commanding expression that he habitually gave to the biblical prophets he painted, forging a visual connection with Old Testament patriarchs (Plate VIII). This was the same imagination that could collapse geographical distance in asking 'And did those feet in ancient time / Walk upon England's mountains green / And was the holy Lamb of God / On England's pleasant pastures seen?'[82]

History unleavened by imagination was alien to Blake, but history as interpreted by historians was worse. 'Acts themselves alone are history', he wrote in the catalogue to his one-man exhibition of 1809, 'and these are neither the exclusive property of Hume, Gibbon nor Voltaire, Echard, Rapin, Plutarch, nor Herodotus. Tell me the Acts, O historian, and leave me to reason upon them as I please; away with your reasoning and your rubbish.' It was, Blake wrote, the artist who was best equipped to present what he called 'the historical fact in its poetical vigour': 'The British Antiquities are now in the Artist's hands; all his visionary contemplations, relating to his own country and its ancient glory, when it was as it again shall be, the source of learning and inspiration.'[83] Blake was writing of his largest ever work, a painting depicting the last battle of King Arthur that had been commissioned by the Welsh antiquary William Owen Pughe, now lost but reported to have measured a gigantic ten by fourteen feet, closer to the size of a tapestry than a conventional picture. In casting his mind back to the ancient Britons and Saxons, Blake was not only reimagining the past but making sure it filled the viewer's entire field of vision.

Once, when Blake was a small boy, he ran excitedly to his mother to tell her that he had seen the Prophet Ezekiel under a tree in the fields. Thinking he was telling lies, she beat him. Yet far from being knocked out of him, this capacity to conduct what his first biographer, Alexander Gilchrist, called 'habitual intercourse with the visionary world' only grew.[84] A great encourager to Blake in this respect was John Varley, a painter of tranquil watercolour landscapes, who became a friend in the latter years of Blake's life. Varley was fascinated by ghosts and spirits, and according to Gilchrist, 'encouraged Blake to take authentic sketches of certain among his most frequent spiritual visitants. The Visionary faculty was so much under control, that, at the wish of a friend, he could summon

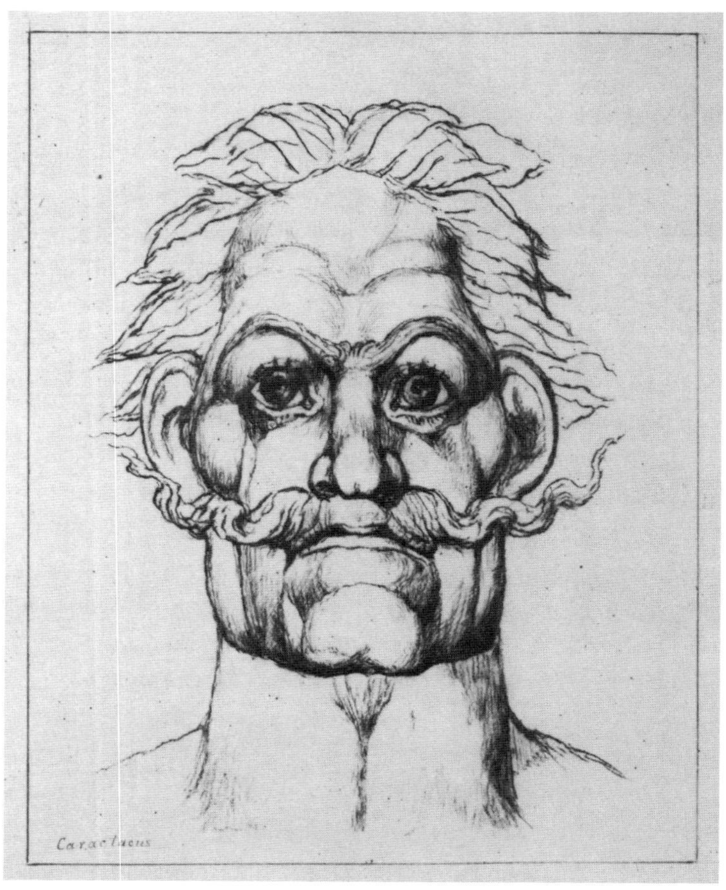

William Blake, 'visionary head' of the first-century British chieftain Caractacus, drawn in a sketchbook around 1819.

before his abstracted gaze any of the familiar forms and faces he was asked for.' As the two sat together late into the evening at Varley's home in Great Titchfield Street,

> Varley would say, 'Draw me Moses,' or David; or would call for a likeness of Julius Caesar, or Cassibellaunus, or Edward the Third, or some other great historical personage. Blake would answer, 'There he is!' and paper and pencil being at hand, he would begin drawing with the utmost alacrity and composure, looking up from time to time as though he had a real sitter before him....
>
> Sometimes Blake had to wait for the Vision's appearance; sometimes it would come at call. At others, in the midst of his portrait, he would suddenly leave off, and, in his ordinary quiet tones and with the same matter-of-fact air another might say 'It rains,' would remark, 'I can't go on, – it is gone! I must wait till it returns;' or, 'It has moved. The mouth is gone;' or, 'he frowns; he is displeased with my portrait of him:' which seemed as if the Vision were looking over the artist's shoulder as well as sitting *vis-à-vis* for his likeness.[85]

Varley would faithfully inscribe Blake's drawings with the sitter's name and the date and time of the visitation. Richard the Lionheart appeared at a quarter past midnight on 14 October 1819, and Wat Tyler at 1am on 30 October, Blake drawing him 'as in the act of striking the Tax Gatherer on the head'. Among the spirits who visited Blake over the following years were Saul, Lot, Job, Socrates, Charlemagne, Merlin, Caractacus, Boudicca, Edward III, Mary Queen of Scots, Ossian, Robin Hood and even Jesus Christ. Poor Varley was left peering around his room in vain, hoping to catch a glimpse of this astonishing cast of characters who apparently popped up so effortlessly in front of his friend.[86]

So was Blake simply pulling his credulous friend's leg? There was a playful aspect to the enterprise, without doubt; and yet it was serious, too. For him, visions conjured up by the imagination were every bit as real as external facts – and, he thought, they could be for others. 'You can see what I do, *if you choose*', he would say to his friends.[87] Few if any shared Blake's temperament or his calm way of traversing great tracts of history and conversing with those plucked from various corners of the 'vasty deep of time', as Gilchrist put it.[88] And yet by the time Blake was taking up his pencil and sketching the historical figures who appeared so vividly to his mind's eye, a writer from the Scottish Borders as successful as his London counterpart was obscure had, in a way, democratized Blake's visionary capacity, making his many thousands of readers feel as though they personally knew some of the most famous characters from British history.

IV

IN THE OLDEN DAYS

Sir Walter Scott's imagination was powerful enough to change the ways his readers experienced places. After his poem *The Lady of the Lake* was published in 1810, tourists rushed to visit its setting, Loch Katrine in the Trossachs. The sun rose and set on the loch and the surrounding mountains as it had always done, but once Scott had pointed out that at sunset 'Each purple peak, each flinty spire, / Was bathed in floods of living fire', everyone wanted to go there.[1] He opened his readers' eyes to beauty and drama, and in time was credited with reimagining Scotland's landscapes for vast numbers of people.

Abbotsford, the baronial mansion he built next to the River Tweed in the Scottish Borders with the proceeds of his bestselling works, is every bit as much a Walter Scott novel as a house: capacious, imposing, rambling, welcoming – perhaps overwhelmingly so. With its turrets, battlements, stepped gables and ranks of chimneys, Abbotsford sprang from the same imagination that created the forbidding Torquilstone in *Ivanhoe* or reconstructed Kenilworth Castle from the ruins in which it stood in Scott's day. Let us pause in the courtyard for a moment before we plunge inside. Come closer, put your hand on the stone and tell me how the corners feel: smoothed by time, or still sharp? One visitor back in 1823 remarked that it 'had not yet had time to take any tint from the weather, and its whole complication of towers, turrets, galleries, cornices, and quaintly ornamented mouldings, looked fresh from the chisel'. Even two hundred years later, one would not mistake it for the late medieval mansion it was built to resemble. But just as Scott included real historical figures in his novels, making them converse with the fictional characters he invented, he built actual history into his house by having his masons incorporate ancient bits of stonework into the walls of Abbotsford; the same visitor recalled the shrubbery in front

The Entrance Hall at Abbotsford, c. 1865,
photograph by George Washington Wilson.

of the windows being strewn with 'grotesque antiquities, for which a place was yet to be found'.[2] Scott even introduced history into the building's new name. 'Cartleyhole' was the name of the farmhouse he bought in 1811 that would eventually be transformed; the locals called it 'clarty hole', clarty being an old Scottish term for dirty. Well, Scott washed that well and truly down the drain: his house was not going to be mired in mud, but would be an elegant junction where past and present met. 'Abbots', the first part of the name, connected it in a general way to the pre-Reformation past and in a particular sense to the nearby ruins of Melrose Abbey, to which he had formed a deep attachment; 'ford' suggested a crossing place, where history might find its way into the here and now.

Everything Scott displayed in the entrance hall is bursting to tell its story. It is a little like being inside his brain. The 'massive' stone chimney piece was carved for Scott by local stonemasons, modelled on the so-called 'Abbots' seat', an ancient decorative arch in the cloisters at Melrose. Other parts of the room were salvaged from old buildings: 'The walls from the floor to the height of eight feet are panelled with black oak which was once the panelling of the pews belonging to the church of Dunfermline.'[3] Gazing around, it is hard to distinguish what is ancient from what is modern; Scott even had the new structural wood stained and stippled so that it resembled old oak. Most eye-catching is the collection of arms and armour, which Scott arranged both in the entrance hall and the next-door armoury. He admitted to being 'quite feverish' about it:

> I have two pretty complete suits of armour – one Indian one, and a cuirassier's, with boots, casque, &c, many helmets, corslets, and steel caps, swords and poinards without end, and about a dozen of guns, ancient and modern. I have besides two or three battle-axes and maces, pikes and targets, a Highlander's accoutrement complete....[4]

In tracking these things down, Scott came to rely on his friend Samuel Rush Meyrick, a historian of arms and armour so passionate about his subject that his own collection filled 'the garrets, the staircase and the back drawing room' of his home, and began, no doubt unnervingly to guests, to occupy bedrooms.[5] Meyrick built himself – or rather his collection – a neo-Gothic castle, Goodrich Court in Herefordshire, that was approached by a drawbridge and included a 'hastilude chamber' – one devoted, in other words, to martial games – that contained a huge tableau of a medieval tournament.[6] After he published his great work *A Critical Inquiry into Antient Armour as it Existed in Europe, but Particularly in England, from the Norman Conquest to the Reign of King Charles II* (1842; Plate IX), illustrated in colour with images of knights in the armour of all periods, his expertise was widely sought: he was consulted by the dramatist James Robinson Planché, who was planning a new production of Shakespeare's *King John*; by the Tower of London for advice on rearranging the national collection; and by George IV when he wished to redisplay the arms and armour at Windsor Castle. Both Eugène Delacroix and Richard Parkes Bonington visited him in order to sketch various items

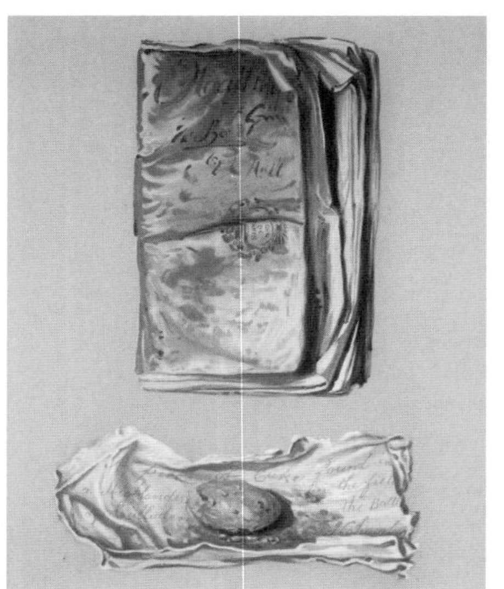

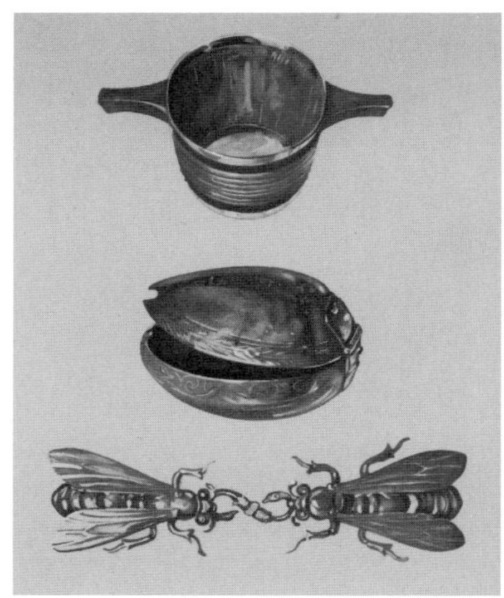

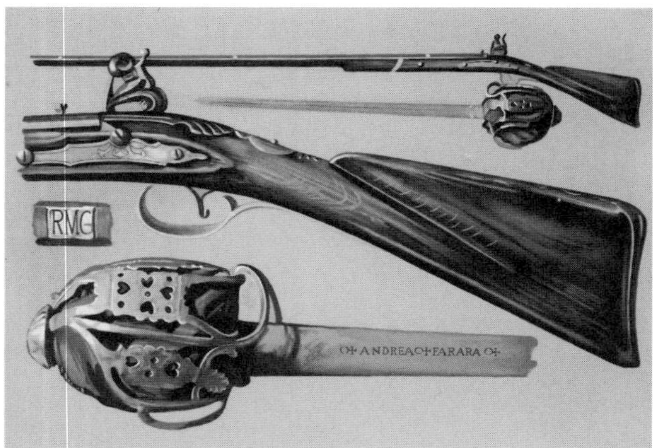

Above and opposite: Illustrations from *Abbotsford: The Personal Relics and Antiquarian Treasures of Sir Walter Scott* by Monica Maxwell Scott (1893).

Clockwise from top left: Fragment of oat-cake found in the pocket of a Highlander on the field of Culloden; Prince Charlie's quaigh, Balfour of Burleigh's snuff-box and Napoleon I's gold bee-clasps; Rob Roy's gun and sword.

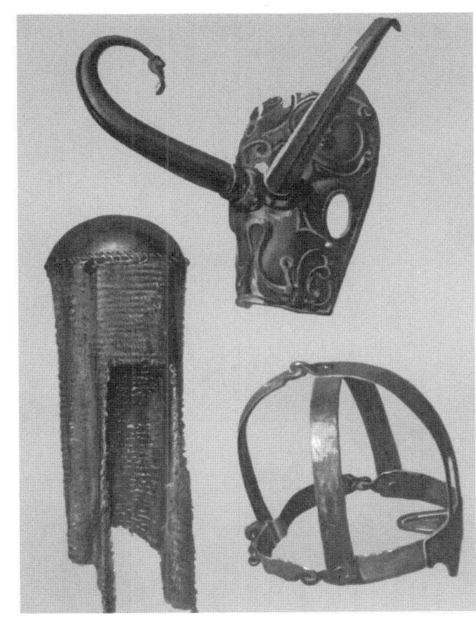

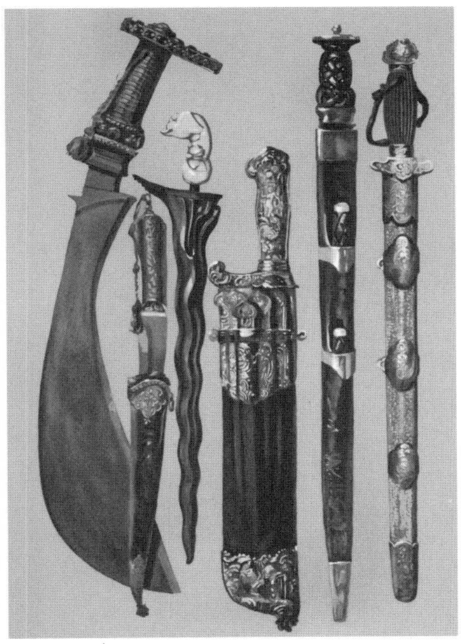

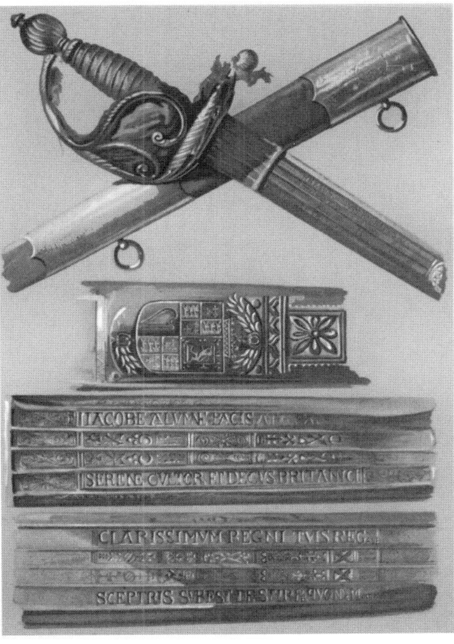

Clockwise from top left: French armour; ancient bronze mask, steel skull-cap with chain-mail and branks; Montrose's sword; weapons including a Persian dagger and Rob Roy's dirk.

in his collection.[7] It had taken nearly three and a half centuries, but John Rous's vision of knights wearing the correct armour for their time had finally been realized.

Above all, Scott prized objects associated with historical figures.[8] In 1811 he breaks off a letter to his friend Joanna Baillie by explaining that he has 'a very important matter to settle – no less than to close a treaty for the gun and arms of old Rob Roy'; a few months later he describes the 'long Spanish barrel'd piece', engraved with the folk hero's initials, to her and also mentions having recently acquired 'a relique of a more heroic character – it is a sword which was given to the great Marquis of Montrose by Charles I and appears to have belonged to his father our gentle King Jamie'. 'I think', he continues, 'a dialogue between this same sword and Rob Roys gun might be composed with good effect.'[9] Whatever they communicated between themselves, they seem to have spoken directly to him; Scott published *Rob Roy* in 1817, and *A Legend of Montrose* followed in 1819. It was as though these objects acted as lightning rods, channelling the highly charged past through the roof of Abbotsford and igniting Scott's imagination. Things did not have to be grand, however, to have this effect. One of the most poignant things at Abbotsford is a fragment of oatcake that had been found in the pocket of a Highlander, dead on the field of Culloden.[10] This small and apparently inconsequential object, that someone had thought to save and wrap up in a scrap of paper, has its own sad story to tell.

Scott may have been deeply serious about these relics, but he could still laugh at his passion for them. He described the arrival of his arms and armour at Abbotsford in May 1812 in a letter to a friend: 'The neighbours have been much delighted with the procession of my furniture, in which old swords, bows, targets, and lances, made a very conspicuous show. A family of turkeys was accommodated within the helmet of some *preux* chevalier of ancient Border fame; and the very cows, for aught I know, were bearing manners and muskets.'[11] When he came to write the character of Jonathan Oldbuck in *The Antiquary* (1816) – his own favourite among his novels – he gave him some of his own traits, repeatedly sending him up for his eccentric obsession with the past.

Scott, who had previously gathered traditional ballads together and published them in his 1802 book *Minstrelsy of the Scottish Border*, makes particular fun of his pursuit of authenticity. When his alter ego Oldbuck visits the Mucklebackits' cottage on the shore, he hears old Elspeth 'chanting forth an old ballad in a wild and doleful recitative' and is rooted to the spot by the sound while he reaches for his pencil and memorandum-book.

> From time to time the old woman spoke as if to the children –
> 'Oh ay, hinnies, whisht, whisht! and I'll begin a bonnier ane than that –
>
> "Now haud your tongue, baith wife and carle,
> And listen, great and sma',
> And I will sing of Glenallan's Earl
> That fought on the red Harlaw.
>
> The cronach's cried on Bennachie,
> And doun the Don and a',
> And hieland and lawland may mournfu' be
> For the sair field of Harlaw – "
>
> I dinna mind the neist verse weel – my memory's failed, and there's unco thoughts come ower me – God keep us frae temptation!'
>
> Here her voice sunk in indistinct muttering.
>
> 'It's a historical ballad,' said Oldbuck eagerly, 'a genuine and undoubted fragment of minstrelsy! – Percy would admire its simplicity – Ritson could not impugn its authenticity.'[12]

While *The Antiquary* is not set very long ago – the summer of 1794, just over twenty years before Scott sat down to write the book – it is all about the ways in which the past overshadows and pinches the present, and about mistakes and misapprehensions that occur when former actions are hidden or misrepresented, or simply occurred so long ago that all one has to go on are sparse material remains. When Oldbuck takes his new friend Lovel to view an earthwork on his estate that he is convinced is the site of a Roman camp, his pompous antiquarian peroration is interrupted by the mocking voice of the local mendicant, Edie Ochiltree: 'Prætorian here, Prætorian there, I mind the biggin' o't [remember it being built]', he reveals, much to Oldbuck's embarrassment. It turns out to have been a temporary shelter built for a wedding. The letters A. D. L. L. inscribed on a stone, which Oldbuck has interpreted as evidence of the presence in the area of Agricola, the Roman general largely responsible for the conquest of Britain, actually stood for 'Aiken Drum's Lang Ladle' – the bridegroom being a well-known trencherman, and what Oldbuck took to be an image of a 'sacrificing vessel' carved alongside the letters, a representation of the ladle itself.[13] Such are the dangers, Scott reminds us, of being so preoccupied with the past that the present drifts out of focus.

Such are the dangers, too, of bringing a novelist's imagination to bear on the past. Abbotsford, with its mix of historical associations and references, was evidently key to Scott's messy creative process, but it can hardly be called a comfortable place. For today's visitors, familiar with the relative harmony of the country-house aesthetic, in which the dates of the tapestries might broadly correspond to those of the furniture, and objects relate in some way to the taste of the whole – give or take the occasional contemporary art installation – Abbotsford presents a nerve-jangling cacophony. Fragments of the past, plucked out of context and jumbled together, bristle out at us. Back in 1838, they scratched irritatingly at the nineteen-year-old John Ruskin. This young man, who cared passionately about truth to materials and honest display of construction in architecture, and was to become one of the most influential of Victorian critics, confessed to the editor of the *Architectural Magazine* to having been distressed by what he called, with heavy irony, the 'splendid combination of the English baronial, the old Elizabethan, and the Melrose Gothic'. What affronted him in particular was the 'actual wooden door of the old Tolbooth of Edinburgh, with lock, bars, and all' that had been presented to the author when the ancient building, which served as a prison, was demolished in 1817: Scott had had this medieval relic inserted into the wall 'twenty feet from the ground' and dressed up with an entirely inappropriate classical architrave. Inside, things were even worse.

> When we enter – through a painted glass door into a hall about the size of a merchantman's cabin, fitted up as if it were as large as the Louvre, or [Christ Church] hall, Oxford – the first thing with which we are struck is a copy of a splendid arch in the cloisters of Melrose. This arch, exquisitely designed for raising the mind to the highest degree of religious emotion, charged with the loveliest carving you can imagine, and in its natural position combining most exquisitely with the heavenward proportions of surrounding curves, has been copied by Scott in plaster, and made a *fireplace*....[14]

In pursuit of the past, Scott – like Walpole before him – had crashed blithely through the barrier separating the spiritual and the domestic. 'I need hardly, I think, go further', remarked an appalled Ruskin with the supreme self-assurance that only a precocious nineteen-year-old could muster.

While Scott was not the first to write historical novels – Walpole had, after all, set *The Castle of Otranto* in the distant past, and other Gothic novelists followed suit because it was an efficient way to convey barbarity and strangeness – he invented the genre we recognize today. He created plausible characters, fitted them deftly between the cogs of known historical events, and then set the plot machinery in motion. Enlivened by their new, fictional element, historical characters themselves lived, breathed, got angry, laughed; rather than the sum of their deeds, as they appeared in history books, they became living men and women with uncertain futures.[15] In the Saxon halls and Norman castles of *Ivanhoe*, Scott introduces us to Friar Tuck, Robin Hood and Richard the Lionheart in disguises that we are meant to see through long before we are told. In *Kenilworth* (1821) we find ourselves at the elaborate reception held in 1575 by the Earl of Leicester for Queen Elizabeth I and her court, while the story of *Woodstock* (1826) unfolds in the mid-seventeenth century, during the English Civil War. Charles II makes an appearance there and in another of Scott's English books, *Peveril of the Peak* (1822). Scott's audacious manipulation of history, his ability to ventriloquize kings and queens, was wildly popular with the public and earned him a fortune – which he subsequently poured back into Abbotsford.

Scott's historical writing did not just enter people's homes in the form of books; it affected the pictures that hung on their walls too. The early nineteenth century saw a fast-growing market for small-scale pictures for the middle-class home – oil paintings, watercolours or reproductive prints, depending on your pocket – which took their subjects from literature, from Chaucer and Shakespeare to Laurence Sterne and Oliver Goldsmith. The most popular were unchallenging, anecdotal and often humorous. William Makepeace Thackeray described this growing taste for 'pleasant pictures, that we can live with – something that shall be lively, pleasing or tender, or sublime, if you will, but...only of a moderate-sized sublimity'.[16] He could have been describing Walter Scott's version of history. It helped that Scott's peculiar love of the material remnants of history prompted him to describe rooms and costumes in great detail. 'I will sit on this footstool at thy feet,' declares Amy Robsart to her finely dressed husband, the earl of Leicester, in *Kenilworth*, 'that I may spell over thy splendour, and learn, for the first time, how princes are attired' – thus giving scope for the Earl's costume to be described in almost fetishistic detail.[17] Artists responded to his pictorial imagination by mining his poems and novels for potential scenes, and from 1805 until 1870 more than a thousand paintings on themes from Scott were shown at the principal exhibition venues, the Royal Academy and the British Institution.[18]

At the height of Scott's popularity, people moved in a cultural climate thick with his works; his dynamic vision of history was all the rage. There were the books themselves, and the numerous illustrated editions; there were the paintings at the Royal Academy and the prints on the wall at home; there were souvenir hand-painted fire-screens and printed handkerchiefs; and even numerous operas and plays based on his novels. Fans of *The Heart of Midlothian* were spoiled for choice in 1819 alone, with six different productions appearing in theatres in London, Edinburgh and Bath.[19] It was the same in France, where in 1830 Scott's works accounted for a third of all novels published there; an astonishing number of people must have spent their evenings engrossed in the *Oeuvres complètes de Walter Scott*.

Scott's novels were so wildly popular in part because, although they were set in a variety of historical periods, they suited the politically unstable times in which they were written. He wrote repeatedly about crises: the clash between Norman and Saxon, Cavalier and Roundhead, or Jacobite and Hanoverian forces. His books seemed on the face of it to offer pleasurable escapism into different eras, but in a period dominated by the recent Napoleonic wars they also shone sidelights onto contemporary conflicts – and helped to shape his readers' responses to the turbulent times through which they were living.[20]

'It would be worth while', wrote Thackeray in 1844, 'for someone to write an essay showing how astonishingly Sir Walter Scott has influenced the world; how he changed the character of novelists, then of historians, whom he brought from their philosophy to the study of pageantry and costume, how the artists then began to fall back into the middle ages and the architecture to follow.'[21] Scott was, however, not quite the singular figure Thackeray suggests. If his historical imagination changed the way people thought about the past, allowing his readers to see it as intimate and personal, it was partly because he had picked up the threads of an existing trend. He may have woven more intricate and beguiling tapestries with these threads than had previously been attempted; and yet by the late eighteenth century a national habit of imagining a romantic view of history through its leading characters had already begun.

When Thomas Gray visited Hardwick Hall in 1762, he would have climbed the same wide stone staircase we might today, walked along the high-ceilinged gallery and through the airy state rooms, made bright by the great windows that offer views far over the Derbyshire fields into the hazy distance. Then, as now, there was much to admire; yet amid the portraits, the plasterwork and the ingeniously carved cabinets, what Gray felt to be most pressing was its historical atmosphere – and the almost tangible presence of Mary Stuart. If, today, we look at the furniture and fabrics of Hardwick with curiosity or appreciation, he regarded them with an emotion that was close to reverential awe: 'one would think', he wrote, 'Mary, Queen of Scots, was but just walk'd down into the Park with her Guard for half-an-hour. her Gallery, her room of audience, her antichamber, with the very canopies, chair of state, footstool, Lit-de-repos, Oratory, carpets, & hangings, just as she left them. a little tatter'd indeed, but the more venerable; & all preserved with religious care, & paper'd up in winter.'[22] But wait – was Hardwick not constructed in the 1590s? And Mary: was she not executed in 1587? By the time the first stone was laid, Mary had been dead three years. Her incarceration had been at nearby Chatsworth House rather than Hardwick; but since the former had been remodelled in the late seventeenth and early eighteenth centuries, it had lost its air of antiquity and there was little left to connect her with it. Hardwick, however, *looked* the part.

Personalities belong not only to people but to houses and rooms. If Gray was thinking of Mary, he was also responding to the atmosphere of Hardwick, which like other houses owned by families whose principal residences lay elsewhere – Cotehele in Cornwall, for instance, or Haddon Hall, also in Derbyshire – was maintained as a historical interior. It was

Mary Queen of Scots under Confinement, 1793, mezzotint by William Ward after a painting by Robert Fulton.

a place to display certain antiquarian objects in the Cavendish family's collections, in this case the furniture and textiles commissioned for the house by Bess of Hardwick herself. At some point in the eighteenth century, rooms at Hardwick were deliberately arranged to suggest their use as Queen Mary's quarters.[23] The creation of such an antiquarian atmosphere was seen as distinctly novel. After a visit to Cotehele in 1789 with its owners Lord and Lady Mount Edgecumbe, even George III's consort Queen Charlotte – no stranger to antique furniture and armour – entered an excited account in her diary describing the 'Old Family seat of theirs where his Ancestors lived at least 200 years before they had Mount Edgecumbe.' The hall, she writes, was

> Full of Old Armor & Swords & Old Carved Chairs of the Times, a Drawing Room Hung with Old Tapestry, the Scirtingboard of which is straw, the Chair Seats made of the Priests Vestments....At Breakfast we Eat off the Old Family Pewter, & used Silver knives Forks & Spoons which have been Time immemorial in the Family & have always been kept at this place.[24]

The Queen had been plunged into a tank filled to the brim with the essence of the olden days, and was entranced.

Gray was not alone in imaginatively recreating Mary Queen of Scots. From around this time, in painting after painting, like the ghost in Horace Walpole's *Castle of Otranto* Mary steps down from her own portrait and begins to re-enact scenes from her life. There she is, looking noble and tragic, at prayer during her confinement; or receiving the news that the warrant for her execution has been signed; escaping from Loch Leven Castle with George Douglas; being admonished by John Knox; at the scene of the murder of David Rizzio; or approaching the executioner's block with grace and dignity. Between the 1760s and the end of the nineteenth century, seventy-three paintings on the subject of Mary Queen of Scots were exhibited at the Royal Academy – substantially more than on any other monarch, including Elizabeth I, and presumably the tip of a more extensive iceberg.[25] Countless reproductions were made of these, bringing this new Mary into the heart of a great many homes.

Why did Mary exert such magnetism at this time? One answer is her variousness: like a doll, or an artist's lay-figure, this charismatic woman could be dressed up and posed in a range of roles: as a resolute woman of action; as a sexually alluring figure; as a dangerous political opponent, possibly even a murderess; as a pious prisoner or tragic Catholic martyr. After Scott published *The Abbot* in 1820, a novel that revolves around Queen Mary's imprisonment at Loch Leven Castle, her escape and her eventual defeat at the Battle of Langside, his version of her story rooted itself even more firmly in the public imagination.

There was a lot to be said for such dramatic scenes, but as British history, particularly of the Tudor and Stuart periods, gripped people's imaginations, portraits became increasingly important. What did these important men and women from the pages of history books actually look like? Could their character be discerned in their faces? How did they dress? These were, at first, questions that could only be answered by a great deal of antiquarian research. In the first half of the eighteenth century the Society of Antiquaries had employed the engraver George Vertue to hunt for true likenesses of historical figures. Although he engraved a portrait of Mary Queen of Scots that turned out not to have been of her at all – rather an occupational hazard when there were so few comparative images to consult – his publications fuelled the growing curiosity about the personal appearance of historical figures, which led in turn to a new and absorbing pursuit: collecting portrait prints and fashioning one's own paper portrait gallery. This was greatly encouraged by James Granger's *Biographical History of England from Egbert the Great to the Revolution* (1769), a book that listed available historical portraits organized in twelve classes from royalty to 'the lowest Order of the People', and included short biographies. A practice known as 'Grangerizing' took hold as cheap printed portraits became ever more available; people took their scissors and paste and stuck likenesses into appropriate books, with the result that published volumes of history and biography became personalized artefacts.[26]

Among those creating new portraits of long-dead monarchs was Joseph Strutt, who brought a unique approach to the enterprise. As a young man he had trained as an artist, enrolling in 1769 at the brand-new Royal Academy of Arts, but what really absorbed him were old illuminated books and medieval manuscripts, and he was increasingly to be found poring over such generally neglected material at a desk in the British Museum.

'Tumbling' and 'Balancing' pictured in Joseph Strutt's *Sports and Pastimes of the People of England* (1801).

Strutt's interest was only partly in likenesses. What fascinated him most of all was the whole context in which they were represented – an aspect of history that, in his view, was not taken seriously enough. 'Hitherto', he complains in his preface to his first book, *The Regal and Ecclesiastical Antiquities of England: Containing the Representations of all the English Monarchs, from Edward the Confessor to Henry the Eighth* (1773), 'our artists have been extremely deficient in their delineations of the early history. – The Saxons are frequently drawn in the habit of the figures on the Trajan and Antonine columns [i.e. as ancient Romans]; and the Normans are put into the dresses and armour worn in Edward the Fourth's time, and indeed are often made still more modern.' His solution to this riot of casual inaccuracy? To seek out 'the most ancient national materials that remain' and to mine these manuscripts for images of 'the dress and personal appearance of our monarchs'. This way, there would be no doubting the authority, he continues, 'since the illuminations were made in, or soon after, the reign of each particular monarch'.[27] They had been there all along, lurking among the manuscript leaves; it was just that no one else had thought to look for them – or had realized, like Strutt, that this quaint old visual material was a valuable resource.[28]

Strutt's focus came to be increasingly on dress, and the oddity of certain costumes kept catching his eye. 'This illumination is very curious', he writes of an image of Richard II enthroned and surrounded by courtiers, 'on account of the extraordinary length of the shoes, when worn at court. That they might not be troublesome to the wearer when he walked abroad, they were fastened up by means of a small chain to his knee. This truly ridiculous fashion continued a long time in vogue.'[29] Strutt's *A Complete View of the Dresses and Habits of the People of England* (1796 and 1799) was the first detailed history of dress in England. Suddenly, a new cast of characters, from eighth-century rustics in their simple tunics and 'The Saxon King in his Martial Habit' (Plate x) to a richly upholstered seventeenth-century Cavalier, saw the light of day. But the book that did most to shape perceptions of the past was his subsequent *Sports and Pastimes of the People of England* (1801). In engaging text and copious illustrations, Strutt covered a gallimaufry of activities: hunting, hawking, horse-racing, ball games and tournaments, mystery plays, minstrels, May-day revels, wassails, bonfires, children's games and acrobatics. The engravings – brightly coloured by hand in many copies – represent simplified human figures dancing or playing games, with little background beyond an indication of the ground on which they stand (or hop, or tumble). Mostly concerned with the medieval period, *Sports and Pastimes* is a capacious scrapbook of the olden times gleaned from Strutt's study of histories, anecdotes, legal documents, legends and public announcements, and it established an indelible image of merrie olde England.

Strutt even marshalled his vast knowledge of the olden days to venture into fiction. In *Queenhoo-Hall, A Romance*, he took some of the figures he had met among the manuscript leaves and set them in motion, as he attempted to bring the customs and manners of late medieval England to life. The book begins with a 'Description of a May-Game in the Fifteenth Century' and the following exchange 'between Gregory the jester and Thomas the reve's son, in the court of Queenhoo Hall, at Tewin, in Hertfordshire, the residence of Lord Edward Boteler, a baron of great opulence in the reign of King Henry the Sixth':

> 'Word me no words,' quoth Gregory; 'I will not perform the hobby-horse; and if the hobby-horse be not performed, wot ye well, the morris will be stark naught; – let Gervas look to it; it comes of his knavery.'
>
> 'But you are so choleric,' said Thomas.
>
> 'Look you now,' answered the jester; 'it is acknowledged on all hands, that no man can jerk the hobby, or rein him, or prance him, like me: I have played the horse with transcendent applause, before this cockerel broke his egg-shell. And shall I be told to my beard by such an howlet, that I know not how to use the bells? May the fould fiend take me, but it were a good deed done to break the hilts of my dagger over the knave's costard!'[30]

And so on; one is forced to admit that Strutt did not wear his learning lightly. Yet his experiment in historical fiction had an important legacy. The manuscript, left unfinished at his death, was handed to Walter Scott to add a concluding chapter, and was published in 1808. That same year, Scott is thought to have begun his own first historical novel, *Waverley*.

It is Christmas time at Haddon Hall in Derbyshire. Everyone has gathered in the banqueting hall and the hubbub is deafening. Look up: the minstrel's gallery is crowded with musicians busy with flutes, horns and fiddles, blowing and bowing as hard as they can to compete with the shouts, laughter and thunder of feet rising up from below. Jesters join hands in a wild dance, legs flailing, while around them men upend huge flagons of ale; someone stokes the fire that is blazing in the cavernous fireplace; a man catches a woman by the waist and tries to kiss her but she pushes him away, laughing. There are flambeaux and pewter chargers, swags of holly and mistletoe, suits of armour and banners. Some revellers are in fancy dress; an armoured knight trots in on a hobbyhorse, while in the foreground a boy rides a toy dragon towards a terrified monkey hobbled by a ball and chain that tries in vain to scamper away. A man dressed head to foot in a wild-man suit, all long hair and great staring eyes, lurches forward, causing more hilarity, while a griffin tiptoes

Joseph Nash, 'The banquetting hall at Haddon Hall in Derbyshire', from *The Mansions of England in the Olden Time* (1839).

theatrically past. It is as though the strange and comic figures monks once drew in the margins of manuscripts have come to life and joined the fun. The artist Joseph Nash had taken hold of time's telescope, pointed it at Christmastide as celebrated in Merrie England, and found it to be everything that the middle-class Victorian would like it to have been – and that they would emulate, too, if only their stays were not quite so tight or the requirements of being respectable quite so inhibiting. Nash's depiction of riotous revelry brought a vicarious unbuttoning into the Victorian home.

Walter Scott had vividly described Saxon feasts in low-ceilinged halls furnished with massive oak settles, shaggy wolfhounds stretched out by the roaring fire and royal receptions in magnificent tapestry-hung, torch-lit halls. For his views of the interiors of great houses, published between 1839 and 1849 as *Mansions of England in the Olden Time*, Nash applied Scott's atmosphere and drama to actual interiors, combining meticulously observed architectural detail with social interaction.[31]

Travelling up and down the country to visit houses built between the fifteenth and the seventeenth centuries – the periods that had become associated with the idea of Merrie England – he treated each of the interior spaces like a toy theatre, adding figures singly and in groups, adults and children whose dress and activities he had carefully researched in the pages of Strutt's books. In the great hall at Hatfield House, three gentlemen in Cavalier dress stand and talk earnestly, while dogs sit by the fire and a servant arrives with a tray: the long table where they will soon gather is set. Servants strew the floor of the presence chamber with straw at Hardwick Hall. Children play a cheerful game of skittles in the gallery at Knole. The figures in each imply a story, whether a pleasant vignette or an incipient drama, and a few even bolster associations with royalty or famous figures. Henry VIII and Anne Boleyn are depicted at her childhood home, Hever Castle – he tenderly takes her hand and draws her towards a seat in a window bay where a lute is waiting – and a bit of literary mythology is perpetuated by the handsome youth Will Shakespeare being caught poaching deer at Charlecote in Warwickshire. These ghosts, forever re-enacting a moment of English history, whether inconsequential or numinous, draw the viewer into the image; we are no longer looking in from the outside, but are invited to join the party.[32]

Nash himself declared that he had intended to show the houses 'in a new and attractive light':

> glowing with the genial warmth of their fire-sides, and enlivened with the presence of their inmates and guests, enjoying the recreations and pastimes, or celebrating the festivals, of our ancestors...in attempting this the artist has endeavoured to place himself in the position of a visitor to these ancient edifices, whose fancy peoples the deserted halls, stripped of all movable ornaments and looking damp and cheerless, with the family and household of the 'old English gentleman' surrounded by their everyday comforts, sharing the more rare and courteous hospitalities offered to the guests, or partaking of the boisterous merriment of Christmas gambols.[33]

The Mansions of England in the Olden Time was a huge success: Nash's plates were engraved for the popular *Saturday Magazine* and pirated so often that the images became part of people's mental furniture. They allowed men and women to picture a shared cultural heritage, one that had deep roots, and to feel a patriotic sense of Englishness. By creating a familiar atmosphere and making historical figures appear so human, the images also drew people to the houses themselves, to walk in the footsteps and breathe the same air as the great men and women who had been there before – visits that were, ironically, made easier by technological advancement in the form of the railways.

Painters responded to the romance of personality. Edward Matthew Ward, who specialized in scenes of seventeenth-century political history, occasionally indulged in more popular subjects. His painting *Charles II and Nell Gwyn* of 1854 (Plate XII) was not an imaginary scene but one closely based on an episode related by John Evelyn in his diary, which describes how the King would often walk in St James's Park with his courtiers and, from the shady Green Walk, flirt with Gwyn, who would appear at the wall of her neighbouring garden terrace. Evelyn, within earshot, describes 'a very familiar discourse between [the King] and Mrs Nellie...I was heartily sorry at this scene,' he adds prudishly.[34] The picture's viewer is presented with options: to be amused by the encounter, admire Ward's expert recreation of seventeenth-century dress and idly wonder what Charles and Nell might be saying to each other; to share in the eavesdropping Evelyn's disapproval; or to indulge in a combination of these. It is remarkable how acceptable Ward's depiction of outrageous flirting could be in the strict moral climate of the 1850s. Such behaviour was evidently tolerated, as long as it was safely confined to the olden times – where they did things differently. A painting of Prince Albert flirting with an actress would have been unthinkable.

Artists also began to create scenes of a picturesque past in which anyone could imagine joining the fun. William Powell Frith is now best known for his incident-packed scenes of bustling modern life in the railway station, at the races and by the seaside – it is no surprise to learn that he and Charles Dickens were lifelong friends – but earlier in his career he specialized in pictures recreating the days of old. This nebulous period could be discovered in fairly recent history; Frith had great success with his painting *An English Merry-Making a Hundred Years Ago* (1849; Plate XI), reproductions of which would have hung in many a home. Even a mere hundred years was enough to put the action firmly in the heart of a pre-industrial England, before the great exodus to the towns and cities, to a place where cheerful folk assembled to dance, eat, drink and court under the shade of a spreading oak tree. Frith's merry-making is a decidedly rural pursuit: the games are being played on the edge of a village, denoted by the gables of old houses, and beyond, fields can be seen stretching away to the far horizon. The picture captured the public mood of nostalgia; it was of course highly romanticized, but it seemed to distill the joyful community and harmony with nature that many believed had drained away from modern life.

Of historic houses, Haddon Hall came to be regarded as among the most precious reservoirs of the sense of the past, and prompted the most romantic reactions. It was so beguiling that it even prompted a lyrical passage from the scholarly architectural historian Nikolaus Pevsner, who described it – with only a hint of critical distance – as 'the large, rambling, safe, grey, loveable house of knights and their ladies, the unreasonable dream-castle of those who think of the Middle Ages as a time of chivalry and valour and noble feelings'.[35] Its appeal lay partly in the fact that after 1703, when the Manners family moved from Haddon to Belvoir Castle, it was uninhabited for two hundred years, apparently suspended in time. But there was more. According to legend, in 1563 Dorothy Vernon, the heiress of Haddon Hall, had eloped with John Manners, the second son of the Earl of Rutland, at a ball held by her father at Haddon, fleeing down its stone steps and through the gardens to where Manners was waiting. A book of 1836 by S. Rayner, *The History and Antiquities of Haddon Hall* (which anticipates Nash in placing figures in period dress in its interior views), includes an illustration that homes in on 'Dorothy Vernon's Doorway'. This feature became a staple of the tour offered to visitors, including the novelist Henry James, who went to Haddon in June of 1872. But James's initial sight of the Hall was in the twilight of the previous evening, when he had walked along a meadow path next to the river and crossed the little bridge in order to see it first in solitude, as he later recalled:

> The great *coup de théâtre* of the young woman who shows you the Hall – it is rather languidly done on her part – is to point out a little dusky door opening from a turret to a back terrace as the aperture through which Dorothy Vernon eloped with Lord John Manners. I was ignorant of this episode, for I was not to enter the place till the morrow, and I am still unversed in the history of the actors. But as I stood in the

> luminous dusk weaving the romance of the spot, I recognised the inevitability of a Dorothy Vernon and quite understood a Lord John. It was of course on just such an evening that the romantic event came off, and by listening with the proper credulity I might surely hear on the flags of the castle-court ghostly footfalls and feel in their movements old heartbeats.[36]

For such a subtle connoisseur of atmosphere as James, one for whom the present was forever being brushed by a sense of the past, it was not even necessary to know the story, so saturated was Haddon in the romance of history. It simply welled up from the stones.

I blame it on spinning jennys and cotton gins, screw-cutting lathes and milling machines, steam power and coke-fuelled blast furnaces. Before the industrial revolution, obsessions with national history – whether Saxons pondering Roman ruins, seventeenth-century antiquaries concocting ingenious theories to account for Stonehenge, or Georgians building tumbledown castles – were a background hum to normal life. But once it had begun, and living conditions began to alter like never before, the balance shifted; the murmur became a roar. While communications and travel were being transformed, mass-produced goods were changing lives, reform of the franchise was reshaping the political and social landscape and the future seemed almost graspable, what did people do? They turned to look wistfully over their shoulders at the days of old. Through the clattering din of machinery, a sweet, bewitching note, *tirra-lirra*, could be heard that promised a continuing connection with King Arthur, and chivalry, and Merrie England.

In the nineteenth century – and particularly in the Victorian era – people fell hopelessly and irrevocably in love with their national past. It became a vast sourcebook of inspiration. This was a time in which history books could become bestsellers: when Thomas Babington Macaulay's *History of England* – a narrative that emphasized the experiences of ordinary people – was published in five volumes between 1848 and 1861, it sold in tens of thousands, rivalling sales of novels by Scott and Dickens. An obsession with the olden days was evident in the ceremonies people held, the plays they attended, the poems they wrote, the novels they read, their architecture, pictures and furniture, the very plates off which they ate. The legacy of this passion is all around us today, in bricks, mortar and encaustic tiles.

Take churches. Church Building Acts were passed by Parliament in 1818 and 1824, making funds available for great numbers of new Anglican 'Commissioners' churches', built to cater for an urban population that, over the century, rose from around twenty per cent to seventy-five per cent.[37] At the same time as this shift from a rural economy to one based on manufacture and commerce, the dominance of the Church of England was being seriously challenged by powerful Nonconformist groups – Methodists, Baptists, Unitarians and Congregationalists – all of which appealed directly to working people and the urban poor.[38] The established church had to assert its authority, and the most visible sign of this was in its new buildings. Today these Victorian churches are such familiar English landmarks that one can almost forget that their design, usually in the Gothic Revival style, was a choice rather than an inevitability. Dressed up as they were with arched windows and tracery, together they created a smokescreen of implied continuity and stability in religious practice, stretching back before the Reformation. Nothing, it seemed, could salve the challenges of the urban, schismatic present as effectively as the balm of the rural, Catholic past.

Other public buildings, too, were remade for the present and future in the terms of the past. After the old Palace of Westminster burned down one terrible October night in 1834, a Royal Commission was appointed to commission a new Parliament building. In June 1835 they organized a competition, with the proviso that submissions be in a Gothic or Elizabethan style – a remarkable decision in itself at a time when most public buildings corresponded to an established neoclassical template.[39] Charles Barry won with a Perpendicular Gothic design – one that recalled a great period of Britain's own past, rather than borrowed splendour.[40] He was assisted by the young Catholic architect A. W. N. Pugin, who created spectacular Gothic interiors throughout the Palace, designing fittings and furnishings from panelling to items for which there was no medieval precedent, such as umbrella stands, post-boxes and gas lamps. This project had huge influence; having in the past been associated with romantic architectural fantasies like Walpole's Strawberry Hill and William Beckford's stupendously extravagant Wiltshire folly, Fonthill Abbey, Gothic had now come of age as the national style.

It was not the only one in town, however. As they arrived in the 1830s, railway stations were clothed in a cacophony of historicist styles. Up and down the land, stationmasters watched for the arrival of trains in front of buildings that could be mistaken for Jacobean gatehouses, Tudor cottages or medieval hunting lodges.[41] In 1858, a leading architect of the Gothic Revival, George Gilbert Scott, was moved to warn of the 'capricious eclecticism' that so readily resulted from 'working with this vivid *panorama* of the past'.[42] Another aspect of this eclecticism was the export of these kinds of architectural fantasies to countries colonized by Britain. From the 1860s Mumbai received a number of Gothic Revival public buildings, including the magnificent Victoria Terminus railway station, now the Chhatrapati Shivaji Terminus, in which the architect's plans were interpreted by Indian craftsmen using local materials and motifs, resulting in a hybrid style that has been called 'Bombay Gothic'.[43] Mumbai University's convocation hall and library were designed by Scott himself from his desk in London. The hall's decorative details were based on fifteenth-century French examples, the library was built in a Venetian Gothic style and the Rajabai Clock Tower was modelled on that of the Palace of Westminster.

There has never before or since been a time like it for ransacking the dressing-up box of history; a passion for the past had spread through the national spirit and coloured virtually every aspect of life. It was as though by donning the costume of the past, people felt that they could keep hold of precious traditions from which they were otherwise in danger of being separated by the forces of modernity.

Let us begin at Westminster Abbey. It is 19 July, 1821: the day of George IV's coronation. George has been king for eighteen months, but, having been created Regent in 1811 because of his father's illness, he has had a full ten years to prepare for this day. And he has used the time productively. Perhaps the most important spur was the example of Napoleon's coronation as Emperor of France in 1804. For one thing, it was provocatively spectacular: so keen was George to outdo it that he persuaded Parliament to contribute an astonishing £240,000 for his own – a sum that made it the most expensive coronation ever held in Britain (by comparison, George III's, held sixty years previously, had cost £70,000).[44] Another needling aspect of the Emperor's coronation was the new ceremony he had designed; although it incorporated revolutionary elements, it also aimed to confer legitimacy by making references to French royal dynasties. Napoleon's splendid coronation mantle, for instance, was embroidered with golden bees based on those discovered in the tomb of the fifth-century king Childeric I when it was opened in 1653. These eye-catching insects created an unmistakeable connection between Napoleon and the Merovingians. George, who had his own reasons for wishing to bolster his position, took note.

The coronation procession, watched from the stands outside the abbey, is an act of extreme pageantry. The King's Herb Woman and her six maids, dressed in white, scatter petals; they are followed by waves of musicians and choristers, dukes and duchesses, earls and countesses. Preceded by two trumpeters, the King's Champion is mounted on a caparisoned charger, escorted by the Lord High Constable and the Earl Marshal; there are heralds in their tabards like so many animate playing cards, a phalanx of bishops, and, walking in a stately gait under a mobile canopy, the King himself, plumed and portly. George, who has been avidly purchasing and poring over prints of former coronations, requested that those not otherwise decked out in their particular regalia wear a version of the dress that had been worn at the English court in the late Tudor and early Stuart periods: doublets, ruffled collars and trunk hose, large red rosettes on shoes – a pantomime costume that makes the Regency hairstyles and side-whiskers of his attendants look somewhat out of place (Plate xv). The King himself is wearing a tinselly doublet made with cloth of silver, a crimson surcoat and trunk hose, but the curly brown wig he has on under his ostrich-feather hat at least lends him a seventeenth-century air.[45] His ermine-lined velvet mantle is so heavy that eight peers' sons are needed to carry it.[46] Is his costume an authentic part of sacred coronation tradition? No. In order to underline his claim to the throne – and to divert attention from the inglorious present to the rich splendour of the past – this Hanoverian king has got himself up in fancy dress.

Not only did George IV persuade Parliament to grant a vast amount of money for his coronation, in 1824 he also talked them into voting £300,000 for the extensive remodelling of the British monarchy's most central symbol: Windsor Castle. We have an excellent idea of what this medieval castle, with its origins in the eleventh century, looked like during the reign of George III, because at that time the watercolourist Paul Sandby painted it from numerous angles, the ancient stones framing the domestic life going on in and around it. George IV, however, wanted it to be more imposing. He wanted it to be more private. But above all, he wanted this medieval castle to be *more* medieval. So he employed an architect, Jeffry Wyatville, who created the profile still visible today, extending the Round Tower at the centre of the site, raising the walls still higher and giving it a more dramatic, battlemented silhouette. Wyatville built further towers, taller than the existing ones, most strikingly the crenellated York and Lancaster towers that form King George IV's Gate in the southern façade and shape the view of the castle from the straight path known as the Long Walk. It was as though George had got hold of a venerable actor, whose every gesture, movement and expression spoke with quiet eloquence of advancing years and the gradual changes wrought by time, and had drawn lines on his face with greasepaint to give him the theatrical appearance of old age. It was carefully done, and effective; but by the time he and Wyatville had finished with Windsor Castle, this ancient edifice was also wearing fancy dress. It had become, as a visiting Frenchman remarked, 'a castle of Walter Scott's own building'.[47]

Travelling north to Eglinton Castle in Ayrshire in August 1839, it would have rapidly become clear that you were not the only one making your way there. Roads were packed with coaches. Busy passenger steamers were chugging up the coast from Liverpool. The Glasgow and Ayrshire railway, spotting an opportunity, had put on extra trains to meet demand on their new line between Ayr and Irvine, the closest station to the castle. (One of the engines was named *Marmion*, the sixteenth-century title character of a poem by Walter Scott.)[48] Cheerful groups made their way on foot. On 28 August 1839, 100,000 spectators arriving from all over the United Kingdom witnessed nothing less than a spectacular medieval-style tournament.

It all began with the coronations that immediately succeeded that of George IV. When William IV was crowned in 1831 he forbade anything that would echo his brother's royal razzmatazz, and in doing so, did away with many of the genuinely medieval parts of the ceremony. He even cancelled the King's Champion, the mounted knight whose role it was to ride through Westminster Hall and throw down a gauntlet to anyone wishing to challenge the monarch's right to reign. The Tories were outraged by this outbreak of Whiggish parsimony, and the event was disparaged as the 'Half Crown-nation'; although a compromise was reached for Queen Victoria's coronation in 1838, the Champion was not revived for her, nor the traditional medieval-style banquet held.

Young, rich and mad about horses, Archibald Montgomerie, the 13th Earl of Eglinton, had succeeded to his title in 1819 at the age of seven – appropriately enough, the year that Scott's fantasy of medieval chivalry, *Ivanhoe*, was published, with its great set-piece tournament at Ashby-de-la-Zouche:

> The scene was singularly romantic. On the verge of a wood, which approached to within a mile of the town of Ashby, was an extensive meadow of the finest and most beautiful green turf, surrounded on one side by the forest, and fringed on the other by straggling oak-trees, some of which had grown to an immense size. The ground, as if fashioned on purpose for the martial display which was intended, sloped gradually down on all sides to a level bottom, which was inclosed for the lists with strong palisades, forming a space of a quarter of a mile in length, and about half as broad. The form of the inclosure was an oblong square, save that the corners were considerably rounded off, in order to afford more convenience for the spectators. The openings for the entry of the combatants were at the northern and southern extremities of the lists, accessible by strong wooden gates, each wide enough to admit two horsemen riding abreast. At each of these portals were stationed two heralds, attended by six trumpets, as many pursuivants, and a strong body of men-at-arms, for maintaining order, and ascertaining the quality of the knights who proposed to engage in this martial game.
>
> On a platform beyond the southern entrance, formed by a natural elevation of the ground, were pitched five magnificent pavilions, adorned with pennons of russet and black, the chosen colours of the five knights challengers. The cords of the tents were of the same colour. Before each

Eglinton Tournament magic lantern slide, *c.* 1839.

> pavilion was suspended the shield of the knight by whom it was occupied, and beside it stood his squire, quaintly dressed as a salvage or silvan man, or in some other fantastic dress, according to the taste of his master and the character he was pleased to assume during the game.

Someone had suggested to the earl that he might stage such a medieval festival at Eglinton Castle – itself only built between 1797 and 1802 – to make up for the diminishment of ceremony at the hands of the Whig government, and somehow the idea had taken hold. Fixing on an August date, Lord Eglinton sounded out potential knights who might take part in a tournament – although many backed out when the costs and difficulty became apparent. Transforming oneself into a medieval knight did not come cheap; and this was quite apart from the physical danger involved in galloping at full tilt while attempting to strike each other's shields with lances. Lord Eglinton himself supplied specially commissioned lances that would break easily on impact – there was real anxiety that someone might be badly injured or killed, especially as none of the combatants had any experience of jousting. 'Rules of the tournament' were set out for the knights to follow, based partly on those laid out in 1465 for Edward IV; in 1839, however, murder was still murder, no matter how it was achieved – as the Sheriff of Ayr pointed out to Lord Eglinton.[49] At the heart of the enterprise was Samuel Luke Pratt, a dealer in medieval armour with a shop in Bond Street. He not only supplied polished steel and decoratively engraved

armour (Plate XIII), but also – with the help of a team of carpenters from the Eglinton estate and from London – seating for four thousand spectators, a fifty-foot-high castellated grandstand and martial tents for the knights, each flying a pennon.

Many of the spectators also dressed in smart costumes supplied by Pratt, made by Messrs Haigh, Theatrical Costumers of Covent Garden, each purportedly copied from a portrait or medieval manuscript (one suspects them of owning several well-thumbed copies of Joseph Strutt's *Complete View of the Dress and Habits of the People of England*). Others invented their own costumes, attending in approximations of archaic Scottish dress, or added a picturesque touch to their normal clothes with wide-brimmed hats or old bits of military uniform.

The tournament, however, did not go as planned. The parade of knights from the castle to the lists was delayed by several hours – do you have any idea how challenging it can be, when wearing armour, to get into the saddle? – and just as the Queen of Beauty (Lady Seymour) was announced, wearing an ermine jacket and a violet velvet skirt covered in gold heraldic wings, there was a flash of lightning, a rumble of thunder, and the first drops of rain began to fall. And fall. As the storm continued, the first day of the tournament collapsed into farce, with armoured knights slipping about in mud and forced to carry highly anachronistic umbrellas, spectators drenched and their outfits and headdresses sadly ruined by the rainstorm. After a few tilts, most of them ineffectual, Lord Eglinton rode up to the stands and apologized for the weather.

Queen Victoria, then just two years into her reign, refused to be impressed by the tournament, remarking tartly to her Whig prime minister, Lord Melbourne, in the weeks leading up to it that it sounded 'very ridiculous' and she considered it 'such folly'. 'Talked of the horrid weather,' she recorded with undisguised satisfaction in her journal of 2 September 1839, after another tête-à-tête with Melbourne, 'of its having poured so at the Tournament, the Queen of Beauty having been obliged to go in a close carriage, and that the whole thing had turned out to be the greatest absurdity.... I said it served them all right for their folly in having such a thing.'[50] Even so, the tournament captured the public imagination and created a market for colourful prints, medals and other souvenirs.[51] These included cheap, mass-produced relief-moulded jugs, manufactured by a process developed as recently as the 1820s: although they celebrated a fantasy of the English past, only an industrialized age could have produced them.

Three years later, Queen Victoria appeared to have had a change of heart. At Buckingham Palace on the evening of 12 May 1842, two years since the young queen had married Prince Albert, guests began to roll in for a *bal costumé*, the couple's first major party. Prince Albert and his family had, it seems, brought her to a new way of thinking. Albert's father, Ernst I, Duke of Saxe-Coburg and Gotha, was bewitched by the medieval past and passionately attached to the works of Walter Scott; to celebrate his own wedding in 1817 he had held a medieval-style tournament at his neo-Gothic house, Schloss Rosenau, and in 1837 had sat for his portrait in the guise of a Gothic knight.[52] On top of that, from 1841 Victoria had a returning Tory prime minister in Robert Peel. Whiggish disapproval of extravagance was drowned out by the promise of a spectacular event – especially one that could be used to shape public opinion.

The theme Prince Albert and Queen Victoria chose for their *bal costumé* was deliberately broad – members of the royal household were required to wear costumes in the style of the fourteenth century, including the appropriate armour and weapons for the gentlemen, but other guests were allowed more latitude.[53] Lady Rosslyn attended as the period-appropriate fourteenth-century Countess of Salisbury, the woman whose garter was, according to legend, the origin of the chivalric Order; but the Duke of Sutherland dressed as the Duke of Ferrara, the Earl of Pembroke as Francis I, and a group including the Marquis of Douro appeared in costumes of the court of Philip II (many guests, perhaps wisely, opted for Continental options, steering clear of dressing up as the Queen's predecessors). The effect, though splendid, must have been somewhat bewildering, as though all Joseph Nash's figures had dropped out of their volumes at once and sprung colourfully to life.[54] Victoria and Albert themselves looked striking in scarlet velvet and cloth of gold as Edward III and his consort, Queen Philippa of Hainault.

A great deal of thought had gone into their appearance in the weeks leading up to the ball; 'there is such trouble in getting the costumes correct', the Queen exclaimed in her journal in mid-April, and shortly afterwards she grumbled in a letter to her uncle Leopold about the 'many silks and drawings and crowns, and God knows what, to look at, that I, who hate being troubled about dress, am quite *confuse*'.[55] As the ball drew closer, however, she was trying on her costume and beginning to be beguiled by her transformation, forgetting about all the 'trouble' and instead finding it 'really very handsome'. There was another fitting at which she admired Albert's; it was, she thought, 'splendid, & so correct, that he seemed to have stepped out of an old frame, & so becoming to his beautiful face & figure'.[56] The man shouldering most of the trouble was the herald, antiquary – and, perhaps most significantly, successful playwright – James Robinson Planché. Planché was instrumental in introducing historically accurate costume into nineteenth-century British theatres, and it was he who suggested that Albert and Victoria's outfits should be closely based on those shown in the tomb effigies of Edward III and Queen Philippa at Westminster Abbey. Shortly afterwards, the Queen and the Prince commissioned Edwin Landseer to paint a joint portrait of them as they appeared at the ball, from which it is apparent that Victoria had not wished to embrace fourteenth-century authenticity so much that she was prepared to abandon the tightly laced stays and multiple petticoats that moulded her figure into a fashionable hourglass shape (Plate XIV). Nonetheless, the message was plain: Queen Victoria may have been the niece of that extravagant preening wastrel George IV, and Albert an insignificant princeling from an obscure German territory, but as Philippa of Hainault and Edward III, this young couple represented the advent of a new and heroic age.

Edward III was an inspired choice: he was considered one of the greatest of the medieval kings, and the period of his sovereignty came to be fabled as a golden age. Over his long reign he restored the royal authority squandered by his father, Edward II, achieved a succession of spectacular military victories and in 1348 founded the Order of the Garter. Queen Philippa, who often acted as regent while her husband was away on military campaigns in France, was widely loved and respected; according to one chronicler she was 'a most noble woman and most constant lover of the English'.[57] And there was an emotional dimension at play here too: the marriage of this medieval couple – second cousins and from different countries, not unlike Victoria and Albert – was an unusually companionable one in the context of royal marriages of the era. By publicly presenting themselves as the heirs of such wise, astute and charismatic royal predecessors, Victoria and Albert were following in the three-hundred-year-old footsteps of Henry VIII, when he planted himself in front of the newly painted round table, fixed his sharp little eyes on Charles V and silently dared him not to remark upon the physical resemblance between him and King Arthur. In among the quadrilles and the candlelight falling becomingly on silk and lace, there was a hard political edge to the 1842 *bal costumé*, as the past was commandeered to cast its magical, transformative glow over the present.

There is another aspect to this royal ransacking of the dressing-up box, relevant to those of us who would not have received an invitation to the ball but instead might have been among the curious onlookers. The extravagance of the two thousand costumes contrived especially for the event was no extravagance at all, but beneficial to the country as a whole; at least, that was the message broadcast from the palace. 'The purpose of this splendid gathering of the brave and beautiful', announced the *Illustrated London News*, having swallowed the bait, 'was to give a stimulus to trade in all the various departments that could be affected by the enormous outlay it would necessarily involve; and we have no doubt that many thousands are this day grateful for the temporary aid which this right royal entertainment has been the means of affording them.'[58] Motivated no doubt by a sense of duty to the silk industry, Queen Victoria and

Prince Albert held two further fancy-dress balls, one in 1845 in costume of the mid-eighteenth century, and another in 1851 in Restoration dress. Neither, however, channelled the power of the olden days with quite such political acuity as the first.

There is an intriguing coda to Queen Victoria's change of heart over fancy dress, apparently triggered by her delight in how attractive she found her husband when he was got up in period costume. In 1844 Prince Albert arranged to sit for a portrait miniature by Robert Thorburn, which was to be a present for his wife's twenty-fifth birthday; it was the kind of intimate work of art that the royal couple were in the habit of exchanging as gifts.[59] Pictures like this were not for public view, but intended solely for one another's eyes: the previous year Victoria had commissioned a provocatively sensual oil portrait of herself *en déshabillé* by the German artist Franz Xaver Winterhalter as a birthday present for her husband, and the Thorburn miniature seems to have been his answer.[60] The couple normally liked to surprise each other with their gifts, but on this occasion it seems as though Victoria had hinted at what she desired – or possibly even dictated it.

'My beloved Albert is painted in armour,' she confided to her journal after she had received the miniature, 'which I so much wished...I cannot say how beautiful it is, nor how it exactly portrays the dear original.'[61] The portrait is an intense, brooding image of the Prince wearing seventeenth-century north German armour, one hand lightly resting on his slender waist, the other on the visored helmet that rests on a table, and gazing into the distance with an expression of bravery and resolve on his handsome face, as though planning a daring campaign.[62] It was pure fantasy: Albert was not a military man, so the armour cannot even be explained as a romanticized version of reality. But in the distorting mirror of the olden times, minor details like that ceased to matter. Adopting a historical persona, Victoria was discovering, could electrify the present with a distinctly erotic charge: Thorburn's portrait miniature of Albert in armour was always said to be her favourite.

When in 1861, Prince Albert died aged just forty-two, the poem to which his grieving widow turned for solace was *In Memoriam A. H. H.* by Alfred, Lord Tennyson. It had been a favourite of Albert's, a fact that had prompted the Queen to offer Tennyson the Poet Laureateship in 1850; now, it was the Queen's melancholy bedside book, one which she would take in her hands in the early mornings and late evenings of those dark days. She was, she wrote in her journal shortly after the Prince's death, 'Much soothed & pleased with Tennyson's *In Memoriam*. Only those who have suffered, as I do, can understand these beautiful poems.'[63]

In Memoriam itself had been written during a period of profound grief; Tennyson had begun it within days of receiving news of the sudden and shocking death in October 1833 of his close friend Arthur Hallam, who had died of apoplexy (a stroke or cerebral haemorrhage) in Vienna and whose body was brought back to England by sea. 'I suffered what seemed to me to shatter all my life so that I desired to die rather than to live,' he said.[64] The profound emotional desolation he experienced changed the way he saw the past: Hallam's death sealed the time they had shared into a golden age to which Tennyson, marooned in the bleak nowadays, no longer had access. He gives the contrast physical form by describing how, sleepless and overwhelmed with longing, early one morning he had walked to the door of Hallam's old lodgings:

A hand that can be clasp'd no more –
Behold me, for I cannot sleep,
And like a guilty thing I creep
At earliest morning to the door.

He is not here; but far away
The noise of life begins again,
And ghastly thro' the drizzling rain
On the bald street breaks the blank day.[65]

In Memoriam, with its pervasive mood of melancholy retrospection, seemed to express the feelings of a generation. In it, Tennyson addressed worries that affected many people: grief, faith, doubt and how to mourn the dead. Queen Victoria had identified with its evocation of a personal olden times, and yet it also spoke to a nation that was undergoing disruption and upheaval on a scale rarely experienced before. The precious days of old from which people had somehow, catastrophically, been cut adrift were a shared concern.

In Memoriam was not the only poem Tennyson was prompted to write by Hallam's death. In the days that followed others began to emerge too: ones that revealed a new preoccupation with loss, time and endings. The narrator of 'Tithonus', begun in October 1833, is a figure from Greek myth, a prince of Troy who asked to be granted immortality but neglected to ask for eternal youth. Narrated by the ancient Tithonus himself, it begins with the most autumnal lines in all of English poetry:

> The woods decay, the woods decay and fall,
> The vapours weep their burthen to the ground,

Time unfolds unbearably for poor Tithonus, a grotesque shadow who has outlived all that was worth living for:

> Man comes and tills the field and lies beneath,
> And after many a summer dies the swan.
> Me only cruel immortality
> Consumes...[66]

Hallam died, the words suggest, as men do – and leaves, and swans. It is the way of things. But he, Tithonus Tennyson, is doomed to stagger through an agonizingly attenuated life of painful disability from which all of value has dropped away.

At this time Tennyson also wrote the intensely contemplative 'Morte d'Arthur', another poem that expresses grief in terms of the long-ago. 'Morte d'Arthur', however, reunites Arthur and his loved friend before their final parting, allowing them time to say their farewells. '"Ah! my Lord Arthur, whither shall I go?"', asks Sir Bedevere,

> 'Where shall I hide my forehead and my eyes?
> For now I see the true old times are dead,
> When every morning brought a noble chance,
> And every chance brought out a noble knight.
> ...
> But now the whole ROUND TABLE is dissolved
> Which was an image of the mighty world;
> And I the last, go forth companionless,
> And the days darken round me, and the years,
> Among new men, strange faces, other minds.'

'"The old order changeth, yielding place to new"', replies the wounded Arthur from his barge, before setting off on his final watery journey to the island-valley of Avilion.[67] And if readers begin to wonder exactly where King Arthur ends and Arthur Hallam begins, it is a grey area that also, perhaps, shades into *In Memoriam*:

> Fair ship, that from the Italian shore
> Sailest the placid ocean-plains,
> With my lost Arthur's loved remains
> Spread thy full wings, and waft him o'er.[68]

Tennyson's passion for Arthurian legends was lifelong, sparked by an edition of Malory in his father's library that was published in 1816, the first for nearly two centuries; it is evident in earlier poems such as the lyrical 'Lady of Shalott'. 'Morte d'Arthur', however, has an extra dimension of grief and longing for reunion with what has been lost. Years later, Tennyson would incorporate a revised version into his cycle of twelve narrative poems, *Idylls of the King*, in which he adapted Malory and other sources to focus on individual tales – Arthur's early kingship, Gareth and Lynette, Vivien and Merlin and so on. Released at various points between 1859 and 1885, *Idylls* would infuse Victorian cultural life with a defining flavour of Arthurian legend and elegiac longing for a former, lost, age.

Not *quite* everyone, though, had fallen under the spell of the past. Among the few major cultural figures of this time for whom it held little romance was Charles Dickens. His amateur antiquary Samuel Pickwick falls for the same sort of 'ancient' inscription as Scott's antiquary, in his case a roughly inscribed stone that he takes to be 'a strange and curious inscription of unquestionable antiquity', and doggedly persists in his view even when it is pointed out that the oddly arranged letters were written by a local man in an idle moment and, when closely examined, turn out to spell the words 'Bill Stumps, his mark'.[69] Jokes of this kind spilled over into Dickens's life. When in 1857 he moved to a spacious Georgian house, Gad's Hill Place in Higham, Kent, he had a set of fake book spines made for his study. Many were humorous: *History of a Short Chancery Suit*, for instance, in twenty-one volumes, and *Cats' Lives* in nine. Among them, however, was one set that betrayed a sharper, more satirical edge: called *The Wisdom of our Ancestors*, its seven volumes were individually labelled

'Ignorance'; 'Superstition'; 'The Block'; 'The Stake'; 'The Rack'; 'Dirt'; and 'Disease'. Rather than being a charmed place to which anyone might turn for respite from the present, in Dickens's novels the past repeatedly extends malevolent fingers into the here and now, to grip its victims and stop them from moving forward into their lives. Think of the apparently interminable legal case of Jarndyce and Jarndyce that holds its victims in suspense in *Bleak House* (1852–3), sucking their present away while making empty promises of a glorious future; or of poor Miss Havisham in *Great Expectations* (1860–1), still wearing the wedding dress she had put on so many years before on the morning she was to be married, and in only one shoe because she had not yet put on the other when she learned of her fiancé's betrayal. An obsession with the past can make us miserable and vindictive, can stunt and damage us.

Dombey and Son (1846–8) is a novel that rings with the clatter of new building and new transport; the narrator describes the erasure of down-at-heel old places by the arrival of the railways, and applauds the smart new streets everywhere proclaiming their obsession with this great modern bringer of prosperity:

> There were railway patterns in its drapers' shops, and railway journals in the windows of its newsmen. There were railway hotels, coffee-houses, lodging-houses, boarding-houses; railway plans, maps, views, wrappers, bottles, sandwich-boxes, and time-tables; railway hackney-coach and cab-stands; railway omnibuses, railway streets and buildings, railway hangers-on and parasites....

The great forces of nature themselves bowed to this new invention: 'There was even railway time observed in clocks, as if the sun itself had given in.'[70] Dickens leaves it to the monstrous Mrs Skewton to hymn the days of old during a visit to Warwick Castle:

> Those darling byegone times...with their delicious fortresses, and their dear old dungeons, and their delightful places of torture, and their romantic vengeances, and their picturesque assaults and sieges, and everything that makes life truly charming! How dreadfully we have degenerated!

Elizabeth I? 'Dear creature! She was all Heart!' Henry VIII? 'So bluff!... So burly. So truly English.'[71]

Dickens, however, was fighting a rearguard action. The romance of the past was thoroughly baked into virtually every aspect of mid-nineteenth-century life. And for others of this period, the spell was only getting stronger. For them, the past offered liberation, not imprisonment. The days of old could be a template for a more soulful and beautiful world. And perhaps a more egalitarian one, too.

V
CRUSADES AGAINST THE AGE

It is a January afternoon in 1854 and the sun is already low; the sky is streaked with pink and dusted with gold. If you happen to be walking along the banks of the Thames near Godstow, through the water meadows just north of Oxford, you might bump into a pale, wide-eyed young man. He is on his way back into the city from what he later described as a 'pilgrimage' to the ruins of Godstow Abbey, the burial place of Fair Rosamond, beloved mistress of King Henry II. He notes the glory of the sky, but it is nothing to the images now forming in his mind 'of the old days, the abbey, and long processions of the faithful, banners of the cross, copes and crosiers, gay knights and ladies by the river bank, hawking-parties and all the pageantry of the golden age – it made me feel so wild and mad', he later recalled, 'I had to throw stones into the water to break the dream'. His medieval vision was, he said, 'quite painful with intensity', and his dreams 'so vivid that they seem recollections rather than imaginations'.[1]

Three years later, and Edward Burne-Jones, having abandoned his undergraduate degree in order to become an artist, is back in Oxford for the summer. He has come to impress his medieval vision upon the heart of the university.

From the new Oxford Union building on Frewin Court comes a sound of banging, accompanied by muffled roaring. Inside, a short man wearing a medieval-style military helmet grips it with both hands and tries desperately to get it off; to make matters worse, the visor has closed over his face and will not open, no matter how hard he pushes and pulls. His friends, helpless with mirth as he bellows and dances with rage, are no help at all.[2] Trapped inside the bassinet is William Morris. He had commissioned this piece of armour, along with a mail surcoat, from a local blacksmith so that he could model as a knight for his friends and fellow artists, who, amid the creaking of ladders, footsteps on scaffolding-boards, jokes, laughter and the frequent popping of soda corks, are busy decorating the upper walls of the long building with murals of Arthurian legends. Morris is suffering for his pursuit of authenticity. He later sports the chainmail at dinner, where it is much admired; 'he looked very splendid', recalled Burne-Jones.[3]

Masterminding the project is Dante Gabriel Rossetti. Earlier that summer Rossetti, accompanied by Morris, had visited Benjamin Woodward, the architect responsible not only for the Union building but also for the university museum, built according to a flamboyantly Gothic design. Woodward was keen to find artists who could paint murals in his new buildings; in fact, his initial proposal to Rossetti had been to create a mural for the museum, representing Newton gathering pebbles on the Shore of the Ocean of Truth. This subject, with its somewhat austere intellectual symbolism, failed to appeal, but Woodward agreed to a more ambitious alternative: scenes from Thomas Malory's *Le Morte d'Arthur*, to be painted high up on the pristine walls of the new Union building. It was evidently too big a project for Rossetti to undertake alone, so he offered to muster a company of artists who would each choose an episode to depict. Along with Morris, Burne-Jones and four others, whom he persuaded to take part for no fee other than travelling and lodging expenses, Rossetti was to transform the new Union into an immersive Arthurian experience, despite having little familiarity with working on this scale or in the demanding medium of tempera. Never mind: as ringmaster to this group of friends, Rossetti was determined to unleash his visual agenda on generations of Oxford undergraduates who were destined to become some of the most influential figures of the future. All young men – and, eventually, women – passing through the university and attending debates at the Union would henceforth find themselves under the gaze of King Arthur and his knights. In their different ways, and with different degrees of practicality, Rossetti, Morris and Burne-Jones used their visions of the past to transform the present.

Rossetti's family background was intellectual, literary and politically engaged. His father was a Neapolitan patriot in exile from Vasto, a Dante scholar and professor of Italian at King's College, London. His mother, the half-Italian Frances Polidori – sister of John Polidori, Lord Byron's personal physician and author of *The Vampyre* (1819) – devoted herself to educating her four children, encouraging them to read and draw. Rossetti's imagination was book-lined; he grew up seeing the world through an inner filter of his favourite authors, including Dante, Shakespeare, Edgar Allan Poe, Coleridge and Goethe. Morris, just twenty-three in 1857, had recently extracted himself from an apprenticeship to a leading Gothic Revival architect, G. E. Street. For the last few months he had been learning to draw and writing medieval-style poems that would be published the following year as *The Defence of Guinevere*, with a dedication to 'MY FRIEND DANTE GABRIEL ROSSETTI PAINTER'. As a child he, too, had read avidly; he claimed to have got through the whole of Sir Walter Scott by the age of seven. His parents had given him a child-size suit of armour, and he would ride his pony through Epping Forest in Essex, near his family's home, exploring its hidden landscapes and visiting small, out-of-the-way medieval churches, imagining himself to be a knight on a quest.[4] For both young men, the visual arts, literature, design and architecture were not discrete entities but interlocking parts of a vast cultural continuum, so close it was hard to tell where one ended and the other began. Or at least that was how they imagined it: the walls of the Oxford Union's new Debating Hall seemed an ideal place to turn their dreams into reality.

Nine years earlier, not long after the twenty-year-old Rossetti had tired of drawing endless plaster casts of antique sculpture and dropped out of the prestigious Royal Academy Schools, he had reached a momentous conclusion: the British art scene was overflowing with sentimental, meretricious rubbish. It urgently needed to be reformed. But how to achieve this? The present, awash with mass-produced goods usually of execrable design, was clearly unable to present a solution. The only answer was to look back into the past for inspiration. So, in 1848, this charismatic young man and a band of like-minded friends including John Everett Millais and William Holman Hunt gathered together to form an artistic group intended to challenge the status quo. They needed a name, so they called themselves the Pre-Raphaelite Brotherhood. It was awkward, but it suited them: in fact, they aimed at awkwardness. They chose it because they thought that Raphael, one of the greatest figures of the High Renaissance, had cast a deleterious shadow over painting ever since. His sweet-faced

Madonnas, elegantly mannered poses and vague approximations of the natural world had launched the careers of ten thousand painters attempting to emulate him, but less skilfully. The Pre-Raphaelites dismissed the majority of contemporary British art and focused instead on what they could learn from the work of the early Renaissance. As John Ruskin later wrote in support of them, 'If they adhere to their principles, and paint... with the earnestness of men of the thirteenth and fourteenth centuries, they will...found a new and noble school in England.'[5]

No amount of earnestness, though, was going to make the Brotherhood's mission easy. At this time, early Renaissance pictures were still considered strange, stiff and awkward – antiquarian curiosities all too clearly demonstrating that lessons in perspective and the illusion of three-dimensionality had yet to be learned. Tellingly, artists of the period were referred to – if at all – as 'primitives'. But it was precisely these qualities, their clear, bright colours and apparent *moral* brightness, that appealed to the Brotherhood. They were mesmerized, for example, by a painting by Jan van Eyck then recently acquired by the National Gallery, the *Arnolfini Portrait* of 1434. Its clarity, sobriety, cool precision and enigmatic atmosphere showed Rossetti and his associates how painting could be. For his own oil painting *The Girlhood of Mary Virgin* (1848–9) – the first to be exhibited with the enigmatic initials 'P.R.B.' – Rossetti adopted an archaic style, borrowing from van Eyck's stiffly formal postures, so unlike the twisting, expressive poses beloved of later old masters, and emulating the purity of colour and contour of early Italian paintings. Originally the painting even had an arched top, in common with many of these pictures: Rossetti was nailing his colours to the mast of art before Raphael, gesturing far back into the past in order to create the art of the future.

As early as 1853, the original Pre-Raphaelite Brotherhood – a disparate group who even at the outset were bound by the loosest of shared ideals – was effectively disbanded. The sculptor Thomas Woolner emigrated to Australia, and Hunt set off for Palestine in dogged pursuit of authentic landscapes for his biblical subjects. Gabriel's younger sister Christina, who had posed for the figure of the Virgin Mary in *The Girlhood*, contributed poems to the Pre-Raphaelite journal *The Germ* and felt so involved in the project that in 1849 she could refer in a letter to her brother William Michael to her 'double sisterhood', composed a mock-

Self-caricature by Edward Burne-Jones in the studio he shared with William Morris, 1856; brass-rubbings are pinned to the walls.

portentous poem about the group's demise. 'The P.R.B. is in its decadence', it lamented, 'For Woolner in Australia cooks his chops; / And Hunt is yearning for the land of Cheops'. And while Millais became an associate member of the Royal Academy, a distinct step in his eventual rise to the very top of the art establishment, Rossetti made a decisive move in the opposite direction and refused to submit his work to be considered for inclusion in the Academy's annual exhibitions. 'D. G. Rossetti shuns the vulgar optic', was Christina's wry comment.[6]

This withdrawal from the London art scene and shrugging rejection of its agenda was a highly eccentric, potentially career-ending move, and meant that, by the middle of the 1850s, Rossetti was in need of new disciples. He found them in the younger figures of Burne-Jones and Morris, whom he had met in 1856 after Burne-Jones had sought him out. These two friends, who had met as undergraduates at Exeter College in Oxford, had soon discovered a shared love of medieval things and jointly embarked on what they called a crusade 'against the age'.[7] After Oxford they shared accommodation in London, eventually settling their books, painting materials, easels, brass-rubbings, old prints and bits of armour in unfurnished rooms in an early eighteenth-century house on Bloomsbury's Red Lion Square, recommended by Rossetti, who had lived there himself at one time. It soon filled up even more with the heavy wooden furniture ('intensely medieval', according to Rossetti) that Morris had commissioned according to his own designs; as a sixteen-year-old, he had so disapproved of the standards of contemporary design and manufacture that he had refused to enter the Great Exhibition when taken there by his family.[8] Morris, Burne-Jones and Rossetti regarded this furniture, which included a huge settle, as a blank canvas, and painted it with bold medieval scenes of knights and ladies, some inspired by Morris's own poetry.[9]

Rossetti was focusing with increasing intensity on the long-ago. He declared Malory's *Morte d'Arthur* and the Bible to be the world's greatest books, and around this time painted his first Arthurian subject of many – a highly charged watercolour representing Sir Launcelot demanding a kiss from Queen Guenevere, now a nun, in front of King Arthur's tomb. Launcelot leans outrageously, if awkwardly, over Arthur's recumbent effigy, thrusting his face towards the Queen.[10] Rossetti rarely felt any need to faithfully represent a text, even one he considered so great, and had conflated two incidents in Malory's text in order to create a bizarrely morbid take on the classic love triangle. For Morris and Burne-Jones, *Le Morte d'Arthur* was every bit as important. They had found a copy in a Birmingham bookshop when they were both still undergraduates, while Morris was staying with Burne-Jones's family. Burne-Jones could not afford it and had resorted to reading it piecemeal in the shop, but Morris, who had family money, bought it outright. What they found in its pages was different from Tennyson's Arthurian poems, 'The Lady of Shalott', 'Sir Galahad', 'Sir Launcelot and Queen Guinevere' and 'Morte d'Arthur'. Offering a seemingly inexhaustible wealth of exciting stories and complex psychological situations, Malory was a vast and unpredictable landscape to Tennyson's carefully tended garden.

In Oxford, the Union building was so new that you could smell the damp mortar, although it was designed to give the impression of a medieval church. The timber roof was left visible and the architect shaped each end like an apse – the effect is rather like being inside an upturned wooden ship. Above a gallery fitted with bookshelves, the walls are divided into ten bays by great wooden roof arches, each bay pierced by two windows shaped like six-petalled flowers. In 1857, over the late summer and into the autumn, intensely dramatic Arthurian subjects began to appear in the newly built bays. Rossetti chose 'Sir Launcelot's Vision of the San Grael (Sir Launcelot prevented by his sin from entering the chapel of the San Grael)'. His knight, dressed in a scarlet robe, slumps against the right-hand edge of the space. The rest of the image comprises Sir Lancelot's dream vision: the Damsel of the Grail appears on the left holding the vessel, but Queen Guinevere rises up between them, raising both arms and holding an apple, symbolic of sin. Burne-Jones chose 'Merlin Lured to his Death by Nimue (Merlin being imprisoned beneath a stone by the Damsel of the Lake)', showing the great magician being seduced and misled by the lute-playing Nimue's beguiling music. And Morris chose to illustrate a dangerously fraught love triangle: 'Sir Palomydes' Jealousy of Sir Tristram (How Sir Palomydes loved La Belle Iseult with exceeding great love out of measure, and how she loved not him again but rather Sir Tristram)'. The subject was to prove horribly prophetic; it was towards the end of the year that he met and fell in love with his future wife, Jane Burden, who was later to have a lengthy relationship with Rossetti.

Each chose a psychologically complex subject, charged with dark and dangerous sexual energy. At the forefront are sin, transgression and exclusion; manipulation, deception and cruelty; jealousy, obsession and unrequited love. Did it occur to any of them to censor or downplay Malory's themes to make them acceptable to a Victorian audience – and appropriate for an educational establishment? If it did, any such scruples faded in the intense Malorean climate that the friends lived and breathed. Medieval legends allowed them to say publicly what was otherwise unsayable.

The group's approach to Malory was in stark contrast to another set of Arthurian murals begun in London ten years earlier. In 1840, the new, Gothic Palace of Westminster began to rise from the ashes of the old. Paintings were naturally required for the interiors, and in 1847 the Scottish painter William Dyce was commissioned to decorate the Queen's Robing Room with scenes from Malory.[11] It had all begun with conversations with Prince Albert, the chairman of the Royal Commission in charge of decorations. Both men were passionately interested in the work of the Nazarenes, a group of idealistic German, Swiss and Austrian artists who gathered in Rome in the 1810s and sought to revive the spirit of medieval and early Renaissance art, and both were keen promoters of fresco painting. One day in 1846, Dyce was at Osborne, Victoria and Albert's house on the Isle of Wight, labouring over a florid mural of *Neptune Resigning his Crown to Britannia*, and he and the Prince were talking about German art. Would 'the stories of King Arthur and in particular Sir Thomas Malory's "Morte D'Arthur"...supply to English artists subjects of legendary history, which, for their great interest, their antiquity and national chivalric character... surpass those of the "Niebelungen-lied", of which so much had been made by the Germans?' wondered the artist.[12] Poor Dyce. If he could have foreseen how the remaining eighteen years of his life would be overshadowed by Malory as a result, he would probably have kept his opinion to himself. To Albert, steeped in his own national legends and fairy tales, Dyce's words were beguiling music. Had either man actually read Malory?[13] A hazily romantic idea of King Arthur and his valorous knights was one thing; Malory's treatment of the legends was quite another. In the event, Dyce – having tried unsuccessfully to shunt the Robing Room project to the history painter Daniel Maclise – found himself in the tricky position of identifying a suite of subjects in Malory that were suitable for the eyes of the Queen herself. His solution? To make a list of moral virtues, and find a scene to illustrate each. Even with such a broad remit, however, he did not find it easy; with Malory, one could, with care, skirt adulterous sex and appalling violence, and yet the clearest of waters always seemed to be muddied by moral problems. 'Hospitality' was relatively easy: *The Admission of Tristram to the Fellowship of the Round Table* (unfinished by the time of Dyce's death in 1864) shows the generous welcome given by King Arthur to Sir Tristram, who had previously fought and defeated a number of his own knights, and his offer of a place at the Round Table. Dyce departed from Malory's account, however, in the marginal part he gives to Guinevere; it seems that he was keen to avoid drawing too much attention to an adulterous queen.[14] He gives her a central role, however, in *Mercy: Sir Gawaine Swearing to be Merciful and Never to be Against Ladies* (1854), which refers to an incident following Arthur and Guinevere's wedding feast. Chased by hounds through the hall is a white hart, which Sir Gawain resolves to follow and bring back; in doing so he gets into a fight and attempts to behead his opponent, but a lady steps between them and he cuts off her head by mistake. When he returns to the court, the Queen – young, just married and therefore still virtuous – appoints a jury of ladies who punish him by making him swear that in the future he will always be courteous and fight on behalf of ladies. Dyce does, however, omit one colourful detail: the lady's severed head, which Malory describes as being suspended around Sir Gawain's neck.[15] In his treatment of other subjects, such as *Generosity: King Arthur Unhorsed by Sir Bors and Spared by Sir Launcelot* (1852) and *Courtesy: Sir Tristram Harping to La Beale Isoud* (1852), it is hard to avoid the impression that he is picking his way unhappily around the edges of Malory's morally compromised world, presenting sanitized and highly selective accounts of these dark and complex tales.[16] On closer inspection, *Le Morte d'Arthur* was far from being the jewel-box of chivalry and honour for which he might have hoped. Which of course was precisely what made it so compelling for Rossetti, Morris and Burne-Jones, each of whom wished to break the conventions of propriety rather than be ruled by them.

Painting in fresco may have been a spirited gesture of allegiance to the days of old. But England is not Italy, and its climate is not kind to wall painting. Exposed to the damp winter air of London, which prevented them from drying properly, Dyce's murals have deteriorated despite his diligent study of fresco technique. In Oxford, the Union murals fared far worse. Their colours must, at first, have been as vividly striking as their subjects. Later that year the poet Coventry Patmore visited the Union and thought them 'so brilliant as to make the walls look like the margin of a highly-illuminated manuscript'.[17] It was not long, however, before things began to go wrong. None of the artists involved had any practical experience of painting in fresco, and the surface on which they painted the murals had not been adequately prepared – it was simply whitewash over a thin skim of plaster that barely covered bricks and still-damp mortar. The colours, initially so brilliant, soon sank into the walls and grew dull, while the brickwork became obtrusive. The fumes from the gas lighting further obscured and darkened the surface; inevitably, paint began to flake off. The paintings were soon sad, barely legible wrecks of what they had been, as they remain today. Even so, the spirit of what they were – both a manifesto for the age, and a shield against it – lived on.

A fair damozel sits in a walled garden, her flowing hair caught up in a clasp. At her feet kneels a gentle knight, who embraces her with reverence, clasping his hands behind her back as though in prayer. Opposite them a youth bends low over a book, *Roman du Quete du Sangral* – the Arthurian story of the quest for the Holy Grail – from which he recites, raising a slender hand to emphasize a point. There are lilies growing in this little plot – their scent must hang heavy in the air – and a fruit-bearing tree, but its foliage does not shield the view of mounted knights beyond, stern and impatient for the road. The kneeling knight must complete his farewell and join his company. The young fellow opposite must be on his way too: his hat is decorated with a cockleshell, identifying him as a pilgrim. The moment should be one of drama and motion, of active leave-taking, but the stillness of the garden works like an enchantment. The lady's face is impassive. The pilgrim's eyes are nearly closed, as though falling into a dream as his story weaves its spell. The little garden's atmosphere of wistful melancholy seems to have paralysed its inhabitants, trapping them like specimens in medieval amber.

Burne-Jones made this mesmerizingly airless little drawing in 1858, in the months following the Oxford Union campaign. The surface he chose was not paper but vellum – prepared animal skin. This eccentric choice had both symbolic and practical value – symbolic because of its associations with medieval scribes, practical because of the smoothness of its surface, which allowed for the finest of detail. He drew on the vellum with an exceptionally narrow, flexible steel nib, which he probably regarded as one of the nineteenth century's more acceptable inventions; it allowed for finer, more reliable lines than the quills that for centuries had been staple tools for writing and drawing. The drawing harked back wistfully to the days of old at the same time as it embraced modern technology. According to Rossetti, Burne-Jones's drawings were 'marvels of finish & imaginative detail, unequalled by *anything* unless perhaps Albert Dürer'.[18]

Morris owned *The Knight's Farewell*, and kept it throughout his life; presumably he bought it from his friend as soon as it was made.[19] Perhaps the two had discussed the subject – Morris might even have commissioned the drawing, which closely echoes part of his poem 'Sir Galahad: A Christmas Mystery', published that year in his collection *The Defence of Guinevere*:

Edward Burne-Jones, *The Knight's Farewell*, ink drawing on vellum, 1858.

Before the trees by autumn were well bared,
I saw a damozel with gentle play,

Within that very walk say last farewell
To her dear knight, just riding out to find
(Why should I choke to say it?) the Sangreal,
And their last kisses sunk into my mind.

Yea, for she stood lean'd forward on his breast,
Rather, scarce stood; the back of one dear hand,
That it might well be kiss'd, she held and press'd
Against his lips; long time they stood there, fann'd

By gentle gusts of quiet frosty wind,
Till Mador de la porte a-going by,
And my own horsehoofs roused them; they untwined,
And parted like a dream.[20]

Whatever the picture's genesis, drawing and verses lock together in a mutual embrace. Morris kept his friend's drawing for the rest of his life.

This and his other drawings with medieval subjects made around this time create the impression that Burne-Jones was scratching away with his nib, removing the surface layer of the present to uncover a miniature medieval world. One might almost suspect him of having wished to scratch a hole big enough to squeeze right through into his own intense medieval vision; but it was really the other way around. Once he had created these portals into the past, the light from his vision of the 'golden age' came streaming through into the modern world. It was not long, in fact, before the prosaic light of day began literally to be tempered by the shades of his medievalizing dreams: at the time of the Oxford Union murals, Rossetti passed on to Burne-Jones a commission from a London firm for the design of a stained-glass window. 'The colour of the whole is beyond all description,' said Rossetti of the design his friend produced, *The Good Shepherd* (1857), while Ruskin, who became one of Burne-Jones's greatest supporters, was – reportedly – 'driven wild with joy'.[21] After the pale colours of eighteenth-century stained glass, the rich azures and crimsons of Burne-Jones's design, divided by lead strips into individual jewel-like sections just like medieval examples had been, burst onto the eye like the colours of a lush spring after an insipid winter. It was the beginning of Burne-Jones's work as a decorative artist, through which he brought medieval legend into the heart of smart drawing-rooms and coloured the very atmosphere in which people lived.

A 'sort of revelation' was how Morris described the effect Ruskin's words had upon him when he first read them. As an undergraduate at Oxford, he would read aloud to his friends from Ruskin's books *The Seven Lamps of Architecture* (1849), *Modern Painters* (from 1843) and *The Stones of Venice* (1851–3), his voice rising in volume until he was chanting the words rather than speaking them.[22] Ruskin wrote not just about medieval art and architecture, but about medieval craftsmen; he thought about human creativity in the Middle Ages and compared it to the present day. In his chapter 'The Nature of Gothic', included in *The Stones of Venice*, he declared:

> You can teach a man to draw a straight line, and to carve it; to strike a curved line, and to carve it; and to copy and carve any number of given s or forms, with admirable speed and perfect precision; and you find his work perfect of its kind: but if you ask him to think about any of those forms, to consider if he cannot find any better in his own head, he stops; his execution becomes hesitating; he thinks, and ten to one he thinks wrong; ten to one he makes a mistake in the first touch he gives to his work as a thinking being. But you have made a man of him for all that. He was only a machine before, an animated tool.[23]

Morris was electrified by the implications Ruskin's words had for the modern world. The industrial revolution had made machines of men and women, and the solution was to learn ways of working from the distant past. As he later wrote, 'in future days ['The Nature of Gothic'] will be considered as one of the very few necessary and inevitable utterances of the century'. A call to action, it seemed 'to point out a new road on which the world should travel'. Well, the world may not have gone that way, but Morris did. The medieval period became for him not the gigantic sourcebook it was for so many others, but a powerful guiding spirit. His imagination was so thoroughly absorbed by the Middle Ages that he did not design medieval-style things, but designed and made things as he imagined medieval craftsmen might, and refused to recognize the modern division between intellect and manual labour. He thought that every detail of domestic surroundings could and should be reformed, from chairs and tables to wall hangings and stained glass. Things were so often ugly and badly made, but it did not have to be that way. 'With the arrogance of youth,' he later admitted, 'I determined to do no less than to transform the world with Beauty.'[24]

Ruskin may have written about medieval craftsmanship with soul-stirring eloquence, but it took Morris to put it into practice. For him, any worthwhile skill, whether it be wood-engraving, embroidery or the ability to write verse, could be acquired by diligent practice; the idea that one needed to wait to be struck by poetic inspiration was, in his words, 'sheer nonsense'. 'If a chap can't compose an epic poem while he's weaving a tapestry,' he once opined rather briskly, 'he had better shut up, he'll never do any good at all.'[25] Burne-Jones drew a caricature of his friend, a stout, determined figure sitting at a loom in front of an

Red House in Bexleyheath.

audience, busily – and possibly incomprehensibly, the drawing slyly suggests – demonstrating the art of weaving.

When Morris and Jane Burden married, he commissioned their first home, Red House in Bexleyheath, south-east of London, from a friend, the young architect Philip Webb – although naturally he involved himself deeply in its design. The house was medieval in spirit, built to resemble a dwelling of the thirteenth century, with steep tiled roofs, oriel windows and a well in the garden. The busy activity under its roof was inspired by the Middle Ages too: it was a workshop for practical crafts. The furniture and decoration – beds, tables, chairs, wall hangings, candlesticks, tiles, and curtains – were, by and large, not bought but designed and made by William, Jane and their friends. They learned crafts, experimented and invented. They regarded walls, ceilings and doors as large-scale canvases for patterns and paintings. In the drawing room, Burne-Jones created a mural depicting the medieval wedding feast of Sir Degrevaunt and Melidor, incorporating portraits of William and Jane, while the artist Elizabeth Siddal, who married Rossetti in May 1860, is thought to be among those who contributed to a scene of characters from the book of Genesis on the bedroom wall.[26] It was the collaborative spirit in which the friends worked that resulted, in 1861, in Morris setting up his decorating company, Morris, Marshall, Faulkner & Co., otherwise known as 'the Firm', which introduced his pared-down, harmonious designs to a wider public.

Jane was already an accomplished needlewoman, but Red House provided the opportunity for her to develop her work on a large scale. She and William bought old textiles and studied their construction together. She began to make wall hangings for their bedroom; inspired by a fifteenth-century manuscript of Jean Froissart's *Chronicles*, she decorated plain, deep blue fabric with bold daisies in simple couched stitches. 'The first stuff I got to embroider on was a piece of indigo-dyed blue serge I found by chance in a London shop,' she remembered. 'I took it home and [William] was delighted with it, and set to work at once designing flowers. These we worked in bright colour in a simple rough way – the work went quickly and when finished we covered the walls of the bedroom at Red House to our great joy.'[27] An even more ambitious project was the creation of large embroidered panels for the dining room, each with a full-length female figure, inspired partly by Chaucer's *Legend of Good Women* and partly by a set of embroideries at Hardwick Hall in Derbyshire that depicted noble and virtuous women of the ancient world. This was another collaboration: Jane worked with her sister Elizabeth 'Bessie' Burden, Georgiana 'Georgie' Burne-Jones (Edward's wife) and Georgie's sister, Alice Macdonald.[28] The panels were sophisticated, made using embroidery techniques based on late medieval examples and with precious materials; she and her collaborators were, Jane recalled, 'making experiments in silk and gold wools afterwards to bloom into altar cloths etc.'[29] Later, Jane channelled her knowledge and experience into managing the needlework commissions for Morris & Co., as well as continuing with her own projects. A coverlet she made for William's bed with the help of her friend Mary de Morgan can be seen at Kelmscott Manor today; she modelled the design on historical patterns and signed it 'Si je puis Jane Morris' – a motto adopted from Jan van Eyck's 'Als ich kann'.

William Morris cared passionately about the quality of materials. And he minded about processes. He worried about dye, which was central to embroidery, weaving and printing. Modern chemical dyes began to be introduced in the early nineteenth century, and by the 1870s aniline dyes, produced by coal-tar, were common. They produced jarring, unnatural colours, Morris thought, looked particularly unpleasant by candlelight, and faded quickly. So he read every tract and treatise about traditional dyeing he could find, from Gerard's *Herbal* to obscure French books of the seventeenth century, delving back as far as Pliny.[30] Then he began to experiment with pigments in the basement of his house; his younger daughter May described the air as 'saturated with dyeing: bits of madder and indigo lay about, papers of the kermes insect brought home and its habits and customs explained.'[31] In 1875 Morris took his research to the centre of the silk trade, persuading a manufacturer in Leek in Staffordshire to allow him to experiment with the firm's equipment, implementing ancient methods and introducing natural pigments back into large-scale industry. Morris loved having the chance to dress in workman's clothes and work with his arms thrust deep into the vats. Indigo was a particular obsession because of its ancient roots, and he frequently returned to London dyed deep blue up to the elbows, much to the amusement of his friends. Georgiana Burne-Jones describes him dining with them 'with two dark blue hands bearing witness that he has plunged into work again'.[32]

To every incidence of nineteenth-century machine-made, mass-produced ugliness, a solution could be found by researching and mastering a traditional craft. Having mastered the art of dyeing, Morris immersed himself in hand-weaving, setting up a tapestry loom in his bedroom and getting up at dawn to make the most of the light. He took old carpets apart and painstakingly learned the technique of hand-knotting. And he took huge pleasure in writing out poems and stories in beautiful calligraphic styles that he had learned from reading sixteenth-century instruction manuals for scribes, decorating the sheets with creeping patterns of leaves and flowers like the medieval manuscripts he had studied at the Bodleian and the British Museum. These he gave as presents to particular friends.

Morris's illuminated manuscripts were a route back into the past, before printing presses made such skills obsolete. For his last great venture, he tackled the problems of modern book design, setting up the Kelmscott Press in 1891. As ever, he threw himself into every detail. The paper was specially commissioned from a firm in Kent, where the

the works of
Geoffrey
Chaucer
now newly
imprinted

HERE BEGINNETH THE TALES OF CANTERBURY AND FIRST THE PROLOGUE THEREOF

Whan THAT Aprille with his shoures soote
The droghte of March hath perced to the roote,
And bathed every veyne in swich licour,
Of which vertu engendred is the flour;
Whan Zephirus eek with his swete breeth
Inspired hath in every holt and heeth
The tendre croppes, and the yonge sonne
Hath in the Ram his halfe cours yronne,
And smale foweles maken melodye,
That slepen al the nyght with open eye,
So priketh hem nature in hir corages;
Thanne longen folk to goon on pilgrimages,
And palmeres for to seken straunge strondes,
To ferne halwes, kowthe in sondry londes;
And specially, from every shires ende
Of Engelond, to Caunterbury they wende,
The hooly blisful martir for to seke,
That hem hath holpen whan that they were seeke.
BIFIL that in that seson on a day,
In Southwerk at the Tabard as I lay,
Redy to wenden on my pilgrymage
To Caunterbury with ful devout corage,
At nyght were come into that hostelrye
Wel nyne and twenty in a compaignye,
Of sondry folk, by aventure yfalle
In felaweshipe, and pilgrimes were they alle,
That toward Caunterbury wolden ryde.

The Works of Geoffrey Chaucer, published in 1896 by the Kelmscott Press.

craftsmen were able to hand-make it to his particular directions: Morris loaned them fifteenth-century books from his library so they could use the paper as a model. He designed three different typefaces, Golden, Troy and Chaucer, based on fonts used in early printed books. He even considered making his own ink. His final project with the press, a gigantic edition of the works of Geoffrey Chaucer, not only returned him to one of his earliest literary passions, but brought him once again into close partnership with Burne-Jones, who drew the illustrations while Morris designed the borders and initial letters. This labour of love took a staggering four years to complete, and Burne-Jones described the magnificent result as a 'pocket cathedral'.[33] In his intensely practical way, Morris had responded to Ruskin's call to arms and given the nineteenth century a final, resounding demonstration of the superiority of medieval materials and techniques over its own tawdry manufactures. He died a few months later – of 'simply being William Morris', said his doctor, 'and having done more work than most ten men'.[34]

'Embroidery is the first thing I learned,' remembered May Morris. 'I sat beside my mother at her embroidery frame and watched the needle come down and begged to be allowed to fasten the thread.'[35] May and her sister Jenny grew up in an environment of craft and making into which their father's enthusiasms would flood; when he was experimenting with dyes, they were given woollen yarns and pigments to play with, and many evenings were spent listening to him reading aloud from his beloved Norse mythology.[36] At sixteen, May enrolled at the National Art Training School in South Kensington, where she continued to study embroidery and took advantage of the school's proximity to spectacular medieval examples in the collections of the South Kensington Museum (later the Victoria and Albert Museum).[37] From 1885, at the age of twenty-three, May ran the embroidery department of Morris & Co., where she oversaw the production of domestic textiles from wall hangings and tablecloths to cushions, bags and chair covers. Her work as an embroiderer and designer of textiles, wallpapers and jewelry (Plate XVII) was underpinned by historical examples such as seventeenth-century crewel work (embroidery with wool) and delicate eighteenth-century beadwork, but her particular passion was for Opus Anglicanum – Latin for 'English work' – a name coined in the thirteenth century to describe the exquisitely fine, luxurious embroideries made with threads of silk, and silver and gold, mostly in the workshops of medieval London.

In an age in which embroidery – or 'work' – was widely practised by middle-class girls and women, and was often no more elaborate than cross-stitch, May had serious ambitions for it. She was, she declared, 'inclined to take needle-art seriously, and regard its simply priceless qualities worth as careful study and appreciation as any other form of art; certainly', she added, 'research into its history and development is as rich and fruitful'.[38] She visited churches in Britain and abroad in search of surviving examples (to her dismay, all too often she was instead shown 'some glittering horror perpetrated in modern times') and, like her parents, acquired and studied medieval fragments for what they could reveal about their making, writing of the 'peculiar pleasure experienced in poring over an old piece of needlework...noting the different ways in which the threads are laid on'.[39]

When May was still in her twenties, she designed several spectacular pairs of hangings, worked by herself and assistants using historical methods. One was 'Fruit Garden', a large-scale silk embroidery depicting a glorious tangle of young fruit trees, flowers and acanthus leaves (Plate XVIII). The composition, described by her friend George Bernard Shaw as 'glowing fruit forests', echoes the teeming, organic patterns of natural forms to be found in Opus Anglicanum. Each pair is embroidered with a text at the top as though emblazoned on a banner; 'Summer is icumen in', promises one, echoing the thirteenth-century song; 'Growth sed & blowth med & springeth wod nu', says another. 'Fruit Garden' bears a motto taken from a poem written by William for his daughter, 'The Flowering Orchard': 'All wrought by the worm in the peasant carle's cot / On the mulberry leafage when summer was hot'.[40] May's hangings, their intricate and painstaking embroidery closely based on techniques and stylistic traits mastered from medieval examples, were an audacious statement in an age of mass production. Through her revival of a medieval art, she recreated embroidery for a new generation.

May also clothed herself in the past. As children, she and Jenny were dressed unconventionally by their parents, in simple serge dresses, sturdy boots and strings of amber beads. Their practical clothes gave the girls such a homespun appearance that an unkind cousin once described their outfits as suitable only for 'medieval brutes'.[41] As an adult May continued to dress distinctively, although the comments excited by her appearance were by this time more flattering: 'she was dressed like the pictures of Raphael', noted one observer at a Grosvenor Gallery exhibition.[42] Part of a generation of women who challenged fashionable clothing for its restrictiveness, May wore dresses in simple, elegant shapes and flowing fabrics of the kind that appeared in paintings by Rossetti, Burne-Jones, James McNeill Whistler and Albert Moore, inspired by medieval and Renaissance examples. In one portrait photograph, taken when she was twenty-four, she wears a simple, untrimmed velvet dress with a natural waistline that would not look out of place in a sixteenth-century painting, while another shows her in a long silk coat with a train and extravagant open sleeves, evidently inspired by Italian Renaissance costume.[43] May, along with other women of the era who were increasingly visible as professionals, artists, teachers and lecturers, moved forward by way of the past.

❖

Previous nineteenth-century reformers had, of course, looked to the past as a model for how the future might be shaped. A book that William Morris knew nearly by heart was *Rural Rides* (1830) by William Cobbett, farmer, roving radical and champion of the rural poor. Cobbett's forthright opinions about the parlous state of the countryside, coupled with an idealistic view of the rural England into which he had been born in 1763, give his book a powerfully nostalgic undertow. He was convinced that the countryside was being depopulated and people forced to make for what he called the 'Great Wen', as he called London. The rot had, he believed, really set in long before, during the Reformation, when there had been a concerted move by the state to dispossess the poor. In former, Catholic times, he implausibly maintained, there were 'no paupers', but 'ease and happiness and harmony and Christian charity'.[44]

Six years later, the twenty-four-year-old A. W. N. Pugin published the forcefully satirical work *Contrasts*, with its self-explanatory subtitle *A parallel between the noble edifices of the fourteenth and fifteenth centuries, and similar buildings of the present day; shewing the present decay of taste*. Pugin made scathing visual comparisons – between, for example, the neoclassical Chapel Royal in Brighton, its theatre-like interior betraying its focus on sermonizing rather than the sacraments, and the solemn grandeur of St George's Chapel, Windsor. However unfair, they were unanswerable.[45] And there was Thomas Carlyle and his biting critique of British society, *Past and Present* (1843). William Morris was profoundly affected by Carlyle's book when he read it as an undergraduate, but found his words disconcertingly grotesque.[46] Cobbett's bluff downrightness and Ruskin's rousing fervour both had greater appeal.

As a young man, Morris absorbed these works that so plainly set out a decline in beauty, morality and standards of living; but when in later life he came to write about them himself he expressed them not as comparisons, but through the literary device of time travel. Imaginatively inhabiting the past had, after all, long been a mental habit for him. 'Not seldom I please myself with trying to realize the face of medieval England,' he once told a lecture audience:

> The many chaces and great woods, the stretches of common tillage and common pasture quite unenclosed...the scarcity of bridges, and people using ferries instead, or fords where they could; the little towns

> well be-churched, often walled; the villages just where they are now (except for those that have nothing but the church left to tell of them); their churches, some big and handsome, some small and curious, but all crowded with altars and furniture, and gay with pictures and ornament; the many religious houses, with their glorious architecture; the beautiful manor-houses, some of them castles once....How strange it would be to us if we could be landed in fourteenth-century England.[47]

Morris channelled his visions of the past into his political books *A Dream of John Ball* (1888) and *News from Nowhere* (1890), both of which feature time-travelling narrators. In the former, the narrator is transported back to the time of the Peasants' Revolt of 1341, thereby linking socialist struggles past and present. In the latter, he wakes in the future, which he finds to be a communist utopia in a medieval-style setting, a place with no private property, no monetary system, no marriage or divorce, no courts and no prisons. The narrator of *News from Nowhere* first begins to realize that something is different when he notices that the ugly modern bridge over which he had walked the evening before has been replaced by a stone structure that far surpasses even Florence's Ponte Vecchio in beauty – and which was built, he is told, in 2003.[48] This narrative technique allowed Morris to construct utopian mind-palaces which he could wander around and scrutinize, describing material things in loving detail, from an entire medieval town 'untouched from the days of its builders of old' to beautiful wrought steel belt-buckles, bright pewter pots and carved oak chairs.[49] His vision of near-equality between the sexes, an absence of authority and a happy balance between work, life and art for all may be framed by an environment of medieval-style architecture, interiors and furniture, but it has little to do with the realities of medieval life as most people would have experienced it. Morris used selective aspects of the pre-industrial world as the building blocks for his future utopia, such as cooperative work and the skilled labour of ordinary craftsmen, along with an absence of miserable urban slums built for factory workers; the other materials he drew from his intensely idealistic imagination.

Burne-Jones never fell out of love with the legendary past. The large-scale projects of his final years were often Arthurian ones, just like his very first in Oxford, in which he sought to draw a medievalizing curtain

CHAPTER V

The Arming and Departure of the Knights, one of six Arthurian tapestries commissioned in 1890 from Morris & Co. for the dining room of Stanmore Hall in Middlesex.

over a distressingly brash modern world. 'I have designed many pictures that are to be painted in Avalon,' he announced to his studio assistant Thomas Rooke in 1886; 'secure me a famous wall, for I have much to say.'[50] He said it at epic length in *The Last Sleep of Arthur in Avalon*, a vast painting upon which he worked for seventeen years. It remained unfinished when he died in 1898; he once wryly remarked that he did not really expect to complete it until around 1970.[51] Perhaps it was unfinishable. Depicting King Arthur surrounded by attendants and lying in a golden tomb in an eerie state of death-that-is-not-death, it was Burne-Jones's impossibly protracted farewell to the once vigorous and commanding mythical figure who had presided over his entire working life. The painting's sheer scale – six and a half metres across – made it a kind of knightly challenge in itself: to conjure up the complex and subtle Arthurian world of the artist's imagination armed only with oil paint, brushes and an expanse of canvas.

While the Kelmscott Chaucer project was underway, he and Morris also collaborated on six tapestries on the subject of the quest for the Holy Grail, the interlinked stories that come towards the end of Malory's *Morte d'Arthur* and relate how the knights set out from the Round Table on their separate journeys – another valedictory subject. 'Back to our old things', said Morris – though whether with satisfaction or with a melancholy apprehension of the passing of time is impossible to say.[52] The tapestries, woven at Morris & Co.'s works in Merton Abbey, were commissioned by a wealthy captain of industry, William Knox D'Arcy, to hang in the dining room of Stanmore Hall, a place Morris described disapprovingly as a 'sham Gothic house of near fifty year ago'.[53] Burne-Jones even supplied set and costume designs for *King Arthur*, a play by Joseph Comyns Carr that opened in 1895 at the Lyceum Theatre in London with Henry Irving as Arthur and Ellen Terry as Guinevere – although he did so with distinct reservations, and refused to enter into practical discussions about the realization of his drawings. How could the Arthurian dream that had sustained and protected his spirit for so many years with its ineffable feelings of glory, chivalry and romance not be violated by the demands of a modern commercial production?[54]

'I can't expect people to feel about the subject as I do, and have always,' he lamented. 'It is such a sacred land to me that nothing in the world touches it in comparison.'[55] Edward Burne-Jones's vision of the past was enchanted. He may once have tried to break the illusion, but the magic that overwhelmed him one afternoon on an Oxford river bank never left him.

The room is crowded and tense. A question has been asked of a little fair-haired boy, just seven or eight years old, so small he has been given a footstool upon which to stand so he can be seen more clearly. He is a touching figure in his blue silk suit; hands clasped behind his back, he is ready, even eager, to answer. Everyone's eyes are now fixed upon him – that is, except for two pairs. One belongs to his sister. She is perhaps two years older – old enough to know what is happening – and hers are overflowing with tears. The other belongs to an impassive, thin-faced clerk sitting at the table who looks down at the notes he is making. In the hush while the boy takes a breath you can almost hear the clerk's pen scratching over the paper. Near the door – which is guarded by two soldiers – the boy's mother half turns away in despair but cannot drag her eyes from her son. A Parliamentarian soldier in a buff coat, cuirass and long riding boots sprawls on a chair and stares hard at the boy's face. Three other men wearing the sober clothes of Puritans gaze at his features from the opposite side of the table with an intensity of purpose that seems to fill the room like a vapour. A room that, incidentally, is in the boy's home, though you would not guess it from the conviction with which these men occupy it. Sitting at the table and facing him is a man – not old, perhaps in his thirties – who leans forward and rests his chin on his folded hands, smiling slightly, as a kind schoolmaster might. Talk to me, his manner implies – confide in me – and I shall listen with sympathy. 'And', he had begun – how that little word softened the question that followed – 'when did you last see your father?'

Does the little Royalist boy answer truthfully, and in doing so bring disaster on his family? Or has his mother schooled him to fib, just this once, for the sake of dear papa and the King? It is impossible to say. But I cannot help fearing the worst.[56] The man who painted *And When Did You Last See Your Father?* (Plate XVI), William Frederick Yeames, was a visual storyteller with a razor-sharp feeling for suspense. In planning this work he sifted everything he could discover about the English Civil War, from individual clashes between Parliamentarians and Royalists to the costume of the time (although the suit worn by the boy being interrogated is an echo not directly of Van Dyck's portraits, but of Gainsborough's famous 1770 painting *The Blue Boy*, in which the boy is in seventeenth-century fancy dress; sometimes imitation has more resonance than the real thing).[57] From these ingredients, Yeames invented a fictional scenario of such emotional resonance that it is hard to believe we are not witnessing a scene from some Royalist household, just as the artist set it out. The painting was popular when it was exhibited at the Royal Academy in 1878, and reproductions circulated widely. The image became so well known that it was manipulated by political cartoonists, secure in the knowledge that Yeames's composition would be recognized. It was even recreated as a waxwork – an accolade awarded to few oil paintings – and exhibited at Madame Tussaud's for over a hundred years, only being taken off display in 1989.[58]

Yeames was not an artist of the avant-garde. Far from it: he belonged to an informal group of painters known as the St John's Wood Clique, founded in 1863 and named after the area of London in which most of them lived. The members courted popular success. Working on small-scale canvases suitable for domestic interiors, they specialized in depicting scenes from British history that ranged from the solemn to the humorous and anecdotal; one critic remarked that their subjects occupied a 'debatable ground between home-life and history'.[59] Yeames's other subjects included *The Meeting of Sir Thomas More with his Daughter after his Sentence to Death* (1863), while another member, David Wilkie Wynfield, was responsible for *The Last Days of Elizabeth: When the Queen Groweth Sad, Mopish and Melancholy* (1865). In 1866, the group rented Hever Castle in Kent for the summer, which served both as a background for their paintings and a site for convivial gatherings that often involved dressing up in historical costume; Wynfield, also an amateur photographer, had high hopes of capturing on camera the ghost of Anne Boleyn, who was said to haunt the premises.[60] *And When Did You Last See Your Father?* can be seen as a swansong for a century of paintings that reimagined scenes from British history, with the Civil War in particular a seemingly bottomless source of dramatic incident. Over the course of the nineteenth century nearly sixty paintings on the theme were exhibited at the Royal Academy alone, not

Self-portrait by David Wilkie Wynfield, 1860s.

to mention many more that were devoted specifically to Charles I, Oliver Cromwell, Cavaliers, Roundheads or Puritans.[61] By the late 1870s it was, frankly, hard to say anything new. And yet despite the conservatism of Yeames's picture, it has a new air – one of suspenseful drama, of frozen time. *And When Did You Last See Your Father?* is an oil painting that has much of the past about it, and yet also reveals the artist's exposure to a very modern artistic medium: photography.

A photographic self-portrait of Wynfield shows him wearing a Tudor-style velvet cap and a cloak fastened at the collar, studying a small book. He could be sitting for a portrait by Hans Holbein; in fact he probably had in mind the pose of a specific figure, the scholarly young John More, absorbed in his book, in Holbein's group portrait of Sir Thomas More and his family (1527–8).[62] Wynfield took photographs of other members of the St John's Wood Clique, too: Philip Hermogenes Calderon wearing a ruff; George Dunlop Leslie dressed as a Tudor courtier; George Adolphus Storey vaguely got up as a medieval friar; Yeames himself in a silk cap and brocade coat. Outside the Clique, Wynfield photographed John Everett Millais dressed as Dante Alighieri, George Du Maurier sporting armour and the historian James Anthony Froude in a high Puritan collar, strangely well complemented by his mid-Victorian chin-beard. When he published a selection in 1864, Wynfield described these portraits as '*Taken in the Style of the Old Masters*', but there was more to it than that. In putting on fancy dress and adopting a pose that recalled a Tudor painting, Wynfield was wrapping himself up in the past. There would have been nothing strange about it if it had been an oil painting, a medium with a sense of its own importance that applauded knowing references and visual echoes. In using photography, though, he was bringing the wires of the past and the present together and creating a distinct and unsettling charge.

Wynfield was not alone in training the camera's lens on the past. Perhaps the oldest camera negative of all, made in 1835 by William Fox Talbot, was of a latticed oriel window at his home, Lacock Abbey – a building founded in the early thirteenth century and converted into a house when it was sold in the wake of the dissolution of the monasteries in the sixteenth. Frederick Scott Archer, who invented the wet-collodion process that produced crisper images than any other photographic method, demonstrated it by photographing the ivy-clad ruins of Kenilworth Castle, while in the 1850s Benjamin Brecknell Turner and Roger Fenton both took their cameras to the ruins of Rievaulx Abbey.[63] The more swiftly technology moved forward, the more compelling, it seemed, the material presence of the olden times became.

In mid-nineteenth-century London, the seven Pattle sisters were celebrated for their verve, cleverness, eccentricity and high social spirits. One of them, the photographer Julia Margaret Cameron, possessed these qualities in highly concentrated form. Her great-niece, Virginia Woolf, remembered her as 'a terrifying apparition' and quoted the artist Mary Seton Watts, who described her as 'short and squat, with none of the Pattle grace and beauty about her, though more than her share of their passionate energy and wilfulness. Dressed in dark clothes, stained with chemicals from her photography (and smelling of them too), with a plump eager face and a voice husky, and a little harsh, yet in some way compelling and even charming.'[64] Cameron was commanding and persuasive. 'The carpenter', Woolf recalled, 'and the Crown Prince of Prussia alike must sit as still as stones in the attitudes she chose....'[65] She would attach weighty swans' wings to children's shoulders and order them to play the parts of angels leaning over the ramparts of heaven. When the distinguished botanical artist Marianne North paid the Camerons a visit she was made to stand 'with spiky coconut branches running into my head' while Cameron instructed her to 'look perfectly natural'. Cameron had not taken up photography until her late forties, after her daughter gave her a set of photographic equipment; over the ten years following, she produced some of the most original compositions of the era. To someone with her profoundly independent manner of looking at the world, there was no reason for one genre not to blend into another: if words from a poem inspired her to create a photograph, the resulting composition would be far too independent to be called an illustration; when she made a portrait, it might more accurately be described as a poetic meditation on a person.[66] She photographed her friend and Isle of Wight neighbour Tennyson in profile, each unruly tendril of hair expressing poetic genius (a great favourite of his, he wryly called this image 'The Dirty Monk'); the astronomer John Herschel appears as an otherworldly being with a halo of white hair, profound wisdom shining from his melancholy, luminous eyes.

Wynfield's portraits of his friends in historical costume – perhaps Cameron's greatest inspiration – had demonstrated how references to historical periods could add qualities of depth and seriousness to the present, and Cameron habitually concealed contemporary clothes with drapery. In 1874, however, an opportunity arose to delve deeper into the past. Tennyson asked Cameron if she would make illustrations for a new edition of *Idylls of the King*, his cycle of poems on Arthurian themes.[67] She threw herself into the project, making nearly two hundred and fifty exposures for the handful she needed. She roped in her husband, friends, nieces and visitors to pose, taking enormous care to fit models to particular Arthurian characters and even upsetting social propriety by her uncompromising attitude. 'Boatmen', recalled Woolf with a degree

Photographer unknown, Princess Louise and Mr Cowell posing in a scene from Tennyson's *Idylls of the King*, 1891.

of snobbery, 'were turned into King Arthur; village girls into Queen Guenevere.'[68] Sir Lancelot proved particularly difficult to track down, until Cameron discovered a porter at Yarmouth Pier with a face and physique that tempered strength and nobility with the requisite sensitivity.[69] She was, inevitably, disappointed by the way the photographs – just three in the end – appeared in Tennyson's book: it was cheaper and more practical for publishers to reproduce images by having them engraved on wood at a reduced size, so that image and type could be set and printed together, than to insert expensive photographic prints. Cameron's basic compositions remained, but not even the most skilful wood-engraver could translate their subtle atmosphere and her deliberate use of soft focus. Matters were not left there, however. Tennyson himself suggested she should publish a selection of her Arthurian photographs at their full size, which she did, in two volumes, each print accompanied by relevant lines from the poems reproduced in her own handwriting.[70] The images do more than capture specific moments in *Idylls* – they seem to express the essence of each character. A melancholy but resolute King Arthur, in chainmail and plumed helmet, clutches his sword-hilt; Lancelot and Guinevere sorrowfully prepare to part; Vivien bewitches Merlin.

Looking at the photographs today is an unsettling experience. There is more than a hint of the Victorian dressing-up box about them; Cameron's husband, Charles, for instance, who posed as Merlin, has quite clearly had his long white beard extended with cotton wool in some images (he was frequently seized with fits of giggling during the sessions).[71] But at the same time, Cameron's close-up focus on individuals, so different from the crowded set-pieces beloved of the St John's Wood Clique, brings a psychological charge so intense that any initial impression of theatricality begins to fall away. Mood and atmosphere replace anecdote and incident as Cameron brings viewers face to face with her subjects.

Episodes from Tennyson's *Idylls* were popular with those planning *tableaux vivants*, which, having begun as staged representations of well-known paintings, were quickly adopted by the aristocracy as private entertainments. Such *tableaux* were even among the amusements arranged for Queen Victoria: in January 1891, the family, then staying at Osborne House on the Isle of Wight, devised an elaborate scene from Tennyson's *Idylls*. Princess Louise posed as the tragic Elaine, who loved Sir Lancelot and died of a broken heart. Not a hair out of place from her fashionable coiffure, she lies in a flower-decked boat in front of a curtain painted with a rocky shore and tall castle walls, while a heavily draped oarsman (a Mr Cowell) gets ready to row her towards Camelot. Naturally, the affecting *tableau* was captured on camera.

VI
NOSTALGIA

20 October 1825: a cold day, with snow on Reigate Hill. Not far from the banks of the River Mole in the Weald of Surrey stands an old farmhouse surrounded by trees. But where you would expect the purposeful bustle of a busy farm, today there is a different sort of commotion: the contents are to be auctioned. The farmer – although he and his forebears have been here a great many years – has given up and left, and now strangers pass through the ancient wooden door with notebooks and measuring tapes, casting keen glances over the family's belongings. In the dim rooms are clothes presses, bedsteads, chests of drawers, joint stools and a great oak table, once burnished by the daily pressure of forearms and elbows; all now stand dusty and awkward, as though they know they are about to be jolted about on the back of a carter's wagon on their way to an unknown future.

William Cobbett has ducked his height through the door and is now edging his bulk between the furniture. He looks around in dismay: everything about the farmhouse's basic structure speaks of what he will later describe in his journal as '*plain manners* and *plentiful living*'; the solidity and gently worn edges of the tables and chairs on which he places his hands can tell him that. But here it is clear that in recent times the old has not been honoured. All appears to be 'in a state of decay and nearly of *disuse*'. It is, he thinks – possibly out loud – a symptom of what is happening everywhere: where formerly farm workers would troop in and sit with the family at the board and be lodged as well as fed, now they are given wages and, with this insufficient money, have to furnish and maintain their own households. And at the same time the family have developed pretensions to gentility, which has left all too obvious a mark on the house: 'worst of all,' says Cobbett, 'there was a *parlour*. Aye, and a *carpet* and *bell-pull* too!...I daresay', he continues, 'it has been '*Squire*

Charington and the *Miss* Charingtons; and not plain Master Charington, and his son Hodge, and his daughter Betty Charington.' It is too much. Before he goes back out into the yard to his horse, Cobbett stops again at the long oak table. He thinks of its history and the 'thousands of scores of bacon, and thousand of bushels of bread' that had been eaten from it, and has an ominous premonition that it will be bought by 'some stock-jobber' – Cobbett's favourite term of abuse – and made to serve as a bridge over 'an artificial river in his cockney garden'. '*By ------- it shant*', he exclaims, and decides to ask a friend to buy the table for him, so he can keep it 'for the good it has done in the world'.[1] It was a piece of old England that could be salvaged, and he could not bring himself to let all it symbolized be forgotten.

Cobbett describes this incident in the journal that was published in 1830 as *Rural Rides*, which describes how over a number of excursions on horseback he took the temperature of the countryside, listening to 'what gentlemen, farmers, tradesmen, journeymen, labourers, women, girls, boys, and all have to say; reasoning with some, laughing with others, and observing all that passes'.[2] It seems safe to say that if Cobbett could have travelled forward in time to 1925, he would have been vociferously appalled. Despite what a contemporary described as his resemblance to 'a great English yeoman of the old time', Cobbett was a radical, on the side of the farm labourers forced to endure miserable living conditions. What he perceived to be happening around him in the mid-1820s – rural labourers being forced to look for work in the 'great Wen', as he called London; stock-jobbers moving to the country with their city attitudes and ignorance of rural traditions – had gained momentum during the Victorian era, taking place on a scale that would have astonished even him. By the mid-nineteenth century, the age-old balance of town and country had been thrown out of kilter as more and more people moved to urban areas. Cities continued to expand exponentially, spreading far from their centres into suburbs and engulfing villages. The young architect Clough Williams-Ellis wrote *England and the Octopus* (1929) in outraged protest against the tentacles of arterial roads, accompanied by ribbon developments, reaching far into what had once been the country. Rural England, it seemed, was being diminished year by year. What was being lost? Meadows, yes, and old farmhouses, heaths and watermills, woods and green lanes. But there was something even more important at stake in the country. It was what Cobbett's farmhouse table symbolized: in the face of all this change, what needed urgently to be saved was a sense of the past.

From the study of Max Gate, the house he had built just outside Dorchester, Thomas Hardy oversaw a new, collected edition of his novels, published between 1895 and 1897. As he cast his mind back over the 'Wessex' about which he had been writing for the past twenty-five years and the occupations, beliefs and superstitions of its people, it was with a sad awareness of how far the modern world had intruded into the most apparently secluded corners of country life. The action of Hardy's novels takes place in what he called 'a partly real, partly dream-country' in which his characters often gaze out over actual landscapes and inhabit existing buildings – many of which were fast disappearing.[3] Hardy had set *Far from the Madding Crowd* (1874) in Weatherbury, which he had based so closely on Puddletown that many locations had once been identifiable, until most of the thatched and dormered cottages were demolished in favour of new houses. Time-honoured customs were disappearing, too. As he wrote in his preface to the new edition, 'The practice of divination by Bible and key, the regarding of valentines as things of serious import, the shearing-supper, the long smock-frocks, and the harvest-home have, too, nearly disappeared in the wake of the old houses.'[4]

Hardy may have been pessimistic, but his readers, encouraged by numerous guidebooks to 'Hardy's Wessex', set out to visit this enchanted region, eager to follow in the footsteps of Tess, Bathsheba Everdene and members of the Mellstock Quire.[5] It was not just literary tourism, but a seeking out of pockets of the past, of quiet places in which the old ways could be imagined to continue undisturbed. The American-born novelist Henry James, out for a walk with a friend in 1877, had been beguiled by his sense of how the landscapes of this 'old, small country' seemed 'charged and interfused' with a long legacy of human presence.[6] The more people left their villages to settle in towns, the more they felt nostalgic for the country. From being an industrial place where crops grew and were harvested, mill-wheels turned and livestock grazed – the kind of working landscape John Constable had painted in the 1820s and

Myles Birket Foster, 'The Country Inn', in
Birket Foster's *Pictures of English Landscape* (1862).

1830s – in the second half of the century, the country was transformed in the imagination into an unchanging haunt of ancient peace. Watercolour became a popular medium for landscape views: its translucency, clear bright colours and capacity for haziness were ideally suited to dream-like pastoral images. Among the most successful watercolourists of the Victorian era was Myles Birket Foster, whose picturesque thatched cottages, mossy banks and shady lanes, inhabited by well-fed country folk in clean smocks, were popular with a picture-buying public who did not have to worry about a stray spark from the chimney setting their thatch on fire or deep mud making the road impassable; a sunken lane he painted at Hambledon in Surrey was subsequently renamed One Hundred Guinea Lane after the staggering price the work fetched. Foster distilled his romantic vision in a book of prints, *Birket Foster's Pictures of English Landscape*, published in 1862 and accompanied by poems 'illustrating' the images by Tom Taylor. The publication did much to reinforce popular perceptions of the countryside: here is an old chair-mender at a cottage door, hay-fields and gleaners and cheerful hayrick-building, smithies and market carts, pools with cattle and ducks and a picturesquely dilapidated old windmill that would have shocked Constable, a miller's son.[7] Foster chose views that gently suggested continuity. And yet in Taylor's poems, the past and the present cannot help but bump into one another. Sometimes these meetings provoke nostalgia. 'The farm-yard of my boyhood! Is it truth', the poet asks, 'That farm-yards were more pleasant then than now? / Or is't the golden morning-light of youth / My memories with a glory doth endow?' Give me a moment to reflect among the bee-haunted limes, then let me hazard a guess. But sometimes change is tangible, even shocking. The old Red Lion that Foster depicts in 'The Country Inn' – where formerly one could be sure of entertainment and simple country hospitality – 'home-brewed ale, sheets clean, if coarse, / And bacon and eggs in last resource' – has, says Taylor, already disappeared. Foster must have been imagining things. The octopus had already extended a malignant tentacle to disrupt this unchanging bucolic world, and the golden age has been replaced – as it always is – by one of iron.

> But now we are ruled by the iron-ways,
> Where no Red Lion swings from its tree;

At the Station Hotel the traveller stays,
And few are the pence and scanty the praise
That come to the landlord of other days,[8]

The old Red Lion might have been a casualty of the modern world, its water trough emptied and its duck pond filled in, but if Old England could be magicked into being with a paintbrush, it could also, surely, be built anew from timber, lath and plaster. In 1863 Foster did just that, designing and building a large Tudor-style house at Witley, near Godalming in Surrey, that he called The Hill. He used weathered tiles salvaged from old cottages for the roof, and employed William Morris and his firm to design tapestries, wallpapers, stained glass, tiles and furniture for the panelled rooms.[9] The Hill was just as much an artistic creation as one of his carefully stage-managed watercolours.

The Hill was not a lone monument to the days of old – far from it. Tudor, Elizabethan, Jacobean and Queen Anne-style houses – and some that were all four at once – became fashionable. Among the most extraordinary of Tudor revival houses of the 1860s was the imposing Cragside outside Rothbury in Northumberland, designed by Norman Shaw for William Armstrong, the immensely wealthy founder of the Armstrong-Whitworth armaments firm. Cragside combined an imposing if rambling exterior of Tudor gables and half-timbering with the most up-to-date facilities: it was the first house in the world to be lit by hydroelectric power and even had an early version of a dishwasher. Towards the end of the nineteenth century and into the twentieth, taste shifted to simpler, more rustic architecture that suggested the Elizabethan cottage of the imagination, a Merrie England of wood and red brick: exaggeratedly tall, decorative chimneys, jettied first floors, half-timbering infilled with herringbone brickwork and even brand-new thatched roofs became common sights in villages and down leafy lanes. One architect of neo-Tudor and Jacobean buildings, Blunden Shadbolt, who often incorporated materials from old barns and cottages into his buildings, created such convincing pastiches that some were even mistaken by English Heritage's early listing inspectors for real survivals.[10] In the hands of architects such as C. F. A. Voysey and Sir Edwin Lutyens, the essential characteristics of sixteenth- and seventeenth-century buildings were infused into elegant and liveable houses that seemed to harbour the deep calm of Old England; their owners could revel in continuity with the past and a patriotic espousal of English values while being protected from the misery of rotting and crumbling timbers, chronic draughts and disintegrating wattle and daub.[11] Many an owner of a Tudor revival house would have hung watercolours of picturesquely dilapidated cottages by Birket Foster or Helen Allingham on their newly built walls without a trace of irony.[12] Features on these new houses in the pages of Edward Hudson's influential magazine *Country Life* further popularized the style. Hudson promoted Lutyens in particular as an example of how contemporary architecture could successfully be steered by tradition.

In *Pillar to Post* (1938), the cartoonist Osbert Lancaster coined the term 'Stockbroker's Tudor' to describe the substantial newly built houses that reflected a profound and 'widespread...post-war devotion to the olde-worlde'. 'Brewer's Tudor', meanwhile, was his name for the style particularly applied to the 'bogus Tudor bars' where, in John Betjeman's 1937 poem 'Slough', 'bald young clerks' gather 'And talk of sport and makes of cars'.[13] The idea of 'homes fit for heroes' – a promise made by the Liberal prime minister, Lloyd George, in a speech delivered the day after Armistice – drove the construction of houses based, however notionally, on traditional English precedents. Modernist houses with flat roofs and expanses of plate glass were associated with avant-garde German design; though not unheard of in England, they were distinctly rare. In the 1920s and 1930s, cheaper construction methods and the expansion of towns into commuter suburbs led to architectural innovations in smaller houses. Lancaster mined the irony of the situation:

> And to-day when the passer-by is a little unnerved at being suddenly confronted with a hundred and fifty accurate reproductions of Anne Hathaway's cottage, each complete with central-heating and garage, he should pause to reflect on the extraordinary fact that all over the country the latest and most scientific methods of mass-production are being utilized to turn out a stream of old oak beams, leaded window-panes and small discs of bottle-glass, all structural devices which our ancestors lost no time in abandoning as soon as an increase in wealth and knowledge enabled them to do so.[14]

Infatuation with the past, it seemed, could turn the most conventional commuter into a Catherine Morland.

F. L. Griggs, *Ex Anglia Perdita*, 1921.

Suburban developments of Tudor-style houses were one thing; unchecked building in historic town and city centres, which saw jaunty new structures popping up cheek by jowl with venerable survivals, was quite another. At the beginning of *Highways and Byways in Oxford and the Cotswolds* (1916) the author, Herbert A. Evans, offers a striking solution to the problem of modern buildings jarring with their traditional architectural surroundings: don't look at them. Just shut your eyes. And, if you wish, you can think of J. M. W. Turner: specifically, a view he painted in 1808 of the London coach making its way down Headington Hill towards Oxford. What, speculates Evans, would the passengers have seen from the windows at that time? They would have passed the picturesque houses of St Clement's, while in the middle distance Magdalen College, with its New Buildings (only some fifty years old at that date, but still very fine) and its tower and bridge would be the first to become visible; and then, from the High Street, the towers of Merton, Christ Church, All Saints', St Mary's, and the dome of the Radcliffe Camera would all appear. But not any more.

> All this is altered now: you take your seat in the express at Paddington, and have hardly scanned your newspaper through, when you are gliding past reservoirs and gas works into Oxford station. If the stranger is resolute enough to close his eyes at Kennington Island [just south of Oxford] and refuse to open them till his cab deposits him at his hotel, he will be the happier man.[15]

The 'Highways and Byways' series, published by Macmillan between 1898 and 1948, were guidebooks to regions of Britain that struck a conversational tone with their readers; turning their pages one encounters verses, anecdotes and history along with folklore and legend. They are handsome books, lavishly illustrated with atmospheric views, whether of Oxford and Cambridge colleges or charmingly crooked cottages in village streets. The artist who illustrated *Oxford and the Cotswolds*, among many more in the series, was Frederick Landseer Maur Griggs – 'Maur' being the baptismal name he adopted when, in 1912, he was received into the Roman Catholic Church. Griggs had always felt the romance of the past; as a child he had fallen under the architectural spell of the chapel he had attended with his parents, which although newly built, was in the Gothic style. Browsing in the Hitchen Mechanical Institute library as a

The early music pioneer Arnold Dolmetsch
in fancy dress, playing a lute, 1895.

schoolboy, he discovered the visionary work of Samuel Palmer, who as a young artist drew and painted the English landscape as though he had crawled through a gap in a hedge and found himself in a paradise of some long-ago time.[16] When Griggs converted to Catholicism, his Palmerish sense of the immanence of the past sharpened into an intense nostalgia for a pre-Reformation England that gave his etchings of churches and cathedrals a strange spiritual dimension.

As though stumbling on a wrinkle in time, he created imaginary or composite views that had all the appearance of topography, but in which walls and towers that had long since collapsed were restored to their medieval grandeur. His etching *Ex Anglia Perdita* (1921) – from lost England – goes even further, showing the towers, windows and buttresses of an imaginary medieval abbey; in Griggs's vision, the past returns with triumphant spiritual authority, tempered with nostalgia. The dissolution had come and destroyed it, just as the First World War came and changed the world; but it could be restored on paper.[17] *Ex Anglia Perdita* was the first etching to be entirely printed on the press he had installed at his home in Chipping Campden; 'for all its faults it aint a bad bit of Old England', he remarked.[18] Griggs was a master of the etching process, and by skilful inking and wiping of his printing plates he created intensely expressive depths of blurry evening shade and atmospheres of softening afternoon haze that make his images all but vibrate with the plangent cello notes of nostalgia.

For all his passion for painting and poetry, William Morris was thought by many to be more or less impervious to music.[19] Morris himself, writing to Burne-Jones in 1896, told him how much he was enjoying his garden, and continues, 'though you think I don't like music, I assure you that the rooks and the blackbirds have been a great consolation to me'.[20] Morris was, however, rehearsing a friendly old joke: two years earlier Burne-Jones had instigated a dramatic change in his friend's musical appreciation. He had persuaded Morris to accompany him to a concert in Dulwich of early English music performed by the French-born musician Arnold Dolmetsch, who had studied at the Brussels Conservatoire under the appropriately named Henri Vieuxtemps. What did Dolmetsch and his group play that evening? Viol music by Orlando Gibbons or Henry Purcell, perhaps, or ayres for the lute by Thomas Campion or John Dowland? Whatever it was, it touched Morris in a way later music never had. 'He understood this music at once', recalled Dolmetsch, 'and his emotion was so strong that he was moved to tears! He had found the lost Art!'[21] When Morris lay dying at Kelmscott House, his home in west London, Dolmetsch rolled up with a pair of virginals and played him a pavane and a galliard by the Renaissance composer William Byrd. These notes seemed to carry the essence of the past; played on a period instrument, they were the same sounds, or near enough, that people would have heard three hundred years before. Morris 'broke into a cry of joy at the opening phrase, and after the two pieces had been repeated at his request, was so deeply stirred that he could not bear to hear any more'.[22]

In order to play the early music he had discovered in the British Museum – in particular a manuscript known as *Henry VIII's Music Book*, containing 109 songs and instrumental pieces – Dolmetsch needed instruments that had become obsolete.[23] So he began to make his own. In 1893 he constructed a lute, and he went on to make copies of virginals, clavichords, harpsichords, recorders and viols. At the concerts he staged with his family, medieval and Renaissance music was heard on instruments of the period, with the performers often in sixteenth-century dress. The musicologist Sir Henry Hadow remarked that Dolmetsch had 'opened the door to a forgotten treasure-house of beauty'.[24] Composers began to turn to these long-forgotten predecessors to make a new kind of music for the twentieth century. In his *Fantasia on a Theme of Thomas Tallis* for string orchestra, first performed in 1910, Ralph Vaughan Williams wove gleaming threads from the sixteenth-century master of polyphony into his opulent, swelling composition, using the old to give lustre – and some of Spenser's 'grace...and auctoritie', perhaps – to the new. Tallis is revived within the piece, precious ballast stowed in the heart of Vaughan Williams's stately barque.[25]

The landscape began to shape music as it shaped the other arts at this time, its prospects, breezes and birdsong telling a new – or perhaps old – story. It is hard to hear Edward Elgar's compositions without thinking of the Malvern Hills; Vaughan Williams's song-cycle *On Wenlock Edge* (1909) gave new form to the landscapes of A. E. Housman's *A Shropshire Lad* (1896); and on the eve of the First World War, the lark ascended. But sometimes pastoral music does not have to be sought out on the downs or in libraries; sometimes it simply walks straight up your garden path and strikes up a tune. The young composer Cecil Sharp first witnessed Morris dancers performing on Boxing Day in 1899 while staying with his mother-in-law at Headington, and, excited by the rasping notes and see-sawing energy of the concertina tunes, he sat down with the musician and noted down some of the pieces. Four years later, in a village in Somerset, he overheard a friend's gardener quietly singing the folk song 'The Seeds of Love' and got the words and tune from him in exchange for a pipeful of tobacco. This brush with the old songs sent him – and Vaughan Williams, who had his own epiphany the same year, in Essex, when he first heard the folksong 'Bushes and Briars' – far and wide collecting many hundreds of songs from old men in villages, who had learned them from their fathers, who had learned them from theirs. Like Percy's ballads a century before, these songs were seen as precious scraps of Old England. Having flourished quite separately from the classical musical tradition, they were now drafted in to revitalize it by leading composers Frederick Delius, Vaughan Williams, Gustav Holst and, later, Benjamin Britten; Morris's vision that the homespun, unpretentious rustic past might shape the future was being realized.

Sounds of a different nature were heard near the south coast, and they were loud enough to wake the dead. The heavy artillery of the Great War boomed across the Channel to English hillsides; it was the first time that noise from the continent had carried so far. Hardy anticipated it with a poem published in May of 1914, 'Channel Firing', written in response to gunnery practice and narrated by a skeleton disturbed by the noise – although it might almost be the land itself speaking:

> That night, your great guns, unawares,
> Shook all our coffins as we lay,
> And broke the chancel window squares,
> We thought it was the Judgement Day...
>
> Again the guns disturbed the hour,
> Roaring their readiness to avenge,
> As far inland as Stourton Tower,
> And Camelot, and starlit Stonehenge.[26]

Existing nostalgia for a vanishing rural past gained a mystic intensity. Hardy's Stourton Tower is a folly in Somerset also called King Alfred's Tower, designed in the 1760s to commemorate the end of the Seven Years' War with France and the accession of George III; it was built near Egbert's Stone, where Alfred rallied the Saxons before the battle of Ethandun at which the Danish army was defeated. At the sonic boom of the guns, King Alfred would stir, and King Arthur awake at last; even Stonehenge, that great cosmic conductor connecting the heavens to the earth, would know of it. These ancient forces in the land would rise up to defend England.

In 1914, R. Hippisley Cox published *The Green Roads of England*, in which he wrote of a network of ancient trackways connecting hillforts and other prehistoric features of the landscape. In a highly critical review of the second edition of 1923 (that had been enlarged with maps and illustrations), the eminent archaeologist O. G. S. Crawford was still forced to acknowledge that the book proved 'a demand for "popular" books dealing with ancient roads and earthworks'.[27] If, two years later, anyone had been foolhardy enough to ask Crawford to review a book by Alfred Watkins called *The Old Straight Track*, they would no doubt have received a crisp refusal; in fact, after he founded the journal *Antiquity* in 1927 he would not even accept advertisements for the book. *The Old Straight Track* set out Watkins's theory of 'ley lines', a network of alignments, some corresponding to discernible tracks, that connected standing stones, hillforts, mounds, beacons and other prominent sites. To archaeologists, this was unscientific speculation and coincidence – in any case, they asked, how could these so-called leys fail to clip numerous sites, in a land in which such features are so densely distributed? But Watkins's ideas struck a chord with a public newly engaged with the archaeological digs and discoveries reported by Crawford in his frequent articles in the *Observer*. They were intrigued by the notion that mysterious forces from deep antiquity might be active within the landscape, pulsing away like arteries and veins under its green skin. Ordnance Survey maps were studied with a new fervour as walks were planned along ancient leys and picnics taken to high spots in the hope that they might reverberate with profound spiritual significance. At a time of war and its aftermath, urban expansion and rapid change in the countryside, ley lines were an anchor down to the bedrock of unimaginable antiquity, which was too deep to be swayed by the currents of the present day.

XIV Edwin Landseer, double portrait of Queen Victoria and Prince Albert dressed as Edward III and his consort Queen Philippa, 1842.

XV 'The King in his Royal Robes wearing a Cap of Estate, 19th July 1821', Edward Scriven after James Stephanoff, plate from *The Coronation of his Most Sacred Majesty King George the Fourth* (London, 1837).

XVI William Frederick Yeames, *And When Did You Last See Your Father?*, 1878.

XVII May Morris, jewelled sleeve clasps designed to fasten puffed fabric in place, *c.* 1905. Morris was inspired by Holbein's portraits of the Tudor court.

XVIII Hanging embroidered by May Morris and assistants in silk yarns with young fruit trees and acanthus leaves, *c.* 1892–93. The design was stitched onto a panel of William Morris's green 'Oak Leaf' damask, creating a rich effect.

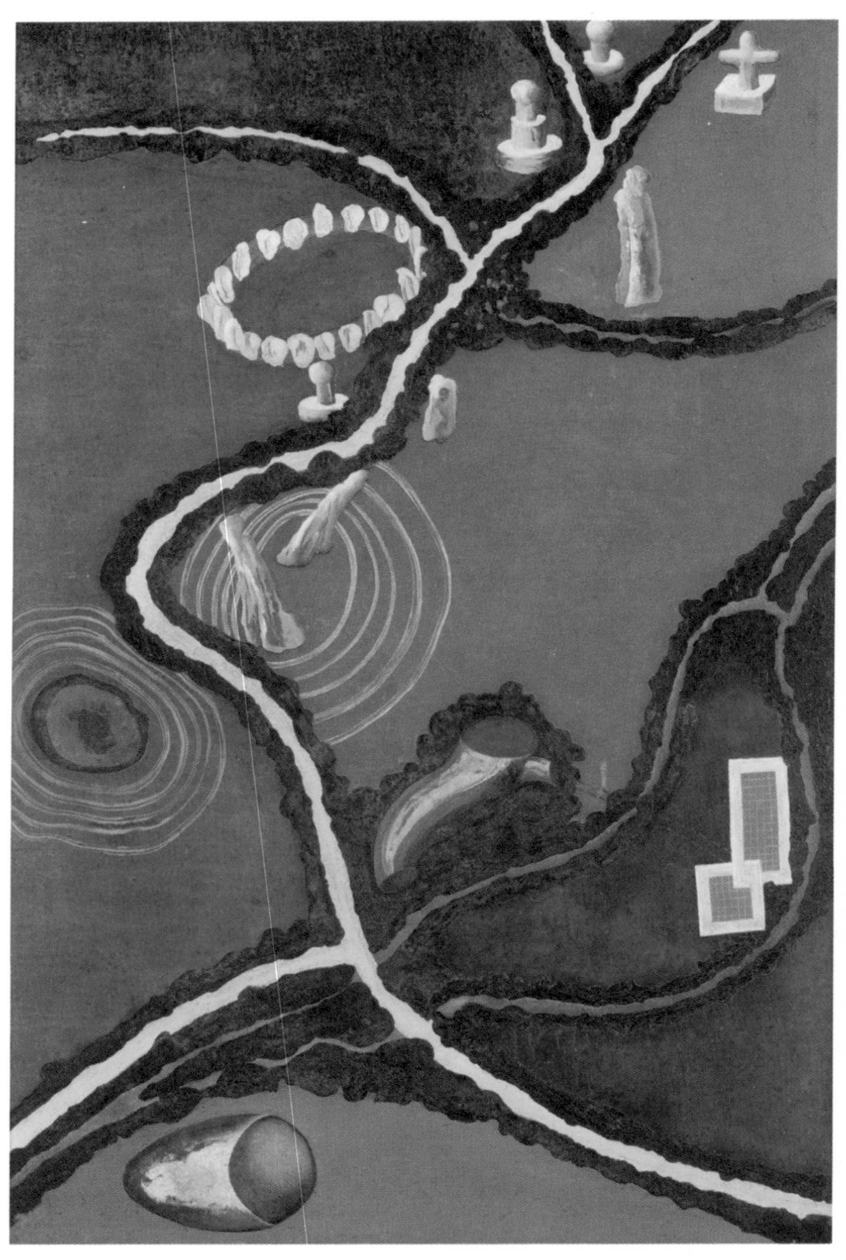

XIX Ithell Colquhoun, *Landscape with Antiquities (Lamorna)*, 1955.

XX John Piper, *Coventry Cathedral, 15 November 1940*, 1940.

XXI Lucina Douglas-Menzies, bedroom in Dennis Severs's house on Folgate Street in Spitalfields.

XXII Barbara Jones, *Savage's Yard, King's Lynn, Norfolk*, 1942, watercolour made for the wartime 'Recording Britain' project.

XXIII Untitled collage by Pauline Boty, *c.* 1964.

XXIV Tessa Farmer, *The Feast*, 2018.

XXV Lubaina Himid, 'The Herbalist', from *Naming the Money* (2004), installed in the Victoria and Albert Museum for the 2007 exhibition 'Uncomfortable Truths'.

DORSET

SCELIDOSAURUS HARRISONI: FORMER NATIVE

SHELL GUIDE

COMPILED
AND WRITTEN BY PAUL NASH

LONDON: ARCHITECTURAL PRESS,
9 QUEEN ANNE'S GATE, S.W.1

Title page to Paul Nash's *Shell Guide to Dorset* (1936).

Ley lines might, on the whole, have been wishful thinking; but there were plenty of tangible relics of prehistory in the landscape, and in the years following the First World War they began to exert a powerful attraction for artists. The landscape painter Paul Nash thought of his own practice as a continuation of ancient habits; reflecting on his career in his autobiography, he acknowledged that he had been 'hunting far afield over the wild country, to get my living out of the land as much as my ancestors ever had done'.[28] Nash had a surrealist's appreciation of the arresting oddity of standing stones in a landscape, or hill figures carved in the turf; they appealed to his love of charismatic objects such as gnarled fallen trees and bleached bones that invited attention and wonder. But more important still was their aura of ancientness, what Nash called their 'primal magic'.[29] The preoccupation with the presence of history in the landscape that prompted him to illustrate Sir Thomas Browne's *Hydriotaphia: Urn Buriall* (1932) also pervades Nash's *Shell Guide to Dorset* (1936), commissioned by the series' general editor, John Betjeman. It is probably the only regional guide to have a photograph of a Scelidosaurus on its title page; the dinosaur, which is shown stalking along a shingle beach, bold as brass, is labelled 'FORMER NATIVE', as though it had perhaps only recently moved away from the area.

Dinosaurs aside, Nash's Dorset is a place of deep enchantment. 'To pass through Chalbury at twilight', he writes, 'shut in by the ridged hills, seeing the long tombs cut against the afterglow, is to experience an almost unnerving feeling of the latent force of the past.' He writes of Maiden Castle as an awe-inspiring place, 'miraculously undisturbed', and of the unique atmosphere of the Iron Age hill fort at Badbury Rings with its crown of trees planted in concentric circles. 'I have read of enchanted places,' he writes,

> and at rare times come upon them, but I remember nothing so beautifully haunted as the wood in Badbury Rings. Long afterwards I read of the tradition that King Arthur's soul inhabited a raven's body which nested there – indeed it is one of the last nesting-places of the wild raven in England – but I needed no artificial stimulus to be impressed. Beyond the outer plateau the rings heave up and round in waves 40 feet high. A magic bird in a haunted wood, an ancient cliff washed by a sea changed into earth.

'There is', he concludes, 'scarcely anything lacking...'.[30] Legend, landscape and history combined for Nash to add an additional dimension to the country: an ongoing relationship with the deep past.

The Scelidosaurus caught on camera wittily sets the scene for Nash's sense that boundaries between past and present can easily dissolve. Nash sometimes played with this permeability, imagining prehistoric sites as they had been in antiquity, representing Avebury, for example, with its great avenue restored; his friend John Piper warped time in the same way in a lithograph of the site he made in 1944.[31] Nash also made the past modern in more subtle ways. Around 1937, he walked up the Berkshire downs to the prehistoric Uffington White Horse and trained his camera on its chalk contours; what from the other side of the vale resolves itself into a coherent image, in close-up can only be perceived in disconnected sections. 'Seen on its own hill', wrote Nash, 'it becomes an affair of violent foreshortenings or tapering perspectives more or less indecipherable.' Lines dip beneath undulations in the turf and are hidden; perspective distorts the whole. In one photograph, the horse's head is unnervingly close – its great blank eye gazing up to the heavens. Under the artist's scrutiny the white horse is reinvented as a modernist image, fractured and contingent. For Nash, though, such loss of perspective led to a more profound understanding of the spirit and history of the place:

> Once the rather futile game of 'picking out' the White Horse is abandoned, the documentary importance of the site fades, and the landscape asserts itself with all the force of its triumphant fusion of natural and artificial design. You then perceive a landscape of terrific animation whose bleak character and stark expression accord perfectly with its lonely situation on the summit of the bare downs.[32]

To feel the force of the past you had to be there in the landscape, up close. Nash, wrote the art critic Myfanwy Evans, 'has no interest in past as *past*, but the accumulated intenseness of the past as present is his special concern and joy'.[33]

Barbara Hepworth moved to Cornwall in 1939, at the outbreak of war. 'Unconquerable and strange,' she wrote of this monument-haunted landscape, 'and my God, how sculptural'.[34] Like Nash, she responded profoundly to the 'primal magic' of ancient sites and found ways of channelling their energy into her work, sometimes creating menhir-like sculptures that echoed the charismatic presence of standing stones. The surrealist Ithell Colquhoun experienced the same enchantment after she began to spend part of each year in Cornwall, at Vow Cave Studio, a hut near Penzance she had bought in 1946 and set about repairing. In the essays published together in 1957 as *The Living Stones*, she describes her exploration of Cornish landscapes and traditions and her discovery that in Cornwall every walk is a path through ancient myth and legend. Colquhoun sought out landscapes shaped by prehistoric hands and compared the degree of 'ancient power' they radiated, finding old wells and stone crosses particularly animated. She visited St Uny's Well and found it neglected and sad: 'Her strange powers, unused, seemed to hover about the grey hill, the unchannelled water, the rank leaf.

A presence that had once been drawn to participate in human affairs had now almost sunk back into soil, weather and plant.' She heard ghostly Celtic music, walked in haunted woods and sketched the annual ritual dance of the 'Obba 'Oss in Padstow.[35] For Colquhoun, the land itself had a 'psychic life' that depended on the nature of the rock from which it was constructed, whether granite, serpentine, slate, sandstone, limestone or chalk; each had 'their special personality dependent on the

Barbara Hepworth, *Two Figures (Menhirs)*, 1964,
carved from Cornish slate.

age in which they were laid down, each being co-existent with a special phase in the earth-spirit's manifestation'.[36] This life also depended on human psychic forces, invested in the rocks in prehistory by worship and ritual.

Colquhoun's picture *Landscape with Antiquities (Lamorna)* (Plate XIX) fuses past and present, reimagining the Lamorna Valley on the Penwith Peninsula. She described it as 'a map-like painting which features the Merry Maidens, Vow Cave, a holed stone and some Celtic crosses to be found in the Lamorna area', monuments placed roughly where they appear, their enhanced scale indicative of their significance.[37] Elsewhere in *The Living Stones* Colquhoun writes of the eerie atmosphere of the Lamorna Valley, 'thinning out here, coagulating there. One could make a map with patches of colour to mark the praeternatural character of certain localities.'[38] *Landscape with Antiquities* is a similar project; it is as though the land itself were under psychoanalysis and expressing its deepest preoccupations. The picture is, of course, also Colquhoun's own mental map, in which the road makes a prominent trail, showing her route from one super-charged site to the next. The deep history of the land had been absorbed into her own memory, psychology and sense of place. As she wrote, 'It seemed that my way home was marked out by ancient stones.'[39]

It was not only deep history that cast a beguiling shadow. There were others who felt the romance of a past that the elderly could still recall, and felt it with intense poignancy because it had not entirely vanished – although it was in grave danger of doing so. 'The old life', wrote George Sturt in his book *Change in the Village* (1912), 'is being swiftly obliterated.' Oh, there had been changes before, of course, not least of which was the enclosure of the common in 1861. But for Sturt, a champion of rural crafts who was born in Farnham in Surrey, the real damage was done at the turn of the century, when the valley was, he writes, using quotation marks as though they were tongs, '"discovered" as a "residential centre"'. After that, it became 'a suburb of the town in the next valley'. The past was not a paradise, of course, and he concedes that in the old days there were problems. 'The want of proper sanitation, for instance; the ever-recurring scarcity of water; the plentiful signs of squalid and disordered living – how unpleasant they must have been!' But even so.

> It were worth something to renew the old lost sense of quiet; worth something to be on such genial terms with one's neighbours; worth very much to become acquainted again at first hand with the customs and modes of thought that prevailed in those days. Here at my door people were living, in many respects, by primitive codes which have now all but disappeared from England....

There was something, Sturt thought, of great value in that 'primitive' way of life; and although it might not be readily accountable to the intellect, it made a powerful appeal to the senses and the emotions.

> Unawares an impression of antiquity would come stealing over the senses, on a November evening, say, when the blue wood-smoke mounted from a cottage chimney and went drifting slowly down the valley in level layers; or on still summer afternoons, when there came up from the hollow the sounds of hay-making – the scythe shearing through the grass, the clatter of the whetstone, the occasional country voices. The dialect, and the odd ideas expressed in it, worked their elusive magic over and over again.[40]

There were also more tangible ways of thinking about change in the country. Just over a decade after *Change in the Village*, Sturt wrote *The Wheelwright's Shop* (1923) – by which time the First World War could be pointed to as the great gulf separating the olden days from modern times. 'One aspect of the death of Old England', he writes, 'and of the replacement of the more primitive nation by an "organised" modern state was brought out forcibly and very disagreeably by the War against Germany.'[41] Sturt's grandfather and then his father had both owned the wheelwright's shop in Farnham, and Sturt himself took over after his father's death in 1884. The chapters of his book linger affectionately over every detail of the craft, beginning with the buying of timber, its transportation and the processes of sawing and seasoning. It is a combination of instruction manual, love letter and obituary that could only have been written at a time at which mechanization was taking over from hand-crafting, and motor cars threatened to make the trade itself obsolete. And it was not only the craft that was being lost, observed Sturt; it was something more fundamental still: a state of mind; a painstakingly won judgment; a wealth of accumulated knowledge that had been passed down from generation to generation for time out of mind. 'A good wheelwright', he wrote,

> knew by art but not by reasoning the proportion to keep between spokes and felloes....He felt it, in his bones. It was a perception with him. But there was no science in it; no reasoning. Every detail stood by itself, and had to be learnt either by trial and error or by tradition.[42]

John Ruskin – whose works Sturt had read and admired – would have approved of this exacting craft, little changed from the medieval period, in which 'a fresh problem confronted the workman's ingenuity every few minutes'.[43] And, indeed, he would have lamented its demise along with Sturt.

In the early 1930s, a tall figure with an oddly angular silhouette could be seen cycling from county to county on a heavy, khaki-coloured army bicycle with a corn-dolly tied to its crossbar. This was Thomas Hennell, and his peculiar shape was due to him having shoved his drawing-board up his jumper to keep it safe and dry; his paints he stored in a specially constructed metal box fixed behind the saddle. Travelling by bicycle, he said, gave him time to see everything – and he found a great deal to look at.[44] He was researching a book that would – with a quiet nod to Sturt – be called *Change in the Farm* (1934). Hennell had not, like Sturt, been born directly into the world about which he wrote, but he was passionate about the crafts and traditions of farming and about old farm equipment. H. J. Massingham, himself the author of many books about rural life and the country, four of which Hennell illustrated, was alarmed by his friend's habit of 'suddenly announcing he may be off to Cornwall or Northumberland or Galway to draw a cart or a haystack or a mill somebody has written to him about', jumping on his bicycle and pedalling off.[45] What drew Hennell were the relics; he was on the scent of old machinery, tools and practices that were slipping away, swallowed up by the demands of the present day, or simply being abandoned as poor economic conditions made many smaller farms unviable. 'In every farmyard, outhouse and contingent building throughout the country', *Change in the Farm* begins,

> Are to be seen – piled-up relics of past generations of farmers – the remains of old ploughs, waggons and implements crumbling away behind the new steam-thresher and brightly-coloured iron rakes and harrows.

> The following compilation is an attempt to collect and arrange some of this lumber....An account of them may be not unlike that of Bunyan's man with the muck-rake, eternally collecting scraps of straw and wood; but all the country's history, and not only a chronicle of small-beer, is written out in the carpentry of broken carts and waggons, on the knots and joints of old orchard-trees, among the tattered ribs of decaying barns, and in the buried ancestral furrows and courses which can still be traced under the turf when the sun falls slantwise across the fields in the long autumn afternoons.[46]

Hennell's last image calls to mind the 'shadow sites' that O. G. S. Crawford was photographing from the air, evidence of prehistoric settlements that can only be seen from above and in the low raking light that picks out patterns invisible when standing on the apparently unremarkable ground. It was all about knowing how to read them; in his 1937 book *The Genius of England*, Massingham would even call ancient history the 'turfscript' of the downs. *Change in the Farm* takes a similar view, shining a light slantways to expose the ancient patterns in the prosaic reality of agricultural work. The cowman, the shepherd, horse-teams, bullock-teams, hedges, ditches, drainage, ploughing, dibbling, drilling, mowing with scythes, haymaking, harvesting, stacking and rick-making, sheaf-knots, rick ornaments, threshing, winnowing, cider-making, turf-cutting and mole-catching: all are described in Hennell's eager, precise words and illustrated with his careful, linear drawings. And yet at the same time *Change in the Farm* is illuminated from within by a subtle nostalgia. Hennell's book could not in itself be a bulwark against change, yet it is a repository for all the valuable things that, as the seasons rolled round each year, were being updated and thrown away as new machinery replaced the old ways.

Among Hennell's drawings is one he intended for the cover. Rejected by his publisher, it was later used as the frontispiece to Massingham's book *Country Relics* (1939), based on the author's own extensive collection of 'bygones'. It is a scene of joyful chaos presided over by a scarecrow in an old smock and tattered hat: a blasted tree is hung about with old bits of plough and everywhere are broken frames, barrels and rakes, all grown over with brambles, or as Hennell himself described it, 'an imaginary composition of a dead tree & a great pile of weeds, bones & junk'.[47] Perhaps only Hennell could have invested a rubbish dump with such life and interest. For him, it was a kind of treasure.

Shortly after the outbreak of war, in the winter of 1939–40, Kenneth Clark, then director of the National Gallery, devised a scheme to employ artists on the home front. It could have been tailor-made for Hennell. Through 'Recording the Changing Face of Britain' – later simply Recording Britain – artists were commissioned to produce views of landscapes and buildings, mostly rural and mostly English, that were in danger of being damaged or destroyed by bombs, invasion or defensive measures. Between 1940 and 1943, artists produced over one and a half thousand drawings and watercolours for this pictorial Domesday Book.

Clark wisely decided to allow Recording Britain artists largely to follow their own inclinations. They sat in front of abbeys and meres, foundling hospitals and manor houses, cottages and castles, terraces and town halls – a selective and conservative version of Britain to record, perhaps; arguably, some aspects were already slipping into the past. The scheme was poised to document the old buildings and traditional crafts already being swept away by what were described in one of its official publications as the 'sinister hands of improvers and despoilers'.[48] Hennell cycled off to Abbotsbury and Wyke for their tithe barns, Hoo in Kent for St Werburgh's church and Rochester for Delce windmill. At short notice he was sent to Lasham in Hampshire to record a magnificent avenue of beeches before it was cut down to make way for an aerodrome. He persuaded Mr Clapp the cooper and Mr Brunt the wheelwright to let him into their workshops in Bath and Newington, and has so much to tell us that it can take some time to interpret what is depicted in the busy, crowded images, from which no detail was left out.[49]

Artists involved with Recording Britain were required to use graphic media or watercolour, the latter because it linked the scheme to an old English tradition: Paul Sandby, John Sell Cotman, Thomas Girtin and J. M. W. Turner had all been masters of the medium, creating powerful visions of the English landscape. Among the most expressive of the Recording Britain images are those by John Piper, who drew churches framed by leaden skies, their stone walls encrusted with the patina of the past. He used the same choppy pen strokes for the masonry as for the clouds, and added colour with a palette of watery greys and pinkish browns, the tones of a fading bruise. His buildings sit snugly into their landscapes, exuding an air of endurance; they could almost have grown there. There was, however, a general feeling that the Recording Britain project was not the place for intense statements of romantic feeling, nor for the fractured and overtly subjective perspectives of modernism. The landscapes and buildings were already at risk of being splintered and cracked apart – that was the point. They did not need it to happen in pictures too. Each sheet produced for the scheme was kept gently in check by the light but firm paperweights of tradition.

Someone had to record the war's bombed and ruined buildings, however, and that task fell to the smaller group of Official War Artists, also under the control of Clark as chairman of the War Artists' Advisory Committee. It included Piper, who was commissioned to produce a series of pictures recording damaged churches.[50] Subjects were not hard to find. The Blitz began in September 1940, with London chief among its targets, and before long around thirty churches had been bombed and large swathes of the East End destroyed. When the city of Coventry was targeted one terrible November night and the medieval cathedral destroyed along with much of the centre, Clark immediately made arrangements for Piper to go there; he arrived the next morning at a scene of desolation, with fires still burning. Years later Piper recalled his reluctance to take out a sketchbook in the shell of the cathedral in front of shocked and mourning bystanders, while bodies were still being recovered from the rubble of surrounding buildings, and described how he had taken refuge in a solicitors' office overlooking the site. Yet how was it possible for an artist who had spent years seeking out and drawing Britain's ruined abbeys – Valle Crucis, Rievaulx, Llanthony – not to find a terrible splendour in the still-smoking ruins of the cathedral?[51] 'Bomb damage is in itself picturesque,' Clark had himself remarked at the height of the Luftwaffe's aerial campaign.[52] Piper's spectacular painting *Coventry Cathedral, 15 November 1940* (Plate xx) reveals a building in shock, seen through what he described as 'a thin fog of smoke and steam', the great window like a gaping mouth, its tracery buckled as though distorted by a heat haze.[53] And yet it also collapses time, bringing the past to bear on the present. The bombing had left a shell that irresistibly recalled others: those that formed such a sublime feature of the British landscape, the former abbeys and nunneries destroyed during the dissolution of the monasteries. New ruins joined hands with old. An 'awful awareness of the extent of time' and a 'dizzy sense of the nearness of the past' could, thought T. S. Eliot, be felt at precisely the same time. He made this observation in the introduction he was writing to a selection of Rudyard Kipling's verse. In particular he was thinking of *Puck of Pook's Hill*, Kipling's children's story of 1906 in which, tucked away near an ancient hill in a corner of Sussex, the fairy Puck magics a sequence of figures – a Roman soldier; a Danish seafarer; a Norman knight – out of England's past to tell their stories. Kipling 'aims I think', wrote Eliot, 'to give at once a sense of the antiquity of England, of the number of generations and peoples who have laboured the soil and in turn been buried beneath it, and of the contemporaneity of the past'.[54] *A Choice of Kipling's Verse* was published in wartime, December 1941, a time during which Eliot was already reflecting on the mysterious relationship between past and present as he served as an air-raid warden in London and wrote the three poems that, along with an earlier piece, would be published in 1943 as *Four Quartets*. The second in the sequence is named *East Coker*, after the village in Somerset where Eliot's ancestors once lived, and from which Andrew Eliot had departed for America in the 1660s; Eliot himself had visited in 1937.

There is plenty of contemporaneity about *East Coker*. The narrator, making his way towards the village down a deep, shaded lane between sunlit fields, is obliged to lean against the bank to allow a van to pass. Eliot's adjectives flirt with modernity: the summer heat is 'electric' and the village is 'hypnotised' by it; even the dahlias that 'sleep in the empty silence' were first introduced to English flower beds in the final years of the eighteenth century. But stop, and listen. When the owl hoots, turn quietly back up the lane to the fields. There are layers of deeper past in this place.

In that open field
If you do not come too close, if you do not come too close,
On a summer midnight, you can hear the music
Of the weak pipe and the little drum
And see them dancing around the bonfire....
Round and round the fire
Leaping through the flames, or joined in circles,
Rustically solemn or in rustic laughter
Lifting heavy feet in clumsy shoes,
Earth feet, loam feet, lifted in country mirth

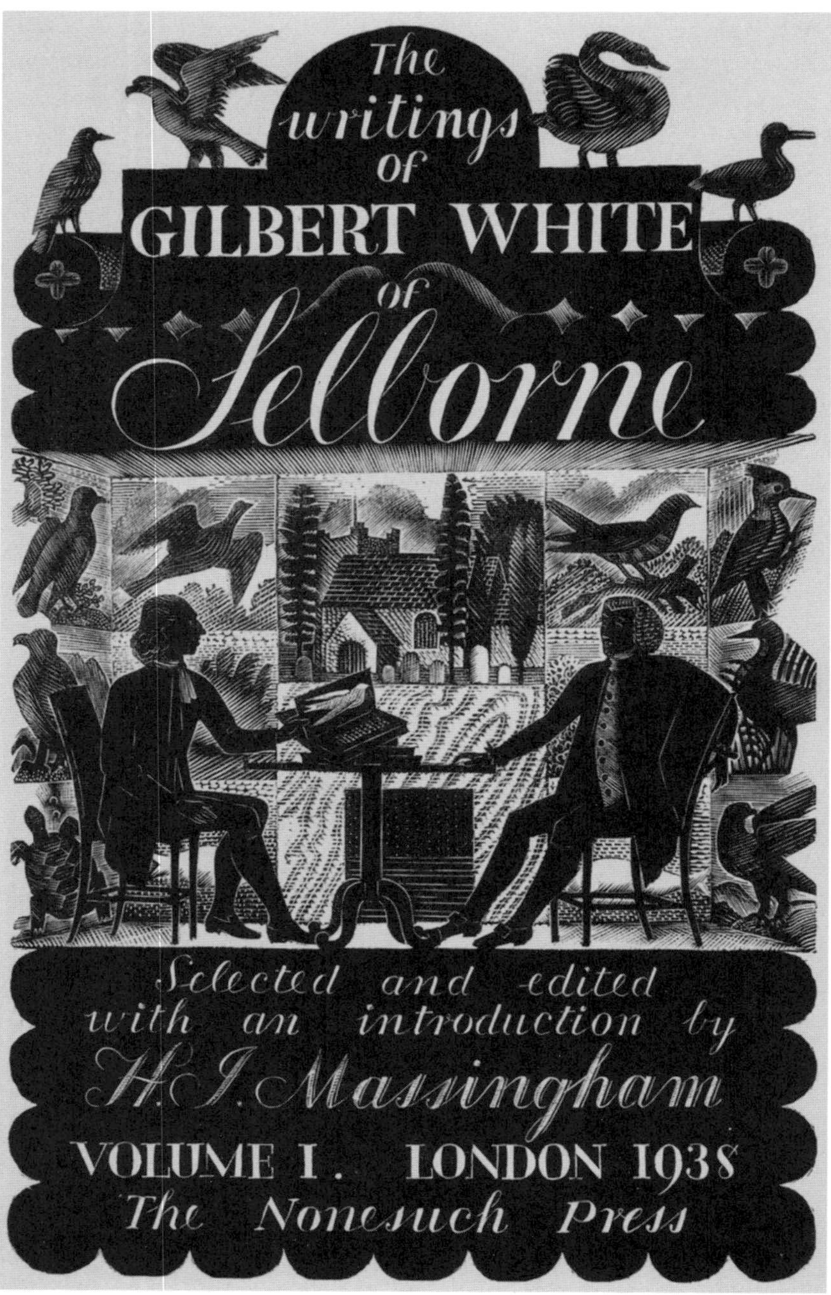

Eric Ravilious, wood-engraved title page for *The Writings of Gilbert White of Selborne*, published in 1938 by the Nonesuch Press.

These rustic ghosts dance on their old familiar ground to the rhythm of a perpetual round of recycling. 'Old stone to new building, old timber to new fires, / Old fires to ashes, and ashes to the earth'.[55] The past, whether manifesting itself as a dancing ghost above the land's surface or as bone-meal fertilizer below it, never quite disappears or loses its value.

In *East Coker*, Eliot went looking for the days of old in Somerset fields and asked how one might catch a glimpse of them, and what they might mean. Cobbett was prompted to ask similar questions when faced with a wooden table; Nash and Colquhoun sought them in the numinous monuments and atmospheric landscapes created in that mysterious stretch of time vaguely called prehistory. Sturt, Hennell, Massingham and the dozens of subsequent mid-century authors of books about olden ways and olden days in Suffolk or Wiltshire or any other county were engaged in the same project of recovery, as were the organizers and artists of Recording Britain. But in *Little Gidding*, the final poem of *Four Quartets*, Eliot suggests another way of thinking about the past, one that unpins it from the conventional rules of time:

> The moment of the rose and the moment of the yew-tree
> Are of equal duration. A people without history
> Is not redeemed from time, for history is a pattern
> Of timeless moments. So, while the light fails
> On a winter's afternoon, in a secluded chapel
> History is now and England.[56]

Ancient feet have shaken off their heavy earth, and the dancers to the music of time join their descendants in an exhilaratingly weightless measure.

'"There are bustards on the wide downs near Brighthelmstone"', wrote Eric Ravilious in 1936 to his friend Helen Binyon. 'Isn't that a beautiful statement?' Ravilious was quoting from a favourite book, *The Natural History of Selborne* by the parson-naturalist Gilbert White, first published in 1789. This 'grand book' had long been part of his mental furniture; he persuaded his students to read it and returned to its pages himself 'every minute I can spare from engraving and other jobs'.[57] Not long after he was inwardly picturing the downs near Brighton – as the small fishing village of Brighthelmstone became – Ravilious was walking up and down the village street in Selborne itself. He had gone there to absorb the atmosphere and to plan a series of illustrations he had been commissioned to produce by the Nonesuch Press, a private press devoted to producing exquisitely designed but affordable books, for a lavish two-volume edition of the *Natural History* to be edited by H. J. Massingham. As Ravilious stood contemplating Selborne and its surroundings, did he attempt to look at it through White's eyes, blinkering out the modern houses, visiting the 'single straggling street', the ancient yew in the churchyard and the adjacent beech wood, trying to focus on unchanged views that the naturalist would still recognize?[58] If he did, he seems to have been disappointed; the modern world evidently kept breaking into his field of vision. The *Natural History*, he concluded, 'is a book I wouldn't care for with pictures to tell the truth', he admitted; 'at least not any contemporary'.[59]

As White's illustrator, Ravilious needed a way of representing the Selborne of the late eighteenth century, of vaulting over the intervening years and offering the book's readers a flavour of the author's world: not only in what he chose to represent, but stylistically too. So he created richly evocative black and white illustrations by engraving them on the hard end-grain of wood, a printmaking technique that had only recently been revived. Its heyday had been in the eighteenth century, when Thomas Bewick was making his finely detailed vignettes of country life and portraits of characterful moles, dogs, bulls and birds. In the nineteenth century, it offered commercial printing firms a cheap method of reproducing pictures alongside type in books and popular periodicals, resulting in many stiff and uninspired images. It was only when photographic methods of reproduction were introduced towards the end of the century and made reproductive wood-engraving unviable that artists began to take fresh advantage of the medium's distinctiveness and expressive possibilities; the Society of Wood Engravers was founded in 1920 by artists including Eric Gill, John Nash and Gwen Raverat. While the old commercial wood-engravers' method involved cutting away the surface of the wood to leave raised lines that printed black in emulation of drawings, this new generation of artists worked in reverse. They used the burin, or engraving tool, more spontaneously, cutting the image directly into the block; as a result, when printed their expressive lines, dots and flecks would emerge

Clare Leighton, 'July: Cottage Gardens',
wood-engraved plate for *The Farmer's Year*, 1933.

sparkling from the solid, inked background. Wood-engraving demanded great manual dexterity and craftsmanship – a revival of traditional, pre-industrial skills for which the recent horrors of mechanized warfare had created a new appetite. In 1933, Clare Leighton used this bold, graphic medium to create twelve powerful images of traditional agricultural labour in *The Farmer's Year*, reimagining the medieval Labours of the Months. The massive figures who stride, build, shear and tend their way through the seasons seem to do so in a timeless world, simultaneously ancient and modern.

Ravilious was an artist for whom past and present coexisted like the two faces of a lenticular picture; a simple turn of the head could transform one into the other. He could paint a Tiger Moth in the manner of John Sell Cotman, and frame the Westbury white horse with a train carriage window. Wood-engraving, for him, offered not only a way of connecting with White's particular era but also of reviving the bold and simplified forms of English folk art. The silhouette and lettering of his title page design for White's *Natural History* would not be out of place on a seventeenth-century headstone, while the hoopoes, pheasants, swallows and tortoise that populate his illustrations could have hopped, swooped and crawled from an old ballad-sheet or chapbook. Each image has a pithily individual character: an owl soars over a moonlit lane and catches our eye, its feathers gleaming; in the tidy kitchen garden, White and his pet tortoise silently contemplate one another. Although wood-engraving was a medium that invited displays of virtuosic skill, its graphic nature could also be used to suggest the charm and naivety of popular imagery. It was an ideal medium for conjuring up White's pre-industrial world, a time before mass-produced goods flattened out local customs and variations and made such skills obsolete.

'Why is it that the eighteenth century so particularly delights us?' Lytton Strachey had asked back in 1926; 'there hangs the picture before us, framed and glazed, distinct, simple, complete. We are bewitched by it, just as, about the year 2000, our descendants, no doubt, will cast longing eyes towards the baroque enchantments of the age of Victoria.'[60] The elegance of the eighteenth century had certainly fitted the mood of the 1920s and 1930s.[61] It suggested aristocratic leisure and foppish dress; it was Cecil Beaton photographing the brightest of the Bright Young Things dressed as eighteenth-century shepherds as they might have been imagined by Marie Antoinette, or the artist Rex Whistler in silk knee breeches tied with ribbons, reclining picturesquely on the grass to strum a guitar. Born in 1880, Strachey *was* a Victorian and therefore could not imagine Victorian things appealing to people so soon, so complete was the rejection of lush nineteenth-century paintings, richly upholstered furniture and heavy ornament after the century's turn. But two years before he wrote those words, the Oxford aesthetes Harold Acton, Robert Byron and Evelyn Waugh – all, perhaps significantly, born in the early years of the twentieth century – were already revelling in the exuberant excesses of Victoriana. Undergraduates at Oxford University together, they were members of the 'Hypocrites', an exclusive social club where on occasion Byron, dressed as Queen Victoria in a black silk cape and lace cap, would entertain fellow members with renditions of Victorian music-hall songs.

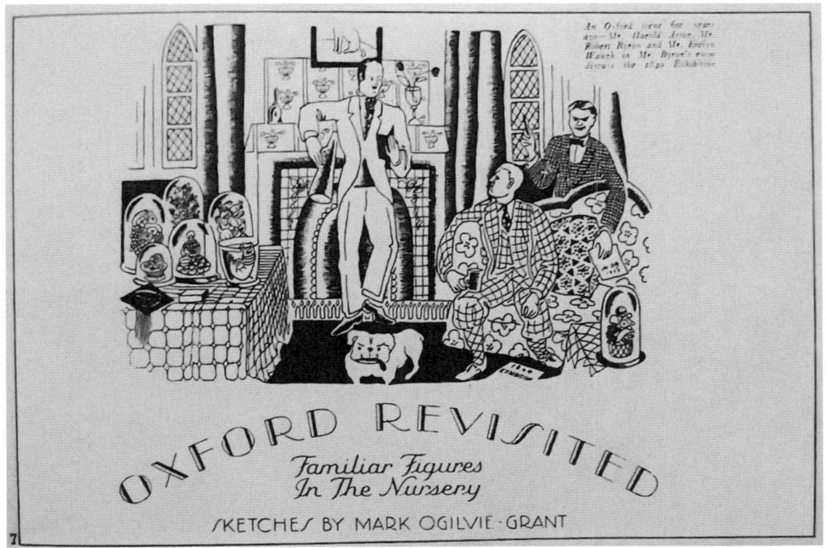

Mark Ogilvie-Grant, *Oxford Revisited*, 1924.

Early in 1924, the three made high-spirited plans to hold an '1840 Exhibition' that was to feature the kinds of objects they felt were most redolent of the period: shellwork, wax fruit, spun-glass sailing ships and Berlin wool flowers under glass domes. A drawing by another member of their circle, Mark Ogilvie-Grant, records a planning discussion in Byron's college room where they are surrounded by these things. When the university authorities forbade the exhibition, the group held a Victorian fancy-dress party in protest, getting themselves up in crinoline cages and top hats.[62]

All this could be taken with a pinch of salt as undergraduate affectation; a provocative defiance of fashion and conventional taste as a way of establishing a sophisticated group identity. And yet any group of objects with such a strong flavour of their time is unlikely to be reviled either completely or for very long. The antics of Byron, Acton and Waugh were an early sign that Victorian things were beginning to be recognized for their potential. Just four years later, Waugh published a well-received critical biography of Dante Gabriel Rossetti to mark the hundredth anniversary of his birth, and went on to form a considerable collection of Victorian narrative paintings. The same year that Strachey airily pre-

Cecil Beaton's romantic portrait of Queen Elizabeth, consort of King George VI, 1939.

dicted a Victorian revival sometime far in the future, Edith Sitwell – who regarded good taste as 'the worst vice ever invented' – published a long poem, *Elegy on Dead Fashion*, for which she rummaged through the silks and velvets of the dressing-up box, pulling them out and piling them up, relishing the names of obsolete garments: tourterelles, crinolines, pelisses, pelerines; Cupid's 'jacket artilleur', the 'toque Hongroise' trimmed with a wing from Venus's pigeons and the 'gowns of green mohair'.[63] Sitwell gave Victorian clothes the air of absurdist fantasies akin to Ballets Russes costumes or the pantomime attire of the commedia dell'arte. In an age of neat tweeds, cardigans and streamlined flapper dresses, she perceived a surreal dimension to the exaggerated Victorian silhouette.

Had it not been for the approach of the Second World War, the 'baroque enchantments of the age of Victoria' may well have remained a minority interest for decades, if not having to wait quite as long as the predicted 2000. The war, however, created a mood of popular nostalgia for the material culture of the nineteenth century, a period reassuringly close and with suitably patriotic overtones. In July 1939, Queen Elizabeth, consort of George VI, was photographed by Beaton wearing a white dress closely based on one worn by Queen Victoria in 1842 in a painting by one of the most extravagantly romantic of Victorian portraitists, Franz Xaver Winterhalter; the gauzy outer layer of her silver-sequined skirt stands out over multiple layers of petticoat, giving the effect of a crinoline.[64] In another portrait the Queen poses in the grounds of Buckingham Palace with a Victorian-style parasol, frothy with lace. Beaton, who had been telephoned by a lady-in-waiting to ask if he would photograph the Queen the next day, had thought at first it was a practical joke; 'my work was still considered revolutionary and unconventional', he noted in his diary.[65] And yet with the knack for evoking the mood of an era he had brought to the *fêtes galantes* of the twenties, he now created a cosy Victorian fantasy. The coming war brought a desire for stability and domesticity, for continuity with the past. In Beaton's photographs, published two months after the outbreak of war, Queen Elizabeth was transformed into the new Queen Victoria: domestic, family-minded and long-lived – those sequins suggesting just a hint of fairy magic.

The war intensified an existing nostalgia for British traditions and sharpened the desire to record and preserve them. In 1941, a new series of books began to appear from the publishing firm Collins, aimed at a wide readership and overseen by the literary editor of the *Spectator*, Walter James Turner. 'Britain in Pictures' was a series of short, illustrated books with distinctive, colourful paper bindings, written by authorities on art, music, literature, sciences, social history, natural history and landscape. The first was *The English Poets* by Lord David Cecil; Edith Sitwell wrote on English women, George Orwell on the British people and Jacquetta Hawkes on ancient Britain. There was Piper on Romantic artists, Hennell on British craftsmen, Beaton on English photographers and Stephen Bone on the English weather. As a series it raises the same question as Recording Britain: was the project one of recording – or salvaging? Were the subjects all still current, or were some in flux, already slipping into the past and needing to be caught by their tails? Among the volumes – one hundred and thirty-two in total, until the series was wound up in 1948, presumably having been considered to have covered every conceivable aspect of British life and culture – one that fell squarely into the second category was *English Popular & Traditional Art* (1946) by the historian Margaret Lambert and the designer Enid Marx. While many of the Britain in Pictures books were about non-tangible subjects, Lambert and Marx – partners in life as well as in writing – were passionate about the material legacy of the past. They looked around villages and towns for old shop and inn signs, visited churchyards for interestingly carved and lettered tombstones and foraged in shops and on market stalls for gingerbread moulds and trade tokens, firebacks and weathercocks, Staffordshire figures and stoneware bottles, cut-paper work and embroidered pictures. The objects they sought were vulnerable in a way that few of the other authors' subjects were: often inherently fragile, they were also in imminent danger of being dismissed as old-fashioned, useless or simply embarrassingly homespun, fit to be thrown on the fire or chucked on the rubbish heap. Through looking, comparing and handling a great range of things, the authors became unofficial curators of the country's popular and traditional art, organizing their material in chapters devoted to paper and printing, pottery and glass, painting, carving, metalwork and textiles. Marx seeded her own creative work with their growing collection, giving salvaged objects a new life by incorporating their images in her pictures and designs. A pair of vases in the form of cornucopias are copied in the repeat pattern

Clockwise from top left: a pin-prick picture; Staffordshire stoneware figures; a painted 'memento mori' panel; and a tinsel picture. Illustrations from Margaret Lambert and Enid Marx, *English Popular and Traditional Art* (1946).

of a modern curtain fabric; a Staffordshire dog guards a jug of tulips in a still-life painting.[66] She was among the artists tasked to Record Britain, and she responded with delicate coloured drawings of the remarkable street-furniture she encountered near her home in St John's Wood in north London: an exuberant plaster plaque on the wall of the Knights of St Johns Tavern; a fierce gold eagle with spread wings perching over an otherwise unremarkable chemist's doorway.[67]

Lambert and Marx were salvaging far more than objects, of course. In the preface to an expanded edition, they explain how the '"innocent eye" was disappearing in England':

> not, we think, entirely due to mechanisation, but rather from changing social habits, bringing a certain lack of initiative and interest in things with a distinctive, individual character. As the countryside becomes urbanised and we buy more from chain stores, the country craftsmen are dying out and with them that individuality in design and decoration that gave life to the old popular art.[68]

But there were urban traditions too, and some of those were also under threat. Another Recording Britain artist drawn to the ebullience of traditional crafts was Barbara Jones, author of *The Unsophisticated Arts* (1951). In this groundbreaking book she documented the visual culture of tattoo parlours, fairgrounds, seaside piers and amusement arcades; it was a blast of rock and roll to Marx and Lambert's gentle Third Programme. Jones went up to King's Lynn to visit Savage's, a firm famous in the Victorian period as a leading manufacturer of steam-powered merry-go-rounds, switchbacks and showmen's engines, but whose trade had begun to dwindle even before the First World War.[69] In a striking watercolour of the yard, Jones captures a balance of visual exuberance and neglect: a painted wooden horse made for a merry-go-round is propped up on a rusty barrel, while another has been tipped upside-down into an unpainted booth, its quarters ruching up the back-cloth and its ghostly white hind legs in the air as though performing some sombre trick (Plate XXII). These bright figures might be dusted down, touched up with paint and sent to the fair, but the overall atmosphere is not encouraging.

Another publication to catch the wartime mood was the *Saturday Book*, a popular annual miscellany published from 1941 that included essays on architecture, literature, art, ballet, music and collecting and was illustrated with wood-engravings and photographs – 'Needlework, furniture, tradesmen's cards and old maps are prominently placed,' noted a reviewer in 1948.[70] It had covers designed by Philip Gough, usually teeming with historical costumes and references such as urns, busts and flowers under glass domes, and with the title framed in an elaborate cartouche. There were essays on the Pre-Raphaelites, on London in the Eighteen Nineties, on rural characters and customs and on collecting Victoriana such as Staffordshire figures, dolls, marionettes, enamels and porcelain. Each issue had a photo-essay with pictures by Edwin Smith and text by Olive Cook, which were reminiscent, thought the editor John Hadfield, of charming Victorian scrapbooks and probably 'exercised no inconsiderable influence on the taste of our times'.[71]

There was a distinct irony in the Victorian era becoming the focus of the intense nostalgia that had been such a factor in its own character. Gough was also involved in a change of direction taken by the publisher Batsford, which from the 1930s had published a series of books on England's architectural and rural heritage, including *The Villages of England* (1932), *The Landscape of England* (1933) and *The Old Inns of England* (1934). Originally packaged with sans serif title lettering and bold and colourful contemporary covers by Brian Cook (a pseudonym: 'Brian Cook' was actually Brian Batsford, a member of the family and later director of the firm), after the war many of its titles were rebranded with traditional, Victorian-style images in muted hues by Gough, based on antique prints and topographical views. Modernism had, it seemed, quite suddenly become old-fashioned.

Sometimes the past becomes visible in the present like ink showing through a fine sheet of paper. We watch as a pilgrim unhoods his falcon and it takes flight. He follows its silhouette against the sky with his eyes as it soars higher and higher; then we become aware of the sound of an engine, and the bird becomes a fighter plane. When the camera comes back down, it rests again on the pilgim's upturned face, but his woollen hat is now a steel helmet. When Michael Powell and Emeric Pressburger's film *A Canterbury Tale* came out in 1944, cinema audiences watched a story unfold of the strange-familiar lives of wartime England – the journeys, the swapped tales, the bizarre occurrences and the chance meeting of disparate people who might otherwise never have encountered each other – and saw how they could be mapped onto a much older template. Through the disruption, the film suggested, an ancient pattern could still be discerned, and events could fall into place as though guided by magnetism. It was the same pattern under the plough that had been discerned by Crawford and that had fired Paul Nash's imagination. When at the end of the film the land-girl Alison Smith hears the sound of medieval pilgrims trotting along the old pilgrim's road to Canterbury, we know that these ghosts have come back to reassure us that history and culture run deep in the land, and that the present is benignly haunted by the past.

VII

BACKING INTO THE FUTURE

'"The point about Merrie England is that it was about the most un-Merrie period in our history. It's only the home-made pottery crowd, the organic-husbandry crowd, the recorder-playing crowd, the Esperanto..."' Jim Dixon does not finish his sentence, but instead collapses at the lecture podium from the combined effects of heat, drink, nerves and guilt.[1] Even so, with these last few words, spoken from the heart, he has made his point. Kingsley Amis's *Lucky Jim*, published in 1954, takes a beady look at nostalgia for England's olden days and stands it up on the firing range along with other kinds of pretension, evasion, manipulation and self-serving hypocrisy. For many at this time, the past was all too present in the shape of bombsites and ruined buildings – and in the painful memories of the spouses and children, parents and friends lost. Few had the appetite to dwell upon it. In general, the 1950s was a time not of retrospection and revival, but of rethinking and rebuilding. A defining exhibition of the era, held in 1956 at the Whitechapel Art Gallery, was called 'This is Tomorrow'; the same year, the art critic John Berger curated his second 'Looking Forward' exhibition of realist artists at the South London Gallery. A national preoccupation with the past was, for a time, replaced by a speculative gaze out into the universe, as the future – in the form of space exploration – captured the public imagination.

Others living in England in the post-war years, however, were experiencing complex, conflicting emotions about the past. Although Black people had been an established presence in the country long before the era of mass migration, after the 1948 Nationality Act awarded British citizenship to any Commonwealth subject, more than half a million West Indians travelled to the UK, responding to calls to help rebuild the country. Some who had come to find work experienced intense home-

Installing the exhibition 'This is Tomorrow'
at the Whitechapel Art Gallery, 1956.

sickness and imagined a future in which they would one day return to reconnect with the past they had left behind in Jamaica, Bermuda or Trinidad.[2] And yet Britain itself had long been the focus of a kind of nostalgia instilled by the teaching of British literature, history, geography and institutions in colonial schools. Views of England, often presented through the filters of canonical writers such as Shakespeare, Wordsworth and Dickens, created a sense of familiarity and belonging.[3] As George Lamming, author of *The Emigrants* (1954), has written:

> Migration was not a word I would have used to describe what I was doing when I sailed with other West Indians to England in 1950. We simply thought we were going to an England that had been painted in our childhood consciousness as a heritage and a place of welcome.

The actual experience of post-war London for those arriving from the Caribbean could be intensely disillusioning. 'It is the measure of our innocence', continues Lamming, 'that neither the claim of heritage nor the expectation of welcome would have been seriously doubted.'[4] All too often, the 'Mother Country' failed to live up to its image. Andrea Levy's 2004 novel *Small Island*, set mostly in 1948, concerns Jamaican migrants to England and their struggle to overcome the hardship and prejudice they faced, and to negotiate the sickening gap between expectation and reality. Hortense, who has travelled from Jamaica to become a teacher, takes great pride in her good manners and is amazed at the slovenly appearance and low standards she constantly finds in those around her: she, it turns out, with her smart hat and matching gloves, is markedly more polite than anyone she encounters – more old-fashioned, too. Her husband Gilbert puts the case more pithily than Hortense ever would. 'Let me ask you to imagine this', he begins.

> Living far from you is a beloved relation whom you have never met. Yet this relation is so dear a kin she is known as Mother. Your own mummy talks of Mother all the time. 'Oh, Mother is a beautiful woman – refined, mannerly and cultured.' Your daddy tells you, 'Mother thinks of you as her children; like the Lord above she takes care of you from afar'....Your finest, your best, everything you have that is worthy is sent to Mother as gifts. And on her birthday you sing-song and party.
>
> Then one day you hear Mother calling – she is troubled, she need your help. Your mummy, your daddy say go. Leave home, leave familiar, leave love....After all you have heard, can you imagine, can you believe, soon, soon you will meet Mother?
>
> The filthy tramp that eventually greets you is she. Ragged, old and dusty as the long dead. Mother has a blackened eye, bad breath and one lone tooth that waves in her head when she speaks. Can this be that fabled relation you heard so much of? This twisted-crooked weary woman. This stinking cantankerous hag. She offers you no comfort after your journey. No smile. No welcome. Yet she looks down at you through lordly eyes and says, 'Who the bloody hell are you?'[5]

Most who wrote directly of their experiences of postcolonial Britain, including Samuel Selvon in *The Lonely Londoners* (1956), Donald Hinds in 'Busman's Blues' (1965) and Beryl Gilroy in *Black Teacher* (1976), framed them in urban terms. Major, shared themes of the search for employment and the struggles of working life for Black people in Britain are reflected in the geographical scope of these stories and other work by writers who had arrived from the Caribbean from the late 1940s onwards. V. S. Naipaul, however, who came to Britain from Trinidad in 1950, reflected instead on the countryside when he based sections of his novel *The Enigma of Arrival* (1987) on notes he had made about life in rural Wiltshire, where for a time he rented a cottage.[6] The narrator at first feels oppressed by what he perceives to be the unchanging sense of the past in the countryside. 'The setting felt ancient', he observes; 'the impression was of space, unoccupied land, the beginning of things.' His observations of his surroundings are filtered through memories of paintings, novels and poems: when he visits Salisbury, he reflects that he has seen it before, in a reproduction of John Constable's *Salisbury Cathedral* in a school textbook, 'Far away in my tropical island, before I was ten.' The sheep-shearing he witnesses reminds him of a novel by Thomas Hardy; an 'exaggeratedly bent' rural labourer appeared 'Wordsworthian'.[7] In time, this literary barrier begins to open and becomes a way in. Having imagined an 'old peasantry, surviving here like butterflies among the explosions of Salisbury Plain, surviving somehow Industrial Revolution, deserted villages, railways', the narrator continues,

> So much of this I saw with the literary eye, or with the aid of literature. A stranger here, and with the nerves of the stranger, and yet with a knowledge of the language and the history of the language and the writing, I could find a special kind of past in what I saw.

One autumn day he has a craving to revisit *Sir Gawain and the Green Knight*, a poem Naipaul had studied at Oxford more than twenty years before, and begins to read himself into the past through the medium of Gawain's wintry journey. He feels 'in tune with the landscape...in that solitude, for the first time in England'.[8]

The 'out-of-placeness' the narrator initially recognizes in himself is also gradually assuaged by daily walks that take him past ruined farm buildings, untidy yards and rotting haystacks – 'superseded things', as he puts it; poverty and squalor. The farm labourer Jack is not the deeply rooted emanation of the English soil the narrator at first takes him for, but a man who has, through constant struggle, created his own world.

The narrator also discovers connections between the estate on which his cottage stands, the former wealth of which derived from imperial subjugation, and his own Trinidadian past and the sugar plantation on which his grandparents were indentured labourers. The postcolonial landscape, he reflects, is fractured and in a state of constant flux; yet there is consolation to be found in the knowledge that by small, personal efforts it can be remade.[9]

In 1965, a folk group from Hull, the Watersons, released the album *Frost and Fire: A Calendar of Ritual and Magical Songs*. It sought to reshape the damaged modern world by tethering it back down to the age-old rhythms of the agricultural year, from cold winter days to the heat of the summer sun and back, assembling songs that encourage the land to produce a good harvest and honour the labour of those who dig and sow and tend and prune. If many in the interwar years battled the changing character of rural life by writing charming books on Victorian traditions or filling their barns with collections of 'rural bygones', the Watersons reached for something darker and more ancient: customs and beliefs with roots older than Christianity, roots that penetrated centuries-deep, all the way down to pagan practices.[10]

The Watersons sang traditional ballads unaccompanied by instruments, powerfully projecting their voices. There is a startling austerity to the sound, even a hint of sacred plainsong; listening to them now gives an eerily vertiginous sense of sonic time-travel.[11] Here we come a-wassailing, they begin, with a song traditionally sung to orchard trees at the beginning of the year to ensure a good harvest. Easter-time is marked by a traditional Pace-egging song, and at harvest John Barleycorn, who has grown tall and strong, must be cut down – a song with roots in ancient rituals of sacrifice, whether actual or symbolic. Autumn comes and, in one of the most haunting of the Watersons' songs, soul-cakes are begged door-to-door, in return for the saying of prayers. Then comes Christmas and the ballad of Herod and the Cock, which relates how Saint Stephen proved the birth of Christ by causing the roast chicken in Herod's dish to rise up and crow 'Christus natus est', before *Frost and Fire* – and the year – ends as it began, with more wassailing.[12] A new year begins, but in its honouring of ancient rites and traditions, it will also be an old year. The album is as much a spell as a collection of songs, each track a trapdoor sending its listeners tumbling into the past.

In an era in which rock and roll was such a powerful cultural force that many British performers found themselves singing with a North American intonation, the Watersons' Yorkshire accents rooted them unequivocally in the English regional ballad tradition, which was about the persistence of the local. As a young man, Peter Bellamy was seduced by the music of Bill Haley and Elvis Presley; but if this enthusiasm ever caused him to modify his Norfolk vowels, it was only temporary. He first began to collect folk songs as a student at Norwich Art School, and once compared himself to the curator of a museum, an apt description that suggests not just the acquisition of songs but his expertise in interpreting and presenting folk music to audiences; he also learned vocal mannerisms from folk-singers like his friends the Copper family of Rottingdean in Sussex, who were born into the tradition.[13] Bellamy founded The Young Tradition, whose eponymous first album of 1966 and its 1967 successor, *So Cheerfully Round*, have been described as 'rustic tapestries of ballads, carols and street cries from the late eighteenth and early nineteenth centuries; a parade of serving-maids, poachers, fishermen, cunning foxes, bold dragoons, pretty ploughboys and hungry children'.[14] Later, he set some of Kipling's verses to music for a solo album, *Oak, Ash and Thorn* (1970), renaming 'A Tree Song' from *Puck of Pook's Hill* and recording it as the title track:

Of all the trees that grow so fair,
Old Engerland to adorn,
Greater than none beneath the Sun,
Than Oak and Ash and Thorn.
Sing Oak and Ash and Thorn, good Sirs
(All of a Midsummer's morn)!
Surely we sing of no little thing,
In Oak and Ash and Thorn!

Oak of the Clay lived many a day,
Or ever Aeneas began;
Ash of the Loam was a lady at home,
When Brut was an outlaw man;

Thorn of the Down saw New Troy Town
(From which was London born);
Witness hereby the ancientry
Of Oak and Ash and Thorn![15]

The tune was not remotely ancient, but written by Bellamy himself, who remarked in the album's sleeve notes that it was 'intended to recall those of some of the old wassail and ritual songs'.[16] The words were not, of course, ancient either, having been composed a mere sixty-five years or so earlier, by someone with a sufficiently traditional education to have heard of the long-defunct Brutus and the myth of Troynovant. But delivered in Bellamy's characteristically nasal voice and Norfolk accent, 'Oak and Ash and Thorn' sounded more thrillingly authentic than many a traditional ballad, and every bit as deeply rooted in the land as the trees themselves. It is not history itself that makes the song shiver with a frisson of 'ancientry', but Bellamy's imaginative vision of it. Bellamy and The Young Tradition were poised between the scholarly revival of medieval music promoted at this time by the historian David Munrow, and avant-garde, psychedelic folk groups such as The Incredible String Band, drawing inspiration from all points on the spectrum. Their 1968 album *Galleries* juxtaposed the traditional Agincourt Carol, played on period instruments with Munrow on shawm (an ancestor of the oboe), with verses from 'Stones from my Passway' by the American blues musician Robert Johnson.

The balance has shifted in our relationship with the past: where once it was regarded as a resource to be plundered, its values refashioned and its protagonists reimagined to suit the times, in recent decades attitudes to history have become more ambiguous. The Watersons, Peter Bellamy and others may have sung about the continuity of the old ways and the observance of rituals and traditions that have roots in the pagan past, but when the theme was taken up on film its darker implications bubbled up to the surface. The past revealed itself to be unquiet and volatile. *Robin Redbreast*, a BBC 'Play for Today' written by John Griffith Bowen and first broadcast in December 1970, tells the story of Norah Palmer, a young script editor who breaks up with her boyfriend and leaves London for an isolated village in the south of England.[17] There she finds herself drawn unwittingly into a long-observed local tradition of human sacrifice when she

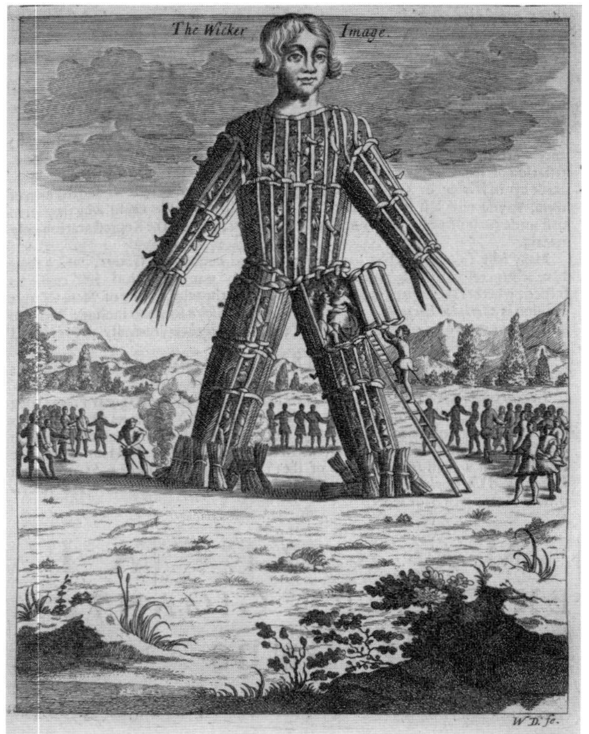

'The Ceremony observed in sacrificing of Men to their Idols, in a Wicker Image': supposed Druidic practice illustrated in Aylett Sammes, *Britannia Antiqua Illustrata* (1676).

sleeps with a local man and becomes pregnant. The man is Edgar, called Rob by the villagers, who lives on the margins of the village and sleeps in the woods, and was destined from birth to be a sacrificial victim, their 'Robin redbreast'; his unborn child is fated to be his successor. Norah is finally allowed to leave the village, but as she does so she turns to look back and sees that the appearance of the villagers has changed. The membrane separating past and present has suddenly been torn: one man now wears antlers like Herne the Hunter, while the others are dressed in strange ceremonial clothes. The 1973 horror film *The Wicker Man* also explores the eruption of ancient pagan practices into contemporary life, concluding with the visually arresting sacrificial device of the giant hollow figure, an

Still from the television play *Penda's Fen* (1974).

image derived from an illustration of supposed Druidic practice in Aylett Sammes's book of 1676, *Britannia Antiqua Illustrata*. In another Play for Today, David Rudkin's *Penda's Fen* (1974), England's restless ancient past disrupts the present in more ambiguous ways. The film culminates in the troubled adolescent protagonist wandering the Malvern Hills, where he receives a blessing from the ghost of England's last pagan king, Penda of Mercia (d. 655). The theme of belonging runs through each of these films, expressed in terms of rites, rituals and the ancient landscape, of rejection or affinity. Each film hinges on the relationship of its characters to a world of spiritual significance that lies underneath the prosaic here and now.

The idea of wiring ancient currents to electrify the present was not only a pastoral phenomenon. In *Lud Heat* (1975), Iain Sinclair plots metaphysical connections between Nicholas Hawksmoor's six London churches: 'Each church is an enclosure of force,' he writes, 'a trap, a sight-block, a raised place with an unacknowledged influence on events enacted within their nome-lines.'[18] *Lud Heat* is a book of apocalyptic dreams and occult visions, of executions and purifications, necropoli and church walls varnished with regular libations of alcoholic piss. Sinclair orchestrates a polyphony of voices, co-opting William Blake, W. B. Yeats, Ezra Pound and Thomas Browne; one of the book's epigraphs is from Thomas de Quincey's *On Murder Considered as one of the Fine Arts* – 'All perils, specially malignant, are recurrent.' In Sinclair's system, past and present are engaged in a perpetual foul-mouthed wrestling bout; there is no romanticized vision of the olden days in these pages. And as if enacting its own argument, *Lud Heat* established the parameters of a future work. Sinclair's speculative proposal that 'From what is known of Hawksmoor it is possible to imagine that he did work a code into the buildings, knowingly or unknowingly, templates of meaning, bands of continuing ritual' challenged Peter Ackroyd to write his novel *Hawksmoor* (1985), with a double time frame that allowed him to interleave a seventeenth-century version of the East End with its twentieth-century story, activating a dialogue between them.[19] For Ackroyd, the East End of London is a palimpsest, continually scrawled upon and only ever imperfectly erased before the next generation comes along to score the surface with the latest sgraffito layer. Ackroyd is among

Poster designed by Paul Christodoulou advertising Elliott's 'Alice Boots', *c.* 1966.

the most keenly alert of novelists to the pattern under the tarmac, and to the spiritual potential of the litter-strewn corners of the city to which crimes, trysts and ghosts stick as fast as chewing-gum.

By the mid-1960s it seemed as though fashion was impermeable to the Victorian era's 'baroque enchantments'. In the years following the Second World War, the appreciation of Victorian art, furnishings and decorative objects had plunged into an abyss, and a great deal of pioneering collecting and scholarly work was needed before it could be hauled back out.[20] Modern women's clothes, designed to be easy to wear and to care for, were dominated by trousers and the iconic minidress, which enabled their wearers to stride purposefully through life. Shoes were slip-on or fastened by a simple stud; boots did up with a zip. This was modernity. No, this was the future.

But not even zip-up, wipe-clean garments are proof against the past. In 1966, the Victoria and Albert Museum held an exhibition devoted to the work of Aubrey Beardsley, the brilliant young illustrator whose work had delighted and scandalized its late-ninteenth-century audiences in equal measure. The exhibition caused a new sensation: having unleashed his transgressive vision on the London of the 1890s, Beardsley was back to do it all again in 1966. For decades, Victorian art had been routinely dismissed as saccharine, sentimental and embarrassingly overblown – it is an irony that even the Pre-Raphaelites, who themselves had run a campaign against precisely those characteristics, were indiscriminately thrown out with their contemporaries. But here on the gallery walls were sharp, uncompromising black and white images; viewers found them knowing, erotic, grotesque and disturbing. Beardsley drew monsters and pierrots, prostitutes and degenerates, dominatrices and flagellants and the smart, dangerously independent New Woman. And he drew them with a conviction and an assurance of line that was almost insolent.

It was not long before Beardsley's characters slipped off the V&A's walls and melted into the shadows. Among the first signs that they had infiltrated English cultural life was an advertisement for a pair of 'Alice boots' issued by the firm Elliott's. The poster, designed by Paul Christodoulou, featured a young woman wearing a white minidress. But rather than the simple shoes one would expect, she wears tightly-fitting boots of a late Victorian style, the kind that lace up laboriously to mid-calf. And as if to explain this retro choice, she is surrounded by figures created by Beardsley at the *fin de siècle*: there is Salome dancing for the head of John the Baptist; next to her is Messalina, the Emperor Claudius's wife, described by the Roman poet Juvenal as so sexually insatiable she attempted to satisfy her lust by working in a brothel at night; there is a horned hermaphrodite, a laughing sorcerer, and three women from Aristophanes's play *Lysistrata*, one of whom makes a bold sexual advance towards her neighbour with a large feather. A boy reaches into a tub to offer the young woman a flower; among the blooms a small masked head bobs past. Beardsley himself appears in a self-portrait, elfin and smirking. Like Lewis Carroll's Alice, the wearer of these boots is surrounded by strange people behaving in transgressive and worrying ways. And yet she remains serene and apparently unperturbed by the company; her boots make her one of them. In an age that had so decisively rejected heavy fabrics, fiddly fastenings and all the unnecessary elaboration associated with Victorian clothes, button-boots were a subversive choice. For five shillings customers could buy a copy of Christodoulou's poster, take it home and pin it to their bedroom walls.[21]

Beardsley was one thing; Lord Kitchener was quite another. And yet in 1965, the shop I Was Lord Kitchener's Valet opened on London's Portobello Road, where it sold items of court dress and vintage military uniform, in particular the red coats worn by Victorian and Edwardian regiments that had been withdrawn from regular use in 1914. These garments became so fashionable among the young and cool that branches of the boutique quickly opened in Wardour Street, Carnaby Street and the King's Road to meet demand. Victoriana including ankle-length skirts, high-necked blouses and men's jackets made up in William Morris patterns, striped velvet and other furnishing fabrics were sold at another King's Road boutique, Granny Takes a Trip.[22]

References to Beardsley harnessed the Victorian era's own transgressions; those to the British Army officer and colonial administrator Lord Kitchener confronted authority head-on. Either way, new conversations were being conducted with history. During this period of rapid social

I was Lord Kitchener's Valet boutique, Portobello Road, London 1966.

change, the past became ever more potent: it could offer anti-establishment positions to take up, and symbols of restriction and conformity to knock down. Wearing items that carried such powerful associations with the British establishment, but doing so casually – a scarlet tunic with long hair, jewelry and jeans, for example – was a political act. Period films with military subjects such as *The Charge of the Light Brigade* (1968) and *Oh! What a Lovely War* (1969), both scathing about establishment ineptitude, further popularized the look. Having been gazed at wistfully for so long, the past was now coming under more critical scrutiny, its symbols of authority and control plundered and subverted as people faced the problems of the present.

History had long served as a gigantic dressing-up box. But the 1960s brought a new, more creative attitude to the past, one that is still current today. Why simply dress up in historical costume or reimagine period scenes when one could bring a haul up to the surface and rearrange it?

The nineteenth century was the principal focus for such forays because of the sheer quantity of literature and visual imagery it had generated. It was the age of periodicals, newspapers, mass-market paperbacks, posters, steel engravings of popular paintings and apparently limitless printed goods, all distributed around Britain in vast quantities by rail and steam. There had never been so much *stuff*. From the vantage point of the late twentieth or early twenty-first century, the nineteenth century was more distinctive than any other era; its imagery could be appropriated, mixed up and juxtaposed with modern visual material without losing any of its own powerful flavour.

Collage was a way of reassembling fragments of the past in a modern framework and setting up a dialogue between them. Just as shoppers at I Was Lord Kitchener's Valet created striking sartorial collages by juxtaposing jeans with vintage uniform, Pop artists made use of Victorian photographs, printed images and typefaces. At the beginning of her career, Pauline Boty made collages by cutting up Victorian engravings and combining them with elements from modern advertisements; the surreal images she created comment on gender, violence and colonialism. In one, a vast pair of pruning shears wielded by a woman's manicured hand is poised to snip the head from a young girl (Plate XXIII); in another, a white European woman's head cut from a fashion plate appears at the top of a crocheted tower, from which it looks down with apparent colonial condescension upon a tropical landscape.[23] Boty's friend Peter Blake was inspired by a screen decorated in the late Victorian period with cut-out flower swags, children and portraits to incorporate nineteenth- and twentieth-century scraps in his own work, in particular his series of 'tattooed ladies'.[24] And if a Victorian air hangs over Blake's collaged design for the cover of the Beatles' 1967 album *Sgt. Pepper's Lonely Hearts Club Band*, it is powerfully reflected by the final track on side one, 'Being for the Benefit of Mr. Kite!' In January 1967, during a break from shooting the promotional film *Strawberry Fields Forever* in Kent, John Lennon went into a local antiques shop where he bought an 1843 poster advertising the Rochdale appearance of Pablo Fanque's Circus Royal, a travelling troupe of acrobats who performed on tightropes, trampolines and horseback. Amused by its bold typeface and extravagant rhetoric – 'Grandest Night of the Season! And positively the last night but three!' – he hung the poster in his home studio and plundered its text for his lyrics. The song's telegraphic phrases were superimposed over a sound-collage made up of the atmospheric fairground clamour of harmoniums, harmonicas and recordings of Victorian steam-organs and calliopes; Lennon wanted, he said, to evoke the feeling of the circus so vividly that he would be able to 'smell the sawdust'.[25]

A previous generation had valued objects created by the Victorians for the comforting sense of tradition they conveyed. Now, when many people looked back on the past, they found something quite different: a playful, carnival world of absurdity and excess; a willingness to question authority and to point out the illogicality of rules; an experimental attitude to perception-altering substances. The counterculture's favourite Victorian heroine was, of course, Lewis Carroll's Alice, whose adventures

Still from Jonathan Miller's *Alice in Wonderland* (1966).

underground and through the looking glass provided inspiration for the Beatles and Blake, among many others.[26] In 1966, three days before the end of the year, television audiences settling down for an evening's viewing might have been surprised to find an adaptation of *Alice's Adventures in Wonderland* (1865) by Jonathan Miller in the schedule. Why was a film of a children's story being shown late in the evening, after most children were in bed? It was because Miller recognized that, in a newly freethinking era, it could just as well be cast as a story for adults. He invited the viewers into the mind of Alice (Anne-Marie Mallik), conveying many of her reflections and questions in a voice-over – a dreamlike experience made more so by a sitar soundtrack written by Ravi Shankar, by turns languid and frenetic. Miller minimized the element of pantomime by dispensing with the elaborate animal costumes that had previously been a staple of dramatic performances of *Alice*, so that the White Rabbit, the Caterpillar, the Mock Turtle, the Mad Hatter, the Mouse and the Gryphon – played respectively by Wilfred Brambell, Michael Redgrave, John Gielgud, Peter Cook, Alan Bennett and Malcolm Muggeridge – are all human figures in ordinary Victorian costume. In so doing, he was able to underline parallels between episodes of Carroll's story and the pompous customs, uncompromising institutions and unbending social codes encountered in real life. In Miller's version the story is not only about the sudden growth spurts, ennui and challenges to authority endemic to adolescence, but about taking a good look at the grown-ups and the rigidly policed and meaninglessly ritualistic world they have created, and declaring, along with Alice, 'nonsense'.

What happens when the collaging scissors are placed not in the hands of artists, innovators and radicals, but philistine big business? What would the consequences be for England's sense of its own history?

The final section of Julian Barnes's satirical novel *England, England* (1998) opens in a village churchyard with a conversation between the heroine, Martha Cochrane, and a local farrier who is taking a scythe to the weeds, having rejected the offer of a petrol mower. '"Mr Harris?"' begins Martha.

> 'You can call me Jez, Missie Cochrane, like others do.' The farrier was a burly fellow whose knees cracked as he straightened himself. He wore a countryman's outfit of his own devising, all pockets and straps and sudden tucks, which had hints of both Morris dancer and bondage devotee.

> 'I think there's a redstart still sitting,' said Martha. 'Just behind that old-man's-beard. Mind you don't disturb her.'
>
> 'Will do, Miss Cochrane.' Jez Harris yanked at a loose strand of hair over his forehead, with possible satiric intent. 'They say redstarts bring luck to them as don't disturb their nests.'
>
> 'Do they, Mr Harris?' Martha's expression was disbelieving.
>
> 'They do in this village, Miss Cochrane,' replied Harris firmly, as if her comparatively recent arrival gave her no right to question history.
>
> He moved off to hack at a patch of cow parsley. Martha smiled to herself. Funny how she couldn't bring herself to call him Jez. Yet Harris was no more authentic. Jez Harris, formerly Jack Oshinsky, junior legal expert with an American electronics firm obliged to leave the country during the emergency. He'd preferred to stay, and backdate both his name and his technology; nowadays he shoed horses, made barrel hoops, sharpened knives and sickles, cut keys, tended the verges, and brewed a noxious form of scrumpy into which he would plunge a red-hot poker just before serving.

Having localized and softened his Milwaukee accent, Jez amuses himself by inventing florid tales of 'witchcraft and superstition, of sexual rites beneath a glowing moon and the tranced slaughter of livestock, all not so very long in the past' for the eager ears of visiting anthropologists pretending to be tourists.[27] Barnes's setting here is Old England, a place that has become an under-populated, agrarian backwater, politically insignificant and cut off from Europe. The Isle of Wight, on the other hand, has been transformed into a highly lucrative theme-park called England, England: a cheerful collage constructed from scaled-down replicas of popular tourist destinations such as Buckingham Palace, all in a conveniently small compass to cater for sightseers. Episodes of English history are re-enacted and myths and legends staged – though bowdlerized and simplified for family visitors from overseas who, decrees the company who runs the place, must not be presented with any offensive or overly complex material. England, England, which serves up a storybook version of the past, becomes a successful independent state and joins the European Union.

England, England is a novel about the national preoccupation with the past, and the fault lines that are exposed when an outrageously megalomaniacal businessman proposes to realize it. Beneath the book's bold, overarching satire, Barnes asks searching questions: can we trust our own sense of history, even our childhood memories? Is it possible to distinguish the authentic from the bogus? And are they truly so different? '"I wish he wouldn't invent these things,"' remarks the earnest schoolmaster Mr Mullin to Martha of Jez's tall tales.

> 'I've got books of myths and legends he's welcome to. There's all sorts of tales to choose from. He could lead a little tour if he wished. Take them up Gibbet Hill and talk about the Hooded Hangman. Or there's Old Mother Fairweather and her Luminous Geese.'
>
> 'They wouldn't be *his* stories, would they?'
>
> 'No, they'd be our stories. They'd be...*true*.' He sounded unconvinced himself. 'Well, maybe not true, but at least recorded.'[28]

And while shabby Old England has apparently invented its own legends, there are aspects of the ersatz England, England that have become all too authentic. The actors who play Robin Hood and his Merry Men identify so strongly with their characters that they begin to hunt local farm animals for food. And the Dr Johnson Dining Experience turns out not to be the entertaining combination of 'Johnsonian soliloquy, repartee among co-evals, and cross-epoch-bonding between the Good Doctor and his modern guests' that had been planned: the actor's marked eccentricities, socially unacceptable attitudes, slovenly dress and doubtful personal hygiene have made him indistinguishable from those of the historical figure.[29] There are, naturally, complaints; who would actually want to encounter the real thing (if you could call it that)? The past, suggests the novel, can be dressed up as a tawdry, compromised theme park and served up to passive consumers; but it retains its own unpredictable life.

The photograph shows a first-floor room in a Georgian house. At the centre is a fireplace in which a coal fire glows behind a screen. On the left is a Regency sofa and on the right a fire screen, an untidy pile of newspapers and a card-table that supports piles of books and a lamp. The walls are of patchy bare plaster hung with framed architectural prints. The room has an appealingly shabby, old-fashioned atmosphere: there are no modern appliances visible and if it were not for a few tell-tale book spines, it could be a room virtually untouched since the Victorian period; one that was perhaps finally abandoned in, say, the 1920s by its elderly inhabitant.

Except that it was not abandoned, and its inhabitant was the energetic, campaigning thirty-eight-year-old architectural historian Gavin Stamp. It looked like that because that is how he liked it, and the photograph was taken for a book of 1986 edited by Alvilde Lees-Milne called *The Englishman's Room*. 'I have a Victorian print entitled "My Den"', Stamp explains in the accompanying text. 'It shows a shabby, bookish old gent seated at a chaotic desk. He is reading a book in a room piled high with books and papers. This is not an ideal to which I aspire but a reality I unfailingly succeed in achieving.' Stamp, who had written in *Private Eye* since 1978 as 'Piloti', under which name he protested against poor planning decisions and the destruction of period buildings, had with his wife Alexandra Artley bought a three-storey late Georgian house in the King's Cross area of London. It was, he wrote,

> once a sleazy lodging house – or worse, for this area used to be better known for red lights than for elegant facades. This was fortunate, and not only because the house was cheap. In smart parts of London, houses have been modernized and restored over and over again, so that practically nothing original is left. Here, the chimneypieces had gone but everything else – doors, staircase, cornices, etc. – had survived.

Even the coal fire, he writes, 'contributes an important element to the character of the room, as it is responsible for a fine layer of ash everywhere'. To Stamp and a small group of like-minded campaigners, the past and its accompanying dust became precious commodities that had to be defended from the destructive attention of property developers. He and Artley were at the centre of what she and the architectural historian John Martin Robinson had defined the previous year as a group of pioneering 'New Georgians', or 'creative conservationists', who recognized the importance and beauty of unloved Georgian and Victorian terraces, which at that time were often boarded up and neglected. They bought houses, lived in them, lovingly preserved remaining period details and hunted in architectural salvage yards for replacements for what had been lost. They were conservers and preservers of the past, battling against those who would prefer to profit by its destruction. 'Their approach to life', write Artley and Robinson, 'is new':

> New Georgians not only know about art and architectural history, they live it. To them art is not a quiet museum study, it is now and for everyone. It is about the quality of life, the new politics to come.
>
> New Georgians can date anything in a flash. They see art in a terrace house, a block of flats, a telephone box, an architectural drawing, a railway bridge, a front-door or the leg of a chair.
>
> The world is full of things to be SAVED. Saving means you must not only know but be practical. With the energy of a high Victorian engineer, who did things as well as designing them, New Georgians campaign, restore, annoy, repair and think, to keep the world looking good.[30]

Thus begins *The New Georgian Handbook of 1985*, a book that aimed simultaneously to define, celebrate and gently poke fun at a social group, just as its predecessor from the same publisher, *The Official Sloane Ranger Handbook* (1982), had so successfully skewered its own tweed-and-pearl-clad subjects.[31]

In 1887 William Morris had founded the Society for the Protection of Ancient Buildings to prevent Victorian architects from damaging structures by over-enthusiastic restoration. It was a long time before Victorian buildings themselves were regarded as vulnerable. 'Too early. We will make ourselves look silly', had been the response in the 1950s when some members of the Society suggested forming a Victorian section.[32] Since the founding of the Victorian Society in 1958, however, those seeking to preserve Georgian and Victorian architecture from neglect, and routine destruction carried out in the name of post-war reconstruction, were increasingly vocal and visible.[33] An early cause célèbre came in 1960, when John Betjeman involved himself in the campaign to save the Euston Arch, the Greek Revival entrance to Euston Station built in 1838, from demolition. But what Artley and Robinson so gleefully describe in their field guide to this social group was not only a passionate wish to conserve period buildings, but to live in them and furnish them with antique furniture and objects to create a suitable atmosphere: 'he [*sic*] likes plenty of clocks at home (boing, boing, boing)'. And not only to furnish their homes in period style, but to dress themselves in a way that evoked the past: 'Mr New Georgian consults a huge half-hunter worn on a watch-chain' while 'Gentle Georgiana...wears layers of crumbling old silk waistcoats' – or 'a lovely silk shirt with a pie-crust frill'. Wherever possible, technology was kept at bay. 'Other accessories include an old, very heavy bicycle for racing to conservation meetings. Sometimes, when cycling, he [*sic*] wears a pair of Thirties leather motoring goggles. New Georgians cycle with an upright Edwardian posture....'[34] The 'New Georgians' were reacting against the primacy of modernism in architecture, the style that had long been accepted as the only appropriate response to the way people lived in the present and would live in the future, and made it their mission to preserve the past – and to demonstrate how it could be inhabited.

Few, however, did so as ambitiously and passionately as Dennis Severs in his house on Folgate Street in Spitalfields, in the East End of London. The tall, terraced houses there were built in the first half of the eighteenth century, where they formed the centre of the silk-weaving industry; many of their first inhabitants were Huguenots, French Protestant refugees fleeing persecution in their country, followed by Irish and Jewish migrants in the nineteenth century and Bangladeshi migrants in the late twentieth century. For a sense of the layers of history that have settled here, stand in front of the Brick Lane Jamme Masjid, on the corner of Fournier Street. From 1743 this building was La Neuve Église, a chapel for the Huguenots, who as Protestant dissenters could not use the local Anglican church, while for most of the nineteenth century it was a nonconformist chapel, first Wesleyan and then Methodist. Then, in 1891, it became the Machzike Hadath, the Spitalfields Great Synagogue, and in 1976, after the synagogue had moved to new premises, the building reopened as a mosque, the London Jamme Masjid (since renamed the Brick Lane Jamme Masjid). Now look up at the sundial: its inscription 'Umbra Sumus', 'we are shadow', has been reminding anyone who cared to notice it of the fleeting nature of human life since the early Huguenot settlers first worshipped there. Since then, the words have become only too fitting for this building that has accommodated successive groups of local people as they have arrived, stayed for a time and then moved on.

By the 1970s, many of the area's houses were derelict, if they were still standing at all; some had been bombed during the war, while others had been demolished to make way for a large wholesale fruit and vegetable market. Those left were under immediate threat from developers. The Spitalfields Trust was formed in 1977 to preserve the early Georgian buildings of the area by a group of architectural campaigners who gained publicity for their cause not only by writing in newspapers, but also by occupying one of the houses at greatest risk. As a result, individuals from city bankers to writers and artists, drawn by the unusual quantity of surviving period details (past occupants mostly having been too poor to make changes), bought houses in deals brokered by the Trust and set about repairing them.[35]

One such was Severs. Born in Southern California, he had grown up beguiled by the atmosphere of historical dramas on television; just five days after graduating from high school he moved to London, drawn, as he said, by the peculiar quality of 'English light'. Often watery or grey, or fading into twilight, it was subtler and more shifting than the bright sunlight that had shone on him before; just the kind of light in which one might, if one were lucky, perceive ghosts. Severs bought No. 18 Folgate Street from the Trust in 1979, moved in with nothing but a candle, a chamber pot and a bedroll and devoted his life to it.[36] He was not able, quite, to make his handsome front door a portal into the past, but he did everything else he could to fill his house from basement kitchen to chimney pots with the distilled essence of the olden days. In his case, this shifting and nebulous period was dictated by the house itself and the tales he felt it could tell of its first inhabitants and their descendants.

Like John Soane before him, Severs told stories by the way he arranged his collection: he used teacups and candlesticks for words, disordered bed-hangings for sentences and table-top arrangements for paragraphs (Plate XXI). He invented the Jervis family (anglicized from Gervaise), originally silk-weavers from France who had moved into the house in 1725 and lived there until 1919, and he began to invite visitors to the house to hear their story. If you knock on the door you are informed that the Jervises are out, but that you are welcome to look around. On entering it takes a moment to acclimatize; there is no doubt that some subtle shift has taken place. Each room contains its own reservoir of historical atmosphere into which one must plunge. Slow and resonant or quick and silvery, clocks tick away the time. There is a pervasive scent of wood smoke. The ground floor parlour is scented with the fragrance of brewing tea from an elaborate silver pot; the Jervises became prosperous when they first moved here. Upstairs, in the elegant drawing room decorated with blue and white china, the clip-clop of horse-drawn carriages drifts in from the street. There is the scent of herbs, where they have been thrown down and swept to the sides to sweeten the air. Downstairs, push open the door of a back room and step forward in time. Blousy roses bloom all over the walls and ornaments mass on mantelpiece and sideboard: Staffordshire dogs, wool-work flowers under glass domes, shell pictures, prints of Queen Victoria, framed photographs, busts and clocks. Up again, on the attic floor, more years have passed, bringing sad changes this time. The Jervis's fortunes have gone downhill as cheaper imports have affected the silk industry. In a room containing a once-grand bed, its drapery now hanging in dusty tatters, the floorboards and walls are bare; the plaster is cracked and washing is strung up to dry. The family has retreated here to a room that must serve every purpose; the unmistakeable smell of boiled cabbage hangs heavily in the air. Fortune has turned her wheel.

The Folgate Street house is alive with activities half-finished and lives interrupted for a moment. The residents may be absent, but everywhere are signs that it is only temporary: letters to the Jervises, plates with half-eaten loaves of bread, strips of orange peel, dregs of wine in a glass, a pair of spectacles left on a pamphlet, abandoned tobacco pipes, rumpled sheets on unmade beds, a waistcoat hanging on a peg. Many objects here are mocked-up: the swags decorating the parlour fireplace are, on closer inspection, not carved wood but varnished walnuts; Severs made the four-poster bed from old pallets and polystyrene. But the house invites its visitors to suspend disbelief and to inhabit the versions of the past it relates so eloquently – to walk like quiet ghosts through its busy rooms.

Severs and the New Georgians – a group that in addition to Stamp, Artley and Robinson included the future director of the National Gallery and later chief executive of the Royal Academy of Arts Charles Saumarez Smith, the writer and broadcaster Dan Cruikshank and the artists Glynn and Carrie Boyd Harte – were outspoken and influential. A consequence of their passion for restoration was a profound alteration of the social character of Spitalfields, as well as other places in similar predicaments. As the architectural status of the earliest terraces began to be widely recognized, their financial value rose steeply. Ironically, some developers at work in Spitalfields today use images of Georgian houses to illustrate their hoardings, when not so long ago they sought to knock them down. And yet a wider group of people were also able to buy into the past at this time, dressing up in styles redolent of Regency prints and Edwardian watercol-

Prairie dress designed by Laura Ashley, 1970s.

ours and escaping, at least in the imagination, from the present. Since 1969, the Welsh designer Laura Ashley had given a commercial dimension to historical style by producing long cotton frocks with puffed sleeves and skirts with tucks, many based on early nineteenth-century and Edwardian dresses in the Platt Hall collection of historical clothing in Manchester, the world's first dedicated costume museum. By the 1980s their dresses were typically of a simpler, more practical design, with square necks and fewer yards of fabric, and were every bit as popular. The patterns, often sprigged, were inspired by historical textiles, particularly nineteenth-century cottons but also the medieval and Renaissance textiles in the Victoria and Albert Museum. Ashley also produced furnishing fabrics for the home: one could take refuge in the simplicity of a Regency-style sitting room or the frills of a neo-Victorian bedroom and draw the prettily patterned curtains against the nowadays unfolding so unpredictably outside the window.[37]

More speculative routes into the past could be forged; in recent years many have embarked on the journey in a creative, do-it-yourself mood. With the countercultural phenomenon of steampunk, escapism itself made a decisive break from pastel shades and sprigged cotton and instead came dressed in an altogether more daring mixture of leather frock coats and corsets, straps and frogging, top hats and flying goggles – often all worn at the same time. Steampunk, which emerged in the 1990s from origins in science fiction books and films, rejected the contemporary post-industrial world and dreamed up an alternative reality – part-Victorian, part-futuristic – in which the industrial revolution had taken a different turn. Steampunks imagine a world of clockwork automata, in which hot-air balloons are a perfectly normal mode of transport and cars are powered by steam. They carry faux-antique fob watches, cover their iPhones in polished walnut cases and tap out emails on tarnished brass keys.[38] Closest to its spirit is the amateur adaptation and inventive repurposing of vintage clothes, although Vivienne Westwood and Alexander McQueen, both plunderers of the past enchanted by the elegant distortions of Victorian fashion, worked Steampunk-inspired styles into their collections, and its atmosphere also hung over the 'Pandemonium' section of Danny Boyle's opening ceremony for the 2012 London Olympics, with its exhilarating spectacle of seven vast factory chimneys emerging from the ground, attended by an army of men in goggles.[39]

I have been wondering how William Morris would have felt about steampunk. On the face of it, they have much in common: as is apparent from *News from Nowhere*, Morris also loved to vault over the irredeemably compromised nowadays to project himself into an alternative future, a utopia constructed from highly selective elements of the past. Yet steampunk's devotion to the shining, whirring, cranking, smoking, sparking machinery of the industrial revolution would have been a stumbling block. And while Morris was battling a rising tide of poorly designed and produced consumer goods, steampunks – along with their less futuristic but equally eccentric relations, hipsters – are facing the opposite: the disappearance of *things* altogether. In the face of e-books and streaming services, leather-bound volumes and wind-up gramophones carry significant emotional heft.

The Victorians had habitually been regarded as spectacular oddities; in part, this accounts for their appeal to successive countercultural groups. It was as though they had been preserved under a great glass dome that descended with Queen Victoria's death in 1901, through the walls of which one could marvel at their monstrous hypocrisies, their bizarre proprieties and their extreme religiosity – until a book of 2001 by Matthew Sweet, *Inventing the Victorians*, irresistibly demonstrated that far from being alien, they were disconcertingly like us. In the intervening years, however,

John Coulthart, 'Steam', from the 2013 *Steampunk Calendar*.

many artists and designers have been on a mission to recover the essential strangeness of Victoriana, particularly in art forms such as taxidermy that express attitudes to death quite at odds with those of the twenty-first century. The celebrated Victorian taxidermist Walter Potter created ambitious tableaux such as *The Death and Burial of Cock Robin* (1861), illustrating the popular nursery rhyme with ninety-eight specimens of British birds, some with glass tears fixed to their eyes. This and his other masterpieces *Rabbits' Village School* (*c.* 1888) and *The Kittens' Wedding* (*c.* 1890) now seem excessive in both their grotesquery and sentimentality; most of us are repelled by the first and unwilling to be coerced by the second. But while some may turn away with a shudder, others such as Damien Hirst, whose creatures suspended in formaldehyde defined 1990s avant-garde art, have recognized that a particular magic is to be found there.

Although Polly Morgan does not recreate Potterian scenes of sentimental anthropomorphy, her taxidermy sculptures tell similarly affecting stories with creatures. *Atrial Flutter* (2010) is constructed from a cast of a human ribcage and spinal column.[40] Caged within the ribs, about where the heart would be, is a small red bird, a cardinal. It is a kind of pun – the morbid flutter of the heart named in the title is replaced by the bird that has ceased to flutter. It is also symbolic: cardinals are traditionally thought to bring messages from the dead to the living. The 'bones' are suspended in the air, apparently held up by colourful balloons – or are they being carried away, conducted into the afterlife? Either way, Morgan's sculpture is about the delicate balance between life and death – the unstable pivot that makes taxidermy itself, so beloved of the Victorians, peculiarly fascinating.

Another taxidermist, Tessa Farmer, engages with the fanciful fairy imagery found in many Victorian paintings and illustrated books by artists such as Richard Doyle. In Farmer's sculptures tiny skeletal fairies, made from parts of insects and plants, capture bumblebees, gang up on ants and swarm over degenerating rodents (Plate XXIV). While Victorian fairies are largely benign, Farmer's are untamed, malevolent and weaponized. She seems to get inside the horror that many feel about taxidermied creatures, cranking it up as she rethinks Victorian conventions and pitches them at the modern world. Jewelers, too, have channelled the arresting power of animal remains into their work: a brooch by Simon Costin made of a taxidermied and gilded fish-head is now in the Victoria and Albert Museum, while Kelly McCallum mounts the heads of small birds and rodents on little plaques like miniature hunting trophies, to be worn as brooches; both artists play on the uncomfortable intimacy of a piece of taxidermy worn on the body. Other jewelers are delving into the culture of Victorian mourning jewelry: Jacqueline Cullen specializes in Whitby jet, while Zoe Arnold has used nineteenth-century daguerreotypes in her reliquary-like pendants.

These excursions into taxidermy have taken place against a backdrop of changing tastes that has allowed some aspects of Victoriana, long considered best forgotten, out of the closet. When the National Trust acquired Calke Abbey in 1985, a Derbyshire house that had become dilapidated and exuded a powerful sense of abandonment, they made a quietly radical decision: not to tidy it up but to preserve the rooms in the state of decline in which they had been left by the family, with peeling wallpaper, stacks of disordered possessions and eccentric arrangements of once-loved collections. At Calke, cabinets are stacked with shells, rock specimens and curiosities; beds are piled high with antlers and mounted animal heads; there are overflowing boxes of children's toys; a crocodile skull that grins quietly to itself in a display case; and flocks of songbirds under glass domes. An entire room is devoted to elaborate dioramas of taxidermied pheasants, foxes, swans, mallards, badgers, weasels and squirrels, carefully posed against backgrounds suggesting their natural habitat. A desire to evoke the enchanted atmosphere, touched by melancholy, that lingers in the rooms and corridors of Calke lay at the heart of an exhibition curated by the designer Mark Hearld in 2015–17 at York Art Gallery, 'The Lumber Room: Unimagined Treasures'. Many years before, he had been entranced by a short story by Saki (Hector Hugh Munro), 'The Lumber Room' (1914), about a boy who contrives secretly to enter a storeroom that has long worked on his imagination, where he finds 'wonderful things for the eye to feast on': a tapestry with a hunting scene, to him 'a living, breathing story'; candlesticks in the shape of snakes and a teapot in the form of a duck; brass figures of bulls and peacocks and goblins; an illustrated book about exotic birds, 'a whole portrait gallery of undreamed-of creatures'.[41] 'Since I heard Saki's story I have always been intrigued by the idea of a locked room that contained treasures so wonderful they are beyond what your mind can imagine,' Hearld has said. 'In this exhibition I wanted to create the sense of excitement and wonder that you get when you discover the key to the room and see the "forbidden" objects for the first time.'[42] For two years he delved into the furthest corners of Yorkshire Museum's and York Castle Museum's stores as well as those of the Gallery to find objects that were otherwise unlikely to have seen the light of day: gawky portraits, florid pub signs, toy theatre prints, ceramic horses, shellwork flowers under glass domes, Victorian capes, fairground gallopers and taxidermied fish of impressive dimensions. It presented a brightly coloured, *Saturday-Book* version of the olden times, a carefully curated Victorian era seen through a lens apparently prepared by Margaret Lambert and Enid Marx. The individual objects in 'The Lumber Room' were less important than the cumulative atmosphere they generated, which promised to transport its visitors back into Hearld's vision of a lost, boyish innocence.

The charming and beautiful mask constructed by museums and heritage organizations around the country has, in the late twentieth and twenty-first centuries, slipped from the face of many gallery displays and historic properties to reveal an ugly truth: that those who assembled the collections or built the houses often had connections, direct or indirect, with the transatlantic slave trade. Modern Britain has been slow to come to terms with the legacies reflected in its culture of five hundred years of colonialism. Ideas of racial and cultural superiority continue to resonate, whether echoing through the grandest historic interior or whispering in the smallest gallery display case. Among the objects visitors to these places might have admired for their beauty are many that were made by enslaved people: some were designed to contain goods like sugar or tobacco, harvested by slave labour; others were created from tropical hardwoods such as mahogany that were gathered under the same conditions; still others depict Black people in ways that unacceptably and distressingly objectify them.

Many objects from the countries invaded or colonized by Britain are displayed in ways insensitive to the cultures in which they were made; they may possess profound spiritual, cultural or historical meaning for their makers and their descendants, who call for their safe return home. They may have been taken by coercion or force, the history of how they came to be in museum collections elided or disguised in the language of 'acquisition' and 'gift-giving'. The stories of people of colour living or working at England's historic houses over the centuries have likewise long gone untold. None of these troubling facts was a startling revelation in 2020. But it took the murder of a Black man, George Floyd, by a white officer of the Minneapolis police force in May of that year and the subsequent momentum gained by the Black Lives Matter movement for many individuals and cultural organizations to accept accountability and to think afresh about the past as it, and its custodians, appeared in the glare of this searching light.

In this climate, can the past still be romanticized at all?

Perhaps not in the same way; but it can be reimagined with creativity and wit. For some time, artists and writers have been asking: can the past be pulled apart and experimented with? Shaken up and rethought?

The British-Nigerian artist Yinka Shonibare took the idea of collage and reversed it. Rather than bringing scraps of the past to the present, he projected himself back into a historical setting. In 1998, he created a

Heather Agyepong, *Too Many Blackamoors* (#8), 2015.

sequence of five photographs representing different times of day, entitled *Diary of a Victorian Dandy*, for which he employed a director of BBC costume dramas, professional actors and make-up artists and a photographer and arranged a three-day shoot on location.[43] Dressed in different costumes and posed in a variety of settings, the artist plays the central role in each scene. *Diary of a Victorian Dandy: 14.00 hours* is set in the library of a grand house, a room that reflects the taste, education and breeding of its inhabitants: there are leather-bound volumes on the shelves, classical busts on top of the bookcases and an eighteenth-century portrait of a man in peers' robes over the chimneypiece. The dandy, wearing a tailored three-piece suit, stands in a commanding position holding papers in one hand as if he has just finished speaking, his expression and posture conveying profound self-assurance. A clerk sits at a desk solemnly recording his words, while the dandy's four assembled friends applaud, laugh and gesture their appreciation. Behind the open door, four housemaids, hidden from the men in the room, listen in rapt admiration. Everything about the scene is conventional – it could be a Victorian painting of a society scene – except for one thing: the dandy is Black. Shonibare uses the figure of the dandy – a man who cultivates his dress, manner and poise to express an inner sense of superiority – because he is an ambiguous figure, an outsider admired by society for the very wit and flamboyance that sets him apart from it. The artist's use of modern colour photography, too, pokes a hole in the partition separating past from present and lets through an unsettling draught. How, Shonibare asks, are images of the olden times constructed in viewers' minds? What part do lingering colonial attitudes play, that write Black people out of England's history? Why can they so easily be disrupted? *Diary of a Victorian Dandy* is both playful and serious as it superimposes the present onto the past, drawing attention to the creative act of picturing history.

Heather Agyepong explores the processes of defining and creating the self against a backdrop of the English past in her work *Too Many Blackamoors* (2015). She takes the series's title from the words of Elizabeth I, who in 1596 wrote an open letter to the Lord Mayor of London announcing that 'there are of late divers black-moores brought into this realme, of which kinde of people there are allready here to manie', following it up a week later by commissioning a merchant to 'take up' certain 'blackamoores here in this realme and to transport them into Spaine and Portugall'.[44] Agyepong was also inspired by carte-de-visite photographs of Sarah Forbes Bonetta (also called Ina or Aina), an Egbado Yoruba woman orphaned as a child and enslaved by King Ghezo of Dahomey (present-day Benin), who subsequently presented her to Captain Frederick E. Forbes of the British Royal Navy as a 'gift' for Queen Victoria, who adopted her as her ward and goddaughter and brought her up to participate in upper-middle-class English society. Agyepong wore Victorian dress and adopted a series of poses for the sequence of black and white photographs. They slip disconcertingly between moods and time frames: in one, she strikes a conventionally graceful posture – it could almost be a nineteenth-century image – while elsewhere, she scrutinizes her own face in a mirror; reflectively handles a piece of wax-printed West African fabric; reads a copy of Peter Fryer's groundbreaking 1984 book *Staying Power: The History of Black People in Britain*; or raises her petticoat to reveal that her long skirts have concealed a pair of Dr. Martens boots. A hall of mirrors, *Too Many Blackamoors* manipulates the past, creating new versions that are unexpected, subtle and arresting.

Shonibare was among the artists invited to create work for an exhibition held at the Victoria and Albert Museum in 2007 to mark the bicentenary of the abolition of the British slave trade.[45] 'Uncomfortable Truths: The Shadow of Slave-Trading on Contemporary Art' was not held in a single place, but existed as a series of interventions dispersed throughout the museum. Shonibare's sculpture *Sir Foster Cunliffe, Playing*, specially commissioned for the exhibition, was positioned in the Norfolk House Music Room in the British Galleries, a room originally constructed for the Duke of Norfolk on St James's Square. The figure, headless, represented the grandson of a prominent Liverpool slave trader, who, when preparing a detailed family genealogy, sought to conceal the origins of the family's wealth and omitted the word 'slavery'. Shonibare exposes Cunliffe's deception by clothing him in the brightly coloured batik cotton often associated with West Africa, made into the conventional coat and breeches of his time. Batik adds another layer of complication to the work, as an art form imported to West Africa from Britain, having previously been developed in the Netherlands as a result of Dutch colonization of the islands that now make up Indonesia. And then another layer: many enslaved people were forced to produce cotton, which was shipped to the islands that now make up Indonesia. And then another layer: many enslaved people were forced to produce cotton, which was shipped to Britain to supply textile mills. The complex trading networks that relied on slave labour, suggests Shonibare, formed a global web that caught a great many between its warp and its weft.

Lubaina Himid's contribution to the exhibition, her 2004 work *Naming the Money*, also concerned the ways in which identity is shaped by colonialism and slavery. Visitors to the museum's galleries negotiated her cut-out figures of Black servants in the style of the dummy-board figures popular in grand houses of the eighteenth century, which were often painted with images of domestic staff (Plate XXV). Through written text or a soundtrack, each of Himid's figures told visitors of their former identities as herbalists, musicians, ceramicists, dancers, cooks, shoemakers and so on, before they were enslaved and assigned new names and roles.[46] Himid has described her desire to 'place black people into historical events, to make the invisible more visible'; during their stay in the galleries, her poignant and engaging figures came out of the shadows to disrupt and enrich the version of the past told by the museum's displays of high-status objects – many of which, as the exhibition pointed out, are tainted by associations with slavery.[47]

Writers, too, have for decades been prising apart established narratives and reimagining them: from Jean Rhys's *Wide Sargasso Sea* (1966), which retold *Jane Eyre* from the perspective of Mr Rochester's first wife, a Creole heiress named Antoinette Cosway, to Angela Carter's neo-Victorian novel *Nights at the Circus* (1984); from Sarah Waters's evocations of lesbian life in the Victorian era, *Tipping the Velvet* (1998), *Affinity* (1999) and *Fingersmith* (2002), to Sally Wainwright's television series *Gentleman Jack* (2019 and 2022), set in 1830s Yorkshire and based on the coded diaries left by Anne Lister detailing her love affairs with women. These authors have reinstated figures marginalized or excluded from conventional histories by their race, poverty, social class or sexuality and given them voices.

Today's artists and writers are engaging imaginatively with the past every bit as much as their predecessors, reframing and rewriting it – not in the sense of falsifying history, but of widening its scope and enriching its texture. In time, as more material comes to light, it will be reimagined again – and again. These are exhilarating times. The past has never been more unpredictable or more enthralling.

EPILOGUE

Most ghost stories, in my experience, fade in the memory as quickly as ghosts themselves are said to; but just occasionally a tale is told that is either so pithy or so bizarre that it lodges in the mind. One such used to be told by a dealer in second-hand books called Eric Barton. One evening, not long after the end of the Second World War, Eric and his wife Irina were in the Seven Dials area of London with their friends Olive Cook and Edwin Smith, the contributors of photo essays to the *Saturday Book*. It was early evening and they were looking for somewhere to have a drink when they noticed a doorway in a wall and steps that led down to a bar. They found themselves in a noisy and boisterous place, dirty and smelling of unwashed bodies, although as the friends were absorbed with each other and their conversation they did not pay a great deal of attention to their surroundings. Later, they wished they had. It was only after they had climbed back up into the evening air that they stopped, suddenly puzzled, and began to tell each other about things that had not felt right: the drab and ragged clothes, the rough manners, the quite unusual number of missing teeth. Now they came to think about it, these historians, they realized that it had had a distinct flavour of the early eighteenth century, a scent of genuinely Hogarthian low-life. But when they turned back to look, the doorway through which they had just passed was no longer there. Long afterwards, each of the four would make a detour whenever they were in the neighbourhood to walk along that street, and would look again for the door and the steps leading down – but they only ever found a blank wall.

Usually, we are told, ghosts visit the present from the past; but in this case the convention turned itself inside out. The four friends – if you are inclined to believe them – were swallowed by the past, before being regurgitated, like Jonah from the belly of the whale, back into the present.

Temporarily, they had become ghosts themselves, phantoms from the future.

Eric Barton's tale opens up a chink through which we glimpse the possibility of quite suddenly being immersed in the past like plunging into a deep pool, so that one is able not just to see it, but to smell and touch it, to hear and taste it.

It is not necessary to believe in ghosts to understand why stories about them continue to be told. If there is a historic house in the UK that is not purported to be haunted by at least one resident spirit, I have yet to hear of it. Ghosts trump the most glamorous painted portraits and expertly re-enact Britain's turbulent history, always dressed in unimpeachably correct historical costumes. The National Trust once ignored them and tried to dampen down any stories that circulated about local hauntings, but no longer; these days it is alive, if that is the word, to their value. Specialist ghost tours are lucrative: the prospect of the Duchess of Lauderdale appearing on the staircase at Ham House, or an immaculately attired Benjamin Disraeli materializing at Hughenden adds an extra dimension to the tour, an emotional frisson half of fear, half of desire.

Ghosts offer a mysterious connection with the past; they remind us of the layers of history pressing upon us. They tell us that the relationship between past and present is an active one, and that the junction between the two can be the finest of membranes. They enchant the present.

For Robert Macfarlane, writing in *The Old Ways: A Journey on Foot* (2012), the land itself is a profoundly haunted place. He imagines the past as a navigable element encompassing both vast stretches of geological time and the smaller span of human time, both prehistoric and recent. Walker-writers of the past trudge alongside him as he explores the ancient tracks of the Icknield Way and the Ridgeway. 'Walking as séance', he calls this imaginative accompaniment, and quotes John Masefield writing of the landscape as 'thronged by souls unseen, / Who knew the interest in me, and were keen / That man alive should understand man dead.' Macfarlane writes of exploring the holloways – ancient sunken paths – of Dorset, and of learning the stories that cling to them: of the refuge they have offered in successive centuries to persecuted groups or individuals, of masses said in the woods by Catholic priests. 'In the dusk of the holloways,' he writes, 'these pasts felt excitingly alive and coexistent – as if time had somehow pleated back on itself.' The feeling of time as non-linear is there again at the end of the book; following ancient footprints at Formby Point, preserved in silt by unusual climatic conditions on the day they were formed, Macfarlane recognizes an uncanny 'feeling of co-presence: the prehistoric and the present matching up such that it is unclear who walks in whose tracks'.[1] Along with Paul Nash – surely among the ghostly company who walk with him down sunken paths and lanes, through woods, over sand and along field selvedges – Macfarlane is alive to the 'accumulated intenseness of the past as present'.[2]

In Hilary Mantel's imagination, ghosts represent memory, desire, warning; paths not taken; unrealized potential; 'the tags and rags of everyday life'; the loose ends.[3] They are the different ways in which the past – which is as much about what did not happen as what did – shadows us, stalks us and speaks to us. In the first of her BBC Reith Lectures in 2017, Mantel made an important distinction between history and the past. 'To retrieve history', she said,

> we need rigour, integrity, unsparing devotion and an impulse to scepticism. To retrieve the past, we require all those virtues – and something more. If we want added value – to imagine not just how the past was, but what it felt like, from the inside – we pick up a novel. The historian and the biographer follow a trail of evidence, usually a paper trail. The novelist does that too, and then performs another act – puts the past back into process, into action – frees the people from the archive and lets them run about, ignorant of their fates, with all their mistakes unmade.[4]

Mantel is describing a kind of haunting: ghosts are said to return when there is unfinished business, when events of the past remain unresolved. If the historian unlocks the door of a historic house, then the novelist and the artist raise its resident spirits.

Open the book and release the ghosts. Let us hear about the *geardagum*, the days of old.

Notes

Prologue

1 John Goodall, 'The Little Castle, Bolsover, Derbyshire: A Property of English Heritage', *Country Life*, 5 December 2002

2 John Summerson, *The Unromantic Castle and Other Essays* (London, 1990), p. 14, quoted in Frank Salmon, '"Those damned Victorians!" John Summerson's changing vision of the Victorians', in *Victorians Revalued: What the Twentieth Century Thought of Nineteenth-Century Architecture*, ed. Rosemary Hill et al (London, 2010), pp. 75–89 (p. 82)

3 Charles Hardwick, *A Manual for Patrons and Members of Friendly Societies* (Manchester, 1859), p. 40, quoted in P. H. J. H. Gosden, *The Friendly Societies in England, 1815–1875* (Manchester, 1961), p. 1

4 For an excellent study of nostalgia, see Hannah Rose Woods, *Rule, Nostalgia: A Backwards History of Britain* (London, 2022)

5 William Cobbett, 4–5 December 1821, 'Kentish Journal' <www.visionofbritain.org.uk/travellers/Cobbett/3> [accessed 30 June 2022]

6 Alfred Tennyson, 'Break, break, break', IV, 3–4, in *Poems*, II (London, 1842)

7 Edward Burne-Jones to his studio assistant Thomas Rooke, in Georgiana Burne-Jones, *Memorials of Edward Burne-Jones*, 2 vols, II (London, 1906), p. 318

8 See in particular Hakim Adi (ed.), *Black British History: New Perspectives from Roman Times to the Present Day* (London, 2019), Helen Carr and Suzannah Lipscomb (eds), *What Is History, Now? How the Past and the Present Speak to Each Other* (London, 2021) and Sathnam Sanghera, *Empireland: How Imperialism Has Shaped Modern Britain* (London, 2021)

9 See Mary Beard, 'Roman Britain in Black and White', *Times Literary Supplement*, for an account of such adverse reactions, these to comments Beard had made on the presence of ethnic and racial diversity in Roman Britain <www.the-tls.co.uk/articles/roman-britain-black-white/> [accessed 27 June 2022]

10 'Of our conceptions of the past, we make a future'. Thomas Hobbes, *The Elements of Law Natural and Politic*, ed. J. C. A. Gaskin (Oxford, 1994), p. 32

11 Glenn Adamson, 'British aisles – the Met's new galleries don't shy away from addressing a complicated past', *Apollo*, 6 March 2020. The reworking of the British Galleries, which reopened in 2020, was initially led by curators Luke Syson and Ellenor Alcorn and taken forward by Sarah Lawrence and Wolf Burchard.

12 See Sally-Anne Huxtable, Corinne Fowler, Christo Kefalas and Emma Slocombe (eds), *Interim Report on the Connections between Colonialism and Properties now in the Care of the National Trust, including Links with Historic Slavery* (Swindon, 2020) <nt.global.ssl.fastly.net/documents/colonialism-and-historic-slavery-report.pdf> [accessed 30 May 2022]; see also Alice Procter, *The Whole Picture: The Colonial Story of the Art in Our Museums & Why We Need to Talk About It* (London, 2021) and Dan Hicks, *The Brutish Museums: The Benin Bronzes, Colonial Violence and Cultural Restitution* (London, 2020). On the interpretation of historic houses, see Corinne Fowler, *Green Unpleasant Land: Creative Responses to Rural England's Colonial Connections* (London, 2020) and Olivia Horsfall Turner and Oliver Cox, 'Comment: can historic houses tell more stories than they have done?', *Apollo*, 4 January 2021

Chapter 1

1 Anonymous Life of Saint Cuthbert in *Two Lives of Saint Cuthbert: A Life by an Anonymous Monk of Lindisfarne and Bede's Prose Life*, ed. and trans. Bertram Colgrave (Cambridge, 1940), p. 123

2 Gnomic poem prefixed to one MS of the *AS Chronicle*, quoted in Dorothy Whitelock, *The Beginnings of English Society* (London, 1954), p. 16

3 Anon., 'The Ruin', lines 1–2 and 21–4. Unless otherwise stated, translations from Old English are the author's own.

4 See James F. Doubleday, '"The Ruin": Structure and Theme', *Journal of English and*

Germanic Philology, 71.3 (July 1971), pp. 369–81 (p. 375)

5 Anon., 'The Wanderer', lines 92–3, 36, 73–4 and 94–6

6 The author of the *Historia Brittonum* is unknown but the work is traditionally credited to Nennius, whose name I use here for the sake of convenience. Nicholas Higham discusses the problems of the *Historia*'s authorship in *King Arthur: The Making of the Legend* (New Haven and London, 2018), pp. 180–3. Nennius, *British History and The Welsh Annals*, ed. and trans. John Morris (London and Chichester, 1980), ch. 11, p. 20

7 Geoffrey of Monmouth, *The History of the Kings of Britain*, ed. Michael D. Reeve and trans. Neil Wright (Woodbridge, 2007), p. vii

8 Higham (2018), p. 245

9 Geoffrey of Monmouth (2007), pp. 6–30

10 Alexandra Villing et al, *Troy: Myth and Reality*, exh. cat. (London, 2020), pp. 187–8

11 Diana Greenway, ed. and trans., Henry, Archdeacon of Huntingdon, *Historia Anglorum* (Oxford, 1996), p. 23

12 Geoffrey of Monmouth, pp. 170–4

13 Henry of Huntingdon to Warin the Breton, 1139; *Historia Anglorum*, p. 559

14 William of Newburgh, *The History of English Affairs*, ed. and trans. P. G. Walsh and M. J. Kennedy (Warminster, 1988), p. 29

15 Gerald of Wales (Giraldus Cambrensis), *The Journey Through Wales and The Description of Wales*, ed. and trans. Lewis Thorpe (London, 1978, repr. 2004), pp. 117–18

16 Nennius, ch. 56, pp. 35–6. The other early account of Arthur occurs in the *Annales Cambriae* probably written at St Davids in 953–4, that chronicles events from the fifth century onwards.

17 Michael Wood, *In Search of the Dark Ages* (London, 1981), p. 57

18 Ronald Hutton, *Witches, Druids and King Arthur* (2003; London, 2006), p. 41

19 William of Malmesbury, *Gesta Regum Anglorum: The History of the English Kings*, ed. and trans. R. A. B. Mynors, R. M. Thomson and M. Winterbottom, 2 vols (Oxford, 1998–9), I, pp. 26–7

20 See Kenneth Hurlstone Jackson, 'The Arthur of History', in Roger Sherman Loomis (ed.), *Arthurian Literature in the Middle Ages: A Collaborative History* (2001; Oxford, 1959), pp. 1–11. See also Hutton (2006); Guy Halsall, *Worlds of Arthur: Facts and Fictions of the Dark Ages* (Oxford, 2013); and Higham (2018)

21 Geoffrey of Monmouth, pp. 196, 198

22 *Ibid.*, p. 194

23 *Ibid.*, pp. 200–2

24 *Ibid.*, p. 212

25 *Ibid.*, p. 198

26 *Ibid.*, p. 252

27 William of Malmesbury, writing *c.* 1125, quoted in Higham (2018), p. 218

28 Gerald of Wales, *De Principis Instructione* (*c.* 1193); E. M. R. Ditmas, 'The Cult of Arthurian Relics', *Folklore*, 75.1 (1964), p. 21

29 See Keith Thomas, 'Perceptions of the Past in Early Modern England', in *The Creighton Century, 1907–2007*, ed. David Bates, Jennifer Wallis and Jane Winters (London, 2009), pp. 181–216 (pp. 186–7)

30 William Caxton, preface to Sir Thomas Malory, *Le Morte d'Arthur*, ed. Janet Cowen, 2 vols (London, 1969; repr. 2004), I, p. 6

31 Nennius, ch. 73, p. 42

32 Society of Antiquaries of London, MS 510; Sarah McCarthy, Bernard Nurse and David Gaimster (eds), *Making History: Antiquaries in Britain, 1707–2007*, exh. cat. (London, 2007), p. 21

33 See 'Troy: Enduring Stories' by J. Lesley Fitton, Alexandra Villing and Victoria Donnellan in Villing et al (2020), pp. 182–271 (p. 191). An example of the Greek soldiers in medieval armour can be seen in the *Histoire ancienne jusqu'a César*, made in Paris in the first quarter of the fifteenth century, British Library, Stowe MS 54, ff. 82v–83r

34 J. G. Mann, 'Instances of Antiquarian Feeling in Medieval and Renaissance Art', *Archaeological Journal*, 89.1 (1932), pp. 254–74 (p. 262)

35 See British Library catalogue entry for Rous Roll, Add. MS 48976 <www.bl.uk/manuscripts/FullDisplay.aspx?ref=Add_MS_48976> [accessed 11 March 2022]

36 T. D. Kendrick, *British Antiquity* (London, 1950), pp. 28–9

37 C. E. Wright, 'The Rous Roll', *The British Museum Quarterly*, 20.4, June 1956, pp. 77–81 (p. 79)

38 *Ibid.*, pp. 34–5

39 Vergil was chosen by Adriano Castellesi da Corneto, an intimate of Alexander VI and collector of Peter's pence, to travel to England in order to act as his subcollector. William J.

Connell, 'Vergil, Polydore [Polidoro Virgili] (*c.* 1470–1555), historian', *Oxford Dictionary of National Biography* <https://doi.org/10.1093/ref:odnb/28224> [accessed 15 December 2020]

40 *Polydore Vergil's English History*, ed. Henry Ellis (London, 1846), I, p. 26. Vergil's *Anglica historia* was completed in 1512, but not published until 1534, in Basel. A second, revised edition, much revised, appeared in 1546 and a new edition with further revisions came out in 1555. Connell, 'Vergil, Polydore'

41 *Polydore Vergil's English History*, pp. 27–9

42 *Ibid.*, p. 31

43 *Ibid.*, p. 33

44 *Ibid.*, p. 122

45 Kendrick (1950), p. 35

46 Edwin Greenlaw, *Studies in Spenser's Historical Allegory* (1932; London, 1967), pp. 172–7 and Kendrick (1950), pp. 36–7

47 *The Anglica Historia of Polydore Vergil, AD 1485–1537*, ed. and trans. Denys Hay (London, 1950), p. 5

48 Martin Biddle, 'The Painting of the Table', in Martin Biddle et al., *King Arthur's Round Table: An Archaeological Investigation* (Woodbridge, 2000) pp. 425–73 (pp. 425–9). See also Sydney Angelo, *Spectale, Pageantry, and Early Tudor Policy* (Oxford, 1969), ch. 5, and Jean Robertson, 'L'Entrée de Charles Quint à Londres, en 1522', in Jean Jacquot (ed.), *Fêtes et cérémonies au temps de Charles Quint* (Paris, 1960), pp. 169–81

49 Corpus Christi College, Cambridge, MS 298, fol. 137v, quoted in Biddle, 'The Painting of the Table' (2000), p. 427

50 Martin Biddle, 'The Making of the Round Table', in Biddle et al. (2000), pp. 337–92.

51 Pamela Tudor-Craig, 'Iconography of the Painting', in Biddle et al. (2000), p. 315; Biddle, 'The Painting of the Table'(2000), pp. 432–73

52 Stuart Piggott, *Ruins in a Landscape: Essays in Antiquarianism* (Edinburgh, 1976), p. 64

53 See Kendrick (1950), p. 86

54 John Leland, *A Learned and True Assertation of the Original Life, Actes, and Death of the Most Noble, Valiant, and Renoumed Prince Arthure, King of Great Brittaine*, trans. Richard Robinson (London, 1582), p. 12

55 *Ibid.*, p. 23

56 John Bale, *A Brefe Chronycle Concernynge the Examinacyon and Death of the Blessed Martyr of Christ Syr Johan Oldecastell the Lorde Cobham* (Antwerp, 1544), fol. 5r

57 Kendrick (1950), pp. 70–1

58 *Ibid.*, pp. 71–2. The author of this book, *Commentaria super opera diversor. auctor. de antiquitatibus loquentium* (Rome, 1498), was a Dominican abbot of Viterbo, Giovanni Nanni, or Annius (d. 1502)

59 See Elisabeth Woodhouse, 'Kenilworth, the Earl of Leicester's Pleasure Grounds Following Robert Laneham's Letter', *Garden History*, 27.1 (1999), pp. 127–44 (p. 127 and 130)

60 Quoted in Elizabeth Jenkins, *The Mystery of King Arthur* (London, 1975), p. 158. See also David M. Bergeron, *English Civic Pageantry 1558–1642* (London, 1971), pp. 30–1

61 Frances Yates, 'Elizabethan Chivalry: The Romance of the Accession Day Tilts', *Journal of the Warburg and Courtauld Institutes*, 20.1/2 (1957), pp. 4–25 (p. 5)

62 Roy Strong, 'The Popular Celebration of the Accession Day of Queen Elizabeth I', *Journal of the Warburg and Courtauld Institutes*, 21.1/2 (1958), pp. 86–103 (p. 86)

63 See Herbert W. Sugden, 'The Grammar of Spenser's Faerie Queene', *Language*, 12.4 (1936), pp. 9–228 (pp. 9–12) and Andrew Zurcher, 'Spenser and Archaism', 2005 <www.english.cam.ac.uk/ceres/haphazard/extra/language/archaism.html> [accessed 12 January 2022]

64 From E. K.'s 'Epistle' to Gabriel Harvey, quoted in Zurcher, 2005

65 Richard Dutton and Richard A. McCabe have both made similar points, the latter aptly calling the 'shared canon of heroic tales' provided by Geoffrey of Monmouth's stories and Bale's pre-Brutus narrative a 'sort of false memory syndrome'. Richard Dutton, 'Shakespeare and British History', *The Oxford Handbook of Holinshed's Chronicles*, ed. Paulina Kewes, Ian W. Archer and Felicity Heal (Oxford, 2012), pp. 527–42 (p. 528) and Richard A. McCabe, 'Spenser and Holinshed', *ibid.*, pp. 543–58 (p. 548)

66 The Holinshed Texts, 1577, vol. 1, p. 1 <english.nsms.ox.ac.uk/holinshed/texts.php?text1=1577_0105> [accessed 12 January 2022]

67 From Richard Dutton (ed.), *Jacobean Civic Pageants* (Keele, 1995), p. 48. See also Sam Smiles, 'John White and British Antiquity: Savage Origins in the Context of Tudor Historiography', in Kim Sloan, ed., *European Visions: American Voices* (London, 2009), pp. 106–12 (pp. 110–11)

68 See Graham Parry, *The Trophies of Time: English Antiquarians of the Seventeenth Century* (Oxford, 1995), pp. 52–3

69 John Milton, *The History of Britain, that Part Especially Now Call'd England* (1670; London, 1695), pp. 9, 10, 11

Chapter 2

1 William Camden, 'Britaine', in *Britannia*, trans. Philemon Holland (London, 1610), section 16 <www.visionofbritain.org.uk/travellers/Camden/2> [accessed 1 February 2021]

2 'it was not in his power to keep within doors: the bent of his own Genius was always pulling him out...' Thomas Smith, 'Life of Camden', trans. Edmund Gibson, in William Camden, *Britannia*, ed. Edmund Gibson (London, 1695), fol. B1v

3 Camden, 'The Author to the Reader', in *Britannia*, section 1 <www.visionofbritain.org.uk/travellers/Camden/1> [accessed 1 March 2021]

4 Thomas Smith, 'Life of Camden', quoted in Stuart Piggott, *Ruins in a Landscape* (Edinburgh, 1976), p. 12

5 Camden, 'Wilshire', in *Britannia*, section 16 <www.visionofbritain.org.uk/travellers/Camden/10> [accessed 2 February 2021]

6 *Ibid.*, 'Cumberland', section 9 <www.visionofbritain.org.uk/travellers/Camden/10> [accessed 2 February 2021]

7 *Ibid.*, 'The Author to the Reader', section 10 <www.visionofbritain.org.uk/travellers/Camden/1> [accessed 4 February 2021]

8 *Ibid.*, 'Wiltshire and Hampshire', sections 16-18 <www.visionofbritain.org.uk/travellers/Camden/10> [accessed 12 March 2021]

9 Graham Parry, *The Trophies of Time: English Antiquarians of the Seventeenth Century* (Oxford, 1995), p. 34

10 Quoted in Camden, 'The Maners and Customes of the Britans', *Britannia*, section 2, 'Caesar' <www.visionofbritain.org.uk/travellers/Camden/2> [accessed 24 June 2022]

11 Quoted *ibid.*, 'Herodian', section 8 <www.visionofbritain.org.uk/travellers/Camden/2> [accessed 24 June 2022]

12 *Ibid.*, sections 2, 8 and 9 <www.visionofbritain.org.uk/travellers/Camden/2> [accessed 11 February 2021]

13 In his preface to the chapter 'The Maners and Customes of the Britans', Camden tells us that a book on the Ancient Britons was being prepared by his friend Daniel Rogers, but was abandoned at his untimely death. He offers instead his 'few notes as touching their ancient maners and customes collected word for word out of ancient authors'. *Ibid.*, section 2 <www.visionofbritain.org.uk/travellers/Camden/2> [accessed 11 February 2021]

14 See Kim Sloan, *A New World: England's First View of America*, exh. cat. (London, 2007)

15 *Ibid.*, p. 153

16 *Ibid.*, p. 160

17 This was not the first time an artist had been inspired to depict ancient Britons by descriptions in classical sources. The painter Lucas de Heere completed two manuscripts, one of which, *Corte Beschryvinghe van Engheland, Schotland, ende Irland* (A Short Description of England, Scotland and Ireland, 1573–5), includes drawings of two ancient Britons. British Library, Add. MS 28330, f.8v. See Kim Sloan, *A New World*, p. 154.

18 For sixteenth-century designs for elite armour, see the Almain Armourers' Album in the Victoria and Albert Museum, D.586-1894 to D.614-1894

19 Compare with an early seventeenth-century woman's jacket now in the Victoria and Albert Museum, T.228-1994. See also Sloan (2007), p. 160

20 See Sloan (2007), pp. 110–11, 153

21 Christina DeCoursey, 'Society of Antiquaries', *Oxford Dictionary of National Biography* <doi.org/10.1093/ref:odnb/72906> [accessed 1 March 2021]

22 Stuart Handley, 'Cotton, Sir Robert Bruce, first baronet (1571–1631), antiquary and politician', *Oxford Dictionary of National Biography* <doi.org/10.1093/ref:odnb/6425> [accessed 1 March 2021]

23 For my description of Sir Robert Cotton's library, I am much indebted to Graham Parry's chapter on Cotton (1995), pp. 70–94

24 James Ussher, *The Annals of the World Deduced from the Origin of Time* (London, 1658), p. 1. See Parry (1995), pp. 148–9

25 *Ibid.*, p. 2

26 Francis Bacon, *Gesta Grayorum* (London, 1688), pp. 34–5. The *Gesta Grayorum* were Christmas festivities of 1594–5 at Gray's Inn for which Bacon wrote parts. See Markku Peltonen, 'Francis Bacon, Viscount St Alban (1561–1626)', *Oxford Dictionary of National Biography* <doi.org/10.1093/ref:odnb/990> [accessed 1 March 2021]

27 Thomas Browne, *Religio Medici* (London, 1643), section 16 <penelope.uchicago.edu/relmed/relmed.html> [accessed 1 March 2021]
28 Parry (1995), p. 93
29 Oliver Impey and Arthur MacGregor (eds), *The Origins of Museums: The Cabinet of Curiosities in Sixteenth- and Seventeenth-Century Europe* (Oxford, 1985), pp. 149–52
30 Richard Verstegan, *The Restitution of Decayed Intelligence in Antiquities* (London, 1605), p. 100
31 Camden, 'Yorkshire: North Riding', in *Britannia*, section 42 <www.visionofbritain.org.uk/travellers/Camden/26> [accessed 4 March 2021]
32 Robert Plot, *The Natural History of Oxfordshire, Being an Essay in the Natural History of England* (Oxford, 1677), p. 111
33 *Ibid.*, p. 113
34 *Ibid.*, p. 122
35 Stuart Piggott, 'Dr Plot, Ring Ditches and the Fairies', *Antiquity*, 59 (1985), pp. 206–9; and *Ancient Britons and the Antiquarian Imagination* (London, 1989), pp. 8–9
36 Plot (1677), pp. 131–2
37 *Ibid.*, pp. 133–9
38 *Ibid.*, p. 138
39 Thomas Browne, *Hydriotaphia, Urne-Buriall, or, A Brief Discourse of the Sepulchrall Urnes Lately Found in Norfolk* (1658; New York, 2010), p. 37. 'Urne-Buriall' is a translation of 'Hydriotaphia': a 'hydria' is a large Greek jar or pitcher meant for carrying water – or, indeed, an urn – while 'taphos' means a grave.
40 *Ibid.*, ch. II, pp. 44 and 37 and ch. III, p. 52
41 *Ibid.*, dedicatory address to Thomas Le Gros, p. 26
42 *Ibid.*, ch. V, p. 81
43 *Ibid.*, ch. V, pp. 89 and 84
44 See Parry (1995), p. 251
45 Browne (2010), ch. V, p. 79
46 *Ibid.*, ch. V, p. 83
47 *Ibid.*, ch. V, pp. 84–5
48 *Ibid.*, ch. V, p. 79
49 Samuel Daniel, *Musophilus* (1599), quoted in Christopher Chippindale, *Stonehenge Complete* (Ithaca, NY, 1983), p. 42
50 Parry (1995), p. 282
51 Edmund Bolton, 'Hypercritica', in Nicolai Triveti et al., *Dominicani, Annales Sex Regum Angliae*, 2 vols (Oxford, 1719-22), II, p. 220
52 Edmund Bolton, *Nero Caesar* (London, 1624), pp. 181–4
53 John Webb, 'To the Favourers of Antiquity', preface to Inigo Jones and John Webb, *The Most Notable Antiquity of Great Britain, Vulgarly Called Stone-Heng on Salisbury Plain Restored* (London, 1655), p. iii. *Stonehenge Restored* was the first work wholly dedicated to Stonehenge.
54 Jones and Webb (1655), p. 51
55 *Ibid.*, p. 66
56 *Ibid.*, p. 63
57 *Ibid.*, p. 101
58 See the engraved portrait by Pierre Lombart in the National Portrait Gallery, NPG D2053
59 Walter Charleton, *Chorea Gigantum, or, the Most Famous Antiquity of Great Britain, vulgarly called Stone-Heng, standing on Salisbury Plain, Restored to the Danes* (London, 1663), pp. 13, 62
60 *Ibid.*, p. 55
61 *Ibid.*, p. xii
62 *Ibid.*, p. 62
63 John Aubrey, *Monumenta Britannica, or, a Miscellany of British Antiquities*, ed. Rodney Legg and John Fowles, 2 vols (Sherborne, 1980 and 1982), I, p. 24
64 *Ibid.*, pp. 19–20
65 *Ibid.*, quoted in Michael Hunter, *John Aubrey and the Realm of Learning* (London, 1975), p. 180
66 Aubrey (1980, 1982), p. 25
67 *Ibid.*, pp. 24–5
68 Hunter (1975), p. 159 and p. 77. The manuscript of *Monumenta Britannica* is now in the Bodleian Library in Oxford, MSS top. gen. c.24 and c.25.
69 Aubrey, MS note in *The Natural History of Wiltshire*, quoted in Hunter (1975), p. 59
70 John Aubrey, *The Natural History of Wiltshire*, ed. John Britton (Newton Abbot, 1969), p. 4
71 John Aubrey, *An Essay towards the Description of the North Division of Wiltshire*, Bodleian Library MS Aubrey 3, 10; quoted in Hunter (1975), p. 150
72 Aylett Sammes, *Britannia Antiqua Illustrata: or, the Antiquities of Ancient Britain, Derived from the Phoenicians* (London, 1676), p. 397
73 *Ibid.*, p. vi
74 The idea had been broached by the Tudor historian John Twyne and, more recently, by the French scholar Samuel Bochart. See Parry (1995), pp. 309–13
75 See *ibid.*, pp. 313–20, and Rosemary Hill, *Stonehenge* (London, 2008), pp. 34–6
76 Sammes (1676), p. 398
77 Parry (1995), pp. 323–4

78 The image of the wicker man derives from an account by Julius Caesar in book VI of *De Bello Gallico* (the Gallic Wars), *c.* 58–49 BC; that of the ancient Briton from one by the Greek geographer and historian Strabo (63 BC to AD 23); the image of the druid from a description by the jurist and scholar John Selden in his *Jani Anglorum Facies Altera* (1610). See Parry (1995), pp. 102–3, 317

79 For material on William Stukeley I am indebted to Chippindale (1983), pp. 71–86 and Hill (2008), pp. 39–49

80 Stukeley's obsession with druids extended to his own garden at Grantham, in which he built a 'temple of the druids' in a grove. See Todd Longstaffe-Gowan, *English Garden Eccentrics: Three Hundred Years of Extraordinary Groves, Burrowings, Mountains and Menageries* (London, 2022), p. 276

81 William Stukeley, *Stonehenge: A Temple Restor'd to the British Druids* (London, 1740), p. 1

82 *Ibid.*, preface, p. vii

83 See David Boyd Haycock, '"A Small Journey into the Country": William Stukeley and the Formal Landscapes of Avebury and Stonehenge', in Megan Aldrich and Robert J. Wallis (eds), *Antiquaries & Archaists: The Past in the Past, the Past in the Present* (Reading, 2009), pp. 46–61

84 *Ibid.*, p. 12

85 *Ibid.*, p. 31

86 Henry James, 'Wells and Salisbury', in *English Hours* (London, 1905), p. 114

87 Jacquetta Hawkes, 'God in the Machine', *Antiquity*, 41 (1967), pp. 174–80 (p. 174)

Chapter 3

1 Alexander Pope to Martha and Teresa Blount, 8 October 1718, in *The Works of Alexander Pope*, ed. Whitwell Elwin and William John Courthorpe, 10 vols (London, 1871–89), IV (1886), p. 289

2 Alexander Pope to George Lyttelton, *c.* 1 November 1738, quoted in Michael Cousins, 'Hagley Park, Worcestershire', *Garden History*, 2007, 35, pp. 1–152 (p. 45). Historic England's listing for Alfred's Hall: <historicengland.org.uk/listing/the-list/list-entry/1298719> [accessed 4 May 2021]. See also William Alvis Brogden, *Ichnographia Rustica: Stephen Switzer and the Designed Landscape* (Oxford, 2017), p. 194

3 Edward Stephens, *A Poem on the Park and Woods of the Right Honourable Allen Lord Bathurst* (Cirencester, 1748), p. 9. Alfred's Hall is on Historic England's Heritage at Risk Register, and unless it receives some attention soon, the 'sudden Fall' with which its walls used playfully to 'Threat[en] the Beholders' (p. 8) looks all too likely. <historicengland.org.uk/advice/heritage-at-risk/search-register/list-entry/46836> [accessed 4 June 2022]

4 Mrs Pendarves to Jonathan Swift, 24 October 1733, *The Works of Jonathan Swift*, 2 vols (London, 1848), II, p. 714

5 See J. M. Frew, 'Gothic is English: John Carter and the Revival of the Gothic as England's National Style', *The Art Bulletin*, 64.2 (1982), pp. 315–19

6 Horace Walpole to Richard Bentley, September 1753, *The Yale Edition of Horace Walpole's Correspondence*, ed. W. S. Lewis et al., 48 vols (New Haven and London, 1937–83), XXXV, p. 148

7 See David Stewart, 'Political Ruins: Gothic Sham Ruins and the '45', *Journal of the Society of Architectural Historians*, 55.4 (1996), pp. 400–11.

8 See Michael McCarthy, *The Origins of the Gothic Revival* (New Haven and London, 1987), pp. 51–2

9 *Ibid.*, pp. 402–3

10 William Shenstone to Richard Jago, 16 June 1754, *The Works, in Verse and Prose, of William Shenstone*, 3 vols (London, 1791), III, pp. 237–8

11 Richard Jago, *Edge Hill* (1767; 2nd edn, London 1784), book I, lines 25–7 and 373–82

12 *Ibid.*, lines 394–401

13 William Shenstone to Mr Graves, 30 May 1758, *Works* (1791), III, p. 275. Historic England's listing for 'The Leasowes' <historicengland.org.uk/listing/the-list/list-entry/1001204> [accessed 18 May 2021]

14 *The Works in Verse and Prose of William Shenstone*, 2 vols (London, 1764), I, pp. 320–1

15 George Colman and David Garrick, *The Clandestine Marriage*, 1766, II.ii

16 William Gilpin, *Observations, Relatively chiefly to Picturesque Beauty, Made in the Year 1772, on Several Parts of England, particularly the Mountains, and Lakes of Cumberland, and Westmoreland*, 2 vols (London, 1786), I, pp. 67–9

17 See Megan Aldrich, *Gothic Revival* (London, 1994), p. 44. As Aldrich points out, at this time 'landscape gardens were a kind of working laboratory for innovations in domestic architecture'. *Ibid.*

18 Paget Toynbee (ed.), 'Horace Walpole's Journals of Visits to Country Seats etc.', *The Volume of the Walpole Society*, 16 (1927–8), pp. 9–80 (p. 36). Walpole was recording a repeat visit he made on 22 August 1761 to Charles Hamilton's house at Painshill near Cobham in Surrey, its design taken from Langley's book.

19 William Shenstone to Richard Jago, 1749, *Works* (1791), III, p. 183

20 John Earle, *The Autograph Manuscript of Microcosmographie* (*c.* 1628; Leeds, 1966), pp. 27–8; see also Rosemary Hill, *Time's Witness: History in the Age of Romanticism* (London, 2021), pp. 27–9

21 Ralph Hyde, 'Samuel Buck (1696–1779)', *Oxford Dictionary of National Biography* <doi.org/10.1093/ref:odnb/3850> [accessed 4 June 2021]

22 Daniel Defoe, *A Tour Through the Whole Island of Great Britain*, ed. P. N. Furbank, W. R. Owens and A. J. Coulson (New Haven and London, 1991), p. 3 (preface) and p. 285 (letter IX, Eastern Yorkshire, Durham and Northumberland)

23 *The Works in Verse and Prose of William Shenstone, Esq.*, 2 vols (Edinburgh, 1768), II, p. 94

24 Ann Radcliffe, *A Journey made in the Summer of 1794, through Holland and the Western Frontier of Germany, with a Return down the Rhine: to which are added, Observations during a Tour to the Lakes* (Dublin, 1795), pp. 487–91

25 See Emma McEvoy, 'Exploring Britain's Ruins', in *Writing Britain's Ruins*, ed. Michael Carter, Peter N. Lindfield and Dale Townshend (London, 2017), pp. 131–57 (pp. 152–3)

26 John Byng, *The Torrington Diaries*, ed. C. Bruyn Andrews, 4 vols (London, 1934–8), I, p. 249

27 John Byng, 'An Excursion taken in the year 1781', Bodleian Library, MS. Eng. misc. d. 237. Byng's frontispiece is reproduced in *With Torrington to Tintern*, a blog by the Gardens Trust <thegardenstrust.blog/2018/11/24/with-torrington-to-tintern/> [accessed 15 August 2022]

28 Jane Austen, 'The History of England from the reign of Henry the 4th to the death of Charles the 1st', British Library, Add. MS 59874, pp. 14–15 < www.bl.uk/turning-the-pages/?id=152707d0-a674-11db-a95e-0050c2490048&type=book> [accessed 27 May 2022]

29 Jane Austen, *Northanger Abbey* (London, 1818), II, chs 5, 6 and 10

30 Laetitia-Matilda Hawkins, *Anecdotes, Biographical Sketches and Memoirs*, 3 vols (London, 1822–4), I, pp. 105–6

31 Horace Walpole to George Montagu, 11 May 1769, *Correspondence* (1937–83), X, p. 278

32 For the passages on Strawberry Hill I am indebted to *Horace Walpole's Strawberry Hill*, ed. Michael Snodin (New Haven and London, 2009), in particular Snodin's chapter 'Going to Strawberry Hill' (pp. 15–57) and chapters by Kevin Rogers and Alicia Weisberg-Roberts, respectively 'Walpole's Gothic: Creating a Fictive History' (pp. 59–73) and 'Singular Objects and Multiple Meanings' (pp. 87–105). I have also made particular use of Clive Wainwright's chapter on Strawberry Hill in his book *The Romantic Interior: The British Collector at Home, 1750–1850* (New Haven and London, 1989), pp. 71–107. The 2010 exhibition at the Victoria and Albert Museum curated by Michael Snodin, 'Horace Walpole's Strawberry Hill', is a valuable memory, as is the exhibition Snodin co-curated with Silvia Davoli, 'Lost Treasures of Strawberry Hill: Masterpieces from Horace Walpole's Collection', held at Strawberry Hill during the winter of 2018–19.

33 From *Description of the Villa of Mr Horace Walpole, at Strawberry Hill near Twickenham, With an Inventory of the Furniture, Portraits, Curiosities Etc.*, printed at Walpole's own press in 1774 and 1784. See Stephen Clarke, 'A Description... of Strawberry Hill', in Snodin (2009), pp. 18–19; also p. 226 and pp. 314–15

34 Horace Walpole to Henry Seymour Conway, 8 June 1747, *Correspondence* (1937–83), XXXVII, p. 269

35 Horace Walpole to Sir Horace Mann, 10 January 1750, *ibid.*, XX, p. 111

36 Horace Walpole to George Montagu, 11 June 1753, *ibid.*, IX, p. 149

37 Horace Walpole to Sir Horace Mann, 12 June 1753, *ibid.*, XX, p. 381

38 Horace Walpole to William Cole, 9 March 1765, *ibid.*, I, p. 88

39 Horace Walpole, *The Castle of Otranto: A Gothic Story*, ed. W. S. Lewis (London, 1964), pp. 23–4. See Snodin (2009), p. 287; Walpole recorded that the idea of a figure walking out of a picture was suggested by this particular portrait in a note he added to his 1784 edition of the *Description...of Strawberry Hill.*

40 Horace Walpole to George Montagu, 5 January 1766, *Correspondence* (1937–83), X, p. 192
41 E. Curll, *The Rarities of Richmond, being the exact descriptions of the Royal Hermitage and Merlin's Cave with his Life and Prophecies* (London, 1736), pp. 111–12
42 Steven Brindle, 'Royal Commissions', in Susan Weber (ed.), *William Kent: Designing Georgian Britain* (New Haven and London, 2013), pp. 271–301 (pp. 285–6), and Judith Colton, 'Merlin's Cave and Queen Caroline: Garden Art as Political Propaganda', *Eighteenth-Century Studies*, 10 (1976), pp. 1–20 (pp. 10–15)
43 Tim Knox, *Sir John Soane's Museum London* (London, 2008), p. 74
44 John Soane, *Description of the House and Museum on the North Side of Lincoln's Inn Fields, the Residence of Sir J. Soane* (London, 1835), p. 27
45 For the idea of Soane as a kind of Gothic novelist, I am indebted to an article by Helen Dorey, 'Sir John Soane's Courtyard Gardens at Lincoln's Inn Fields', *The London Gardener, or the Gardener's Intelligencer*, 5, 1999–2000, pp. 14–21. Dorey points out that Soane owned two copies of Matthew Lewis's famous Gothic novel *The Monk* (1796), one bought in the year of its publication.
46 Thomas Gray to William Mason, 24 or 31 May 1757, *Thomas Gray Archive* <www.thomasgray.org/> [accessed 23 June 2021]
47 William Whitley, *Artists and their Friends in England, 1700–1799*, 2 vols (London, 1928), I, p. 169
48 James Macpherson, ed., *Fragments of Ancient Poetry* (Edinburgh, 1760), pp. iii and vi
49 *Ibid.*, p. 23
50 *Ibid.*, p. vii
51 Anna Seward to unknown correspondent, November 1762, *The Poetical Works of Anna Seward; With Extracts from her Literary Correspondence*, ed. Walter Scott, 3 vols (Edinburgh, 1810), I, p. lvii
52 Thomas Gray to Horace Walpole, *c.* April 1760, *Thomas Gray Archive*, letters.0357 <www.thomasgray.org> [accessed 8 August 2021]
53 Thomas Gray to Thomas Wharton, *c.* 20 June 1760; *ibid.*, letters.0361 <www.thomasgray.org> [accessed 8 August 2021]
54 For discussions of the debate, see Edward D. Snyder, *The Celtic Revival in English Literature 1760–1800* (Cambridge, MA, 1923, repr. 1965), pp. 78–85; Howard Gaskill, '"Ossian" Macpherson: Towards a Rehabilitation', *Comparative Criticism – an Annual Journal*, 8 (1986), pp. 113–46; and Sam Smiles, *The Image of Antiquity: Ancient Britain and the Romantic Imagination* (New Haven and London, 1994), pp. 61–9
55 On the relevance of Macpherson's poems/translations to their times, see John L. Greenway, 'The Gateway to Innocence: Ossian and the Nordic Bard as Myth', *Studies in Eighteenth Century Culture*, IV (1975), pp. 161–70
56 Percy's note inside the cover of the MS, in J. W. Hales and F. J. Furnivall, eds, *Bishop Percy's Folio Manuscript: Ballads and Romances*, 3 vols (London, 1867–8), I, p. lxxiv
57 Nick Groom, *The Making of Percy's* Reliques (Oxford, 1999), p. 6
58 *Ibid.*, pp. 42–3; and M. E. J. Hughes, *The Pepys Library and the Historic Collections of Magdalene College Cambridge* (London, 2015), p. 32
59 Thomas Percy, *Reliques of Ancient English Poetry; consisting of Old Heroic Ballads, Songs, and other Pieces of our earlier Poets*, 3 vols (London, 1765), I, p. ix
60 'Robin Hood and Guy of Gisborne', Percy (1765), I, 1, viii, lines 171–2; 'Little Musgrave and Lady Barnard', III, 1, xi; 'The Lady Isabella's Tragedy', III, 2, xiv, lines 93–4.
61 Percy (1765), pp. xvi–xvii
62 S. H. Harlowe, 'Letters from Dr Percy to T. Astle, esq.', *Notes & Queries*, IV.3 (1869), pp. 25–7
63 As Rosemary Hill nicely puts it in *Time's Witness: History in the Age of Romanticism* (London, 2021), Ritson's *Robin Hood* anthology 'reflected the contradictions in Ritson's character by combining research so thorough that it has never been substantially superseded, with violent political polemic' (p. 74)
64 Edward Bell, 'Memoir', in *The Poetical Works of Thomas Chatterton*, ed. Walter W. Skeat, 2 vols (London, 1871–83), I, pp. xx
65 Nick Groom, 'Thomas Chatterton', *Oxford Dictionary of National Biography* <doi.org/10.1093/ref:odnb/5189 > [accessed 5 October 2022]
66 *The Confessions of William-Henry Ireland* (London, 1805), pp. 17–18
67 Groom, 'Chatterton', pp. 3–4
68 *Ibid.*, pp. 6–7
69 Quoted in Daniel Wilson, *Chatterton: A Biographical Study* (London, 1869), pp. 116–17

70 Bell, 'Memoir', p. lviii
71 Thomas Chatterton, *Poems, Supposed to have been Written at Bristol, by Thomas Rowley, and Others, in the Fifteenth Century* (3rd edn, London, 1778), p. 24
72 *Ibid.*, pp. 278–9
73 Groom, 'Chatterton', pp. 5–6
74 See Joseph Cottle, 'Account of Rowley's MSS', in *The Works of Thomas Chatterton*, ed. Joseph Cottle and Robert Southey, 3 vols (London, 1803), III, pp. 497–520; Groom, 'Chatterton', p. 5
75 Cottle (1803), pp. 513–14
76 Walpole, *Correspondence* (1937–83), XVI, pp. 101–5 (pp. 103–4)
77 Horace Walpole to Thomas Chatterton, 28 March 1769; *ibid.*, p. 105; see also an incomplete, unsent letter from Walpole to Chatterton written between 27 July and 4 August 1769, *ibid.*, pp. 116–18
78 Groom, 'Chatterton', p. 11
79 William Blake, 'The Body of Edward I in his Coffin', 1774, pen and ink, Society of Antiquaries, London <www.blakearchive.org/work/pid> [accessed 1 September 2021]
80 Smiles (1994), p. 72
81 William Blake, *A Descriptive Catalogue of Pictures, Poetical and Historical Inventions* (London, 1809), p. 43
82 Blake's lyric poem 'And did those feet in ancient time', now known as the hymn 'Jerusalem', was first published in 1810 in the 'Preface' to *Milton*
83 *Exhibition of Paintings in Fresco, Poetical and Historical Inventions by Wm. Blake* (London, 1809), pp. 44 and 40, here quoted from David V. Erdman, *The Complete Poetry & Prose of William Blake* (New York, 1965; rev. edn 1988), p. 544 and p. 542; <erdman.blakearchive.org/> [accessed 15 August 2022]
84 Alexander Gilchrist, *Life of William Blake, 'Pictor Ignotus'*, 2 vols (London and Cambridge, 1863), I, p. 250
85 *Ibid.*, I, p. 251
86 On the Visionary Heads, see Martin Butlin, *The Blake-Varley Sketchbook of 1819*, 2 vols (London, 1969) and David Bindman, *Blake as an Artist* (Oxford, 1977), p. 202
87 Gilchrist (1863), I, p. 321
88 *Ibid.*, I, p. 252

Chapter 4

1 Walter Scott, *The Lady of the Lake* (Edinburgh, 1810), canto I, lines 186–7
2 J. G. Lockhart, *Memoirs of the Life of Sir Walter Scott*, 4 vols (Paris, 1838), III, p. 176
3 Letter written by Scott, *c.* 1816, quoted in Clive Wainwright, *The Romantic Interior: The British Collector at Home 1750–1850* (New Haven and London, 1989), pp. 199–200
4 Walter Scott to Daniel Terry, 23 January 1818; *The Letters of Sir Walter Scott*, ed. H. J. C. Grierson, 12 vols (London, 1932–7), V, p. 63
5 Sarah Barter Bailey, 'Sir Samuel Rush Meyrick', *Oxford Dictionary of National Biography* <doi.org/10.1093/ref:odnb/18644> [accessed 16 October 2021]
6 Ian Anstruther, *The Knight and the Umbrella: An Account of the Eglinton Tournament, 1839* (London, 1963), pp. 125–6
7 *Ibid.*
8 For a detailed exploration of Scott's creative engagement with objects, see Lucy Majella Linforth, 'Fragments of the Past: Walter Scott, Material Antiquarianism and Writing as Preservation', unpublished PhD thesis (University of Edinburgh, 2016)
9 Walter Scott to Joanna Baillie, 17 December 1811, and Walter Scott to Joanna Baillie, 4 April 1812, *Letters* (1932–7), III, pp. 39 and p. 99. I am grateful to Kirsty Archer-Thompson, Collections Manager at Abbotsford, for her guidance on Scott's collection and his creative process. I am also indebted to Dr Anna Groundwater, Principal Curator of Renaissance and Early Modern History at National Museums Scotland, for her kindness in providing me with the label texts written for the exhibition 'Inspiring Walter Scott' (National Museum of Scotland, Edinburgh, 6 August 2021 to 9 January 2022). See also Stuart Kelly, *Scott-Land: The Man who Invented a Nation* (Edinburgh, 2021), pp. 127–41
10 Mary Monica Maxwell Scott, *Abbotsford: The Personal Relics and Antiquarian Treasures of Sir Walter Scott* (London, 1893), p. 38
11 Walter Scott to Lady Alvanley, 25 May 1812, *Letters* (1932–7), III, p. 122
12 Walter Scott, *The Antiquary* (Edinburgh, 1816), ch. XL
13 *Ibid.*, ch. IV
14 John Ruskin to John Claudius Loudon, September 1838, *The Works of John Ruskin*, ed. E. T. Cook and Alexander Wedderburn, 37 vols (London, 1903–12), XXXVI, p. 17
15 A. N. Wilson has written that Scott's was 'the first mind in history to enquire what people in the past were actually like'; introduction to Penguin Classics edition of Walter Scott, *Ivanhoe* (London, 1986), p. xiii

16 Thackeray, 'An Exhibition Gossip', in *Sultan Stork and Other Stories and Sketches* (London, 1887), pp. 49–50
17 Walter Scott, *Kenilworth: A Romance* (Edinburgh, 1821), ch. VII
18 Catherine Gordon, 'The Illustration of Sir Walter Scott: Nineteenth-Century Enthusiasm and Adaptation', *Journal of the Warburg and Courtauld Institutes*, 34 (1971), pp. 297–317 (p. 297)
19 Allardyce Nicoll, *A History of English Drama 1660–1900*, 5 vols (Cambridge, 2009), IV, p. 93, n. 5
20 See Hannah Rose Woods, *Rule, Nostalgia: A Backwards History of Britain* (London, 2022), pp. 210–11
21 'May Gambols, or Titmarsh in the Picture Galleries', in *The Works of William Makepeace Thackeray*, 26 vols (London, 1885), XXV, pp. 242–3
22 Thomas Gray to Thomas Wharton, 4 December 1762, *Thomas Gray Archive* <www.thomasgray.org/cgi-bin/display.cgi?text=tgal0416> [accessed 16 October 2021]
23 See 'Preserving the "false...romance of history"', in Jonny Yarker, 'Continuity and the Country House: Preservation as a Strategy of Display from 1688 to 1950', in *Art and the Country House*, Paul Mellon Centre, 2020 <www.artandthecountryhouse.com/> [accessed 25 October 2021]
24 Quoted in John Cornforth, 'Cotehele House, Cornwall - II', *Country Life*, 184.6 (8 February 1990), p. 68. See also Jonny Yarker, '"Gothic it was, and more Gothic it will be"', *ibid.*
25 See Roy Strong, *And When Did You Last See Your Father? The Victorian Painter and British History* (London, 1978), pp. 128–35 and pp. 162–3
26 On the practice of Grangerizing, see Lucy Peltz, 'A Friendly Gathering: The Social Politics of Presentation Books and Their Extra-Illustration in Horace Walpole's Circle', *Journal of the History of Collections*, 19.1 (2007), pp. 33–49
27 Joseph Strutt, *The Regal and Ecclesiastical Antiquities of England* (1773; 3rd edn, London, 1793), preface (unpaginated)
28 See Jennifer Harris, 'Joseph Strutt', *Oxford Dictionary of National Biography* <doi.org/10.1093/ref:odnb/26684> [accessed 5 October 2022]
29 Strutt (1793), p. 37
30 Joseph Strutt, *Queenhoo-Hall: A Romance* (London, 1808), ch. 1
31 Peter Mandler refers to Nash's 'humanizing of the past' in *The Fall and Rise of the Stately Home* (New Haven and London, 1997), p. 34. His chapter 'The Victorian Idea of Heritage', pp. 21–69, provides a thoughtful, nuanced account of the idea of the 'olden days' as applied to country houses throughout this period.
32 See Mandler (1997), p. 34
33 Joseph Nash, 'Descriptions of the Plates', in *The Mansions of England in the Olden Time*, 4 vols (London, 1839), I, pp. 1–2
34 Entry for 1 March 1671; *The Diary of John Evelyn*, ed. John Bowle (Oxford, 1985), p. 233
35 Nikolaus Pevsner and Judy Nairn, eds, rev. Elizabeth Williamson, *The Buildings of England: Derbyshire* (2nd edn, Harmondsworth, 1978), p. 221
36 Henry James, *English Hours* (London, 1905), pp. 76–7
37 Chris Brooks, introduction to Chris Brooks and Andrew Saint (eds), *The Victorian Church: Architecture and Society* (Manchester, 1995), p. 1. A similar scheme, though on a smaller scale, had been instigated a century before. The New Churches in London and Westminster Act of 1710 resulted in twelve new churches; these became known as the Queen Anne Churches.
38 *Ibid.*, p. 4
39 See Andrea Fredericksen, 'Parliament's Genius Loci: The Politics of Place after the 1834 Fire', in Christine Riding and Jacqueline Riding (eds), *The Houses of Parliament: History, Art and Architecture* (London, 2000), pp. 98–111 (p. 105)40 See Alexandra Wedgwood, 'The New Palace of Westminster', *Ibid.*, pp. 112–35 (p. 115)
41 As Simon Jenkins has pointed out, Isambard Kingdom Brunel 'seems to have regarded gothic as the language of the future' (Simon Jenkins, *Britain's 100 Best Railway Stations* (London, 2017), p. 144). See also Andrew Sanders, *In the Olden Time: Victorians and the British Past* (New Haven and London, 2013), p. 26
42 George Gilbert Scott, *Remarks on Secular and Domestic Architecture, Present and Future* (London, 1858), p. 265
43 See Srinath Perur, 'Chhatrapati Shivaji Terminus, Mumbai's Iconic Railway Station', *Guardian*, 21 April 2015 <www.theguardian.com/cities/2015/apr/21/chhatrapati-shivaji-terminus-cst-mumbai-railway-station> [accessed 10 August 2022]

44 Christopher Hibbert, *George IV: Regent and King 1811–1830* (London, 1973), p. 190. For detailed accounts of George IV's coronation, see Kate Heard and Kathryn Jones (eds), *George IV: Art and Spectacle*, exh. cat. (London, 2019), pp. 206–13; <www.rct.uk/collection/1005090/ceremonial-of-the-coronation-of-his-most-sacred-majesty-king-george-the-fourth> [accessed 20 October 2021]; and Steven Parissien, 'Romancing the Past: Image and Theatre at the Coronation of George IV', in Riding and Riding (2000), pp. 68–79

45 Heard and Jones (2019), pp. 207–9

46 Parissien (2000), p. 73. I would also like to thank Keith Levett for his observations on the coronation costumes of George IV and the court. According to Parissien, more than once the King nearly fainted from the weight.

47 Quoted in Mark Girouard, *The Return to Camelot: Chivalry and the English Gentleman* (London, 1981), p. 30

48 For much of the detail of the Eglinton Tournament given in this and the following paragraphs I am indebted to Ian Anstruther, *The Knight and the Umbrella: An Account of the Eglinton Tournament, 1839* (London, 1963)

49 *The Eglinton Tournament: The Quest for Authenticity*, National Museums of Scotland <www.nms.ac.uk/explore-our-collections/stories/scottish-history-and-archaeology/the-eglinton-tournament/> [accessed 10 November 2021]

50 Queen Victoria, journal entries for 5 August 1842, 11 August 1842 and 2 September 1842 <www.queenvictoriasjournals.org/home.do> [accessed 30 November 2021]

51 See examples in *The Eglinton Tournament*, National Museums Scotland <www.nms.ac.uk/explore-our-collections/stories/scottish-history-and-archaeology/the-eglinton-tournament/> [accessed 10 November 2021]

52 See catalogue entry for Robert Thorburn's 1844 portrait of Prince Albert in the Royal Collection, 'European Armour in the Royal Collection' <www.rct.uk/collection/themes/trails/european-armour-in-the-royal-collection/prince-albert-1819-1862> [accessed 30 November 2021]

53 See Sara Stevenson and Helen Bennett, *Van Dyck in Check Trousers: Fancy Dress in Art and Life 1700–1900* (Edinburgh, 1978), p. 67

54 *Illustrated London News*, 14 May 1842, 7–9. See also Stevenson and Bennett (1978), pp. 67–8

55 Queen Victoria, journal entry for 18 April 1842 <www.queenvictoriasjournals.org/home.do> [accessed 30 November 2021]; Queen Victoria to the king of the Belgians, 19 April 1842; *The Letters of Queen Victoria: A Selection from her Majesty's Correspondence Between the Years 1837 and 1861*, ed. Arthur Christopher Benson and Viscount Esher, 3 vols (London, 1908), I, p. 392

56 Queen Victoria, journal entries for 9 May 1842 and 11 May 1842 <www.queenvictoriasjournals.org/home.do> [accessed 30 November 2021]

57 Quoted in Juliet Vale, 'Philippa of Hainault', *Oxford Dictionary of National Biography* <doi.org/10.1093/ref:odnb/22110> [accessed 30 November 2021]

58 *Illustrated London News*, 14 May 1842, p. 7

59 Royal Collection Trust, RCIN 421665

60 Royal Collection Trust, RCIN 406010

61 Queen Victoria, journal entry for 24 May 1844 <www.queenvictoriasjournals.org/home.do> [accessed 1 December 2021]

62 Catalogue entry in 'European Armour in the Royal Collection' <www.rct.uk/collection/themes/trails/european-armour-in-the-royal-collection/prince-albert-1819-1862> [accessed 2 December 2021]

63 Queen Victoria, journal entry for 5 January 1862 <www.queenvictoriasjournals.org/home.do> [accessed 12 March 2022]

64 Alfred Tennyson to Princess Alice, *c.* 23 December 1861 (draft), *The Letters of Alfred Lord Tennyson*, ed. Cecil Y. Lang and Edgar F. Shannon, Jr, 3 vols (Cambridge, MA, 1987), II, p. 290

65 Alfred Tennyson, *In Memoriam A. H. H.* (London, 1850), VII, stanzas 1–3

66 Alfred Tennyson, 'Tithonus', begun 1833, completed 1859, first published in the *Cornhill Magazine*, February 1860; lines 1–6

67 Alfred Tennyson, 'Morte d'Arthur', *Poems* (London, 1842), stanza 23, lines 2–6 and 9–13 and stanza 24, line 2

68 Tennyson, *In Memoriam*, IX, stanza 1, lines 1–4

69 Charles Dickens, *The Pickwick Papers* (London, 1836), ch. 11

70 Charles Dickens, *Dombey and Son*, 2 vols (London, 1848), II, ch. 15

71 *Ibid.*, ch. 27. In *A Child's History of England* (first published in *Household Words* between 1851 and 1853), Dickens introduces Henry VIII as 'one of the most detestable villains that ever drew breath' (ch. 27).

Chapter 5

1 Georgiana Burne-Jones, *Memorials of Edward Burne-Jones*, 2 vols (London, 1906), I, p. 97
2 Fiona MacCarthy, *William Morris: A Life for Our Time* (London, 1994), p. 133
3 J. W. MacKail, *The Life of William Morris*, 2 vols (London, 1899), I, pp. 120–1
4 MacCarthy (1994), pp. 5 and 14
5 John Ruskin, 'Pre-Raphaelitism', 1851, in *The Complete Works of John Ruskin*, ed. E. T. Cook and Alexander Wedderburn, 39 vols (London, 1903–12), XII, pp. 336–93 (p. 358, note)
6 'The P.R.B.', in Christina Rossetti, *The Complete Poems*, ed. R. W. Crump and Betty S. Flowers (London, 2001) p. 755. On Rossetti's 'double sisterhood', see Susan Owens, 'The Appearance of Christina Rossetti', in *Christina Rossetti: Poetry in Art*, ed. Susan Owens and Nicholas Tromans (New Haven and London, 2018), pp. 43–81 (pp. 49–64). She used the phrase in a letter to William Michael Rossetti in April 1849; *The Letters of Christina Rossetti*, ed. Antony H. Harrison, 4 vols (Charlottesville, VA, 1997–2004), I, p. 17
7 MacKail (1899), I, p. 63
8 MacCarthy (1994), p. 121
9 See Frances Collard, 'Furniture', in Linda Parry (ed.), *William Morris*, exh. cat. (London 1996), pp. 155–79 (pp. 155–6)
10 *Ibid.*, p. 97; Dante Gabriel Rossetti, *Arthur's Tomb*, 1854/5. British Museum 1982,0619.23
11 See William Vaughan, '"God Help the Minister who Meddles in Art": History Painting in the new Palace of Westminster', in Christine Riding and Jacqueline Riding (eds), *The Houses of Parliament: History, Art and Architecture* (London, 2000), pp. 224–39 (pp. 247–9)
12 J. S. Dyce, *Life, Correspondence and Writings of William Dyce, RA 1806–1864, Painter, Musician and Scholar by his Son*, 4 vols (MS, Aberdeen Art Gallery), III, p. 992
13 Christine Poulson also poses this question in *The Quest for the Grail: Arthurian Legend in British Art 1840–1920* (Manchester and New York, 1999), p. 28
14 *Ibid.*, p. 31
15 *Ibid.*, pp. 31–2
16 *Ibid.*, pp. 35–6
17 Coventry Patmore, *Saturday Review*, 26 December 1857, p. 584; quoted in John Christian, *The Oxford Union Murals* (Chicago and London, 1981), p. 47
18 Dante Gabriel Rossetti to William Bell Scott, 7 February 1857; *The Correspondence of Dante Gabriel Rossetti*, ed. William E. Fredeman, 10 vols (Woodbridge, 2002–15), II, letter 57.12, p. 171
19 See Stephen Wildman and John Christian, *Edward Burne-Jones: Victorian Artist-Dreamer*, exh. cat. (New York, 1998), pp. 58–9
20 William Morris, 'Sir Galahad, A Christmas Mystery', *The Defence of Guenevere* (London, 1858), p. XX. On 'The Knight's Farewell' see *The Pre-Raphaelites*, ed. Leslie Parris, exh. cat. (London, 1984), pp. 285–6; Colin Cruise, *Pre-Raphaelite Drawing* (London, 2011), pp. 135–6; and 'The Knight's Farewell', *Burne-Jones Catalogue Raisonné* <www.eb-j.org/browse-artwork-detail/NTk4> [accessed 23 June 2022]
21 Quoted in Aymer Vallance, *The Decorative Art of Sir Edward Burne-Jones* (London, 1900), p. 2
22 MacKail (1899), I, pp. 46–7
23 *Works of Ruskin*, X, pp. 191–2
24 Quoted in Jan Marsh, *William Morris & Red House* (London, 2005), p. 65
25 MacKail (1899), I, p. 186
26 See Tessa Wild, *William Morris & his Palace of Art: Architecture, Interiors & Design at Red House* (London, 2018), pp. 158–63 (p. 163)
27 Jane Morris to May Morris, n.d. [between 1901 and 1912], British Library Add. MS 45341, ff. 91–110; see also *ibid.*, pp. 172–4
28 Wild (2018), p. 86; see also Marsh (2005), pp. 52–3
29 Wild (2018), p. 100 and British Library, Add. MS 45341
30 MacKail (1899), I, p. 314
31 Quoted in MacCarthy (1994), p. 352
32 Georgiana Burne-Jones to Rosalind Howard, 28 March 1876; quoted *ibid.*, p. 353
33 Edward Burne-Jones to Charles Eliot Norton, December 1894; quoted in Martin Harrison and Bill Waters, *Burne-Jones* (New York, 1973), p. 164. Burne-Jones, as Douglas E. Schoenherr has pointed out, was referring to Ruskin's *Praeterita*: 'a well-illuminated missal is a fairy cathedral full of painted windows, bound together to carry in one's pocket' (Douglas E. Schoenherr, 'A Note on Burne-Jones's "Pocket Cathedral" and Ruskin', *Journal of William Morris Studies*, 15.4 (2004), pp. 91–3)

34 MacKail (1899), II, p. 336
35 Ida B. Cole, 'May Morris, Daughter of Master Craftsman', *The Women's Magazine, The St Louis Star and Times*, 16 January 1910, p. 59; quoted in Lynn Hulse, '"When needle work was at its very finest": *Opus Anglicanum* and Its Influence on the Work of May Morris', in Lynn Hulse (ed.), *May Morris: Art & Life* (London, 2017), pp. 87–110 (p. 95)
36 Jan Marsh, '"A remarkable woman – though none of you seemed to think so": The Overdue Re-evaluation of May Morris's Career', in Hulse (2017), pp. 9–24 (p. 10); and Jan Marsh, 'A Well-Crafted Life', in Anna Mason et al., *May Morris: Arts & Crafts Designer* (London, 2017), pp. 8–31 (p. 13)
37 Hulse (2017), p. 95
38 May Morris, 'Chain Stitch Embroidery', *The Century Guild Hobby Horse*, 3 (1888), pp. 24–9; quoted in *ibid.*
39 May Morris, 'Medieval Embroidery', *Journal of the Society for Arts*, 42.2207 (8 March 1895), pp. 384–96 (pp. 387–8); 'Chain Stitch Embroidery', p. 102
40 Mason et al. (2017), pp. 91–2
41 May Morris, *The Introductions to the Collected Works of William Morris*, 2 vols (New York, 1973), I, p. 99
42 Quoted by Jenny Lister, 'Dress and Costume', in Mason et al. (2017), pp. 176–87 (p. 176)
43 *Ibid.*, p. 177
44 William Cobbett, *Political Register*, 28 February 1829; and William Cobbett, *A History of the Protestant Reformation in England and Ireland*, 2 vols (London, 1829), I, letter 1; both quoted in Ian Haywood, 'Illuminating Propaganda: Radical Medievalism and Utopia in the Chartist Era', in *The Oxford Handbook of Victorian Medievalism*, ed. Joanne Parker and Corinna Wagner (Oxford, 2020), pp. 370–93 (p. 371)
45 Pugin's biographer, Rosemary Hill, describes *Contrasts* as 'tendentious, passionate and plain, morally and literally black and white... an attack on the world of the Regency, that Vanity Fair of stucco-fronted manners, high taste and low principles'. Rosemary Hill, *God's Architect: Pugin and the Building of Romantic Britain* (London, 2007), p. 153
46 MacCarthy (1994), p. 71
47 William Morris, 'The Hopes of Civilisation', *Signs of Change, Seven Lectures Delivered on Various Occasions* (London, 1888), p. 88
48 William Morris, *News from Nowhere* (London, 1890), ch. 2
49 William Morris, *A Dream of John Ball and a King's Lesson* (London, 1888), ch. 1
50 Burne-Jones (1906), II, p. 169
51 Fiona MacCarthy, *The Last Pre-Raphaelite: Edward Burne-Jones and the Victorian Imagination* (London, 2011), p. 475
52 MacKail (1899), II, p. 245
53 Quoted in MacCarthy (2011), p. 434
54 On this episode, see *ibid.*, pp. 441–5
55 Burne-Jones (1906), II, p. 247
56 For a detailed discussion of the painting, see Roy Strong, *And When Did You Last See Your Father? The Victorian Painter and British History* (London, 1978), pp. 136–45
57 See Juliet Carey, 'Boy Wonders', *Apollo*, January 2022, pp. 50–5 (p. 55)
58 Andrew Sanders, *In the Olden Time: Victorians and the British Past* (New Haven and London, 2013), p. 99
59 Tom Taylor, *The Portfolio*, 12, 1870, p. 177; here quoted from Juliet Hacking, *Princes of Victorian Bohemia: Photographs by David Wilkie Wynfield*, exh. cat. (London, 2000), p. 36
60 Colin Cruise, 'St John's Wood Clique', *Oxford Dictionary of National Biography* <doi.org/10.1093/ref:odnb/96393> [accessed 23 June 2022]
61 For a list of the Civil War subjects exhibited at the Royal Academy in the nineteenth century under the subject headings 'The Civil War', 'Charles I', 'Henrietta Maria', 'The Children of Charles I', 'Oliver Cromwell', 'Cavaliers' and 'Roundheads and Puritans', see Strong (1978), pp. 163–7. In the 1840s the Royal Commission on the Fine Arts chose the Civil War as a suitable subject for murals to decorate two important spaces in the Houses of Parliament, the Commons Corridor and the Peers Corridor. The schemes were carried out in the 1850s and 1860s by Charles West Cope and Edward Matthew Ward. T. S. R. Boase, 'The Decoration of the New Palace of Westminster, 1841–1863', *Journal of the Warburg and Courtauld Institutes*, 17.3/4 (1954), pp. 319–58 (pp. 341 and 345–6); see also William Vaughan, '"God Help the Minister who Meddles in Art": History Painting in the New Palace of Westminster', in Riding and Riding (2000), pp. 225–39 (pp. 231–3)
62 Holbein's painting was destroyed in the eighteenth century, but his large preparatory

studies of individual figures, including John, survive in the Royal Collection. In the 1790s the Royal Librarian had published a series of large-scale reproductions of the Holbein drawings by Francesco Bartolozzi, engraved and printed in colour.

63 See Mark Haworth-Booth, *The Golden Age of British Photography 1839–1900*, exh. cat. (London, 1984), p. 48

64 Virginia Woolf, 'Julia Margaret Cameron', 1926, reprinted in Virginia Woolf, Julia Margaret Cameron and Roger Fry, *Julia Margaret Cameron* (Los Angeles, 2018), p. 27

65 *Ibid.*, pp. 41 and 37

66 An example of Cameron taking a line from a poem as inspiration for an independent composition is *The Minstrel Group* (1866), prints of which she inscribed with lines from Christina Rossetti's poem 'Advent'. Owens and Tromans (2018), pp. 153–4

67 See Julian Cox and Colin Ford, *Julia Margaret Cameron: The Complete Photographs* (London, 2003), pp. 467–81

68 *Ibid.*, p. 37

69 Julian Cox et al., *In Focus: Julia Margaret Cameron: Photographs from the J. Paul Getty Museum* (Los Angeles, 1996), p. 96

70 *Ibid.*, p. 136

71 See Cox and Ford (2003), p. 468

Chapter 6

1 William Cobbett, 'Oct. 19th to 21st, 1825: Across Surrey' (Reigate, Thursday evening, October 20), *Rural Rides* <www.visionofbritain.org.uk/travellers/Cobbett/16> [accessed 24 January 2022]

2 Quoted in Ian Dyck, 'William Cobbett (1763–1835)', *Oxford Dictionary of National Biography* <doi.org/10.1093/ref:odnb/5734> [accessed 24 January 2022]

3 Author's preface to 1895 edition of *Far from the Madding Crowd*; quoted in Penguin edition (London, 1978), p. 48

4 *Ibid.*

5 On Hardy and literary tourism, see Nicola J. Watson, *The Literary Tourist* (Hampshire, 2006), pp. 176–200

6 Henry James, *English Hours* (London, 1905), p. 212

7 On *Birket Foster's Pictures of English Landscape*, see Malcolm Andrews, *A Sweet View: The Making of an English Idyll* (London, 2021), pp. 189–202

8 *Birket Foster's Pictures of English Landscape (engraved by the brothers Dalziel), with Pictures in Words by Tom Taylor* (London, 1863), XI

9 Andrews (2021), pp. 174–9

10 On Shadbolt, see Donald Campbell, 'Blunden Shadbolt 1879–1949: Architect of the House Desirable', *Journal (Thirties Society)*, 3 (1983), pp. 17–24

11 See Timothy Brittain-Catlin, *The Edwardians and their Houses* (London, 2021), which focuses on the extraordinary number of Liberal politicians who commissioned houses in the Tudor and Jacobean revival style, and their dislike of the Palladian houses built by the Whig aristocracy, which were powerfully influenced by foreign architecture.

12 On the romanticization of thatched country cottages, see Anna Gruetzner Robins, '"South Country" And Other Imagined Places', in Kim Sloan (ed.), *Places of the Mind: British Watercolour Landscapes 1850–1950* (London, 2017), pp. 92–117 (p. 93)

13 John Betjeman, 'Slough', first published in *Continual Dew: A Little Book of Bourgeois Verse* (1937), stanza 6, line 1; stanza 8, lines 1–2

14 Osbert Lancaster, *Pillar to Post* (London, 1938), p. 62

15 Herbert A. Evans, *Highways and Byways in Oxford and the Cotswolds* (London, 1916), p. 2

16 Palmer himself wrote of 'wax-jointed pipes and poetic sheep which never come to mutton' in relation to pastoral poetry in the introduction to his book *The Eclogues of Virgil: An English Version* (London, 1883), p. 1

17 On *Ex Anglia Perdita*, see Jerrold Northrop Moore, *F. L. Griggs (1876–1938): The Architecture of Dreams* (Oxford, 1999), p. 139, pp. 142–3 and pp. 168–70

18 Quoted in Francis Adams Comstock, *A Gothic Vision: F. L. Griggs and his Work* (Oxford, 1966), p. 127

19 See Mary Lago, ed., *Burne-Jones Talking* (London, 1982), p. 69

20 J. W. MacKail, *The Life of William Morris*, 2 vols (London, 1899), II, p. 325

21 Arnold Dolmetsch, *Dolmetsch and his Instruments* (Haslemere, 1930), preface; see also Andrew Heywood, 'William Morris and Music: Craftsman's Art?', *The Musical Times*, 139.1864 (Autumn 1998), pp. 33–8 (p. 38)

22 MacKail (1899), II, p. 334

23 British Museum, Add. MS 31922

24 H. C. G. Matthew and Julia Craig-McFeely, '(Eugène) Arnold Dolmetsch', *Oxford Dictionary of National Biography* <doi.org/10.1093/ref:odnb/32853> [accessed 24 January 2022]

25 In *Electric Eden: Unearthing Britain's Visionary Music* (London, 2011), Rob Young aptly descibes the *Fantasia* as 'glid[ing] serenely out of the dock like a gigantic galleon' (p. 76)

26 *The Variorum Edition of the Complete Poems of Thomas Hardy*, ed. James Gibson (London, 1979), p. 305

27 O. G. S. Crawford, 'The Green Roads of England – R. Hippisley Cox', *Geographical Journal*, 63.5 (May 1924), pp. 442–3

28 Paul Nash, *Outline: An Autobiography and Other Writings* (London, 1949), p. 123

29 Paul Nash, 'Picture History', November 1943; one of a collection of typescripts sent by Nash to his dealer Dudley Tooth, now in the Tate Archive (769/1/29-50). Quoted in Andrew Causey, *Paul Nash: Landscape and the Life of Objects* (London, 2013), p. 157. On Nash and prehistory, see Sam Smiles, 'Ancient Country: Nash and Prehistory', in *Paul Nash: Modern Artist, Ancient Landscape*, ed. Jemima Montagu, exh. cat. (London, 2003), pp. 31–7

30 Paul Nash, *Dorset* (London, 1936), p. 10

31 See Paul Nash, *Landscape of the Megaliths*, c. 1937, colour lithograph (an example is in the Victoria and Albert Museum, E.4801-1960) and John Piper, *Avebury Restored*, 1944, colour lithograph (reproduced in 'Topographical Letter from Devizes', *Cornhill Magazine*, 1944); see also Sam Smiles, *British Art: Ancient Landscapes*, exh. cat. (London, 2017), pp. 84–91

32 Paul Nash, *Country Life*, 21 May 1938; quoted in Montagu (2003), p. 66

33 Myfanwy Evans, 'Paul Nash, 1937', *Axis*, 8 (1937), pp. 12–15 (p. 12)

34 Barbara Hepworth to John Summerson, 3 January 1940; quoted in Sally Festing, *Barbara Hepworth: A Life of Forms* (London, 2005), p. 141

35 Ithell Colquhoun, *The Living Stones* (1957; London, 2016), pp. 57–8; p. 70

36 *Ibid.*, p. 57 and p. 58

37 Ithell Colquhoun in *Cornish Banner*, June 1978, quoted in Richard Shillitoe, *Ithell Colquhoun: Magician Born of Nature* (NC, 2009), p. 313

38 Colquhoun (2016), p. 55

39 *Ibid.*, p. 220

40 George Sturt, *Change in the Village* (London, 1912), p. 17, pp. 6–7 and pp. 8–9

41 George Sturt, *The Wheelwright's Shop* (Cambridge, 1923), p. 23

42 *Ibid.*, pp. 19–20

43 *Ibid.*, p. 45

44 Recollection by Thomas Hennell's sister Betty, quoted in Jessica Kilburn, *Thomas Hennell: The Land and the Mind* (London, 2021), p. 154

45 *Ibid.*, p. 168

46 Thomas Hennell, *Change in the Farm* (Cambridge, 1934), p. ix

47 Quoted in Kilburn (2021), p. 156

48 Lord Macmillan, introduction to Arnold Palmer, *Recording Britain*, 4 vols (Oxford, 1946–9), I, p. v; see also Gill Saunders, *Recording Britain* (London, 2011), p. 12

49 Victoria and Albert Museum, E.2056-1949 and E.1669-1949. The Recording Britain watercolours were given to the Victoria and Albert Museum in 1949 by the Pilgrim Trust, which funded the scheme. For many years they were lent around the country, but in 1990 were recalled; most can now be seen on request in the Prints and Drawings Study Room at the Victoria and Albert Museum.

50 Frances Spalding, *John Piper, Myfanwy Piper: Lives in Art* (Oxford, 2009), p. 179

51 David Fraser Jenkins, *John Piper: The Forties* (London, 2000), p. 30

52 Quoted in Christopher Woodward, *In Ruins* (London, 2001), p. 212

53 John Piper, 'The Architecture of Destruction', *Architectural Review*, 14.535, July 1941, p. 25, here quoted from Spalding (2009), p. 180

54 *A Choice of Kipling's Verse*, ed. T. S. Eliot (London, 1941), p. 32

55 T. S. Eliot, *East Coker* (London, 1940), part I, stanza 3, lines 1–5, 11–15 and part I, stanza 1, lines 5–6

56 T. S. Eliot, *Little Gidding* (London, 1942), part V, lines 19–24

57 Eric Ravilious to Helen Binyon, 30 January 1936; quoted in Jeremy Greenwood, *Ravilious: Engravings* (Woodbridge, 2008), p. 254; see also Simon Martin, *Drawn to Nature: Gilbert White and the Artists* (Chichester, 2021), p. 62

58 Gilbert White, *The Natural History of Selborne* (London, 1789), letter I (to Thomas Pennant)

59 Eric Ravilious to Diana Low, 15 March 1939; quoted in Greenwood (2008), p. 256

60 Lytton Strachey, 'The Eighteenth Century' (1926), in *Characters and Commentaries*

(London, 1933), pp. 297–302 (pp. 299 and 300)

61 See Alexandra Harris's chapter 'A Georgian Revival' in her book *Romantic Moderns: English Writers, Artists and the Imagination from Virginia Woolf to John Piper* (London, 2010), pp. 59–85; I am also indebted to her chapter 'Victoriana', pp. 86–100

62 On the Hypocrites' club and Acton, Byron and Waugh's proposed '1840 Exhibition' see Stephen Hoare, 'Hypocrites', in the *Anthony Powell Newsletter*, Winter 2016 (vol. 65), pp. 22–4 (pp. 23–4); see also Martin Green, *Children of the Sun: A Narrative of 'Decadence' in England after 1918* (London, 1977), p. 190

63 Edith Sitwell, 'Elegy on Dead Fashion', in *Collected Poems* (London, 1958), pp. 197–209 (pp. 199 and 202)

64 Franz Xaver Winterhalter, *Queen Victoria*, 1842; Royal Collection Trust, RCIN 401413

65 Cecil Beaton, *The Wandering Years: Diaries 1922–1939* (London, 1961), p. 372

66 The Marx–Lambert Collections, which include many of Marx's works, can be seen at Compton Verney in Warwickshire <www.comptonverney.org.uk/collections-pages/marx-lambert/> [accessed 19 February 2022]

67 Victoria and Albert Museum, E.1842-1949 and E.1840-1949

68 Margaret Lambert and Enid Marx, *English Popular Art* (London, 1951), p. v

69 Lorraine Ward, *Frederick Savage, Victorian Fairground Manufacturer of King's Lynn* (Norfolk, 1989), pp. 7–8

70 M. Wilson Disher, 'Bits and Pieces', *The Times Literary Supplement*, 20 November 1948, p. 650. See also Stephen Calloway, 'Recording Britain: Patriotism, Polemic and Romantic Psychogeography', in Saunders (2011), pp. 54–75 (p. 66)

71 John Hadfield, preface to Oliver Cook and Edwin Smith, *Collectors' Items from the Saturday Book* (London, 1955), p. 10

Chapter 7

1 Kingsley Amis, *Lucky Jim* (London, 1954), ch. 22

2 In *Lovers and Strangers: An Immigrant History of Post-War Britain* (London, 2017), Clair Wills describes this period of work in Britain 'as a kind of interregnum' for many, 'a period to be endured or enjoyed because it would make possible a future that was envisaged, as often as not, as a return to the past made viable again'. (p. 4)

3 Alison Donnell, 'Looking Back, Looking Forward: Revisiting the Windrush Myth', in Susheila Nasta and Mark U. Stein (eds), *The Cambridge History of Black and Asian Writing* (Cambridge, 2020), pp. 195–211 (p. 200)

4 George Lamming, 'Sea of Stories', *Guardian*, 24 October 2002 <www.theguardian.com/books/2002/oct/24/artsfeatures.poetry> [accessed 25 February 2022]

5 Andrea Levy, *Small Island* (London, 2004), ch. 12, 'Gilbert'

6 On the long and complex history of Black people in the British countryside, see Caroline Bressey, 'Cultural Archaeology and Historical Geographies of the Black Presence in Rural England', *Journal of Rural Studies*, 25 (2009), pp. 386–95

7 V. S. Naipaul, *The Enigma of Arrival* (London, 1987), pp. 8, 5, 12, 15

8 *Ibid.*, pp. 17, 20–1

9 *Ibid.*, pp. 13, 98–100

10 The Watersons and other folk groups could be described as part of what Ronald Hutton has called the 'Second Romantic Movement'. 'One aspect of this', he has written in a chapter called 'Arthur and the Academics', 'was a profound desire to reinvest the world with magic and mystery.' Ronald Hutton, *Witches, Druids and King Arthur* (London, 2003; 2006), p. 50

11 See Rob Young, *Electric Eden: Unearthing Britain's Visionary Music* (London, 2010), p. 193

12 A. L. Lloyd, sleeve notes to The Watersons, *Frost and Fire: A Calendar of Ritual and Magical Songs* (London, 1965)

13 Ken Hunt, 'Peter Franklyn Bellamy (1944–1991)', *Oxford Dictionary of National Biography* <doi.org/10.1093/ref:odnb/75736> [accessed 25 February 2022]

14 Young, *Electric Eden*, pp. 196–7

15 'A Tree Song / Oak, Ash and Thorn', *Mainly Norfolk: English Folk and other Good Music* <mainlynorfolk.info/peter.bellamy/songs/atreesong.html> [accessed 25 February 2022]. The song was included on Bellamy's solo album *Oak, Ash and Thorn* (London, 1970)

16 Quoted in 'A Tree Song', *Mainly Norfolk*

17 'In Gothic narratives, the village is the locus of premodern survivals,' writes Roger Luckhurst in *Gothic: An Illustrated History* (London, 2021), p. 91

18 Iain Sinclair, *Lud Heat* (London, 1975), p. 19

19 *Ibid.*

20 As the Victorian art expert John Christian wrote of Christopher Wood (1941–2009), a dealer specializing in Victorian art, 'He certainly [did] not exaggerate the disrepute into which Victorian art had fallen [in the 1950s and 1960s] or the sense of excitement that so many of us felt at its rediscovery. Although a few pioneers had long been active, and the Victoria and Albert Museum had mounted its great exhibition of *Victorian and Edwardian Decorative Arts* as far back as 1952, ignorance, vandalism and arrogant disdain were rife throughout our early years.' John Christian, 'Tailpiece', in *Christopher Wood: A Very Victorian Eye*, exh. cat. (London, 2007), pp. 10–11 (p. 11)

21 Jennifer Harris, Sarah Hyde and Greg Smith, *1966 and All That: Design and the Consumer in Britain 1960–1969*, exh. cat. (London, 1986), p. 67

22 A classic example is a striped velvet suit designed by Mr Fish for David Mlinaric around 1968, now in the Victoria and Albert Museum; T.310&A-1979

23 Pauline Boty, *Untitled* (hand, secateurs and children), *c.* 1964; the Murray Family Collection, included in Patrick Elliott, *Cut and Paste: 400 Years of Collage*, exh. cat. (Edinburgh, 2019), p. 141; and Pauline Boty, *Untitled* (seascape with boats and island), *c.* 1960; Pallant House Gallery <pallant.org.uk/our-art/untitled-pauline-boty/> [accessed 20 August 2022]

24 Helen Barrett, 'Peter Blake, the Beatniks and their Lost Pop Art Furniture', *Financial Times*, 7 February 2020; see, for example, Peter Blake's *Tattooed Lady*, 1958, in the Victoria and Albert Museum, P.3-1972

25 Ian MacDonald, *Revolution in the Head: The Beatles' Records and the Sixties* (2nd ed.; London, 2005) pp. 237–8

26 In 1970–71 Peter Blake made a series of watercolour illustrations to *Through the Looking Glass*. See *Peter Blake*, exh. cat. (London, 1983), pp. 113–14

27 Julian Barnes, *England, England* (London, 1998), part III, 'Anglia'

28 *Ibid.*

29 *Ibid*, part II, 'England, England', ch. 3

30 Alexandra Artley and John Martin Robinson, *The New Georgian Handbook* (London, 1985), p. 4

31 Ann Barr and Peter York, *The Official Sloane Ranger Handbook* (London, 1982)

32 Ivor T. Idris, foreword to Violet Wood, *Victoriana: A Collector's Guide* (London, 1960), p. 9

33 On 'the change in attitudes that took place over the first fifteen years of the [Victorian] Society's existence', see Gavin Stamp, 'What Did We Do for the Victorians?', in *Victorians Revalued: What the Twentieth Century Thought of Nineteenth-Century Architecture*, ed. Rosemary Hill, Colin Cunningham and Aileen Reid (London, 2010), pp. 7–25; 'the 1960s was the crucial period when the Victorians came back into fashion', writes Stamp, 'both popular and intellectual' (p. 7). The Georgian Group, initially part of the SPAB, was founded in 1937.

34 Artley and Martin (1982), pp. 13, 21, 5

35 <www.thespitalfieldstrust.com/spitalfields-a-brief-history/> [accessed 28 February 2022]

36 <dennisevershouse.co.uk/about/dennis-severs> [accessed 27 February 2022]

37 See Jane Clifford, *Laura Ashley Decorates a London House* (London, 1985), *passim*. I am grateful to Jane Clifford for sharing information on Laura Ashley's sources.

38 See Katty Pearce, 'Steampunk', in Sonia Solicari (ed.), *Victoriana: A Miscellany* (London, 2013), pp. 78–83 (p. 81)

39 See Claire Nally, *Steampunk: Gender, Subculture and the Neo-Victorian* (London, 2019), p. 249

40 *Atrial Flutter* was shown in 'Psychopomps', an exhibition of Polly Morgan's works held at Haunch of Venison gallery in London in 2010.

41 Saki (Hector Hugh Munro), 'The Lumber Room', in *Beasts and Super-Beasts* (London, 1914), pp. 274–84 (pp. 279–81)

42 <www.yorkartgallery.org.uk/exhibition/the-lumber-room-unimagined-treasures/> [accessed 20 May 2022]

43 See the Victoria and Albert Museum catalogue entry for E.235-2013 to E.239-2013 <collections.vam.ac.uk/item/O1263374/diary-of-a-victorian-dandy-photograph-shonibare-yinka/> [accessed 20 May 2022]

44 Queen Elizabeth to the Lord Mayor et al., *c.* 11 July 1596, in *Acts of the Privy Council of England*, 26 (1596–7), ed. John Roche Dasent (London, 1902), pp. 16–17; quoted in Emily C. Bartels, 'Too Many Blackamoors: Deportation, Discrimination and Elizabeth I', in *Studies in English Literature, 1500–1900*, 46.2 (2006), pp. 305–22 (p. 305)

45 'Uncomfortable Truths: The Shadow of Slave Trading on Contemporary Art' was curated by Zoé Whitley and was shown in galleries around the Victoria and Albert Museum from February to June 2007.

46 See <lubainahimid.uk/portfolio/naming-the-money/> [accessed 23 May 2022] and Michael White, '"Uncomfortable truths": The Intervention of the Past at the Victoria and Albert', in *1807 Commemorated: The Abolition of the Slave Trade* <archives.history.ac.uk/1807commemorated/exhibitions/art/uncomfortable.html> [accessed 23 May 2022]

47 Imelda Barnard, 'Artist of the Year', interview with Lubaina Himid, *Apollo*, 21 November 2017 <www.apollo-magazine.com/author/imelda-barnard/> [accessed 23 May 2022]

Epilogue

1 Robert Macfarlane, *The Old Ways: A Journey on Foot* (London, 2012), pp. 21–2 and p. 362

2 Myfanwy Evans, 'Paul Nash, 1937', *Axis*, 8 (1937), pp. 12–15 (p. 12)

3 Hilary Mantel, *Giving Up the Ghost: A Memoir* (London, 2003), p. 233

4 Hilary Mantel, 'The Day is for the Living', BBC Reith Lectures 2017, part 1 <medium.com/@bbcradiofour/hilary-mantel-bbc-reith-lectures-2017-aeff8935ab33> [accessed 5 March 2022]

Select Bibliography

Ackroyd, Peter, *Albion: The Origins of the English Imagination* (London, 2002)

Adams, Max, *The First Kingdom: Britain in the Age of Arthur* (London, 2021)

Aldrich, Megan, and Robert J. Wallis (eds), *Antiquaries & Archaists: The Past in the Past, the Past in the Present* (Reading, 2009)

Alexander, David, *Affecting Moments: Prints of English Literature Made in the Age of Romantic Sensibility 1775–1800* (York, 1993)

Alexander, Michael, *Medievalism: The Middle Ages in Modern England* (New Haven and London, 2007)

Alt, Kasie, 'Fictions and Fabrications: The Gothic Folly at Wimpole, Cambridgeshire', *Garden History*, 44.1, (2016), pp. 74–89

Arscott, Caroline, *Edward Burne-Jones and William Morris: Interlacings* (New Haven and London, 2008)

Ashe, Geoffrey, *From Caesar to Arthur* (London, 1960)

— (ed.), *The Quest for Arthur's Britain* (London, 1968)

— *Camelot and the Vision of Albion* (London, 1971)

— *The Landscape of King Arthur* (London, 1987)

Aubrey, John, *Monumenta Britannica, or, a Miscellany of British Antiquities*, ed. John Fowles and Rodney Legg, 2 vols (Sherborne, 1980 and 1982)

Banham, Joanna, and Jennifer Harris, *William Morris and the Middle Ages: A Collection of Essays* (Manchester, 1984)

Bann, Stephen, *The Clothing of Clio: A Study of the Representation of History in Nineteenth-Century Britain and France* (Cambridge, 1984)

— *The Inventions of History: Essays on the Representation of the Past* (Manchester, 1990)

— *Scenes and Traces of the English Civil War* (London, 2020)

Barnes, Julian, *England, England* (London, 1998)

Bending, Stephen, *A Cultural History of Gardens in the Age of Enlightenment* (London, 2016)

Bennett, Helen, and Sarah Stevenson, *Van Dyck in Check Trousers: Fancy Dress in Art and Life 1700–1900*, exh. cat. (Edinburgh, 1978)

Biddle, Martin, et al., *King Arthur's Round Table: An Archaeological Investigation* (Woodbridge, 2000)

Boase, T. S. R., 'The Decoration of the New Palace of Westminster, 1841–1863', *Journal of the Warburg and Courtauld Institutes*, 17.3/4 (1954), pp. 319–58

Boyes, Georgina, *The Imagined Village: Culture, Ideology and the English Folk Revival* (Manchester, 1993)

Brassley, Paul, Jeremy Burchardt and Lynne Thompson, *The English Countryside Between the Wars: Regeneration or Decline?* (Woodbridge, 2006)

Brooks, Chris and Andrew Saint (eds), *The Victorian Church: Architecture and Society* (Manchester, 1995)

Brown, David, *Walter Scott and the Historical Imagination* (London, 1979)

Bump, Jerome, 'Hopkins, Pater and Medievalism', *Victorian Newsletter*, 50 (1976), pp. 10–15

— 'Hopkins's Imagery and Medievalist Poetics', *Victorian Poetry*, 15 (1977), pp. 99–119

Cannadine, David, *The Pleasures of the Past* (London, 1989)

Carr, Helen, and Suzannah Lipscomb (eds), *What is History, Now? How the Past and the Present Speak to Each Other* (London, 2021)

Carter, Michael, Peter Lindfield and Dale Townshend, *Writing Britain's Ruins* (London, 2017)

Causey, Andrew, *Paul Nash: Landscape and the Life of Objects* (London, 2013)

Chamberlin, Russell, *The Idea of England* (London, 1986)

Chambers, E. K., *Arthur of Britain* (Cambridge, 1927, repr. 1964)

Chandler, Alice, *A Dream of Order: The Medieval Ideal in Nineteenth-Century English Literature* (Lincoln, NE, 1970)

Chapman, Raymond, *The Sense of the Past in Victorian Literature* (London and Sydney, 1986)

Chippindale, Christopher, *Stonehenge Complete* (Ithaca, NY, 1983)

Christian, John, *The Oxford Union Murals* (Chicago, 1981)
Clarke, Stephen, 'Rosamond's Bower, The Pryor's Bank, and the Long Shadow of Strawberry Hill', *Journal of the History of Collections*, 26.2 (2014), pp. 287–306
Clifford, Sue, and Angela King, *England in Particular: A Celebration of the Commonplace, the Local, the Vernacular and the Distinctive* (London, 2006)
Cohen, Richard, *Making History: The Storytellers Who Shaped the Past* (London, 2022)
Colton, Judith, 'Merlin's Cave and Queen Caroline: Garden Art as Political Propaganda', *Eighteenth-Century Studies* 10.1 (Autumn 1976), pp. 1–20
Cooper, Suzanne Fagence, *How We Might Live: At Home with Jane and William Morris* (London, 2022)
Coote, Lesley, *Storyworlds of Robin Hood: The Origins of a Medieval Outlaw* (London, 2020)
Corbett, David Peters, Ysanne Holt and Fiona Russell, *The Geographies of Englishness: Landscape and the National Past 1880–1940* (New Haven and London, 2002)
Cousins, Michael, 'Hagley Park, Worcestershire', *Garden History*, 35, supplement (2007), pp. iii–iv, vi–xii, 1–152
Cruise, Colin, *Pre-Raphaelite Drawing* (London, 2011)
Curran, John E. Jr., 'The History Never Written: Bards, Druids, and the Problem of Antiquarianism in Poly Olbion', *Renaissance Quarterly*, 51.2 (1998), pp. 498–525
D'Arcens, Louise (ed.), *The Cambridge Companion to Medievalism* (Cambridge, 2016)
Ditmas, E. M. R., 'The Cult of Arthurian Relics', *Folklore*, 75.1 (1964), pp. 19–33
Duffy, Maureen, *England: The Making of the Myth from Stonehenge to Albert Square* (London, 2001)
Ferguson, Arthur B., *Utter Antiquity: Perceptions of Prehistory in Renaissance England* (Durham, NC, 1993)
Gelling, Margaret, *Signposts to the Past: Place-Names and the History of England* (London, 1978)
— *Place-Names in the Landscape* (London, 1984)
Gibson, Marion, *Imagining the Pagan Past: Gods and Goddesses in Literature and History Since the Dark Ages* (Oxford, 2013)
Girouard, Mark, *The Return to Camelot: Chivalry and the English Gentleman* (New Haven and London, 1981)
Gosden, P. H. J. H., *The Friendly Societies in England, 1815–1875* (Manchester, 1961)
Gransden, Antonia, *Historical Writing in England* (1974; London, 1998)
Groom, Nick, *The Making of Percy's Reliques* (Oxford, 1999)
Guilding, Ruth, *Owning the Past: Why the English Collected Antique Sculpture, 1640–1840* (New Haven and London, 2014)
Halsall, Guy, *Worlds of Arthur: Facts and Fictions of the Dark Ages* (Oxford, 2013)
Harney, Marion, *Place-Making for the Imagination: Horace Walpole and Strawberry Hill* (Farnham, 2013)
Harris, Alexandra, *Romantic Moderns: English Writers, Artists and the Imagination from Virginia Woolf to John Piper* (London, 2010)
— 'Squint', *International Literature Showcase*, 2017; <litshowcase.org/content/squint/> [accessed 27 February 2022]
Haskell, Francis, *History and Its Images: Art and the Interpretation of the Past* (New Haven and London, 1993)
Hauser, Kitty, *Shadow Sites: Photography, Archaeology, and the British Landscape 1927–1955* (Oxford, 2007)
Hawkes, Jacquetta, *Early Britain* (London, 1945)
Headley, Gwyn, and Wim Meulenkamp, *The English Folly: The Edifice Complex* (Swindon, 2020)
Higham, Nicholas J., *King Arthur: Myth-Making and History* (London, 2002)
— ed., *Britons in Anglo-Saxon England* (Woodbridge, 2007)
Hill, Rosemary, 'Reformation to Millennium: Pugin's "Contrasts" in the History of English Thought', *Journal of the Society of Architectural Historians*, 58 (1999), pp. 26–41
— *Stonehenge* (London, 2008)
— Colin Cunningham and Aileen Reid (eds), *Victorians Revalued: What the Twentieth Century Thought of Nineteenth-Century Architecture* (London, 2010)
— *Time's Witness: History in the Age of Romanticism* (London, 2021)
Hobsbawm, Eric, and Terence Ranger, *The Invention of Tradition* (Cambridge, 1983)
Holt, J. C., *Robin Hood* (London, 1989)

Howkins, Alun, 'The Discovery of Rural England', in Robert Colls and Philip Dodd (eds), *Englishness: Politics and Culture 1880–1920* (1986; 2nd edn London, 2014)
Hunter, Michael, *John Aubrey and the Realm of Learning* (London, 1975)
Hutton, Ronald, *Witches, Druids and King Arthur* (London, 2003)
— *Blood and Mistletoe: The History of the Druids in Britain* (New Haven and London, 2009)
Jenkins, Elizabeth, *The Mystery of King Arthur* (London, 1975)
Jenkins, Geraint H. (ed.), *A Rattleskull Genius: The Many Faces of Iolo Morganwg* (Cardiff, 2005)
Jones, Chris, *Strange Likeness: The Use of Old English in 20th Century Poetry* (Oxford, 2006)
Jones, Peter, 'Bladdersticks and Fools: William Nicholson and the Morris', *British Art Journal*, IX.3 (2009), pp. 55–61
Kelly, Stuart, *Scott-Land: The Man Who Invented a Nation* (Edinburgh, 2011)
Kendrick, T. D., *British Antiquity* (London, 1950)
Kilburn, Jessica, *Thomas Hennell: The Land and the Mind* (London, 2021)
King, Andrew, *The Faerie Queene and Middle English Romance: The Matter of Just Memory* (Oxford, 2002)
Knox, Tim, *Sir John Soane's Museum London* (London, 2008)
Lange-Berndt, Petra, 'A Parasitic Craft: Taxidermy in the Art of Tessa Farmer', *Journal of Modern Craft*, 7.3 (2014), pp. 267–84
Lindfield, Peter, 'Serious Gothic and "doing the Ancient Buildings": Batty Langley's "Ancient Architecture" and "Principal Geometric Elevations"', *Architectural History*, 57 (2014), pp. 141–73
— *Georgian Gothic: Medievalist Architecture, Furniture and Interiors 1730–1840* (Woodbridge, 2016)
Linforth, Lucy Majella, 'Fragments of the Past: Walter Scott, Material Antiquarianism, and Writing as Preservation', unpublished PhD thesis (University of Edinburgh, 2017)
Lively, Penelope, *Treasures of Time* (London, 1979)
Longstaffe-Gowan, Todd, *English Garden Eccentrics: Three Hundred Years of Extraordinary Groves, Burrowings, Mountains and Menageries* (London, 2022)
Loomis, Roger Sherman, 'Edward I, Arthurian Enthusiast', *Speculum*, 28.1 (1953), pp. 114–27
— 'Arthurian Tradition and Folklore', *Folklore*, 69.1 (1958), pp. 1–25
— *Arthurian Literature in the Middle Ages: A Collaborative History* (Oxford, 1959)
Luckhurst, Roger, *Gothic: An Illustrated History* (London, 2021)
MacCarthy, Fiona, *William Morris: A Life for Our Time* (London, 1994)
— *The Last Pre-Raphaelite: Edward Burne-Jones and the Victorian Imagination* (London, 2011)
Maccoll, Alan, The construction of England as a Protestant "British" nation in the sixteenth century', *Renaissance Studies*, 18.4 (2004), pp. 582–608
Macfarlane, Robert, *The Old Ways: A Journey on Foot* (London, 2012)
Mackail, J. W., *The Life of William Morris*, 2 vols (London, 1899)
Mandler, Peter, *The Fall and Rise of the Stately Home* (New Haven and London, 1997)
— '"In the Olden Time": Romantic History and English National Identity, 1820–50', in Laurence Brockliss and David Eastwood (eds), *A Union of Multiple Identities: The British Isles, c. 1750–c. 1850* (Manchester, 1997), pp. 78–92
— *History and National Life* (London, 2002)
Mann, J. G., 'Instances of Antiquarian Feeling in Medieval and Renaissance Art', *Archaeological Journal*, 89.1 (1932), pp. 254–74
Mantel, Hilary, *Giving Up the Ghost: A Memoir* (London, 2003)
— 'The Day is for the Living', BBC Reith Lectures, 2017, part one; <medium.com/@bbcradiofour/hilary-mantel-bbc-reith-lectures-2017-aeff8935ab33> [accessed 25 February 2022]
Marsh, Jan, *Back to the Land: The Pastoral Impulse in Victorian England from 1880 to 1914* (London, 1982)
— *William Morris & Red House* (London, 2005)
Mason, Anna, et al., *May Morris: Arts & Crafts Designer* (London, 2017)
Matless, David, *Landscape and Englishness* (2nd edn, London 2016)
Matthews, David, *Medievalism: A Critical History* (Cambridge, 2015)
McAra, Catriona (ed.), *In Fairyland: The World of Tessa Farmer* (London, 2016)
McCarthy, Michael, *The Origins of the Gothic Revival* (New Haven and London, 1987)

McCarthy, Sarah, Bernard Nurse and David Gaimster (eds), *Making History: Antiquaries in Britain, 1707–2007*, exh. cat. (London, 2007)

Meyrick, Samuel Rush, *The Costume of the Original Inhabitants of the British Isles from the Earliest Periods to the Sixth Century* (London, 1815)

Miles, David, *The Land of the White Horse: Visions of England* (London, 2019)

Mitchell, Rosemary, *Picturing the Past: English History in Text and Image, 1830–1870* (Oxford, 2000)

Murphy, Erin, 'Sabrina and the Making of English History in Poly-Olbion and A Maske Presented at Ludlow Castle', *Studies in English Literature, 1500–1900*, 51.1 (2011), pp. 87–110

Myrone, Martin, and Lucy Peltz (eds), *Producing the Past: Aspects of Antiquarian Culture and Practice, 1700–1850* (Aldershot, 1999)

Nennius, *British History and the Welsh Annals*, ed. and trans. John Morris (London and Chichester, 1980)

Parker, Joanne (ed.), *Written on Stone: The Cultural Reception of British Prehistoric Monuments* (Newcastle upon Tyne, 2009)

— and Corinna Wagner (eds), *The Oxford Handbook of Victorian Medievalism* (Oxford, 2020)

Parry, Graham, *The Trophies of Time: English Antiquarians of the Seventeenth Century* (Oxford, 1995)

Payne, Ann, *Views of the Past: Topographical Drawings in the British Library* (London, 1987)

Payne, Christiana, *Pre-Raphaelites: Drawings and Watercolours*, exh. cat. (Oxford, 2021)

Piggott, Stuart, *The Druids* (London, 1968)

— *Ruins in a Landscape: Essays in Antiquarianism* (Edinburgh, 1976)

— *William Stukeley: An Eighteenth-Century Antiquary* (1950; London, 1985)

— *Ancient Britons and the Antiquarian Imagination* (London, 1989)

Porter, Bernard, *The Battle of the Styles: Society, Culture and the Design of a New Foreign Office, 1855–1861* (London, 2011)

Poulson, Christine, *The Quest for the Grail: Arthurian Legend in British Art, 1840–1920* (Manchester, 1998)

Pryor, Francis, *Britain AD: A Quest for Arthur, England and the Anglo-Saxons* (London, 2004)

Reeve, Matthew M., 'Gothic Architecture, Sexuality and License at Horace Walpole's Strawberry Hill', *The Art Bulletin*, 95.3 (September 2013), pp. 411–39

Riding, Christine, and Jacqueline Riding (eds), *The Houses of Parliament: History, Art and Architecture* (London, 2000)

Ritson, Joseph, *Robin Hood: A Collection of all the Ancient Poems, Songs and Ballads, Now Extant, Relative to that Celebrated English Outlaw*, 2 vols (Cambridge, 2015)

Robichaud, Paul, *Making the Past Present: David Jones, the Middle Ages, and Modernism* (Washington, DC, 2007)

Salisbury Museum, *British Art: Ancient Landscapes*, exh. cat. (Salisbury, 2017)

Sanders, Andrew, *In the Olden Time: The Victorians and the British Past* (New Haven and London, 2013)

Saunders, Gill (ed.), *Recording Britain* (London, 2011)

Sellar, Walter Carruthers, and R. J. Yeatman, *1066 and All That* (London, 1930)

Semple, Sarah, *Perceptions of the Prehistoric in Anglo-Saxon England: Religion, Ritual and Rulership in the Landscape* (Oxford, 2013)

Severs, Dennis, *18 Folgate Street: The Tale of a House in Spitalfields* (London, 2002)

Sloan, Kim, *A New World: England's First View of America*, exh. cat. (London, 2007)

Smiles, Sam, *The Image of Antiquity: Ancient Britain and the Romantic Imagination* (New Haven and London, 1994)

— *Eye Witness: Artists and Visual Documentation in Britain 1770-1830* (Aldershot, 2000)

—'John White and British Antiquity: Savage Origins in the Context of Tudor Historiography', in Kim Sloan, ed., *European Visions: American Voices*, exh. cat. (London, 2009), pp. 106–12

— *British Art, Ancient Landscapes*, exh. cat. (London, 2017)

Snodin, Michael (ed.), *Horace Walpole's Strawberry Hill* (New Haven and London, 2009)

Snyder, Edward D., *The Celtic Revival in English Literature, 1760–1880* (Cambridge, MA, 1923)

Spalding, Frances, *The Real and the Romantic: English Art Between Two World Wars* (London, 2022)

Stamp, Gavin, 'I was Lord Kitchener's Valet or, How the Vic Soc Saved London', in Elain Harwood and Alan Powers (eds), *Twentieth Century Architecture, 6. The Sixties: Life: Style: Architecture* (London, 2002), pp. 129–44

— 'Neo-Tudor and its Enemies', *Architectural History*, 39 (2006), pp. 1–33

Stewart, David, 'Political Ruins: Gothic Sham Ruins and the '45', *Journal of the Society of Architectural Historians*, 55.4 (1996), pp. 400–11

Strong, Roy, *And When Did You Last See Your Father? The Victorian Painter and British History* (London, 1978)

Sweet, Rosemary, *Antiquaries: The Discovery of the Past in Eighteenth-Century Britain* (London, 2004)

Thomas, Keith, 'The Perception of the Past in Early Modern England', in *The Creighton Century, 1907–2007*. ed. David Bates, Jennifer Wallis and Jane Winters (London, 2009), pp. 181–216

Tolstoy, Nikolai, *The Quest for Merlin* (London, 1985)

Turner, Olivia Horsfall, 'Perceptions of Medieval Buildings in England, c. 1640–c. 1720'; unpublished PhD thesis, University College London (University of London), 2009

Vaughan, William, '"God Help the Minister who Meddles in Art": History Painting in the New Palace of Westminster', in Christine Riding and Jacqueline Riding (eds), *The Houses of Parliament: History, Art and Architecture* (London, 2000), pp. 225–39

Vine, Angus, *In Defiance of Time: Antiquarian Writing in Early Modern England* (Oxford, 2010)

Wainwright, Clive, *The Romantic Interior: The British Collector at Home 1750–1850* (New Haven and London, 1989)

Weber, Susan (ed.), *William Kent: Designing Georgian Britain* (New Haven and London, 2013)

Whitelock, Dorothy, *The Beginnings of English Society* (London, 1952)

Whittaker, Jason, *William Blake and the Myths of Britain* (London, 1999)

Wild, Tessa, *William Morris & his Palace of Art: Architecture, Interiors & Design at Red House* (London, 2018)

Williams, Raymond, *The Country and the City* (London, 1973)

Wood, Andy, *The Memory of the People: Custom and Popular Senses of the Past in Early Modern England* (Cambridge, 2013)

Wood, Michael, *In Search of England: Journeys into the English Past* (London, 1999)

Woodhouse, Elisabeth, 'Kenilworth, the Earl of Leicester's Pleasure Grounds Following Robert Laneham's Letter', *Garden History*, 27.1, 1999, pp. 127–44

Woods, Hannah Rose, *Rule, Nostalgia: A Backwards History of Britain* (London, 2022)

Woodward, Christopher, *In Ruins* (London, 2001)

Woolf, Daniel R., 'The Dawn of the Artefact: The Antiquarian Impulse in England, 1500–1730', *Studies in Medievalism*, 4 (1990), pp. 5–35

— *The Social Circulation of the Past: English Historical Culture 1500–1730* (Oxford, 2003)

Wragge-Morley, Alexander, 'Inigo Jones and the Ruins of Stonehenge', in *Picturing Places*, British Library; <www.bl.uk/picturing-places/articles/inigo-jones-and-the-ruins-of-stonehenge> [accessed 27 February 2022]

Wright, C. E., 'The Rous Roll: The English Version', *The British Museum Quarterly*, 20.4 (June 1956), pp. 77–81

Yarker, Jonny, 'Continuity and the Country House: Preservation as a Strategy of Display from 1688 to 1950', in *Art and the Country House*, Paul Mellon Centre, 2020; <https://www.artandthecountryhouse.com/> [accessed 27 February 2022]

Yates, Frances, 'Elizabethan Chivalry: The Romance of the Accession Day Tilts', *Journal of the Warburg and Courtauld Institutes*, 20.1/2 (1957), pp. 4–25

Acknowledgments

As part of this book was written during the lockdowns brought by the COVID-19 pandemic, my first thanks should go to the UK's ever resourceful and expeditious second-hand book dealers. I am also grateful to the staff of the British Library and the Paul Mellon Centre Library, who guided and supported readers in the uncertain days of reopening. In writing a book with as broad a scope as this one, I have been aware throughout of my indebtedness to those scholars who have made particular subjects their own; I sincerely hope I have sufficiently acknowledged their work throughout my endnotes and bibliography.

At Thames & Hudson I should like to offer warm thanks to my commissioning editor, Ben Hayes, for supporting the idea for this book and to Kate Edwards for her attentive editing. I am also grateful to the book's editorial assistant, India Jackson, to the picture researcher, Nikos Kotsopoulos, and to the production controller, Celia Falconer. Peter Burgess has created an elegant design for the interior and Stephen Hickson for the cover. Grateful thanks too go to my agent, Andrew Gordon.

Any author looks forward to the moment at which it is possible to express gratitude to those who have helped them. It is a pleasure to thank the following who have debated ideas with me, recommended books and articles, been generous with their expertise, offered valuable observations and insights, insisted I consider particular artists or writers I was inexplicably overlooking, or simply shared my enthusiasm for the project: Leila Anani, Kirsty Archer-Thompson, Nirmala Bigden, David Bindman, Bronwen Burgess, George Carter, Rachel Church, Stephen Clarke, Jane Clifford, Catherine Davidson, John Deben, Penelope Deben, Thomas Faggionato, the late Roseline Greenwood, Anna Groundwater, Benedict Gummer, Mark Haworth-Booth, Lucy Holmes, Olivia Horsfall Turner, the late Kevin Jackson, Thomas Jayne, Kirstin Kennedy, Christine Kyle, Francis Kyle, Petra Lange-Berndt, Keith Levett, Lucy Majella Linforth, Paul Mendez, Frances Parton, Anthea Pender, Kate Retford, the late Marcus Rowell, Beatriz Chadour Sampson, Gill Saunders, Tessa Solomon, Hew Stevenson, Xanthe Wilde, Martin Williams, Viktor Wynd and Jonny Yarker.

The word 'late' occurs too often in this list; 2021, the year in which much of this book was written, was marked by premature bowings-out. I should like particularly to mention Roseline Greenwood, with whom I discussed many of the ideas for this book and whose encouragement and wisdom were of great value to me; and Marcus Rowell, who read more widely than anyone else I know and was the most loyal and generous of friends. I am profoundly sorry that both conversations have come to an end.

It was my husband, Stephen Calloway, who first suggested that I might write a book about the olden days. For that, and for everything else, my thanks and love.

Picture Credits

Colour plates

I British Library, London. Cotton MS Claudius D VI, f. 6r. Photo British Library/Bridgeman Images; **II** British Library, London. MS Egerton 3028, f. 30r; **III** Great Hall, Winchester Castle; **IV** British Library, London. Royal MS 20 A II, f. 4r; **V** Yale Center for British Art, Paul Mellon Collection, New Haven; **VI** British Library, London; **VII** National Museum of Wales, Cardiff; **VIII** Yale Center for British Art, Paul Mellon Collection, New Haven; **IX** Royal Academy of Arts, London; **X** Photo Chronicle/Alamy Stock Photo; **XI, XII** Victoria and Albert Museum, London; **XIII** Victoria and Albert Museum, London. Photo The Stapleton Collection/ Bridgeman Images; **XIV** Royal Collection Trust, London/His Majesty King Charles III. Photo Royal Collection Trust/His Majesty King Charles III, 2022/Bridgeman Images; **XV** Private collection; **XVI** Walker Art Gallery, National Museums Liverpool. Purchased by the Walker Art Gallery in 1878; **XVII** National Museum of Wales, Cardiff; **XVIII** Museum of Fine Arts, Boston. Photo Museum of Fine Arts, Boston. All rights reserved/Scala, Florence; **XIX** Tate. Photo Tate. © Tate; **XX** Manchester Art Gallery. Gift of H.M. Government War Artists' Advisory Committee. © Transferred to MCGs from the War Artists Advisory Committee, Ministry of Information (1947). Photo Manchester Art Gallery/Bridgeman Images; **XXI** Photo © Lucinda Douglas-Menzies; **XXII** Victoria and Albert Museum, London. Recording Britain Collection. Given by the Pilgrim Trust. © Victoria and Albert Museum; **XXIII** Courtesy the Pauline Boty Estate; **XXIV** Courtesy the artist. Photo Anima Mundi Gallery; **XXV** Courtesy the artist and Hollybush Gardens, London. Photo © Victoria and Albert Museum, London

Black and white illustrations

1 The Metropolitan Museum of Art, New York. David Hunter McAlpin Fund, 1952; **6** Victoria and Albert Museum, London. Recording Britain Collection. Given by the Pilgrim Trust. © Victoria and Albert Museum; **14** Beinecke Rare Book and Manuscript Library, Yale University Library, New Haven; **17** Photo akg-images/ Richard Booth; **28** Bibliothèque nationale de France, Paris. BnF Latin 8501A, f. 108v; **31** J. Paul Getty Museum, Los Angeles; **35** College of Arms, London; **46** University of Illinois Urbana-Champaign; **52** Roy G. Neville Historical Chemical Library, Science History Institute, Philadelphia; **56** Stanford University Libraries; **62** Luna Community College, Las Vegas; **64, 65** Wellcome Library, London; **70** British Library, London. Add MS 28330, f. 36r; **78** Beinecke Rare Book and Manuscript Library, Yale University Library, New Haven; **80** Widener Library, Harvard University, Cambridge, MA; **84** Photo Martin Charles/RIBA Collections; **90** British Library, London. Photo British Library Board. All Rights Reserved/ Bridgeman Images; **91** Getty Research Institute, Los Angeles; **92–93** The Metropolitan Museum of Art, New York. Purchase, Brooke Russell Astor Bequest, 2013. Photo The Metropolitan Museum of Art/Art Resource/Scala, Florence; **96** Victoria and Albert Museum, London. Photo Heritage Image Partnership Ltd/Alamy Stock Photo; **98, 99** Lewis Walpole Library, Farmington; **104** British Library, London; **110** The British Museum, London. Photo The Trustees of the British Museum; **112** Beinecke Rare Book and Manuscript Library, Yale University Library, New Haven; **118** Getty Research Institute, Los Angeles; **124** Fitzwilliam Museum, Cambridge; **128** J. Paul Getty Museum, Los Angeles; **130, 131** Robarts Library, University of Toronto; **138** The Metropolitan Museum of Art, New York. Gift of Georgiana W. Sargent, in memory of John Osborne Sargent, 1924; **141** Robarts Library, University of Toronto; **144** Getty Research Institute, Los Angeles; **154–55** The Metropolitan Museum of Art, New York. Gift of Ed and Pieper Dittus, 2013;

169 Mark Samuels Lasner Collection, Special Collections, University of Delaware Library; **175** Ashmolean Museum, University of Oxford. Photo Heritage Image Partnership Ltd/Alamy Stock Photo; **178** Photo Richard Gardner/Shutterstock; **181** Birmingham Museums Trust/Birmingham Museum and Art Gallery; **186** Photo Heritage Image Partnership Ltd/Alamy Stock Photo; **190** National Portrait Gallery, London; **193** Royal Collection Trust, London/His Majesty King Charles III; **198** Getty Research Institute, Los Angeles; **202** Gerrish Fine Art, London; **204** Photo Look and Learn/Bridgeman Images; **209** Yale Center for British Art, New Haven. Gift of Elisabeth Fairman; **212** Tate. Photo Tate. Barbara Hepworth © Bowness; **220** Private collection; **223** Reproduced courtesy of the artist's estate; **225** Published in *Vogue*, January 1929; **226** Victoria and Albert Museum, London. © Cecil Beaton/Victoria and Albert Museum, London; **229** © Estate of Enid Marx; **234** Photo Sam Lambert/Architectural Press Archive/RIBA Collections; **240** British Library, London; **241** © BBC Archive; **242** Courtesy T. Elliott & Sons; **245** Photo Richard Frieman-Phelps/Gamma-Rapho via Getty Images; **247** © BBC Archive; **256** Courtesy Laura Ashley; **258** © John Coulthart; **262** Originally commissioned by Autograph ABP. © Heather Agyepong

Index

Page references in *italics* indicate illustrations.

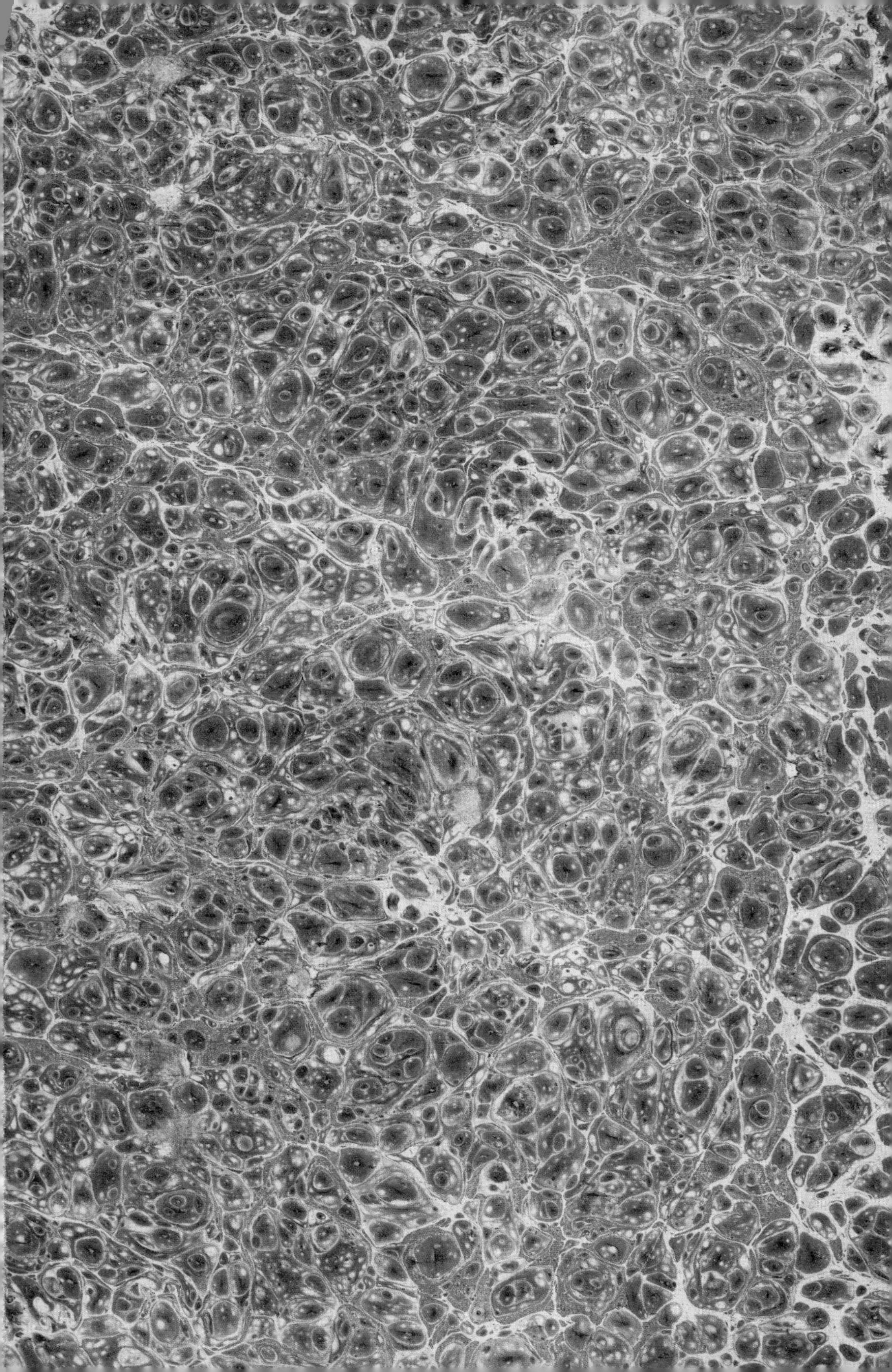

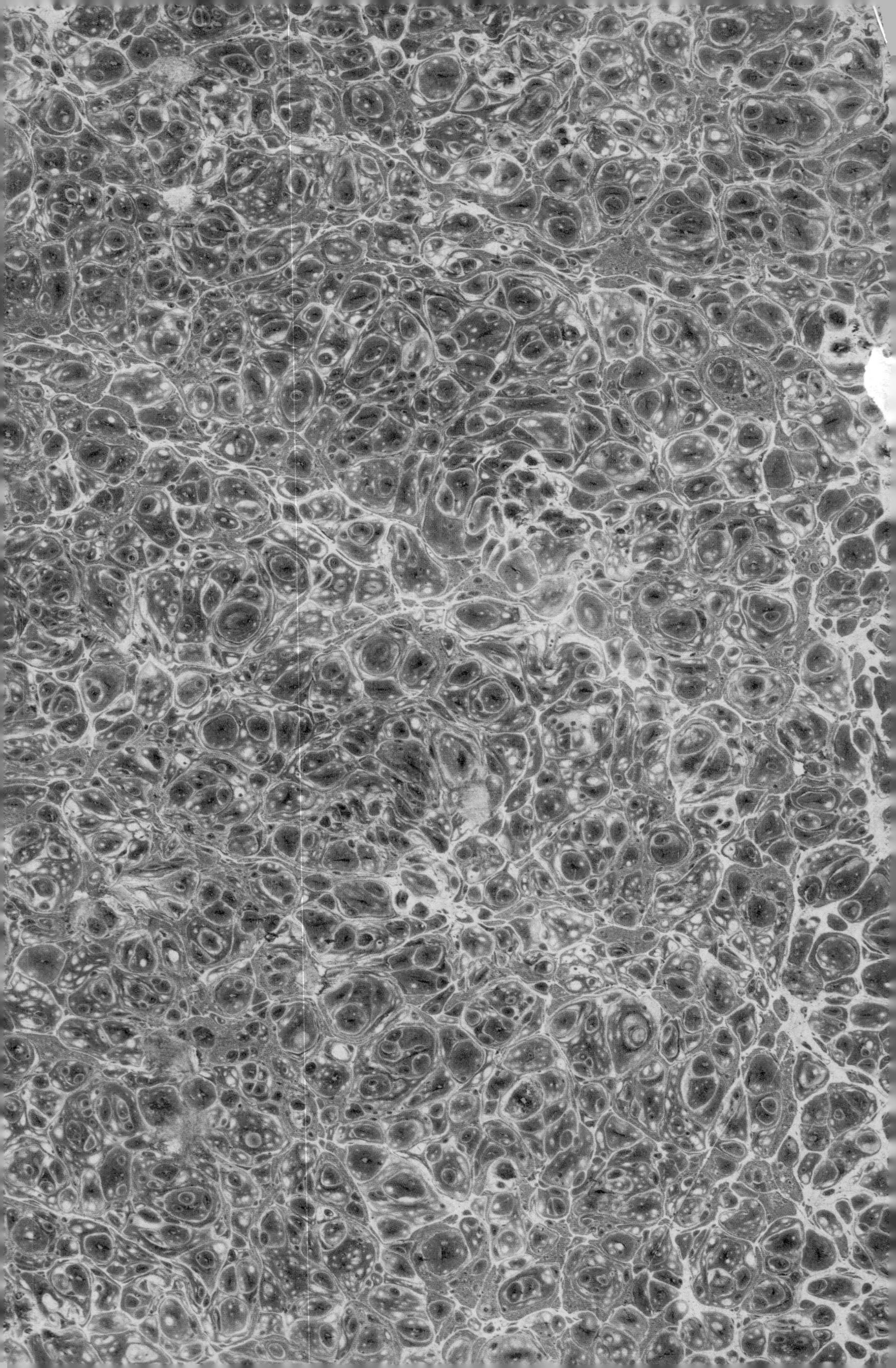